Hostage on the Yangtze

HOSTAGE

Malcolm H. Murfett

NAVAL INSTITUTE PRESS
Annapolis, Maryland

ON THE

Yangtze

Britain, China, and the *Amethyst*
Crisis of 1949

© 1991
by the United States Naval Institute
Annapolis, Maryland

Library of Congress Cataloging-in-Publication Data

Murfett, Malcolm H.
    Hostage on the Yangtze : Britain, China, and the *Amethyst* crisis
of 1949 / Malcolm H. Murfett.
      p.   cm.
    Includes bibliographical references and index.
    ISBN 0-87021-289-3
    1. China—Foreign relations—Great Britain.   2. Great Britain—
Foreign relations—China.   3. China—Foreign relations—1912–1949.
4. Great Britain—Foreign relations—1945–.   5. *Amethyst* (Sloop)
I. Title
DS740.5.G5M87   1991
327.51041—dc20   90-42359

Printed in the United States of America on acid-free paper ∞

9   8   7   6   5   4   3   2

First printing

Title page calligraphy by Helene Sze McCarthy

For Stephanie

Contents

Illustrations

Preface

ANYONE picking up a British newspaper on Thursday 21 April 1949 would have found the main headlines reserved for a new crisis in international relations that had suddenly and dramatically broken out in China on the previous day. *The Times* carried the story under the headline "British Warships Shelled on Yangtze." Although its report was written in far more restrained language than that used by the popular tabloids, the story still sounded alarming and intriguing; it conjured up images of evil deeds being done by a group of unidentified assailants to a variety of unsuspecting British victims in a far corner of the globe.

> Two British warships were attacked to-day by artillery fire in the Yangtze river near Chinkiang, which has been the scene of bitter fighting between Chinese Nationalists and Communists during the past few days, and 72 British naval ratings are reported killed or wounded.
> The sloop H.M.S. Amethyst, commanded by Lieutenant-Commander B. M. Skinner, steaming up-river to Nanking from Shanghai, was hit by shell fire from the north bank and went aground on Rose Island, 15 miles east of Chinkiang. The destroyer H.M.S. Consort, which came from Nanking to assist the Amethyst, was also fired on. She returned the fire, but was unable to stop on reaching the Amethyst because of the heavy shelling. Proceeding down-river with her guns blazing back at the shore batteries, the Consort lay up at the Nationalist naval anchorage of Kiangyin to tend her own wounded and await a better chance to help the crippled Amethyst.[1]

The report went on to reveal that two other British warships, a frigate HMS *Black Swan* and a cruiser HMS *London*, had joined the destroyer *Consort* at Kiangyin and were waiting there to see whether they were needed to mount a rescue operation for the *Amethyst*. This was ominous news because it sounded as though the crisis might not yet be over. It wasn't.

A day later the official Communist New China News Agency published its own compelling and radically different account of what had taken place on the Yangtze that previous Wednesday. Far from being cast as the villains of the piece, the Communist artillery troops on the northern bank of the river were alleged to have been merely defending themselves against a concerted assault upon their positions by units of the Royal Navy and those of the Kuomintang.

> People's Liberation Army (after called P.L.A.) defeated joint naval attack of the K.M.T. and British Imperialist Navy on April 20th and 21st during the river crossing battle about Chinkiang and Kiang Yin. The battle started on the forenoon of the 20th when the P.L.A. attacked the K.M.T. bridgeheads on the northern banks of the river and the islands in the middle of the river. Just at that moment, two enemy war vessels from the east suddenly opened fire on the P.L.A. positions northwest of Taihsing and north of Yangchung countries to halt the crossing of the P.L.A. The P.L.A. returned fire and hit one of the vessels which subsequently sank while the other steamed westwards and was half sunk near Chinkiang. Then another enemy war vessel steaming eastward from Chinkiang reached the spot and opened fire.[2]

From the outset, therefore, this latest crisis in Anglo-Chinese relations looked as though it would be difficult to resolve. It was. As the days passed, the crisis deepened, frustration and resentment grew, and an acceptable settlement of the Yangtze incident appeared to become less rather than more likely. This sense of ultimate failure created the circumstances for the final denouement in late July. Once again for a few days, the *Amethyst* recaptured the press headlines around the world. Hero or villain, applauded or reviled, this small British frigate had somehow managed to become an unlikely symbol of the enduring cold war in Asia.

This book explains the importance of the *Amethyst* episode in the history of Anglo-Chinese naval relations and why it may be seen as a final poignant break with the past. Ironically, out of glorious victory sprang ultimate defeat.

Acknowledgments

MY INTEREST in the *Amethyst* crisis was first aroused in the spring of 1985 when I came across a few cryptic messages in the files of the Ministry of Defence in London about an incident that had taken place on the Yangtze River in April 1949. Although a number of my colleagues in the History Department of the National University of Singapore (NUS) knew far more than I did about what had been at stake in China at this time, I decided that the story sounded fascinating and ought to be followed up. Later that year, I spent four weeks in the Public Record Office in London carrying out a preliminary investigation into the feasibility of writing a new account of the incident. While I was there I met and discussed the project with Dr. Nicholas Rodger, a naval expert whom I knew I could count upon to answer candidly any question about the suitability or otherwise of this venture. He agreed that a new study of this incident might reveal something useful about British policy making, particularly because neither Lawrence Earl's *Yangtse Incident* (London, 1973) nor C. E. Lucas Phillips's *Escape of the "Amethyst"* (London, 1958) had been based upon the official government records, most of which had only been subsequently opened for inspection by the general public under the terms of the thirty-year rule.

Once I began the project, I could rely on the unfailing interest and support of Professor Ernest Chew, head of the History Department, and Professor Edwin Thumboo, dean of the Faculty of Arts and Social Sciences, at the NUS. Four of my former students in Singapore—John Gu, G. Uma Devi, Tan Soo See, and Henry Yeung—assisted me in undertaking some of the useful background research in a variety of English and Chinese sources.

I first presented my initial findings on this topic in a video program directed by Stewart Arrandale of the Educational Technology unit at the NUS, which was shown to a research seminar in the Asian Studies Centre at St. Antony's College, Oxford in November 1986. Shortly thereafter, I showed several exploratory chapters of my manuscript to Professor Ralph Smith of the School of Oriental and African Studies at London University (SOAS). His wise suggestions and encouragement at this stage also proved to be immensely beneficial to me.

Thanks to the support of Dr. Peter Carey and Professor Arthur Stockwin, my application to become a senior associate member of St. Antony's for the 1986–87 academic year was successful, and this enabled me to return to Oxford for the whole of Trinity Term in 1987. While there, I had the good fortune to meet and discuss my topic on several occasions with Dr. Steve Tsang and Shao Wenguang, both of whom were attached to the college and were working on aspects of modern Anglo-Chinse history. I found their insights into the Chinese character and criticism of my interim conclusions to be unfailingly helpful.

In September 1987, I went on a short lecture tour of the United States, during which time I gave a paper on the Yangtze crisis to the History Department at the University of Kansas in Lawrence. I benefited from the lively discussion that followed my presentation on this occasion and am especially obliged to Professors Grant Goodman, Dan Bays, and David Katzman for their comments and high level of interest in my work. My next stop was the Pennsylvania State University where I had the opportunity to discuss the project with Professor William Duiker, a dear friend and former colleague of mine, and Professor E-Tu Zen Sun, a noted sinologist. A couple of days later I delivered a paper on "Britain and China in 1949" at a formal session of the Eighth Naval History Symposium in Annapolis. I was fortunate to have Professor William Braisted of the University of Texas as the commentator on my panel. He has proved to be a constant source of support to me ever since, and my gratitude to him remains marked. Professor Daniel Baugh, an accomplished expert on the Royal Navy in the age of sail, also brought his considerable talents to bear on my paper. A critique from him is always instructive, and his subsequent friendship has meant a lot to me.

Apart from my teaching duties in Singapore, I divided my time in the following months between additional research and writing. I spent several weeks in London working mostly in the Public Record Office, where the staff has always been helpful (even if the food is expensive) and paying useful visits to the manuscript section of the Imperial War Museum, the National Maritime Museum, the Liddell Hart Archive Centre of King's College, and the libraries of the University of London and SOAS. Further help was rendered by the staff

of the Archive Centre at Churchill College in Cambridge and by those working in the Bodleian Library, Rhodes House Library, and Modern History
Faculty Library in Oxford. A trip to Hong Kong in February 1988 enabled me
to visit Dr. Lau Yee Cheung at the Public Records Office and to give a research
paper in the History Department of the University of Hong Kong. In particular, Professor Mary Turnbull, Dr. Chan Lau Kit-ching, and Dr. Thomas
Stanley were very kind to me, and I appreciated their hospitality.

Another spell of research in the early summer of that year took me to
Castletown on the Isle of Man where Mark Stevenson and his wife were
gracious hosts and allowed me full access to Sir Ralph's private collection of
papers. They simply could not have been more pleasant to me than they were
on this occasion.

Once I felt I was coming to the end of my research, I arranged to meet or
correspond with some of the principal personalities who had been in China
during the *Amethyst* crisis. My earlier contact with Sir Edward Youde, the
governor of Hong Kong, had been broken by his sudden death in early
December 1986. Fortunately, I could always count upon Rear-Admiral Vernon D'Arcy Donaldson to assist me with information about what was happening in China during 1948–49 as seen from the British Embassy. He has been
immensely helpful to me not only in what he has been able to recall of those
troubled times but also in suggesting I contact the remarkable U Myint Thein,
the former Burmese ambassador to China. Vice-Admiral Sir Peter Berger was
also very helpful to me when I went to meet him at Selwyn College in
Cambridge in June 1988.

Once the research was over and writing began in earnest, I badgered various
people for their assistance. Technical support came from Captain Charles
Baker, Royal Navy (Ret.), and Richard Burton. Dr. Robert Lumsden, Professor Robert Scott Dupree, Dr. Andrew Robertson, and my wife Ulrike
examined the manuscript for errors of grammar and style. Professors John
Hattendorf, Barry Hunt, Don Schurman, and Gerald Jordan all read and
commented on parts of the work; Barry Gough not only did that, but also gave
me all the material he had been collecting on the Yangtze crisis, an act of true
scholarly cooperation for which I remain indebted to him.

On the production side of things, Dr. Avi Gupta of the Geography Depart-
ment at the NUS made all the arrangements to get my maps drawn in the
Cartography Lab by Lee Li Kheng. Ian Thomas, of the National Portrait
Gallery Archive and Library, supplied three of the photographs, and Mark
Stevenson lent me a photograph of his father for reproduction in this book.
Although I had put much of the book onto computer disks while I was in

Singapore, there was still quite a lot to do once I arrived in Canada in the summer of 1989. As a result, I was a more or less constant visitor to the Secretarial Services Department of the Faculty of Arts at York University in Toronto as the final deadline for submission of the typed manuscript approached. Pat Cates, Grace Baxter, and Susan Rainey helped me to iron out the technical problems I experienced with my computer software. Without their consistent support, this manuscript could not have been submitted on schedule. I am also deeply grateful to Paul Wilderson, Judith Grumstrup-Scott, Mary Lou Kenney, and Deborah Farrell, my editors at the Naval Institute Press, for being interested in my manuscript from the outset and for keeping the pressure on me to produce it on time.

All Crown-copyright material in this book is reproduced by permission of the Controller of Her Majesty's Stationery Office. Material from other public archives and private collections is reproduced by permission of the appropriate authorities identified in the Notes.

Finally, I must thank my family for putting up with me during the course of this project. My wife Ulrike has been a constant source of strength to me. Apart from relying on her perceptive criticism and sound judgment to draw my attention to errors of language or logic in the text, I am grateful to her for shielding me from the attentions of my four young children, Marianne, Caroline, Nicolas, and Stephanie, who saw no particularly valid reason why daddy was invariably locked away in his study when they either wished to play with him or required his assistance with their homework! All of them deserve my heartfelt thanks.

Hostage on the Yangtze

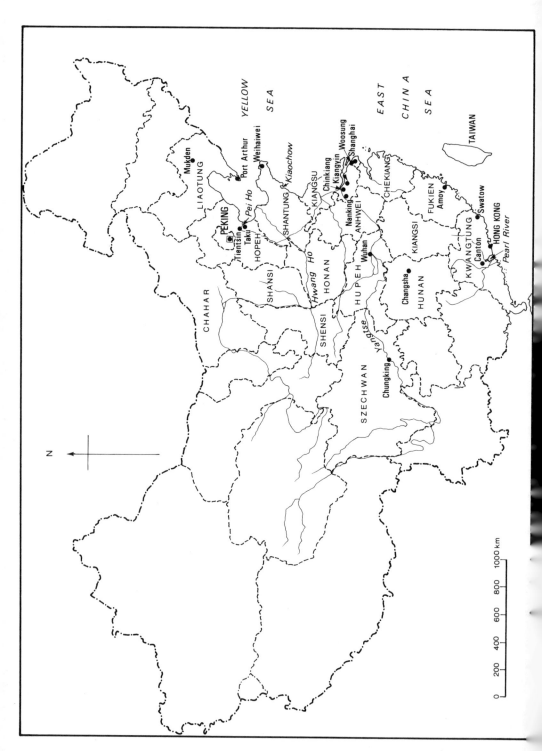

Map 1. The China Coastline

1. Gunboat Diplomacy

$\mathcal{E}$ NGLAND'S interest in China awoke rather late in the day. One hundred and twenty years after the Portuguese had originally landed in the country, the first English expedition of four ships under the command of Captain John Weddell finally arrived at Macao in the Gulf of Canton toward the end of June 1637. Weddell quickly realized that direct methods were required if he was to attain his objective of opening trade with the inhabitants of the Celestial Kingdom. Under attack from the Bogue forts at the entrance to the Canton River, Weddell turned his ships' armory upon the Chinese forts with such élan that they were rapidly cajoled into silence. Afterward he continued his passage upriver to Canton, where he sold his cargo of merchandise and took on a full load of sugar and ginger before departing from Chinese waters for the first and last time.[1]

Strangely perhaps, the allure of China—which had already captivated some of the other leading European maritime powers, such as the Russians, Spanish, and Dutch—did not immediately assert itself in English minds. It took another twenty-seven years after Weddell's foray into southern China before the next English ship docked in the Macao Roads. Despite the opening of trade with Amoy and Formosa in 1670, English vessels remained an unusual sight in China for some years to come. In fact, it was only after an imperial edict opened all Chinese ports to foreign trade in 1685 that English mercantile interests began to pay much attention to the potentialities of this eastern connection. Even so, it was thirty years before the East India Company felt confident enough about the China trade to open its first permanent factory at Canton in 1715. Its early hesitancy was hardly inappropriate, given the history of the trading relationship and the level of fees demanded by the Chinese on this

3

trade. By 1757 all the Chinese ports, with the solitary exception of Canton, had been closed to foreign trade.[2]

Following the infamous *Lady Hughes* affair in November 1784, when a gunner firing a salute from the English ship managed to kill two Chinese in a boat alongside his own at Whampoa, Pitt's government in London was forced to think seriously about the measures it could take to improve relations between itself and the Chinese authorities in the future. It was with the dual intention of establishing official relations with the imperial government in Peking and likewise improving the trading position between the two countries that the British government sent out Earl Macartney from Portsmouth in September 1792 to seek an audience with the Chinese emperor. Despite the extraordinarily elaborate nature of his embassy, Macartney's diplomatic mission failed ultimately to secure improved access for His Majesty's Government in the China trade or to convince the Chinese that King George III was anything more than the monarch of a barbarian tributary of the Celestial Kingdom. Macartney finally left the Chinese capital on 7 October 1793, his task of establishing a formal official relationship between London and Peking unfinished.[3]

By the time of Lord Amherst's ill-fated embassy to China in 1816, the vast potentialities of a trading relationship with this exotic Asian country were swiftly being appreciated by British merchants, shipowners, and government alike. At the outset, much of the trade was in Chinese tea, a beverage that had become highly sought after in England by as early as the beginning of the Hanoverian succession. As the eighteenth century had passed, this trade had risen steeply, so that by the end of the 1820s, annual consumption of Chinese tea reached nearly 30 million pounds.[4]

While the demand for Chinese imports of tea, silk, jade, and spices seemed insatiable in a Europe revelling in the peace of the post-Napoleonic period, the British made a discovery that would totally transform the terms of their trade in the East. After running a large deficit in its China trade in the past, Britain found that in Indian opium they possessed a commodity that the Chinese apparently wanted in almost inexhaustible amounts. In the hands of such merchants as William Jardine, James Matheson, and Lancelot Dent, the lucrative opium trade flourished in Chinese waters. By 1829 the value of British opium exports to China exceeded by $1.83 million that of their imports of Chinese tea. By 1833 the gap between the two had risen to over $4.25 million.[5]

In 1833 the British government decided to break the East India Company's monopoly of the China trade. This action did more than anything else to open up the China coast to the attentions of independent British merchants. Their ships, laden with opium, having made the journey across the Indian Ocean and through the South China Sea, began plying up and down the southern shore of Kwangtung province, discharging their cargo where they could and finding a ready home for much—if not all—of it at Lintin, an island in the Gulf of Canton, and at the other outer anchorages in the vicinity. Ships lying off these islands acted as opium receiving stations, and from this location, smaller vessels were chartered to run further up the coast selling their immensely popular contraband to whoever wished to purchase it.[6]

It did not take long for the results of this illegal trade to have a profound effect in China. Opium sales soon reached such a scale that they far exceeded the current operating revenue earned through the sale of Chinese exports to Britain. This yawning gap between imports and exports could only be bridged by paying the British an ever-increasing quantity of silver from the imperial exchequer. It was an unprecedented situation and one that the emperor was determined to stop at all costs. In 1839, therefore, he appointed Lin Tse-hsü as his high commissioner at Canton with the express purpose of bringing this illegal trade to an end.[7]

Lin's zealous attitude in discharging his duties soon achieved results. On 28 March 1839, Captain Elliot, chief superintendent of British trade in China, agreed reluctantly to comply with the high commissioner's instructions that all British-owned stocks of opium held in Chinese waters should be yielded to the imperial authorities. Over 20,000 chests of opium were surrendered in this way by 21 May and all were systematically destroyed in the following month. Harassed and then under virtual house arrest in Canton for nearly two months while the stocks of British opium were being collected, Elliot responded to the final delivery of this contraband by instructing the local British community to leave the city and forbidding all British vessels from entering the Canton River in the foreseeable future. Elliot sailed for Macao on 24 May.

It is difficult not to see Elliot's withdrawal from Canton as a calculated step on the road to war. In professing to have no confidence in the justice and moderation of the Chinese authorities, Elliot provided Lord Palmerston, the ebullient British foreign secretary, with a second motive for some form of military intervention in China, if the confiscation and destruction of British property worth an estimated £2.5 million was not already a good enough pretext for it. A month later on 23 June 1839, the imperial authorities in Canton added further to the controversy by demanding that from that date onward all foreign interests intent on trading in Chinese waters would have to render a signed bond guaranteeing that their ships were not carrying opium and permitting an on-board inspection by the appropriate Chinese officials for the purposes of authenticating the cargo manifest that each ship was obliged to possess.[8]

During the next two months, Anglo-Chinese relations worsened to the point of total rupture over the dubious circumstances surrounding the death in early July of a Chinese civilian, Lin Wei-hi, at the hands of a party of British sailors in Kowloon. Unable at his own inquiry to establish exactly what had happened on that fatal occasion—let alone identify the culprit responsible for the homicide—Captain Elliot comprehensively failed to satisfy Commissioner Lin about the efficacy of British justice in this case. Hostility between the two sides therefore increased. Elliot finally left Macao for Hong Kong on 23 August 1839 and was followed by the remaining members of the British community three days later. As the weeks passed, so the crisis deepened, and the two countries appeared to be on the verge of war. Jurisdictional disputes over the presence of British nationals on Chinese soil, together with strident demands made by the high commissioner about the long-running and unresolved Lin Wei-hi incident, added fuel to the flames of war.[9]

On 3 November 1839, hostilities began with a clash between twenty-nine Chinese war junks and HMS *Volage* and HMS *Hyacinth*. Victory on this occasion went to the British, as it ultimately did in what has become popularly—if a little inaccurately—known as the Opium War of 1839–42. Within a few months after the outbreak of this first Anglo-Chinese War, the British government had equipped and sent a force of 16 warships mounting 540 guns, 4 armed steamers, 1 troop ship, 27 transports, and roughly 4,000 troops to China from various naval stations around the globe. Their arrival in Chinese waters did not have the anticipated impact on the war that Lord Palmerston had either wished or expected. Far from swiftly subduing their Oriental foe, the British forces encountered firm and spirited resistance from the Chinese troops who defended their homeland against the ravages of what were depicted as barbarian hordes. In due course as the debilitating effects of malaria and dysentery began to take a severe toll of the British forces, substantial reinforcements were needed to supplement those already battling the enemy. Nonetheless, even with 25 warships boasting 668 guns, 14 steamers with another 56 guns, 9 other vessels including hospital and surveying craft, a host of transport ships, and 10,000 troops, it took the British forces until 17 August 1842 before the city of Nanking surrendered without a fight and the Chinese authorities were finally forced to the negotiating table.[10]

As a result of the Treaty of Nanking signed on 29 August, the five ports of Canton, Amoy, Foochow, Ningpo, and Shanghai were opened to foreign residency and trade, while Hong Kong was ceded to Britain in perpetuity for use as a military and commercial base for British trade in China. Besides being able to station a warship at each of the so-called treaty ports, the Royal Navy was permitted to deploy additional vessels in Chinese waters if their express intention was to protect commerce. This settlement and other accompanying treaties negotiated by various international powers with the Chinese over the next couple of years, did much, as one might have expected, to stimulate and vastly increase foreign trade and shipping along the China coast. Notwithstanding the active presence of the United States in this region, the lion's share of this rich new market still fell to Britain.[11]

Greater commercial involvement in China was not attained, however, without some cost to the principal foreign powers. Friction between the imperial authorities and the foreign powers was evident, inspired as much by the distaste of the former for the newly won rights of the latter as by the traditional suspicion that had plagued their unequal relationship in the past. Cases of brawling, rioting, stoning, and murder by groups of incensed locals against British citizens toward the end of the 1840s did nothing to subdue the fiery temperament of Lord Palmerston or lure him away from the temptation of issuing scarcely veiled threats of military reprisals against the Chinese should these incidents continue in the future.

After Palmerston had been forced to resign over his incautious declaration of support for Louis Napoleon's coup d'état in France of 2 December 1851, however, a distinct change came over British policy toward China. For a couple of years at least, the British government followed a more accommodating and less pugnacious path with the Chinese authorities in the hope of reducing animosity between their two peoples and improving opportunities for even greater future trade. Some success was achieved for a while, particularly with respect to cooperation against acts of piracy, but unfortunately, by 1856 an innate and seemingly mutual intolerance between the races undid the solid work of Palmerston's successors at the Foreign Office, namely, Granville, Malmesbury, and Clarendon, respectively.[12]

In 1856 a fresh crisis erupted over the lorcha *Arrow*, a Hong Kong–registered ship apprehended by four Chinese officers and sixty soldiers as it lay off the port of Canton on the morning of 8 October. As well as hauling down both the British ensign and the Blue Peter, the boarding party summarily arrested all twelve Chinese crew members of the lorcha. Although nine of these men were later returned to the boat, the Chinese authorities at Canton under High Commissioner Yeh Ming-chin held the other three crew members for further questioning. Claiming extraterritorial rights under the Treaty of the Bogue in 1843, the British government demanded the return of the three men forthwith. Its request was refused.

Matters then swiftly degenerated, and war broke out on 23 October. It lasted—with French and to a lesser extent American encouragement and assistance—until the fall of Canton on 29 December 1857 and the arrest of Commissioner Yeh a few days later on 4 January 1858. These events marked the end of the first phase of the war; the second and final part was concluded with the capture of the Taku forts on the Peiho River on 20 May 1858 and the signing of the Treaty of Tientsin on 26 June 1858.[13] This latter document was supposed to ensure among other things that from this date onward, foreign envoys could reside in Peking and that diplomatic missions would be established in the city. Apart from further extending the rights of extraterritoriality enjoyed by foreign nationals in China, it also conjured up the prospect of greater commercial opportunities for them by opening eleven more treaty ports, including several along the middle and lower reaches of the Yangtze and others at important locations up the coast. Although the destabilizing effects of the Taiping Rebellion ensured that several of the designated ports, particularly those in the Yangtze valley, were not opened on schedule, the principle of further expansion of foreign trade in China had been secured, and the leading commercial powers were poised to exploit it.

Ratification of this latest treaty wrought by force of arms upon the imperial court was to prove impossible, however, without a show of steely defiance from the emperor's subjects. As a result of what the British saw as a further blatant example of Chinese intransigence, a third war erupted between them in the following year. It arose specifically out of the British government's wish that the Treaty of Tientsin should be ratified by the emperor himself. Finding such an arrangement extremely distasteful and having no desire to sign what amounted to an instrument of surrender, the imperial court refused to sanction the plan when it was put to the test in the early summer of 1859. By preventing the Honourable Frederick W. A. Bruce, chief superintendent of British trade, from sailing unmolested up the Peiho River to Peking, the Chinese gave notice that unless His Majesty's Government was prepared to do something about it, the provisions of the Tientsin treaty were worthless.

Incensed by this discovery and impatient for some action, Bruce passed the issue for resolution to the British naval force—consisting of one ship of the line, two frigates, and thirteen gunboats—which was drawn up under the command of Admiral Sir James Hope at the mouth of the river. Hope delivered an ultimatum to the Chinese forces and then launched an attack on 25 June 1859 designed to smash through a heavy boom laid across the entrance to the river and force a passage up the Peiho to the Chinese capital. Hope's tactical battle plan lacked subtlety and finesse, merely consisting of a bludgeoning frontal attack on the booms and forts by the massed force at his disposal. Its naive deficiencies were soon exposed, as the attack was severely repulsed by accurate fire at close range from the guns of the restored Taku forts. Six British gunboats were put out of action, 89 sailors and marines were killed, and a further 345 were wounded, including Admiral Hope. Not even the American Commodore Tatnall's welcome but equally surprising intervention in the battle and his famous explanation that "Blood is thicker than water" could disguise the fact that the British had suffered a stunning and unexpected defeat at the hands of the Chinese on this occasion. That such a reverse would have to be answered was just as obvious.[14]

Under the leadership of Lord Elgin, who was appointed ambassador extraordinary, with Lieutenant-General Sir Hope Grant assuming command of the 10,500 land forces at his disposal and Admiral Hope leading 7 frigates, 34 smaller vessels, and 143 transports, the British prepared to bring their errant opponents to heel. As the French government pronounced itself just as keen as the British to see the Chinese honor their treaty obligations, an additional force of 6,300 French troops was assembled to support the latest allied attack on China. Not wanting to repeat the same mistake they had made in 1859 when they conducted a full frontal river attack on the Taku forts, the allies decided to land at Peitang to the north of the river defenses on 1 August 1860 and capture the forts by artillery and infantry assault after seizing the towns of Sinho and Tangku along the route southward to the banks of the Peiho. This strategy was as eminently sensible as it was successful; the forts were taken on 21 August, a mere four days before the allies began to enter the undefended city of Tientsin. Despite renewed efforts by the Chinese envoys to stall the foreign advance, the British and French forces resumed their steady march toward Tungchow and Peking. Allied victories in the battles of Chanchiawan on 18 September and Palichao Bridge three days later were achieved at the cost of running perilously short of ammunition. As a result, Lord Elgin and General Hope Grant decided to play a waiting game with the Chinese, during which time they could call up their reinforcements and restock their equipment for the expected battle for Peking, which now lay open to attack. This offensive was finally launched on 5 October and was greeted with further parleying and ultimata for eight more days before the allies, bent on capturing the city, discovered to their immense relief that the Chinese defenders had stolen away, leaving Peking undefended. By staging such a withdrawal, the imperial troops delivered the population into the rapacious hands of the victorious foreign troops. Sadly, the outcome was all too predictable: allied excesses—including burning down the emperor's summer palace at Yuenmingyuen—disfigured the final settlement, which otherwise was a satisfactory one from a British perspective. Apart from the payment of indemnities to the allies, the opening up of Tientsin as a treaty port, and the ceding to Britain of Kowloon Point in perpetuity, the foreign powers were accorded the right to a permanent legation in Peking.[15]

In many ways the end of this third Anglo-Chinese war marked a watershed in the relations between the British government and the imperial authorities. Thereafter under the benign influence of Lord Elgin's younger brother, the Honourable Frederick Bruce, the intense acrimony diminished, and a new spirit of effective cooperation slowly began to prevail. Evidence of this more helpful attitude was seen in the months following the signing of the Conventions of Peking in October 1860, with growing British support for the imperial authorities in their gruelling struggle with the Taiping rebels. Abandoning the strict neutrality observed since the outbreak of this civil war nearly two decades before, the British military response became increasingly interventionist and sympathetic to the existing imperial government. Although admittedly much of this change could be attributed to a pragmatic and mercenary desire to safeguard their trading and treaty privileges, the British also recognized that with the death of Emperor Haifeng in August 1861 and the reduction of much of the virulent xenophobia expressed by his court, the opportunity presented itself at last for some kind of Anglo-Chinese rapprochement.[16]

This possibility became a reality during the next few years as military collaboration aimed at defeating the Taiping rebels helped to do just that by 1864. In addition to the feats of General Staveley, Major Gordon, and Admiral Hope in helping to subdue the rebel forces, the British were instrumental in establishing a maritime customs inspectorate as an effective vehicle for collecting tariffs on all foreign trade with China. Three events—the legalization of opium in 1858, the end of the third Anglo-Chinese War two years later, and the end of the Taiping Rebellion in 1864—provided the circumstances necessary for a growth in international trade. Under Robert Hart, the inspector general of the Chinese Customs from 1863 onward, the service became an efficient arm of government. His pro-Chinese stance was much appreciated in Peking and his influence at court increased with time. If not solely responsible for encouraging a more open attitude on the part of the imperial government, Hart did as much as anyone to get it to realize the importance of being represented in the capitals of the other treaty powers.[17]

It was in this atmosphere of improved Anglo-Chinese relations that Lord Clarendon, the British foreign secretary, proposed a major policy change toward China on 28 December 1868. He indicated that the British government did not wish to put any "unfriendly pressure" on China to increase the pace of the reform process and improve its relationship with foreign powers.

Although dispensing with an aggressive approach, Clarendon made it clear that the British government was far more interested in dealing with the central government in China than with any local or provincial authority.[18]

This new directive was to have a most profound effect upon British naval policy in Chinese waters. In the recent past, apart from their constructive role in the suppression of piracy along the coast, gunboats had been called upon regularly to apply direct coercive force against those elements that acted against foreign missionaries, merchants, and consular officials in the provinces. In such cases, it was not unusual for these vessels to open fire or to land marines for some sortie ashore. Naturally, this kind of armed belligerence did nothing to endear the British to the Chinese people or lessen the xenophobic reaction of the Chinese to foreigners in their midst. Although Clarendon's policy did not end gunboat diplomacy per se, it did lead to a much greater control by the Admiralty over the use of naval force to support British mercantile and other interests in China. Whether coincidental or not, the new, less assertive role of the navy had an almost immediate and beneficial effect upon Anglo-Chinese relations. This marked improvement also made possible a reduction in the number of His Majesty's ships in Chinese waters to one ironclad, four corvettes or sloops, sixteen gunboats, one troop ship, and three other assorted vessels in the early months of 1869.[19]

Unfortunately, this newfound spirit of cooperation kept xenophobia at bay only for a time, a fact which was evident in the Tientsin massacre of 1870, in various anti-French incidents in the years thereafter, and in the murder in Yunnan province of A. R. Margary, a British consular interpreter from Peking, in February 1875. It was the circumstances of Margary's death that made it difficult for His Majesty's Government to ignore the murder.[20] In the months that followed, the two sides once again flirted disconcertingly with the specter of war before a settlement—the Convention of Chefoo—was reached between them on 13 September 1876. Sir Thomas Wade, the British plenipotentiary, ably supported by the intimidating presence at Talienwan of a British "flying squadron" of four frigates, induced the Chinese government to make some recompense, including the opening of Ichang, Wuhu, Wenchow, and Pakhoi as treaty ports, with six other towns on the Yangtze designated as ports at which steamers would be allowed to call. Although the threat of force had again been evident, and perhaps even because of it, this convention finally persuaded some members of the imperial court that it was not in China's long-term interests to be complacent and to dwell indefinitely upon the luster of its glorious past, however strong the temptation might be, but to accept that it had a role to perform in the modern international system. As a result of the convention, therefore, China at last opened its first permanent legation in London in February 1877 and followed this with diplomatic representation elsewhere in Europe, the United States, and Japan in the following months.[21]

Thereafter, peace brought important commercial benefits to both Britain and China. Far more ships than ever before came to do business in Chinese waters, a fact encouraged both by the opening of the Suez Canal in 1869 and the greater access these vessels now had to China's ports and inland waterways. British ships established an early dominance in this trade, accounting for roughly 63 percent of all tonnage in Chinese waters in 1883 and 65.6 percent ten years later.[22] In particular, British merchants had tried with some success to exploit the vast potential of the Yangtze River and the basin it drains, an area of some 750,000 square miles and with a population estimated in excess of 170 million. Shallow draught vessels were able to make the journey from Shanghai to Chungking throughout the year, a distance of 1,427 miles, and during the spring to autumn months of high water, even oceangoing ships could usually get up to Hankow, some 595 miles from the sea. Shanghai at the mouth of the Yangtze rapidly became a crucial trading port for the British in their attempt to impose themselves on the China trade. Its importance lay not only in its strategic location for the river trade, but also as a distribution center for the central and northern regions of the country.[23]

Trade was the main attraction for the British in their early relationship with China, but a disturbing blend of strategic, military, and imperialistic factors began to make their presence felt as the nineteenth century drew to a close. Much of the responsibility for this change came in the wake of China's comprehensive defeat in the Sino-Japanese War of 1894–95, a result that did much to underline and expose China's more obvious limitations. After the punitive terms of the Treaty of Shimonoseki were announced in April 1895, the major European powers recognized that they too could secure substantial advantages for themselves from such a weakened power.[24]

Once this idea was born, the "Scramble for China" could not be long delayed. Germany, Russia, and France all wrung concessions from the Chinese in the form of territorial acquisitions, business ventures, and other favors during the next three years. Worried by the prospect of increasing foreign competition in the China trade, the British government sought to protect its dominant position by demanding equal treatment with the other powers. It did not shrink, for instance, from dispatching nine of its warships to Chemulpo in Korea on 7 December 1897 to shadow a Russian fleet of the same size that had supposedly anchored at the same port. This blatant show of force that was based, alas, on wrong information seemed to indicate that the Russians were not alone in desiring a northern port from the enfeebled Chinese government. Unfortunately, the British naval demonstration—a source of acute embarrassment to Lord Salisbury's government—seems to have touched off a state of near panic in European capitals and may indeed have been partly responsible for convincing the Germans to hold onto Kiaochow and the Russians to remain in the market for Port Arthur. Thwarted on this score and that of a £12 million loan to the Chinese government, which the other powers opposed, the British cabinet was finally bought off on 1 July 1898 with the lease of Wei-hai-wei, a port that had no great material value save that it could be retained for as long as Port Arthur remained in Russian hands.[25] If Wei-hai-wei was merely a pawn in the game, the British made some amends by reaffirming their special interest in the Yangtze valley and by negotiating an immensely important concession in the south. A ninety-nine year lease on the entire Kowloon peninsula from Deep Bay to Mirs Bay did much to enhance the already formidable reputation of Hong Kong in commercial circles by increasing its size and making it less vulnerable to attack.[26]

By plundering China in this way, the foreign powers contributed to the imperial government's demoralization and instability. They also reawakened the latent xenophobia that many Chinese nationalists needed little stimulus to express at the best of times. But these were not the best of times. A bewildering succession of poor harvests, disastrous floods, severe drought, and locust plagues combined to wreak havoc in China's provinces. Bad omens were often depicted as a running commentary on the emperor's conversion to the need for modernization, which vested itself in a succession of reform decrees promulgated by the court during the hectic period from June to September 1898. After the empress dowager had removed the reformist emperor and reasserted her own conservative influence on the court, those movements that fed on antiforeignism and a hatred of Christianity were tacitly encouraged. By far the most fearsome of these sects was the Fist of Patriotic Union, which the world was soon to know more widely as the Boxers.[27]

By early June 1900, the situation in many of China's provinces had become virtually anarchic. In wreaking a terrible vengeance on all their enemies, the Boxers' extremism created a sense of justifiable alarm, bordering upon panic, among the foreign community in China. This unnerving situation—where executions of Christians were commonplace and foreigners feared for their lives—had underlined the necessity for troop reinforcements to be moved up to Peking to guard the various international legations from the excesses of the militant xenophobes. As this plan failed to restrain the Boxers from continuing to cause mayhem in the province of Chihli, the naval commanders of the great powers decided to take matters into their own hands. By 6:30 A.M. on 17 June, they had seized the Taku forts at the mouth of the Peiho River after a short but violent struggle.[28]

Within a matter of hours, the foreign powers found themselves in a virtual state of war with the Chinese government. Although none of the major powers were disposed to see it as a war between themselves and the imperial government--all preferring instead to see the Boxers as their natural enemies--the fact remained that some of the more powerful members of the imperial court were considered to be sympathetic to the Boxers' cause. This much was made clear on 20 June when the foreign legations in the capital came under fire for the first time from troops of the imperial army, and the infamous siege of Peking began. Elsewhere too, the Boxers and imperial troops cooperated in their quest to exterminate foreigners and eliminate their doleful influence in China. A savage and bloody repression resulted during the following weeks.

Britain, caught up in the morass of the Boer War in South Africa, was not in a position to drop everything and redeploy large forces in East Asia. This did not prove to be a great handicap, however, because all the other leading foreign powers recognized that they had vested interests to protect in China and were, therefore, prepared to work together to bring the Boxer Rebellion to an end. An international army of some eight thousand American, British, French, Japanese, and Russian troops eventually wrested the city of Tientsin from Chinese control on 14 July. After a nearly three-week delay, during which the contingent of foreign troops in the city had risen to more than eighteen thousand, the international force left Tientsin on 5 August to begin its advance on Peking, which was finally entered on 14 August 1900. Once the siege of the city had been raised, it was discovered that the imperial court had beaten a hasty and undignified retreat to Sianfu in Shensi province. Thereafter, the foreign troops took their revenge upon Peking and its inhabitants in an unrestrained, ruthless orgy of pillage and destruction.[29]

After the city had been duly sacked and the Boxers routed from the surrounding areas, the British government became anxious lest the allied powers should begin squabbling over the spoils of their victory in China. It was particularly concerned about what might happen to its predominant position in the Yangtze valley if China suffered an internal collapse or fell victim to dismemberment by the other powers. From the outset of the troubles, Lord Salisbury's cabinet had approved the Admiralty's plan to maintain at least one of its gunboats at each of the treaty ports on the river, both to deter potential troublemakers and to quell any unrest and disorderliness that might break out if the Boxers' influence began to prevail in any of these cities. Although a few of the gunboats had been withdrawn from some of the more exposed spots on the river by the end of July, a small cabinet committee of three (Goschen, Hamilton, and Lansdowne) used the prime minister's absence to order a British occupation of Shanghai on 15 August. This decision soon backfired as France, Germany, and Japan all began expressing an interest in the future of the city and the region as well. Far from consolidating Britain's position on the Yangtze, therefore, the occupation looked likely to undermine it. As a result, worried by the intensity and querulousness of the French, while wishing to contain the spread of Russian influence in the northern regions of the country, Britain reached an agreement with Germany on 16 October 1900 that established the principle of free trade and what would later be graphically described as the Open Door.[30] Although neither government wished to see China plunged into chaos by the collapse of the state, the two powers could hardly be said to have been successful in swaying the other allies to moderate the terms of the final protocol on 7 September 1901 or reduce the price the imperial government was forced to pay for its complicity in the Boxer Rebellion. China's humiliation was complete, or so it seemed at the time.[31]

It was in this mood of unusual frailty that Britain approached its naval dilemma in the Far East. Since 1898, the Russians had substantially increased their naval strength in this region, surpassing that of the Royal Navy. If one added the smaller French naval contingent to that of its Russian ally, the British position looked even worse. This unusual situation of being relatively as well as numerically inferior to other European naval powers, at least in the Far East, was not appreciated by either the British Admiralty or indeed by serving officers and gentlemen brought up in the era of the Raj and Pax Britannica. Informed comment in some of the London daily newspapers dwelled upon the matter and suggested that something ought to be done before long to redress the balance of advantage in Britain's favor.[32] It was partly to assuage this feeling of vulnerability, coupled with the lack of a suitable alternative power with whom it could do mutually satisfactory business, that some of the leading members of the British cabinet turned their attention eastward toward Japan in a bid to end the era of "splendid isolation." Apart from any other effects it might have in the Far East, the alliance would immediately ensure naval supremacy for the two powers in the region.[33]

Although the British saw the Anglo-Japanese Alliance of 30 January 1902 as a strategic expedient designed to forestall Russian aggression in Manchuria and Korea, the Chinese—whose hatred for the Japanese was well known—regarded the agreement as a deadly compact designed to exploit their country by two powers that had the capacity to do so. Britain, which often claimed to be

China's erstwhile friend, had shown just how deep that supposed friendship went by failing to explain adequately just what this latest act of diplomacy was designed to achieve. Sadly, it would not be the last time that Britain demonstrated what some would say was a callous and blatant disregard for Chinese sensitivities. Such was the humble role assigned to China in the early twentieth century. Its five millennia of civilization had failed to save it from such an indignity.

While the British vainly sought peace and stability in China so that their merchants could get on with the business of making money by developing their interests in the country, the omens for such a prolonged period of calm were not good. Two years after renouncing isolationism by signing its defensive alliance with Japan, Britain found itself on the brink of yet another major conflagration in the region with the opening of the Russo-Japanese War in February 1904. Worried by the potential implications of this unwelcome event, Balfour's Conservative government in London sought to avoid being pulled by its Japanese ally into this limited war in the Far East. It was relieved to discover that the French felt the same way and that an entente between them would ensure that neither power would become an actual belligerent in the struggle over Korea.[34]

Although the British were delighted not to be involved in the war, they found themselves benefiting greatly from the Japanese victory both on land and at sea. After the almost total eclipse of the Russian fleet in the battle of Tsushima Strait on 27 May 1905, for example, Britain no longer needed to maintain such a relatively large number of capital ships in Chinese waters. Apart from the persuasive argument for a redeployment of its battleship fleet in one or other of the European theaters, the dramatic improvement in Britain's strategic position in China did not lead to a marked reduction in the other classes of warship it had in the region. Part of the reason for this reluctance to disengage its naval force from eastern waters can be found in the government's continued support for those merchants who were engaged in the profitable enterprise of opening up China to British goods and services.[35] It displayed (one might accuse it of openly flaunting) its commitment on this score by retaining a fleet of gunboats and other warships in Chinese waters to protect this trade from the attentions of pirates and others who might have otherwise been tempted to interfere with it. In this way the commercial exploitation (His Majesty's Government was wont to describe it as "development") of China was greatly enhanced. Consequently, the metaphorical expression of an Open Door policy was not merely an example of political rhetoric dreamed up by a Tory government and abandoned by its Liberal successor. On the contrary,

Asquith's government remained every bit as concerned to keep that particular door ajar, or to push it open further, as Lord Salisbury's cabinet had been in 1900.

Whatever the situation was elsewhere in East Asia, the wearisome fact remained that Anglo-Chinese relations were hardly likely to reach a truly satisfactory state while the xenophobic empress dowager remained the dominant figure in framing imperial policy in Peking. Her death at the age of seventy-three on 15 November 1908, however, following the fatal collapse on the previous day of the thirty-seven-year-old Emperor Kuang-hsu, appeared to offer the British the most enticing prospect yet of forming a better, more constructive, and less enigmatic relationship with the Manchu court than had been the case in the past.[36] In reality, the baleful influence that the empress dowager had exerted upon the throne in her lifetime—especially in its idiosyncratic behavior toward foreign powers—was not substantially eroded by her demise. Therefore, while Britain may well have wished for commercial purposes, if for no other higher motive, to pose as China's friend, the hollowness of the claim was evident to the authorities in Peking. As a result, it would be fair to say that a basic level of distrust remained to bedevil their relationship in the few years left to the Ch'ing dynasty. Nonetheless, this official reserve did not amount to much in practice, for the Chinese authorities were no longer in a position to dictate terms to any of the great powers, least of all to Great Britain, which had shown in the past that it possessed the industrial and military muscle to impose its will upon the Manchu court when and if called upon to do so.

By the time of the Chinese Revolution in 1911, British investments in China ranged from railways and mining concessions to textiles, poultry, and tobacco. Financial credit was provided by the Hong Kong and Shanghai Banking Corporation, and many firms in Shanghai and Tientsin availed themselves of these benefits. In addition to the import-export trade, many firms were involved in a wide variety of other commercial tasks in the treaty ports. Ownership of both large tracts of land and buildings was also a source of considerable wealth for the British in China at this time.[37]

While these investors quite naturally desired more than just a token element of political stability, the Chinese Revolution ensured that they were denied even this during the next two years. In the ensuing turmoil brought on by the eclipse of the Ch'ing dynasty and the birth of the republic, Britain had little option but to keep its ships in place and trust in their deterrent value. On the whole, this policy worked, as the various belligerents chose not to widen the scope of the conflict by attacking or even meddling with the economic interests of the great powers.

Relieved that it had emerged relatively unscathed from the tumultuous events that had taken place in China, the British government was beginning to come to terms with Yuan Shih-k'ai's presidency when the European situation deteriorated to the point of war in August 1914. After the Japanese entered the fray on 23 August, the threat posed by the German squadron based hitherto at Tsingtao was swiftly removed by Vice-Admiral Graf von Spee's decision to leave Chinese waters in search of a safer harbor and richer pickings—such as unprotected merchant ships—plying along the South American coast.[38]

Von Spee's decision to withdraw from China—welcome though it undoubtedly was to the Admiralty in London—did not result in the British removing all their warships from the region, even if it led ultimately to a reduction in the number of vessels on Far Eastern duties. A number, admittedly a fluctuating one, were still deemed necessary to continue policing the vast area, in excess of 16 million square miles, covered by the China Station. Apart from recommissioning the 12,175-ton battleship HMS *Triumph*, which had been in reserve at Hong Kong at the outset of the campaign, Britain had a variety of warships on hand to patrol Chinese waters, show the flag, and assist in trade protection. Although there was much coming and going on the China Station throughout the war, the Admiralty insisted upon retaining a naval presence in the region and not relying entirely upon expressions of good faith from its eastern ally, the Japanese, who professed a willingness to look after British interests for them.[39]

Although alarm about the unscrupulousness of the Japanese grew in British circles after the presentation of the infamous Twenty-One Demands in January 1915, Asquith's government hoped it could avoid being dragged into the controversy or becoming identified too closely with its ally's imperialistic ambitions in China. In British eyes, the Japanese action was reprehensible, not least because it was likely to alienate the Chinese and make them more inclined to lapse into another bout of destructive antiforeignism. Although President Yuan Shih-k'ai's acceptance of the Japanese ultimatum in May 1915 resolved the matter temporarily, it left the British apprehensive about the future.

When China finally entered the war on the side of the British and Japanese on 14 August 1917, it did so out of a conscious fear of the future. On the face of it, the decision to ally with two nations that had done most in both the distant and recent past to embarrass and molest it appears curiously perverse. Yet far from being foolish and illogical, China's late entry into the war achieved one of its government's primary objectives, namely, securing a berth for itself at a future international peace conference. Unfortunately, the presence of China's delegates at the Versailles Conference from January 1919 onward did little to safeguard Chinese interests, and they withdrew in disgust four months later because Japan was awarded the former German rights and concessions in Shantung and Manchuria. This contentious decision by the allies, which gave formal approval to what had been the basis of Japan's earlier notorious ultimatum to Yuan's government in January 1915, took the Chinese government by surprise and convinced many in Peking and far more in the provinces beyond that the European nations could not be trusted. This award did considerable damage to the European cause by stimulating Chinese nationalism, in particular the May Fourth Movement, while strengthening the already widespread belief that ultimately on issues concerning their sprawling country, the Chinese people could only rely on themselves. Xenophobia, which was never far from the surface in the world's most populous country, thereafter reasserted itself with a vengeance.[40]

At the same time that antiforeignism was gaining ground in the coastal cities and treaty ports, the entire country began to be wracked by rebellion and the breakdown of law and order. Without an imperial authority, China rapidly disintegrated into provincial particularism and warlordism. In this atmosphere of almost perpetual crisis, warships of the European powers and the United States returned in greater numbers to the rivers and ports of China, determined to uphold the national interests of the governments that had sent them into these waters. As the north-south divide grew ever deeper, with the Yangtze forming a natural barrier between the geographical halves of the country, the foreign naval forces in China assumed an increasing responsibility for policing the areas in which they were situated. Unwilling to surrender their economic interests to the safekeeping of others in what was rapidly becoming a near anarchic state, Britain had four warships, including the 10,000-ton cruiser HMS *Hawkins* and fifteen modern gunboats on the Yangtze alone by the summer of 1920.[41]

It soon became obvious that a China engulfed by civil war and teetering on the verge of collapse benefited no state except Japan. Unsympathetic to Japan's cause, the United States used the China card deliberately in support of its bid to see the Anglo-Japanese Alliance dissolved and a new deal struck over the future of the Far East. Britain responded sluggishly to these American overtures, realizing that it had gained substantial strategic benefits from the alliance during the First World War.

In the end, of course, Britain's fragile, war-torn economy and the nature of its financial indebtedness to the United States proved to be the two most decisive factors in forcing the coalition government of David Lloyd George to the conference table in Washington D.C. from November 1921 to February

1922. Once there, however, its representatives played a constructive role in the eventual settlement. On paper at least, the results of the conference appeared to favor the Chinese, in that the signatory powers recognized that if they continued to deny China its sovereign rights by insisting upon the retention of their own extraterritorial rights and tariff privileges, they could arouse the Chinese masses against them, thereby risking the very investments they wished to preserve.[42]

As so often happened in the past, the foreign powers said one thing and then did another. Several years elapsed before the Nine Power Treaty was actually ratified and its clauses implemented. In the meantime, the chronic political instability in China worsened with the resumption of the civil war in November 1922, to the point that the foreign warships stationed in the country were sometimes drawn into the fray. British warships, by virtue of their numbers and the scale of the investments they were assigned to protect, were often to the fore in these incidents. Many of their activities from Canton northward along the coast and into the interior of China in the post-1922 period can be classified as relatively modern examples of gunboat diplomacy.[43] Whether or not force was actually used to gain specific objectives, the vessels involved in these incidents were prepared to use their weapons if necessary. Moreover, the actions of these foreign ships constituted an interference in Chinese affairs that was contrary to the spirit and letter of the Nine Power Treaty.

By the end of 1924, many Chinese people, not just the radicals and militants, agreed with Dr. Sun Yat-sen that extraterritoriality and the entire apparatus of the unequal treaties were an unjustifiable anachronism that ought to be abolished. A series of unfortunate and tragic mistakes made by the British in the spring and early summer of the following year, culminating in the incident at Shanghai on 30 May and the Shameen massacre on 23 June 1925, greatly increased this awareness and led to the imposition of a general strike in Hong Kong and boycotts against British and Japanese goods in Canton and throughout the province of Kwangtung.[44]

If 1925 was a bad year for the British in China, 1926 was even worse. One controversial incident stalked the other as the British found themselves the chief target of the Nationalist leaders' rhetoric and the enduring symbol of foreign repression. General Chiang Kai-shek's announcement in July 1926 of the opening of his Northern Expedition to reunify the republic under a Nationalist government did much to touch off this new wave of xenophobia that swept along the Yangtze valley. Whenever it became threatening, British naval vessels were called into action to try to curb the excesses of the Kuomintang's (KMT) more volatile supporters. Anyone with a sense of history witnessing the unrestrained naval bombardment of Wanhsien on 5 September 1926, for example, would have recognized a Palmerstonian dimension to the shelling of the old city by HMS *Widgeon* and HMS *Cockchafer.*[45]

Fortunately, sanity soon prevailed; the British government came to the rather belated conclusion that incidents like that at Wanhsein were harmful and that an accommodation would have to be made with the most vibrant force in Chinese politics at the time, namely, the Nationalist government installed in the south of the country. Once this realization dawned, Stanley Baldwin's Conservative government in London began to adopt a two-track policy regarding China. While its embassy personnel were encouraged to retain their diplomatic links with the authorities in Peking, its representatives in south China were urged to open negotiations with the KMT administration at Canton. It was hoped that in return for British support for the systematic implementation of the Nine Power Treaty, the Nationalists would use their influence among the people of Hong Kong and Kwangtung province to call off the anti-British strikes and boycott. As an act of apparent good faith, the British government drew up the December Memorandum, which it circulated to the other signatory members of the Nine Power Treaty. This document, despite its diplomatic hyperbole, seemed nonetheless to be a commitment on behalf of His Majesty's Government toward satisfying, as far as possible, the legitimate aspirations of the Chinese people, especially in regard to tariff autonomy and a revision of the international treaties forced on the imperial court and the republican governments that had succeeded it.[46]

Far from leading to a rapid improvement of the British position in China, the December Memorandum failed to receive the blessing of either of the two main factions in the Nationalist leadership. Both the leftists, who had established a provisional government with Russian backing at Hankow in January 1927, and those of a more moderate political persuasion who sympathized with the aims of the Northern Expedition, had used antiforeignism as a popular rallying cry to gain popular support in the past, and neither group would lay this attitude aside for the time being. Within the first fortnight of the new year, this wave of xenophobia had swept away the British concessions at Hankow and Kiukiang and made life virtually untenable for foreign merchants in Changsha. British warships picked up the evacuees on each occasion. Encouraged by the scale of their success, the Nationalists began to make threatening suggestions about the future existence of the International Settlement at Shanghai. Rumors of this sort led to a massed naval demonstration off the port by thirty warships drawn from eight nations with interests in China. By the end of the month, some forty thousand foreign troops were assembled and ready for combat should the KMT or its supporters attempt to overrun the Settlement. This firm response on behalf of the international powers ensured that any plan of action against Shanghai that had been considered by the KMT was now suspended indefinitely.[47]

Far from ending the crisis in China, the assertive role played by the foreign powers over Shanghai alienated the two wings of the Nationalists even further. In Nanking, matters came to a head in March 1927 when serious looting and mob action became once again the norm. Aggravated by what was happening in the city and anxious lest the situation deteriorate even more, the British and Americans retaliated by instructing their warships to bombard Nanking until order was restored.[48] After shelling the city without restraint, the British cruiser HMS Emerald—together with the two American destroyers the USS Noa and the USS Preston—anchored, put men ashore, and began evacuating their nationals from the city. Other ships performed similar tasks elsewhere on the Yangtze. By the end of the month, forty-seven warships were concentrated at Shanghai; Britain supplied an aircraft carrier, five cruisers, a destroyer, and two gunboats to the collective effort.[49]

After being at such a low ebb, Anglo-Chinese relations began to make a dramatic recovery in the following months, mainly as a result of Chiang Kai-shek's decisive action in April 1927 against the leftists in the KMT who had congregated at Wuhan. Thereafter, as the moderate faction began to establish its ascendancy within the party by purging the Communists and their sympathizers from its ranks, a more pragmatic, less confrontational policy was adopted toward the business interests of the foreign powers in China. This more realistic attitude survived the resignation of General Chiang in August and encouraged British shipping to begin recovering some of the ground it had lost over the last three tumultuous years. As the Yangtze opened up once more to foreign commerce, British merchants and traders began returning to the ports from which many had been driven by mobs of frenzied Chinese earlier in 1927.[50]

While the political carousel continued to turn in China with the resignation of Wang Ching-wei in September and Chiang Kai-shek's return from Japan in November 1927, official British policy remained supportive of the Nationalists without identifying anyone in particular with whom they were openly consorting. They maintained this position until General Chiang and the Nationalist forces he commanded had completed the second and final phase of the Northern Expedition in June 1928. Meanwhile, the Royal Navy discontinued the convoy system it had operated for British shipping on the upper Yangtze since December 1927.[51] Thereafter, the contentious question of treaty revision could not be long delayed because the essential requirement of the foreign powers—that is, that there must be a unified government in China with which to discuss these issues—now appeared to be an indisputable fact.

Once full tariff autonomy had been restored to the Chinese by an agreement signed with the British on 20 December 1928—the very day that Baldwin's government in London officially recognized Chiang Kai-shek's regime as the National government of China—talks got under way on ending the entire concept of extraterritoriality. Neither Sir Austen Chamberlain, of the Baldwin government, nor his successor at the Foreign Office, Arthur Henderson, doubted the depth of feeling on this issue in China. Both were informed that if an acceptable solution to this problem could not be negotiated, the Nationalists would resort to a unilateral repudiation of what they described as the "unequal treaties." Under pressure to reach agreement with the Nationalists before 1 January 1930, Ramsay MacDonald's Labour government formally announced the return of the British Concession at Chinkiang on 15 November 1929. Shortly afterward, Henderson agreed that the deadline of 1 January would be seen as beginning the process of abolishing extraterritoriality. This agreement had the effect of further improving relations between the two governments. It did not take long to reach agreement on the abrogation of the lease at Wei-hai-wei, which came into effect on 1 October 1930, or the return to Chinese control of the British Concession at Amoy in the previous month.[52]

Just when it appeared that political stability had settled upon China in 1930, the country was plunged once more into the maelstrom of a civil war. British gunboats saw a great deal of action during this turbulent year, none more so than HMS *Teal,* HMS *Aphis,* and HMS *Bee,* all of which were caught up in the fight for control at Changsha in late July. Well known for the depth of its antiforeign feeling, Changsha displayed this characteristic with some ferocity as the month drew to a close, forcing the British, Americans, Italians, and Japanese to intervene decisively and evacuate those foreigners who did not wish to stay and risk the wrath of the mob.[53]

By November 1930, the latest bout of civil and military unrest to sweep over China had at last ended in Chiang Kai-shek's favor. If he thought that consolidating his hold on power by being appointed to the presidency of both the National government and the Executive Yuan would impress the foreign powers, he was to be sorely disappointed. Such had been the history of bitter feuding and factional politics since the revolution of 1911 that neither the British nor the Americans had much confidence that restoring peace on this occasion would presage a long, uninterrupted period of political calm in China.

In this mood, the foreign powers began to drag their feet over the question of ending extraterritoriality. There had been little progress on this issue before the Nationalists, at their convention in May 1931, revived the threat to abolish the unequal treaties by their own action if necessary. Although a draft treaty was hurriedly prepared by Sir Miles Lampson and Dr. C. T. Wang, representatives of the British and Chinese governments respectively, in the form of notes exchanged between them on 6 June 1931 covering the terms of their agreement, that was as far as the quest for an end to extraterritoriality went for more than a decade.[54]

Thereafter, the attention of the Chinese government shifted to more immediate problems, namely, the danger posed by Japan. In using the Mukden incident of 18 September 1931 as a pretext for its seizure of Manchuria, Japan demonstrated its conversion to military rule and to the imperial doctrine of *Nanshin-ron* or southward expansion.[55] When Japan extended the scope of its invasion to Shanghai at the mouth of the Yangtze in January 1932, the British responded by ordering five of their 10,000-ton, 8-inch gun cruisers of the *Kent* class to the port. Once there they joined units of the French, Italian, and U.S. navies in a successful bid to deter the two belligerents in the Sino-Japanese encounter from disrupting or endangering the continued existence of the International Settlement in the city.[56]

Japan's interest in the economic penetration of China, much stimulated by its wretched experience in the wake of the Wall Street Crash of October 1929, became more evident as the 1930s proceeded. Beginning in the northeast, Japanese merchant shipping interests sought to increase their share of China's lucrative coastal and riverine trade at Britain's expense. It failed comprehensively to do this. Whatever success it may have had in Manchuria was cancelled out by its dismal performance elsewhere in China. While Japanese shipping in Chinese waters went into an accelerated decline in the post-1931 period—measured by both the number of ships entering and clearing customs as well as by actual tonnage—the British share of the China trade held relatively steady and only began to decrease appreciably in the years after the Sino-Japanese conflict began in 1937 (see Appendix 2).

Throughout the 1930s as one crisis followed another in the Far East without diplomatic resolution, British commercial interests in China were once more vulnerable to forces beyond their control. Ultimately, military conflict—whether of a civil war nature against the Communists or as a defense against invasion by the Japanese—was bound in the long term to distort trade patterns in China. Nonetheless, Britain could and did still derive substantial benefits from providing a service to the community in the interim period. It was particularly anxious to protect its most important commercial assets in and along the Yangtze basin and did so by retaining a total of thirteen gunboats and one cruiser on the river. Once the undeclared Sino-Japanese War had broken out after the Marco Polo Bridge incident of 7 July 1937, however, British shipping interests in China experienced a rapid fall in business and prosperity. Their commercial vessels encountered difficulties in honoring contracts because they were excluded from certain ports and rivers for indefinite periods owing to the military operations being waged in the country. This acute dislocation of the British-China trade had major consequences, for once this decline set in, it proved to be irreversible.

In the past, conventional wisdom dictated that in this period of great instability when British and other foreign vessels were prevented from using, say, the Yangtze, Japanese shipping interests stepped in to take up the slack. In fact, there is very little evidence to support this view, and if anything, the available statistical information points to another, quite different, conclusion.[57]

Although the British disliked what was happening in China, there was not much they could do about it on their own. In the absence of any agreement on concerted action by the signatories to the Nine Power Treaty, Anthony Eden, the British foreign secretary, tried in vain during the late autumn and early winter of 1937–38 to interest the Roosevelt administration in some form of naval demonstration off the China coast to warn the Imperial Japanese forces that they should behave or face the consequences. His view that the time had come for a showdown with the forces of totalitarianism seemed to be borne out by a series of rash acts committed by the Japanese military against foreign shipping on the Yangtze in December 1937. For a few days at least, the latest Far Eastern crisis provided Eden with his best chance yet to persuade the Americans that some form of punitive action was necessary to bring the Japanese to their senses. Whatever prospects there had been for some form of joint or parallel action with the U.S. Navy in eastern waters, however, were soon disspelled by astute Japanese diplomacy. After the government in Tokyo had issued a fullsome apology and agreed to pay an indemnity for the *Panay* incident, the U.S. government decided not to pursue the matter any further. Eden's hopes of a more trenchant response were dashed, and he was left reflecting on what might have been.[58]

Despite the growing difficulties that they faced by remaining in a country convulsed by war and subject to an irksome measure of Japanese military rule, British ships were not withdrawn from Chinese waters. They had been sent there to protect British investments in China and to encourage bilateral trade. No government in London at any stage of the economically ruinous 1930s could afford to neglect, let alone turn its back on, these sizeable assets.[59] Neville Chamberlain's administration followed the trend set by its predecessors in this respect. When war broke out in Europe in September 1939, therefore, the British government saw good reasons for retaining the services of four cruisers, four destroyers, seventeen submarines, five escort vessels, and twenty gunboats in Chinese waters. Usually, the larger vessels in the fleet were on patrol. It was their task to intercept, detain, or sink any German merchant ships they found on the high seas and to investigate all reports of enemy sightings in northern waters. Because the reports were rarely accurate, the warships on the China Station spent an inordinate amount of their time chasing elusive shadows.[60]

Once the phoney war in Europe finally gave way to the real thing in the spring of 1940 and Japanese imperial ambitions began to grow in East Asia, the Admiralty wisely concluded that conditions had changed and the deployment of a large fleet in Chinese waters had become redundant. As a result, the headquarters of the China Station was transferred from Hong Kong to Singapore, and the vessels assigned to it were expected to operate in Southeast Asian waters. By November 1941 as Anglo-Japanese hostility increased, British naval activity in China had virtually come to a halt; the Royal Navy's presence in these waters was reduced to three cruisers (*Danae, Dauntless, Durban*) and nine gunboats, the rest having been either pensioned off or withdrawn for duties elsewhere.[61]

By the time the Japanese cast aside peace for war in December 1941, the cruisers had gone, all but three of the gunboats had been withdrawn to Hong Kong or Singapore, and British investments in China—built up at great cost over at least two centuries—were summarily left to await their fate. British power had at last been turned back from China; an era had passed.

2. Renewal of an Old Adventure

*B*Y THE time the Second World War shuddered to a halt shortly after the atomic devastation of Hiroshima and Nagasaki in early August 1945, Britain had already elected a Labour government into power by a landslide majority. If its election promises could be believed, Clement Attlee's government was pledged to usher in a new and much-needed era of modernization and social reform for a nation that had emerged drained from nearly six years of warfare.

Although the government did honor its election pledges on many domestic issues in the coming months, its attempt to dispense with the trappings of imperialism on the foreign stage was not so successful. In fact, Britain's financial indebtedness was such that the government could not afford to be politically squeamish about retaining its overseas investments, especially when those assets were the source of much-needed foreign currency. This was particularly the case in commodities such as Malayan rubber and tin, which had a lucrative market in the United States and whose dollar earnings could then be used to bolster the flagging British exchequer.[1] Whereas this economic exploitation of Malaya was encouraged by the return of British rule to parts of Southeast Asia in the immediate aftermath of the war, the same plausible excuse cannot be advanced as the rationale for Britain's ultimately disastrous foray into China at the height of the cold war in 1948.

In contrast to later developments, the British Labour government behaved with a sensible degree of circumspection toward China in the immediate postwar period. Its wartime predecessor had, after all, signed a treaty with the Chinese government on 11 January 1943 renouncing all British extraterritorial rights in the country. Attlee's administration had little difficulty resisting the blandishments of those of its business fraternity who were most inclined to see the government support a renewed British commercial offensive in China once that country had reverted to a peacetime setting.

China did not, however, experience a long, uninterrupted spell of calm once the Japanese had sued for peace. Indeed such was the enmity between the KMT and its Communist opponents that the threat of civil war was in the air well before the Second World War had officially ended. In these disturbed conditions, opportunities for a full-scale resumption of British trade with China were poor and likely to remain so for an indefinite period. It was, therefore, wise of the British government not to push the issue at the outset and join the other major world powers at Moscow in December 1945 in officially adopting a policy of nonintervention in the Chinese civil war. For some time thereafter the British government avoided making any decisions or implementing any action in the region that might compromise its relations with either belligerent.[2] This arrangement suited the British admirably in the coming months as disenchantment with Generalissimo Chiang Kai-shek and his corrupt, neofascist regime continued to grow, and concern about the long-term threat to regional security posed by Mao and the forces of the Communist party remained a nagging problem that refused to go away.[3] Embarrassed by the one and disturbed by the other, the Labour government tried to postpone making any controversial decisions on the China question until the political and military situation was resolved either in favor of the KMT or the Peoples Liberation Army (PLA).[4]

Although it made a lot of sense for the British to keep their options open and preserve as neutral a stance as possible in the civil war, it was a task that proved to be easier said than done.[5] More than anything else, diplomatic accreditation tied the government in Whitehall to that of the KMT. Attempts to construct some form of diplomatic liaison with the Communist authorities consistently foundered on this formidable obstacle.[6] According to the accepted wisdom of the time, because a policy of dual recognition was out of the question, the British could only expect to be represented with the Communists if they withdrew their recognition of the Nationalist government. Even though they were unlikely to carry out such a radical initiative in the foreseeable future, Attlee's administration, along with the other leading western powers, tried vainly to pursue a compromise, which managed, as is so often the case, to satisfy no one.[7]

When the KMT decided to move the seat of its government from Nanking to Canton in February 1949, for example, the British decided to keep its ambassador in the former capital despite the likely occupation of that city by the PLA in the near future. A counselor was sent to maintain an official diplomatic link with the Nationalists in Canton, and consular officers in areas controlled by the Communists were told to remain at their posts to keep an eye on the activities of the Chinese Communist party (CCP) cadres.[8] In this way the British hoped that local contacts might be encouraged with the CCP and that from these somewhat ad hoc arrangements, a decent working relationship might be formed in the future between London and Peking. This plan was doomed to failure from the beginning. It smacked of the kind of unequal treatment that the Communists despised but expected from western governments. As a result, whenever British consular officials in Communist areas attempted to establish a measure of liaison with members of the CCP or the PLA, their efforts were spurned from the outset and proved to be utterly ineffective.[9]

Not surprisingly, perhaps, frustration with this situation ran high in the British consulates at Mukden, Tientsin, and other major northern Chinese cities where the officials—who were willing to deal with the local Communist authorities on a de facto basis—found themselves entirely powerless and completely unable to implement the official policy of building diplomatic bridges between the British government and the Communists, which was required of them by the foreign secretary. Peter W. Scarlett, an assistant under secretary assigned to the China desk at the Foreign Office in London, sympathized with those who felt that few if any benefits accrued to the United Kingdom from maintaining a presence where it was not wanted. In a memorandum drafted on 12 February 1949, referring to the plaintive opinion expressed by the consul general at Mukden that there was little point in him remaining in the city if the Communists would not do business with him or recognize his official existence in their midst, Scarlett noted:

> He has of course very few British interests to defend & probably feels that a political listening post which cannot report what it hears is not worth maintaining. However we cannot do anything at present.[10]

British irritation with the Chinese was not solely confined to their dealings with the Communists, as they had discovered when cooperating with the Nationalists in the immediate postwar period. Many of the difficulties faced during this time stemmed from honoring agreements made during the Second World War when Churchill's government and that of Chiang Kai-shek were allies against the Japanese. Attlee's administration had, for instance, given in to pressure from the KMT authorities in January 1946 and gone ahead with a scheme agreed on earlier by the War Cabinet in October 1944 to lend the Chinese navy a certain number of British warships. Whatever its doubts on the wisdom of the proposed transfer might have been, the Admiralty hoped that the ships, by assisting in postwar reconstruction of the Chinese fleet, might strengthen the bonds linking the two navies and thereby help to increase or at least maintain British maritime influence in the region. Under the terms of the agreement announced on 23 January 1946 by the first lord of the Admiralty, the British government loaned a sloop (HMS *Petunia*), a 1000-ton destroyer (HMS *Mendip*), a light cruiser of 5,270 tons (HMS *Aurora*), two submarines, and eight harbor defense motor launches to the KMT navy for a five-year period.[11] Conscious that the PLA would see this as more than mere favoritism, the Attlee administration trusted that the loan period would somehow pass without any incident. It was not to be so fortunate. As well as being more than a mere technical infringement of the Moscow Declaration on nonintervention, the transfer of these British vessels to the KMT at a time when the civil war was being fought was bound to create an element of controversy in Anglo-Chinese relations even if a specific crisis did not occur involving any of the ships.

Unfortunately, crises dogged the enterprise from the outset. Shortly after being put into service, HMS *Petunia* was sunk in a collision off Formosa in March 1947. If this was not a sufficient cause for the British government to regret its decision to lend the ships in the first instance, a further complication arose in the spring of 1948. On 3 April, the Nationalist government pressed the British to abrogate the loan and agree instead to give the vessels to the Chinese navy as a gift for services rendered during wartime. After a month of talks on the matter, a compromise was agreed upon whereby the *Aurora*, the nonexistent *Petunia*, and the eight motor launches would be passed to the Chinese government on 19 May 1948, providing that China withdrew its outstanding claim for compensation against the British government for its requisition in 1941 of six Chinese customs cruisers for use in the war against the Japanese.[12] This agreement did not end the matter, for on 25 February 1949 the officers and crew of the *Aurora* (which was by that time renamed the *Chungking*), the most potent vessel in the Nationalist fleet, defected to the Communists. Enraged by this embarrassing defection, KMT aircraft managed to locate, bomb, and sink the *Chungking* off Hulutao, in the Liaotung Gulf of northeastern China, on 19 March 1949.[13]

By this time, Attlee's government had also found the KMT's strict interpretation of the January 1943 treaty, by which the British had finally relinquished their extraterritorial rights in China, to be too narrow for its taste. Despite its theoretical commitment to removing the last vestiges of the unequal treaties, the Labour government in London had come to realize by the early months of 1948 that, unequal though they had been, there was still something to be said for these former special privileges that their predecessors had enjoyed in the past. Under pressure from British commercial and mercantile interests in the Far East, who made no secret of their desire to reestablish themselves as a major force in and beneficiary of the valuable Chinese coastal and inland trade, the Foreign Office was forced to reexamine its position on British shipping in China.[14] An enquiry of this kind soon revealed the extent of the financial loss incurred by British merchants as a result of the abrogation of their treaty rights in 1943 and the overtly nationalistic policy pursued by the powerful Chinese shipping lobby thereafter.

> Prior to the relinquishment of British extraterritorial rights in China under the 1943 Sino-British Treaty British shipping interests, like those of the other Treaty Powers, enjoyed cabotage rights along the China coast and rivers and rights by navigation in Chinese inland waters. In 1937 British shipping carried 42.4% of China's domestic trade and 36.5% of her ocean trade. Since the abolition of extraterritoriality foreign shipping has been excluded from the cabotage trade and from Chinese rivers and inland waters. Certain ports are open to direct overseas trade, but none of the deep-water Yangtze river ports have been so opened.[15]

Although the Chinese government did not possess a merchant fleet capable of handling all its peacetime commerce in China, it had refused to call for assistance from any of the British companies, such as Jardine Matheson or Butterfield and Swire, who had the capacity to take on what the local merchant fleet could not cope with. While it was evident that Attlee's government could not unilaterally reassert these lapsed privileges in China on behalf of British companies—no matter what ingenious interpretations of the 1943 agreement were dreamed up by their businessmen in the region—it remained aware of the possible use of other naval schemes that might be contemplated if the turmoil and chaos spawned by the civil war worsened in the future.

This particular scenario was soon created, for once the PLA had embarked upon its major drive southward on 6 November 1948, the KMT's position began to deteriorate markedly.[16] As the days passed and the scale of the Communist victory in northern and central China began to be appreciated by western diplomats residing in Nanking, it was difficult for them not to be extremely pessimistic about the future prospects of the Nationalists, who seemed to lack the vitality, vigor, and commitment of their adversaries.[17]

Alarmed by reports that the KMT forces were encountering stiff resistance from the PLA and concerned that the Yangtze region would soon become the focus of extensive military operations, the Commonwealth envoys residing in

Sir Ralph Stevenson (courtesy of Mark B. Stevenson).

Nanking reached a unanimous conclusion that Sir Ralph Stevenson, the British ambassador in China, should approach Chiang Kai-shek's government with a request for the British to exercise rights of passage along the Yangtze river from Shanghai to Nanking and to station a Royal Navy frigate or destroyer in the capital.[18] He issued the appeal on the basis that a warship could provide protection for British nationals living and working in the city and afford them both moral support and a means of escape from the area at short notice, should it be necessary.[19] Significantly and ominously, given the course of later events, neither the Foreign Office nor the Admiralty appear to have raised any particular objections to this scheme either at the time it was debated or at any time thereafter.[20]

Although concern for the fate of Nanking and those living there was justifiable, the western powers were even more anxious about the future of the port city of Shanghai. Neither the British nor the Americans wished to surrender their investments in this city or the area surrounding it and looked ahead without enthusiasm to the prospect of a long, grim struggle for supremacy in the Yangtze basin between the PLA and the forces of the KMT.[21] Aware of the dangers of becoming entangled in the civil war and wishing to avoid this fate if at all possible, both governments still managed to adopt controversial policies that endangered those very goals. For example, the British continued to allow a number of warships to dock at Shanghai, and the Americans actually dispatched a navy transport ship, the USS *Bayfield,* and two infantry companies of marines to the port. They were to be on hand in case an emergency developed in the near future that would necessitate an evacuation of American citizens from the city.[22]

If the British needed an additional excuse to support their request for the resumption of their lapsed extraterritorial rights in China, they could point to the fact that it would enable them to provide regular supplies for the British Embassy, an important consideration in a likely war zone when the usual methods of communication and supply were likely to be disrupted.[23] By the end of 1948, for instance, the road between Shanghai and Nanking had deteriorated so markedly that hauling bulk stores along this route was totally impracticable. In addition, rail traffic, particularly freight transportation, was uncertain and continually subject to the needs and whims of the Nationalist government and military. Although access by air to Nanking was still a possibility, how long it would remain so was far from clear. While the airfield at Nanking remained in Nationalist hands, it was still possible to provision the embassy. Once Nanking became a battle area, however, the continued use of air transportation for this purpose or to afford either relief or evacuation for British citizens in the region was bound to become more problematic.[24]

British naval authorities in the Far East preferred using warships on the Nanking route because they possessed two crucial advantages over any other form of transport. As well as providing a boost to expatriate morale in the area, a warship could act as an additional communications facility for handling the large amount of semioperational radio traffic that flowed between Nanking, Shanghai, Hong Kong, and Singapore at this time. In the past, WT (wireless telegraphy) communications with Nanking had always been poor and subject to long delays. Unfortunately, being slow was not the only flaw in the system. Another irritating feature of the service was its persistent and uncanny knack for corrupting many of the messages it handled. Anything that could be done to reduce mistakes and improve this frustrating situation was thought to be highly desirable. As a result, the presence in port of a ship that could deal with many cables from different locations was a relief to those in the city endeavoring to communicate with the outside world. Whether or not the vessel could

HMS Amethyst *(courtesy of Captain Charles Baker).*

assist in gathering classified information by monitoring the wavelengths used by the KMT and PLA was never made clear by those on the Far East Station. Sophisticated eavesdropping techniques could provide vital information for the British at all times. Since its importance in a crisis is readily apparent, one suspects—admittedly without corroboration—that the Nanking guardship may well have been secretly performing this task and relaying the crude data back to the Far East Station and from there on to the Admiralty in London.[25]

Stevenson's request for restricted rights of passage on the Yangtze was approved in principle by the Nationalist authorities in November 1948, with the understanding that the British would inform them in advance of the details of each journey they intended to make on the river.[26] This understanding with the KMT was reached despite a warning given by the Central Committee of the CCP on 1 February 1947—which the KMT ignored—that it would refuse to recognize any agreement made after 10 January 1946 between the Nationalists and other powers on such matters as the concession of special navigation rights for foreigners in Chinese waters.[27]

In view of later events, it was ironic that the first vessel to make the 200-mile journey upriver from Shanghai to Nanking was the frigate HMS *Amethyst*. She arrived in November with emergency food supplies destined for the embassy's use in the event of war.[28] HMS *Constance,* a destroyer, was sent as her replacement in December, and *Amethyst's* sister ship HMS *Alacrity* played a similar role later in the month; *Constance* evacuated the Czech ambassador and his family from Nanking, and the *Alacrity* brought further emergency stores—such as camp beds, bedding, and mess gear—for the embassy compound. HMS *Concord,* another destroyer, arrived in January with antifreeze for the embassy vehicles and a stock of personal items for the chain-smoking ambassador. She was relieved later in the same month by the frigate HMS *Black Swan,* who after completing her tour of duty returned to Shanghai with a number of embassy personnel bound for the new seat of the Nationalist government at Canton.[29]

At the beginning of 1949, the Nationalists were still reeling from the Communist offensives of the previous three months. As pressure on the KMT mounted and the confidence of the PLA increased, Mao had felt emboldened enough to publish an eight-point program for peace on 14 January 1949.[30] Controversial and provocative as always, Mao had indicated that Chiang Kai-shek did not figure in his long-term plans for the political development of China. Chiang had no difficulty understanding what this meant for him personally. Although he found Mao's plans for China highly objectionable, he did not wish to issue an outright rejection of the Communist ultimatum at this time and immediately resume the war with the PLA. Instead he played for time by dramatically retiring from the fray, leaving Li Tsung-jen as acting president to piece together a mutually acceptable settlement. A more Herculean task could hardly be imagined. As General Li tried unsuccessfully to square the circle over the next few months, a cease-fire on the war front brought much-needed relief to China.[31]

While Li was engaged in his task of stalling for time and because no one seriously expected the KMT to agree to Mao's demands, a decision was made by his government to move the seat of its power from Nanking to Canton where the Nationalists were more entrenched and less vulnerable. When the KMT administration decided to move south, it issued a formal request for the withdrawal of all foreign vessels from the Yangtze by 8 February.[32] According to the British interpretation of this instruction, however, the Nationalists were not objecting to the presence of foreign naval craft on the river per se, but were going through the motions in order to indemnify themselves in advance should some mishap involving any foreign vessels occur on the Yangtze in the future.[33] Confident that they would not offend the Nationalists by ignoring their request, the British preferred to take their chances and continue to maintain a naval presence at Nanking for the foreseeable future. Their belief in the deterrent value of the white ensign was totally misplaced, as later events would prove.

By February 1949, the Yangtze was no longer solely in Nationalist hands. As a result of their burgeoning military strength and recent run of successes in the campaigns of the last few months of 1948, the Communists had swept down to and were now in control of the northern bank of the river.[34] Any further journeys made by British ships up the Yangtze, therefore, would need the permission as much of the PLA as of the KMT. Unfortunately, diplomatic contact between the British and the Communists was virtually nonexistent at this time, which meant that vital information about the passages their ships were going to make on the Yangtze could not be given to the PLA. This situation made it impossible for the British to undertake these journeys with the expressed consent of the Communist authorities. One would have thought the heightened risk for the vessels embarking upon the river passage would have been only too obvious to the naval authorities both in China and at the Far East Station in Singapore.

Despite this considerable drawback, the British naval authorities had continued their Yangtze voyages, informing the KMT each time and hoping for the best as far as the Communists were concerned. On 22 March 1949, HMS *Consort*, a 1,710-ton destroyer, reached Nanking carrying 2,250 gallons of diesel fuel for the British embassy generators. She had also brought provisions and other supplies for the staff who had remained at their posts in the Australian, Canadian, and Swiss embassies in the city. *Consort* had sufficient fuel and stores to remain at anchor in Nanking for 36 days, that is, up to 27 April, if necessary, but was originally scheduled to be relieved by the Australian frigate HMAS *Shoalhaven* on 12 April.[35]

Before this changeover could be put into effect, however, events on the political stage began to take their toll. Although a general ceasefire had proved reasonably effective during the first quarter of the year, by the beginning of April the Communists were becoming restive and increasingly dissatisfied with the prevaricating tactics used by the Nationalists in settling matters between them. Buoyed up by their military strength and confident that nothing could deny them ultimate victory if the Nationalist authorities decided to reject the idea of a negotiated end to hostilities, the Communists let it be known that they would no longer tolerate further delay in the acceptance of their conditions for peace.[36] Evidence of this more trenchant stand was not slow in coming to the fore.

On 5 April 1949, Li Tsung-jen, the KMT acting president, was informed in a note—which he correctly interpreted as a thinly veiled ultimatum—that either he or General Ho Ying-ch'in, his prime minister, was expected to be present at a specially convened meeting of the Army Reorganisation Committee, which would commence its deliberations in Peking on 9 April. According to the Communists, these talks were expected to last only three days because they were designed to do little more than give formal effect to the KMT's acceptance of Mao's terms for peace. Li was warned that if the KMT failed to send a high-ranking representative to these talks as directed or refused to agree to the eight-point program for peace, the PLA would begin crossing the Yangtze on or after 12 April. It was also intimated by the PLA that regardless of what the KMT did, whether it opted for peace or war, the naval operation could not be delayed indefinitely, and Communist troops would eventually cross the river and take up their new positions on the southern bank.[37]

Li's reply was a skillfully crafted plea for moderation and compromise, dwelling upon the need for reconstruction and urging a spirit of cooperation rather than conflict between the KMT and CCP. This shrewd piece of diplomacy encouraged a moderate response from Mao, the text of which was broadcast over Peking radio on 11 April. Despite the usual rhetoric, his message appeared to offer the prospect of conciliation and a postponement of the ultimatum. Not surprisingly, Mao's answer was welcomed by the Nationalists and foreign observers alike as representing a new and more positive development in this long-running crisis.[38]

Within a few days, however, the Communists veered away from the moderate stance they had assumed in the wake of Mao's message and demanded that they be allowed to establish bridgeheads on the southern bank of the Yangtze at Kiangyin and at a point opposite Anking.[39] This demand was refused by the KMT. In fact, the acting president dispatched an appeal to the American ambassador asking whether it would be possible for the U.S. government to issue a statement that would deter the Communists from crossing the river. Ambassador Leighton Stuart was unable to give General Li such an assurance, although personally he was extremely sympathetic to the Nationalist cause and believed its leaders to be negotiating in good faith.[40]

On 16 April the screw was turned even tighter by the Communists when they presented the Nationalist envoys with an extremely harsh draft peace agreement. Huang Shao-hung, one of General Li's emissaries, was told that this document would have to be accepted in its entirety, without possibility of further revision, by the KMT government within four days. If no such consent was forthcoming by 20 April, the CCP would immediately break off the peace negotiations and resume the war without further ado.[41]

At a meeting between the acting president and the American, Australian, British, and French ambassadors in Nanking on 17 April, General Li predicted that his government would not be able to accept these terms and that a genuine peace settlement with the Communists was unlikely. Nonetheless, he professed himself anxious to discover what China's former wartime allies felt about the situation.[42]

Sir Ralph Stevenson, the British ambassador, pointed out that as a signatory to the Moscow Declaration of December 1945, his government remained committed to a policy of complete noninterference in Chinese internal affairs. Consequently, although sympathizing with General Li in his present predicament, Stevenson believed that there was nothing the British government could do for him. This chilling news was echoed by the other diplomats at the meeting and must have been profoundly disappointing for Li. Yet the alternative—acceptance of the Communist ultimatum—seemed out of the question.[43]

Under these circumstances and being well aware that the western governments were unwilling to do anything for him, General Li attempted to stall for time by making an official request to the CCP authorities in Peking for an extension of the deadline on its peace terms until 25 April.[44] Initially, this request, which eventually would be refused by the Communists, had elicited no response from them until the situation was transformed by an incident that occurred on the Yangtze during the morning of 20 April.

While events on the political stage in Peking were reaching a delicate stage, the British destroyer HMS *Consort* stood waiting to be relieved at Nanking. After the Communists issued their first ultimatum to General Li, with its scarcely veiled threats to cross the Yangtze if the Nationalists had not agreed to peace terms by 12 April, Sir Ralph Stevenson, the British ambassador, met his Australian counterpart to discuss the deteriorating situation in China. As both diplomats felt that the passage of the Australian frigate *Shoalhaven* up the Yangtze on this date might be recklessly provocative, Stevenson sent a cable on 7 April requesting permission from Vice-Admiral Alexander Madden—the flag officer second in command of the Far East Station—to postpone the trip.[45] A week later he again signaled Madden that because he was still unable to forecast what was likely to happen in the Yangtze region in the short term, nothing should be done about relieving *Consort* as yet. Stevenson's message fell victim to more than the usual transmission delays and took twenty-four hours to be received in Hong Kong. When it was eventually decoded, the flag officer proposed on 16 April that HMS *Amethyst* should be substituted for *Shoalhaven* as relief, because the latter was scheduled for operational duty in Japan under *Comnavfe* forces at the end of the month.[46]

Although Madden was prepared to await developments on the political stage, he was not disposed to cancel his plans to relieve *Consort* by *Amethyst*.

Despite the prevailing air of crisis in the Yangtze region, he decided to make the changeover on 20 April. He reached his decision before information had been received in Nanking to the effect that a second Communist deadline had been set, coincidentally for that very same day. In light of what happened subsequently, this fatal decision of Madden's perhaps was based more on the need to relieve *Consort* than as a result of his concern about the prevailing politico-military situation in China.

According to established practice, ships on the Far East Station were never supposed to let their stock of usable fuel fall below 35 percent. Madden was aware that he had no more than a week to spare before *Consort* reached this stage. By 20 April she would have only 53 percent of her fuel left, a figure that would be reduced by a further 10 percent by the time she had steamed down to Shanghai.[47] Madden may have felt that if *Consort* had remained at anchor in Nanking she would have soon urgently required additional supplies of fuel and food and that this task might have proved difficult to arrange from purely local sources.[48] Under these circumstances, therefore, a more comprehensive and effective system of supply would somehow have to be arranged from Shanghai if the task of keeping *Consort* operational in the long term was not to be gravely imperiled.

There is no evidence to suggest, however, that the flag officer thought seriously about the prospects of keeping *Consort* stranded in port at Nanking indefinitely or until such time as it was politically expedient to move her. Apart from the obvious practical objections to withdrawing a destroyer from active duty for an indefinite period, there was also the question of the logistics involved in attempting to provision such a ship while she remained in a city to which access from Shanghai was tortuous at the best of times.

Madden can hardly be faulted for wishing to avoid such a scenario as this, nor is it particularly surprising that he sought the earliest possible date for *Consort*'s passage downriver. When he made his decision, a ceasefire was being observed over the greater part of the lower Yangtze, and his desire to extricate his destroyer while peace reigned was both understandable and justifiable.[49] If this was all that had been contemplated, one could have sympathized with him had there been an incident involving *Consort* on her downward voyage.

What remains utterly indefensible, however, given the volatile politico-military situation in China and the perils associated with it, was his inexplicable decision, supported at least tacitly by the British ambassador, to send another warship to Nanking in order to relieve *Consort*.[50] Although it is true that maintaining a naval presence on the Yangtze had yielded some useful advantages for the British in the past, it is highly improbable that these were of such magnitude that they could not be done without in the future. It is still simply astonishing to think that this policy was not subject to critical reexamination, modification, or suspension in light of events in China at this time. In fact, it says much about the adroitness of British foreign policy concerning the Far East in 1949 that a closer watch was not kept on regional decision making by British government officials in China. It may say even more about the lack of perception or foresight of those same specialists in the field whose inflexibility, complacency, and above all, perhaps, arrogance were sufficient to maintain a policy that was inappropriate and dangerous under the circumstances, partial because permission could only be obtained from one of the two protagonists, and offensive because it smacked of old-style imperialism.

By no stretch of the imagination could the relief of *Consort* by *Amethyst* be regarded as merely routine. Yet the matter appears to have been handled as if it were a procedural item of little international significance. A decision about whether to send the *Amethyst* upriver was not referred to higher authority, but appears to have been made in the first instance by the flag officer and endorsed subsequently by the British ambassador.[51] Alas, at no stage other than after the crisis had broken on 20 April was the wisdom or validity of this policy ever seriously questioned by either the Admiralty or Attlee's cabinet in London.

Madden's original suggestion of 16 April for the relief of *Consort* by *Amethyst* on 20 April was based on the assumption that it would take up to three days for the Nationalist authorities to grant permission for this scheme.[52] By the time Stevenson had proffered his own advice on 18 April, he had learned that the Nationalists were virtually certain to reject the Communist peace terms and ignore the deadline for the second ultimatum, which had been fixed for midnight two days later.[53] He knew that failure to accept the Communists' conditions was likely to lead to an immediate forcible crossing of the Yangtze by the PLA, and he pointed out this probability in a cable to the Foreign Office in London on 18 April.[54] Yet on the same day and despite anticipating such action, he had nonetheless sanctioned the changeover desired by Madden—a grievous miscalculation by an experienced key diplomat. Stevenson's decision not to oppose the sailing of the *Amethyst* upriver to Nanking, an area that was almost bound to be a battle zone within a matter of days, must be judged as being both reckless and ill conceived.[55]

His error was compounded by the unwillingness of the flag officer to alter his plans. Even without receiving the necessary clearance from the Nationalist government, Madden still resolved to begin the relief mission early on the morning of 19 April.[56] In fact, he did not obtain permission from the KMT for the passage of the two British warships on the Yangtze until some hours after *Amethyst* had left Holt's Wharf at Shanghai for the voyage upriver.[57]

Vice-Admiral Sir Alexander C. G.
Madden (courtesy of the National Por-
trait Gallery, London).

Captain (later Rear-Admiral) Vernon
Donaldson (courtesy of Rear Admiral
V. Donaldson).

Shortly after *Amethyst*'s departure and more than four hours before he sent a message to Hong Kong confirming the news that the Chinese authorities had agreed to the visit, Captain Vernon Donaldson, the British naval attaché in Nanking, had sent a priority wire to Madden that made it clear that the latest Communist ultimatum was unlikely to be accepted by the Nationalists.

> If Nationalist reply fails to gain further time, Nanking Garrison Commander expects Communists to commence crossing river early on morning of 21st April. Most likely crossing places below Nanking are in vicinity of Ku-an. . . .[58]

Despite the cable's priority status, the vagaries of the WT system in China were such that this cable would still take some time to reach the flag officer's desk on board HMS *London*. Even when it was deciphered, Madden may have felt that the news was not likely to jeopardize the relief operation or endanger either vessel involved in it. Consequently, little material change was made to the original plan for the changeover. There appeared to be no need to do anything about *Amethyst* in any case, as she was scheduled to reach Nanking at 1500 hours local time on 20 April, nine hours before the expiry of the ultimatum.[59] In the case of *Consort*, the naval authorities in Nanking only advanced her departure time thirty minutes to 1130 hours on 20 April, because they were satisfied that her speed downriver would enable her to pass the dangerous spot of Ku-an before nightfall. *Consort* would be allowed to continue her passage toward Shanghai only during daylight hours. At night she would be obliged to respect the regulations governing river traffic on the Yangtze and anchor until first light the following morning.[60]

These arrangements may be criticized on the grounds that they did not leave much leeway should anything delay *Consort* on her passage downriver. One is entitled to ask why the destroyer was not instructed to leave port earlier, given the fact that she would not be on hand to conduct the customary turnover procedure when *Amethyst* arrived at Nanking? After all, the river had become a no-man's-land between the two front lines during the ceasefire, and the latest indications were that a revival of warfare was predictable within a matter of hours. Tension in the area was, therefore, bound to be high. Furthermore, because the Communists had not approved travel for either the *Amethyst* or *Consort* on the river at this time, it would be difficult for them not to see the British destroyer's passage downriver a few hours before the expiry of their ultimatum as anything other than a direct provocation by a colonial power, which was disdainful of local authority and intent upon exercizing its former privileges. If there was any discussion of this feature of the situation by either the senior embassy personnel in Nanking or the flag officer on board the cruiser HMS *London* bound for Shanghai from Hong Kong, no message was exchanged about it. Once again, the optimistic sentiment of "It will be all right on the night" seems to have prevailed at a time when the danger of an imminent resumption of the civil war ought to have dictated a far more cautious approach.

In the end, of course, it was not the voyage of the *Consort* that triggered off the famous Yangtze incident, but that of HMS *Amethyst,* her intended replacement at the Nanking outpost of the Far East Station. Although it is easy enough to be wise after the event, the whole concept of maintaining a warship at Nanking does appear to be flawed. In the first instance, it is difficult to justify using a warship on standby duty at Nanking as a means of evacuating Commonwealth nationals from the locality, particularly because those in non-government professions had been asked to consider leaving the area several months earlier.[61] In the case of the small number of government employees involved, evacuation was very much a last resort as it flew in the face of the policy—endorsed by British Foreign Secretary Ernest Bevin—that required the diplomatic corps to remain at their posts in China regardless of whether the area was controlled by the KMT or the PLA.[62]

Using a ship as a psychological weapon may have certain merits in particular circumstances; at Nanking, however, the morale-boosting effect it was expected to have upon the expatriate community could hardly compensate for the further alienation of the Communists, with whom the British hoped to forge a useful working relationship in the future. How could Britain claim to be neutral or noninterventionist in the civil war, when it was exercizing special privileges in China as a result of bilateral agreements it had made with the Nationalists? Although the Admiralty may have wished to keep the Yangtze open for vessels of all nations, the cost of doing so seems to have been prohibitively high, especially because it would reinforce the impression that Britain was nothing other than an unreformed colonial power, insensitive to change and unwilling to accept any external constraints being placed upon its conduct of foreign affairs.

One is left, therefore, with the feeling that the only tangible value a ship had at Nanking was to supplement the rudimentary WT communications network at the embassy. Useful though this service undoubtedly had been in the past, no one either in the Foreign Office or the Admiralty ever claimed that it was absolutely indispensable. This verdict could also be applied to a warship's possible use as an intelligence-gathering facility.

All of this evidence seems to suggest that the policy of maintaining a ship at Nanking was actually unnecessary and to some extent both provocative and irresponsible. If this charge appears harsh, one only needs to think of what was likely to happen when the *Amethyst* completed her tour of duty at Nanking and needed relieving. Would another naval operation have to be mounted by the British, and if so, could it be accomplished particularly if the city had fallen by this time to the Communists? Even if there was to be no replacement for *Amethyst,* would the PLA allow the frigate to leave the port and make her way downriver to Shanghai?

Although these questions ought to have been addressed by the British naval authorities, the disturbing fact is that they were not. Once the emergency on the Yangtze broke out on 20 April, the British found themselves in an exceedingly difficult situation that took them completely by surprise. That the unexpected had happened can hardly be offered by them as a suitable defense of their bankrupt policy, even if it does ring true. In essence, an initiative that had been created to protect British interests ended up endangering them. It was not just the operators of the system who were to blame for poorly orchestrating a plan that had the opposite effect of what was intended, although their responsibility was considerable; the fault lies as much with those who conceived a policy that appears to have been both opportunistic and imperious.

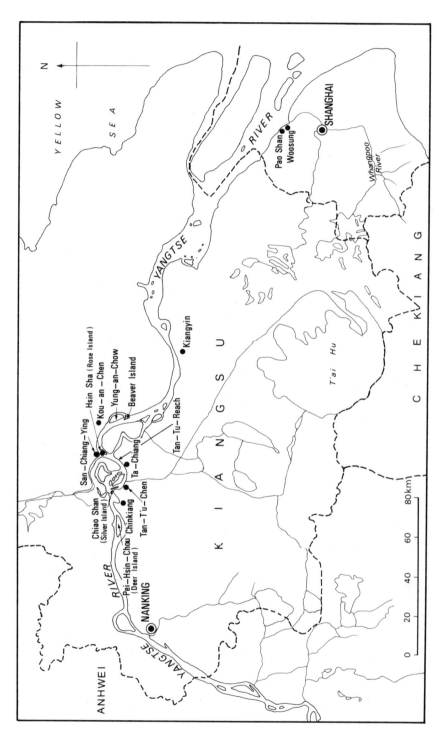

Map 2. The Course of the Lower Yangtze

3. Under Attack

AT THE END OF February 1949, after completing several weeks of antibandit patrol work off the east coast of Malaya, HMS *Amethyst* sailed to Hong Kong for her annual refit. She had not been there long before Vice-Admiral Madden, the flag officer at the Far East Station, decided to postpone the refitting program and send her as the replacement for HMS *Consort* as the Nanking guardship.[1] At 1,430 tons deadweight and nearly 300 feet in length, the frigate *Amethyst* was much smaller and perhaps more suitable for work on the treacherous Yangtze than the destroyer she was ordered to relieve.[2]

During the springtime, the Yangtze is undoubtedly one of the most difficult and formidable rivers in the world on which to navigate. Apart from its hazardous shoals, which must be negotiated with the greatest care, the navigable channel tends to be a narrow, unpredictable, and constantly shifting menace. Over the years, the Yangtze had become established as a river on which British naval captains usually employed two experienced local pilots to take their vessels up- or downstream.[3]

Amethyst sailed from Hong Kong on the first leg of her journey to the Yangtze on 12 April. She arrived at Shanghai at the mouth of the river on 15 April and expected to leave for Nanking at any time. Her sailing orders were finally given to Lieutenant-Commander B. M. Skinner on Monday 18 April. He was told to leave on the following morning and to pick up his two local river pilots off the Woosung forts shortly after moving off from Shanghai.[4]

According to Lieutenant Geoffrey Weston, the ship's crew had few apprehensions about making their way up the Yangtze, even though it meant doing so less than forty-eight hours before the expiry of the Communists' second ultimatum to the KMT. Nonetheless, they prepared themselves for possible trouble enroute, as his later report makes clear.

> Large painted union flags had been made and placed ready for display; ammunition had been got up; and it was decided to close up at action stations before proceeding through areas where the Naval Attache, Nanking, had signalled the Communists were concentrated and where crossings might take place.[5]

It was wise of them to be ready for anything since *The Times* correspondent had begun relaying dispatches on 18 April to the effect that fighting was going on between troops of the PLA and KMT in the Yangtze area.[6]

Leaving Holt's Wharf at 8:00 A.M. on Tuesday 19 April, *Amethyst*, flying the white ensign as well as the union flag at the jack staff and with another union flag painted on her hull, picked up her two Chinese pilots as arranged and made steady progress upriver against a strong tide.[7] It took some eight and a half hours to reach the town of Kiangyin where the frailty of the Nationalist position in the civil war was readily apparent. An important naval redoubt, Kiangyin stood as a painful and constant reminder of the KMT's precarious hold on the Yangtze region. Although it remained in Nationalist hands for the time being, the town and especially the harbor area were already covered by a PLA battery position dug in on the northern bank of the river a short distance away.

Upon arrival, Lieutenant-Commander Skinner observed standard orders and requested permission from the senior Chinese naval officer on board the Nationalist destroyer *Yat Sen* to drop anchor for the night. After receiving the necessary consent, Skinner anchored his ship not far from where a number of KMT warships lay.[8] Movement on the river during the hours of darkness was forbidden by the Nationalists, but even if it had not been, *Amethyst* would hardly have risked making the rest of her journey to Nanking at night. Although Skinner's original intention had been to keep his ship lit up while she lay at anchor—on the grounds that she could then be plainly distinguished as a vessel belonging to a neutral power—he immediately complied with a request from the officer on board the *Yat Sen* to darken his ship.[9]

Aware from reports he had received that further north the Communists had already begun shelling some of the Nationalist positions, Skinner addressed his crew and warned them that in the morning they would be entering a fighting zone. He ordered his men to position the union flags, which had been painted on canvas, on either side amidships even though they were not unfurled at this time.[10]

At 5:10 A.M. on Wednesday 20 April, *Amethyst* weighed anchor and wear-

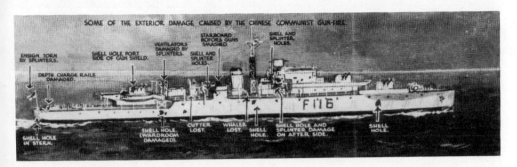

Figure 1. HMS Amethyst *after the Action on the Yangtze, 20 April 1949 (courtesy of the* Illustrated London News, *London).*

ing an additional white ensign proceeded upriver toward Nanking. Unfortunately, the advantage of an early start was all but canceled out when a large bank of fog enveloped the ship and reduced visibility to such an extent that the local Chinese pilot advised Skinner to anchor and wait for the fog to lift. *Amethyst* came to halt at 6:38 A.M. In about an hour, visibility on the river improved sufficiently for the frigate to continue on her journey. As *Amethyst* would soon reach one of the areas where the Communists were gathered in some strength, the ship's company was piped to action stations at 8:00 A.M.[11]

If called on to defend herself, *Amethyst* had an armory complement of six 4-inch caliber dual-purpose guns, four of which were mounted forward of the bridge in two pairs to form A mounting and B mounting, while the third pair, known as X mounting, was situated aft to sweep both to port and starboard and overhead if need be. In addition, there were two 40-mm Bofors guns and two single Oerlikons that could be used, if necessary, against aircraft.[12]

Shortly after closing up for action stations, the gun crews both fore and aft were asked to test their firing circuits. This was a straightforward task that should under normal circumstances create little or no noise. Strangely enough, however, when the official report was circulated later in the year, mention was made of the possibility that the noise of this testing procedure might conceivably have been heard by the Communist forces on the northern bank of the river.[13]

While the gun crews prepared for all possible contingencies, those in the engine room were advised that at 8:30 A.M., when the *Amethyst* would be passing a Communist battery position, the ship's oil-burning twin boilers

Figure 2. HMS Amethyst *(courtesy of the* Illustrated London News, *London).*

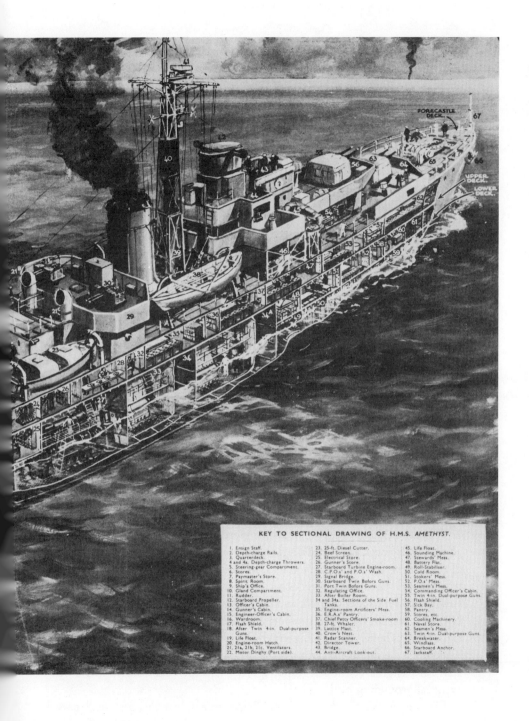

FORECASTLE DECK.

UPPER DECK.

LOWER DECK.

KEY TO SECTIONAL DRAWING OF H.M.S. AMETHYST.

1. Ensign Staff.	23. 25-ft. Diesel Cutter.	45. Life Float.
2. Depth-charge Rails.	24. Beef Screen.	46. Sounding Machine.
3. Quarterdeck.	25. Electrical Store.	47. Stewards' Mess.
4 and 4a. Depth-charge Throwers.	26. Gunner's Store.	48. Battery Flat.
5. Steering-gear Compartment.	27. Starboard Turbine Engine-room.	49. Roll-Stabiliser.
6. Stores.	28. C.P.O.s' and P.O.s' Wash.	50. Cold Room.
7. Paymaster's Store.	29. Signal Bridge.	51. Stokers' Mess.
8. Spirit Room.	30. Starboard Twin Bofors Guns.	52. P.O.s' Mess.
9. Ship's Office.	31. Port Twin Bofors Guns.	53. Seamen's Mess.
10. Gland Compartment.	32. Regulating Office.	54. Commanding Officer's Cabin.
11. Rudder.	33. After Boiler Room.	55. Twin 4-in. Dual-purpose Guns.
12. Starboard Propeller.	34 and 34a. Sections of the Side Fuel	56. Flash Shield.
13. Officer's Cabin.	Tanks.	57. Sick Bay.
14. Gunner's Cabin.	35. Engine-room Artificers' Mess.	58. Pantry.
15. Engineer-Officer's Cabin.	36. E.R.A.s' Pantry.	59. Stores, etc.
16. Wardroom.	37. Chief Petty Officers' Smoke-room	60. Cooling Machinery.
17. Flash Shield.	38. 27-ft. Whaler.	61. Naval Store.
18. After Twin 4-in. Dual-purpose	39. Lattice Mast.	62. Seamen's Mess.
Guns.	40. Crow's Nest.	63. Twin 4-in. Dual-purpose Guns.
19. Life Float.	41. Radar Scanner.	64. Breakwater.
20. Engine-room Hatch.	42. Director Tower.	65. Windlass.
21. 21a, 21b, 21c. Ventilators.	43. Bridge.	66. Starboard Anchor.
22. Motor Dinghy (Port side).	44. Anti-Aircraft Look-out.	67. Jackstaff.

would have to forsake economy for a substantial increase in turbine revolutions and an injection of speed that would take her from 11 to 16 knots, but still short of the 19.25-knot capacity of this vessel.[14]

Shortly after the frigate moved into what was thought to be a possible danger zone to the north of Low Island—some 30 miles upriver from Kiangyin—a battery on the northern bank of the river opened fire on her without warning. According to the official report of the incident, at 8:30 A.M. small arms fire and, later, medium-range artillery were directed toward the ship from the starboard side. Although the guns were difficult to locate exactly from the bridge of the *Amethyst,* they appeared to be sited in the vicinity of Hsi-hsin-wei on the island of Yung-an-chow.[15] Ten shells missed their target: some fell short, and others passed harmlessly overhead. Even so, the situation was not without danger, and the captain responded quickly to it by calling for full speed ahead. He ordered the guns to be trained on the target and to open fire once the armaments director could plainly distinguish it.[16] At the same time, X mounting crew was ordered to unfurl the union flags down the sides of the ship where they were bound to be seen by the forces attacking it from the northern bank.[17] Before *Amethyst*'s guns could engage the target, the firing ceased. It had lasted fourteen minutes. Lieutenant-Commander Skinner drafted a signal recording the incident for coding and dispatch to the flag officer at the Far East Station, but before the message could be sent, other matters intervened to prevent its transmission.[18]

Amethyst continued upriver at speed. She had proceeded about 9 miles from the scene of the first incident and was passing to the east of Rose Island—at a point some 60 miles northeast of Nanking—when she came under sustained heavy artillery fire from a Communist battery situated at the mouth of a tributary leading to the Kao-yu Lakes at San-chiang-ying. It was exactly 9:30 A.M.[19]

From the time that a 75-mm armor-piercing shell struck the ship four feet above the flag deck and bored a 3-inch diameter hole in the wheelhouse, the fate of the *Amethyst* was probably sealed. In this devastating burst of gunfire, her wheelhouse was suddenly reduced to a shambles; one rating was hit in the stomach and mortally injured; and the coxswain, Chief Petty Officer Rosslyn Nicholls, was hit by flying shrapnel and badly wounded in both the head and right leg. As he fell over to his left, he involuntarily pulled the wheel to port with him as he slid to the floor. At the same time, the shell managed to jam the starboard engine room telegraph, a crucial factor that contributed to the eventual grounding of the ship.[20]

Lieutenant Weston had been on B gundeck when the first shell passed harmlessly over the ship. As he scrambled to get to the bridge, he had to pick his way through the shattered wheelhouse, which was victim to a direct hit from the second shell fired in the attack. By the time Weston reached the bridge, the captain had ordered full speed ahead. As the ship's gunnery officer, Weston was told by Skinner to open fire on those attacking the *Amethyst*. Before he could put the order into effect, the bridge received its first direct hit. A 75-mm shell entered the frigate at an angle of 30 degrees and four feet above the bridge deck on the starboard side. It punched a hole into the bridge, traveled 15 feet, and exploded on impact in the forward corner on the port side with appalling force, wreaking havoc with virtually everyone on the bridge at this time. Before any respite could be gained, however, another shell smashed into the bridge and further aggravated the chaotic situation.[21] Weston's report of the incident is sobering.

> Everyone there was killed or wounded, except the Yeoman of signals. I received a wound in the chest, a piece of shrapnel passing through my lung. My communication number died within a few minutes; the Captain and Chinese pilot were seriously wounded (mortally as it proved). I tried to con the ship into the middle of the river, but the first hit had jammed the steering hard to port, and the ship's head swung towards the South bank.[22]

Once it became obvious that Skinner was in no state to issue further orders, Weston promptly assumed command.[23] Despite ordering full astern both, he found *Amethyst* unresponsive. Although the port telegraph worked normally, stopping the port engine as directed, the starboard telegraph had been jammed from the moment the shell had struck the wheelhouse, so the starboard engine remained at full ahead. Once Weston realized that something was dreadfully amiss, he unsuccessfully attempted to establish voice-pipe contact with the engine room. In the end and without receiving any orders to do so, Leonard Williams, the engine room artificer, decided on his own initiative to stop both engines.[24] By that time, however, the *Amethyst*—her low power room wrecked and gyro compass useless; her electrical, gunnery, lighting, and navigational circuits damaged, unable to steer or defend herself adequately—had ground to a halt on a mud bank about 150 yards from the western shore of Rose Island. All attempts to use the engines to get her bows out of the mud failed. She was trapped. It had taken only five minutes to cripple the frigate. It was now 9:35 A.M.[25]

After ordering stretcher parties to remove the casualties from the bridge to a more sheltered part of the ship on the port side well forward, Weston left the bridge and made his way to the wireless room where he drafted an urgent signal reporting what had occurred and that he had assumed command of the ship.[26] He did not know at this point that the main transmitters had been put out of action and that an emergency transmitter would have to be rigged up to send a shortened version of this message. Even so, a flash signal to all ships was dispatched at 9:46 A.M., which said simply:

> Under heavy fire am aground in approx. position about 31 degrees 10 North 119 degrees 60 mins. East. Large number of casualties.[27]

Stuck fast in the mud, the *Amethyst* was in an intensely vulnerable position. She was virtually defenseless because she had gone aground in such a way that neither her A nor B guns could be brought to bear on the target, and they were, therefore, abandoned as useless. Although peppered by shells from the battery on the northern shore and sustaining a number of serious casualties among its crew, X gun mounting remained operational for a few minutes and fired about thirty rounds in reply before the right gun received a direct hit and ceased firing. Two men were killed in this explosion, and another three were wounded by flying shrapnel.[28] Undeterred, Leading Seaman Mullins, the captain of the X gun mounting, kept the left gun in action for a few more rounds until he was ordered by Weston to withdraw in the hope of preventing further loss of life.[29]

For all Weston's good intentions, the plan failed to halt the persistent shelling of the frigate. Instead the Communist batteries continued to rake the ship with both medium and heavy artillery fire, causing more casualties as each shell registered a hit on the stricken vessel. In these circumstances, with the Communist offensive still at its height, Weston contemplated the possibility of having to defend the *Amethyst* with what remained of the ship's company against any assault force the PLA might send to subdue her. He hurriedly arranged for the distribution of bren guns, rifles, and small arms to the crew and told them to take up their positions along the upper deck to repel boarders should they attempt to come alongside.[30]

Meanwhile, stretcher parties were taking the dead and wounded from the places where they lay to the after mess deck and quarterdeck, where it was hoped they would have more shelter. Lieutenant Peter Berger, the navigation officer, had recovered consciousness by this time and was roaming the ship, as best he could, ensuring that the acting captain's orders were obeyed to the letter.[31] Amid this frenetic activity, the shelling continued unabated, and the casualty toll mounted aboard the frigate. There seemed no end in sight, for the Communists appeared intent on destroying the ship, whatever the cost in human lives.[32]

As the situation deteriorated, so the injured—who required attention from Surgeon-Lieutenant J. M. Alderton, the ship's doctor, and Baker, the sick-berth attendant—grew in number. They could do little on board ship for either the mortally wounded or those who had been seriously hurt, and Weston must have been aware of this situation from the outset. It was clear that the medical resources of the *Amethyst* were incapable of dealing with the scale and nature of this kind of crisis. It was imperative, therefore, that some plan be devised that would enable the wounded to be ferried safely ashore to receive hospital treatment while it was still possible to help them. Before anything of this kind could be arranged, however, an inspection of the boats revealed that only one, the starboard whaler, remained undamaged and in a seaworthy condition. It was lowered, and the Carley floats were towed round to the port side of the quarterdeck in order to disembark the wounded.[33]

After giving Weston an injection of morphia to deaden the pain from his shrapnel wound, Alderton and Baker were making their way to the quarter-deck to attend to some of the injured men gathered there when a shell exploded nearby, killing them both instantly.[34] This calamity underlined the gravity of the situation; it was now essential that the most seriously injured be evacuated because there was no experienced medical team aboard the frigate who could administer to their needs.

Soon afterward, sometime between 10:00 and 10:30 A.M., as the shelling wore on, Weston decided reluctantly that the only effective way to ensure the safety of the ship's company was for the majority of them to abandon the *Amethyst* and try to get to the south shore of Rose Island. Although it was hoped they could rejoin the ship later, much would obviously depend on what the Communists decided to do about the beleagured vessel. Since the first lieutenant had no way of knowing what their intentions were, he kept a steaming party on board as well as a group of about a dozen volunteers who would look after some of the stretcher cases until they were finally evacuated from the ship.[35]

Berger was assigned the task of executing this order and he did so promptly, encouraging members of the crew who could swim to go over the side and strike out for the shore and urging those who could not to man the whaler.[36] According to the official report of the incident, between sixty to seventy ratings left the ship, most of them in the boat or on the floats, but many others never received the order to abandon ship or, if they did, chose to ignore it. In all, ninety-five men, seventy of whom were uninjured, appear to have re-mained on board the *Amethyst* after the evacuation call.[37]

Commissioned Gunner Monaghan took command of the whaler as it made its way toward the shore with some of the nonswimmers and a few of the wounded on board. As the boat closed with the shore, the Communists put it under heavy machine gun fire. They soon claimed a victim. Able Seaman Sinnott, who had been wounded earlier in the morning's action, was hit once more and died soon afterward.[38] As the boat was about to reach the bank, a shell exploded nearby. Not surprisingly, perhaps, the crew panicked, and in the melee that followed, the whaler capsized, throwing both the fit and the incapacitated into the water. Some scrambled up the bank to relative safety, and the rest were dragged out of the water and beyond the range of direct fire from the northern bank.[39] Unfortunately, this incident was not the end of the matter, for now the Communist batteries concentrated their artillery as well as small arms fire on those men swimming for the shore from the *Amethyst*. How successful the Communist batteries were is difficult to judge, but it is well known that two of those who had opted to swim to safety never made it.[40]

After the men were ashore, Monaghan took charge and ordered the ratings to keep to the bank and crawl through the high grass that bordered the beach until they reached the southern edge of the island, where it was hoped they could find refuge until the situation on the Yangtze quieted down. At this stage, the general plan was for the men to stay out of range of the Communist guns and be ready to return to the *Amethyst* if and when the shelling stopped and orders for their recall were received from the acting captain. Before Monaghan's instructions could be followed, however, the survivors were met by Nationalist soldiers and directed inland to the nearest village through the minefields that had been sown all along the beach and western shore of Rose Island.[41]

At about 11:00 A.M. and for no apparent reason, the shelling of the frigate stopped, and the Communists contented themselves with raking the upper deck with machine gun fire. By this time, an inspection of the damage on board ship had revealed an urgent need for running repairs to be made to the steering gear and much more below deck. Although the attack had only lasted roughly ninety minutes, *Amethyst* had been hit repeatedly during this period, and the damage caused by this concentrated shell fire was considerable. Some of the crew were detailed to begin the long process of clearing up the debris of the assault and repairing vital equipment so the frigate could function as an operational ship again once she had extricated herself from the mud bank.[42]

Meanwhile, Monaghan, wishing to take advantage of the lull in the shelling in order to pick up more of the ship's wounded, returned from the shore in the whaler with three ratings who had volunteered for the assignment.[43] One of the rowers was Telegraphist Jack French, a young man who was to be a vital link in reestablishing contact with the outside world in the coming weeks. It was fortuitous that he had returned to the *Amethyst* because all the other wireless office personnel had jumped overboard when they heard Berger's earlier call to abandon ship.[44]

Unfortunately, shortly after the first lieutenant had decided upon a strategic withdrawal of some of his ship's company and before the firing had stopped, standing orders were complied with and Berger oversaw the destruction of all secret and confidential equipment, such as radar sets and the Typex cypher machines. They were broken into pieces with mallets and heavy spanners and thrown into the muddy brown, swirling waters of the Yangtze.[45] At the same time all code books, special cypher pads, and charge documents were collected in canvas bags and placed on the quarterdeck, ready for transfer if possible to a rescue ship. Even so, the two most secret ones were burned immediately in the galley stove in accordance with Berger's instructions. All the remaining classified material was burned on the afternoon of 21 April, after it had become evident that no early rescue could be arranged.[46]

About three hours after the attack had begun, Lieutenant Wilkinson, the engineer officer, who was ashore on Rose Island, spotted two Nationalist aircraft at a height of about 500 feet apparently attacking Communist batteries in the vicinity of the *Amethyst* with rockets and tracer shells. One of these aircraft flew over the ship at a low altitude, which suggested, of course, that *Amethyst*'s flash signal had been picked up and her distress call noted. This event increased the hope of the ship's company that in the next few hours their lonely vigil would be over; most of them confidently expected that HMS *Consort* would hasten to leave Nanking in order to come to their aid.[47]

If and when the destroyer arrived, *Amethyst* would be ready to be pulled off the mud bank on which she was grounded. In the midst of some of the heaviest shelling and before the order to abandon ship had been given, Leading Seamen Frank and Petty Officer Freeman managed to crawl along the length of the deck with a wire from the hawser wheel before fastening it in place astern for use as a towing line once *Consort* reached her.[48]

Owing to the persistent sniping from the northern bank, no one was allowed on deck except the lookout who was on B gun deck. It was he who spotted a vessel approaching at speed from the direction of Nanking at about 1:40 P.M. Although he informed Weston and they assumed it to be *Consort,* it was not positively recognized as such for another ten minutes.[49] In the meantime, Weston asked Signalman Roberts to go up on deck to signal the oncoming vessel by Aldis lamp. Roberts, still unaware that he had been blinded in one eye during the morning's shelling, took up position through an overflow port on B gundeck. Beginning by identifying his ship, he advised the destroyer to turn back if the batteries in the area opened fire upon her. *Consort* replied by asking where the enemy guns were sited and slowed from 27 to 15 knots as she waited for the frigate to reply. Perhaps Roberts did not read this signal in the bright sunlight that bathed the Yangtze at this time of day because nothing is mentioned about it in the official report. In any event, Commander I. G. Robertson, the captain of the destroyer, soon discovered the Communist guns without further assistance from the *Amethyst*. One field gun opened fire on *Consort* from a distance of about 2,800 yards.

> After two salvoes had near-missed, I opened fire with air bursts and later when emplacements could be distinguished, with H.E. After about four salvoes one gun emplacement was soon to suffer a direct hit, and fire was shifted to the next—a battery of three guns which were effectively silenced, and then a four-gun battery was engaged at 1,200 yards. No hits were obtained mainly due to the large line spread.[50]

At a distance of about $1^1/_2$ miles from the stranded *Amethyst,* Roberts saw that *Consort* was firing all her guns at the Communist batteries and was coming under fire herself. When she was about 1,400 yards away, *Consort* at last replied to the Aldis by lamp, and Roberts was able to relay the two messages he had been ordered to send to her. His first dealt with the need for urgent medical attention for the wounded, and the second asked the destroyer to set watch on 2,990 kilocyles TCS so that further messages could pass between them.[51] *Amethyst*'s radio set was operating on batteries at this time, and Lieutenant George Strain, the flotilla electrical officer, hoped that it would prove strong enough for the emergency job. He need not have worried, however, as no communication other than by lamp was exchanged between the two vessels when they met. As soon as she had passed the frigate's stern, *Consort*'s light flashed out a message asking whether it was possible to tow the *Amethyst* off the mud bank where she was embedded and whether her main engines were sound. Weston gave instructions to Roberts, who signaled that under the present circumstances a tow was only possible if the batteries were put out of action beforehand. Even as Roberts frantically tried to send this message, *Consort* disappeared around the bend and was lost to view.[52]

She reappeared soon afterward having turned around a short distance downstream. As she approached the stricken vessel once more, *Consort* came under intense fire from well-hidden, 37-mm antitank weapons and 105-mm artillery pieces on the northern bank. She received several direct hits—most notably on her bridge, wheelhouse, and gunnery control room—sustaining serious casualties among the crew and damaging her steering gear at the same time.[53] During these exchanges, *Consort* was firing constantly with every gun at her disposal. According to Geoffrey Birch, her torpedo officer, *Consort* fired between three to four hundred 4½-inch shells, plus a similar number of smaller caliber shells at the Communist positions, knocking out eight gun emplacements as she did so. This degree of accuracy could not be maintained once the calculator room had been knocked out of action on the return leg up the Yangtze. Thereafter the gunners aboard *Consort* had to resort to direct fire through open sights to engage the PLA batteries.[54]

It became clear as *Consort* closed with the *Amethyst* that the shell fire from the Communist batteries was far too heavy for any successful rescue mission to be performed at this time. Both A and B gun mountings on the destroyer had been knocked out, forward supply and director support had also been hit, and the X gun mounting was forced to go into quarters firing, that is, local control without the benefit of the fire control system. Robertson, commenting on the situation, wrote later:

> Half a mile from *Amethyst* I stopped the ship, turned and proceeded slowly down river firing all the time. We were still coming under accurate anti-tank fire from point-blank range. As my Medical Officer was overwhelmed with our casualties I reluctantly decided to withdraw.[55]

Consort steamed past the forlorn figure of the *Amethyst* for the last time and plowed her way downriver out of the original danger area and on toward Kiangyin.[56]

Although discouraging, the events of the afternoon did not entirely destroy hope of another rescue operation being mounted after dark. Weston was certainly more inclined to optimism on this score than he would have been had he known the extent of the damage inflicted on the destroyer as a result of her engagement with the PLA. Not only had the shelling killed ten of her crew and seriously wounded four others, it had caused so much damage to her vital equipment that she was forced to steer from aft, a far more complicated maneuver than usual, particularly when it had to be done on one of the most hazardous stretches of water in the world.[57]

Weston had already decided to try to refloat the *Amethyst* after nightfall when, he hoped, most of the temporary repair work would have been completed so as to make the ship serviceable again. Until such an attempt could be made, work proceeded on board at a hectic pace: the steering gear and telegraphs were restored to working order, the hole in the tiller flat was plugged, the wireless set was repaired, fuel stocks were transferred and stores from the forward part of the ship were placed ready for jettisoning once darkness came.[58]

Meanwhile, administering to the wounded on board was causing further grave concern. Apart from the rapidly dwindling stock of morphia and other pain-relieving drugs available to the seriously wounded, the sad fact was that until they were hospitalized and given urgent medical attention, their condition could only be expected to worsen. Weston realized the extent of the problem, and it strengthened his resolve to extricate the *Amethyst* from her present precarious position and make some effort to reach Nanking, if that still proved possible.[59]

Meanwhile back on Rose Island, some of the evacuees from the frigate, after being pinned down by accurate sniper fire for several hours and forced to find shelter in the long grass growing close to the shore, were eventually able to make contact in the late afternoon with two Nationalist soldiers who had come to the shoreline to lay additional landmines. Since none of the eight ratings in this party spoke any Chinese and the two Nationalist soldiers could not speak English, communication between the two sides must have been an object lesson in using what nonverbal skills each possessed. Whatever sign language was used, an understanding of sorts was soon reached between them, and it was demonstrated most vividly when the two soldiers led the ratings to where Wilkinson, the engineer officer, and another crew member of the *Amethyst* waited on the bank.[60]

As the only officer among the group of ten assembled on the shore, Wilkinson took charge and hailed those aboard the frigate, requesting the services of an interpreter so that it could be established where the other crew members of the ship had been taken. Once their location was known, he hoped a message could be taken to them ordering them to reassemble on shore for reembarkation at some suitable time during the evening.[61]

Wilkinson's call was answered by Lieutenant Keir Hett, the director-control officer, who was standing at the ship's rail facing the shore. Hett brought the only uninjured Chinese pilot up on deck to shout to the Nationalist soldiers on the shore. At that distance, however, conversation was difficult, so the whaler boat was immediately sent back to Rose Island in the hope of settling matters more expeditiously than at long range. Monaghan was again put in charge, and he decided to take two different-dialect-speaking Chinese with him ashore. He opted for the tailor who spoke Cantonese and the second pilot who spoke a northern dialect. He did not realize that Weston had already forbidden the uninjured pilot to leave the ship on the grounds that his knowledge of the navigable channel would be vital once the *Amethyst* had gouged her way off the mud bank and back into the Yangtze proper.[62]

Having rowed safely ashore, Monaghan, accompanied by the tailor and the pilot, was guided by the two Nationalist soldiers inland to the local KMT army headquarters on the island.[63] Once there, arrangements were quickly made for a Chinese doctor from a local regiment to board the ship and attend to the wounded. In addition, the Nationalists offered to supply bearers and transport to take the injured to hospital if the acting captain of the *Amethyst* decided to land them on Rose Island after dark. Monaghan then asked the whereabouts of the other crew members on the island. A colonel in the KMT army informed him that although Petty Officer Heath was in charge of a number of ratings in a village several miles away, the group could not possibly be guided back through the minefield at night. As a result, Heath's group was essentially cut off from the frigate, because Weston hoped to leave the area that evening. Once this fact was established, there was no alternative for those evacuees but to proceed to Shanghai by the safest route the KMT could devise for them.[64]

Monaghan returned to the *Amethyst* at about 7:15 P.M. with Wilkinson and the nine ratings who had been hiding close to the shore all afternoon. Once aboard ship, the commissioned gunner and engineer officer reported to Weston, and a decision was reached to flash the boilers and raise steam. Later in the evening when sufficient pressure had been reached, an attempt would be made to get off the mud bank. Despite the gloomy tone of the latest intelligence reports brought back from KMT headquarters, Weston clung stubbornly to the increasingly forlorn hope that *Consort* might reappear after dark. As a result, he was still not inclined to land any more of the wounded at this stage, preferring instead to wait for any developments that might take place in the next few hours.[65]

Although the engine room at once became a center of activity and anticipated excitement, the failure of the Chinese pilot to come back on board the frigate severely handicapped *Amethyst's* chances of steaming under her own power to relative safety. While the loss of the ship's pilot was a bitter blow, Weston still resolved to try to escape if he could.

By 10:30 P.M. with power restored to the frigate, Weston ordered the engine room to obey telegraphs, and WT contact was finally made with Hong Kong. After Wilkinson informed him that the time had arrived to coax the *Amethyst* off the mud, Weston ordered both engines full astern, but the maneuver failed to free the ship. Whatever variations Wilkinson tried in the following hour—whether port engine full astern and starboard full ahead or vice versa—the result was the same: *Amethyst* remained stuck in the mud.[66]

Having failed in these attempts, the acting captain had little alternative but to reduce the weight of the ship on the raised upper deck. A party was duly sent to the forecastle shortly before midnight to remove and throw overboard any heavy items of equipment that were not permanent fixtures and that could be safely dispensed with. At the same time the engine room was ordered to pump about 10 tons of oil overboard from numbers one and two fuel tanks.[67]

One minute before midnight, Weston ordered Wilkinson to renew his efforts to free the ship. As before, he began by using variations of engine power, and at 12:15 A.M. success occurred when some movement astern was detected by those assembled on the bridge. Once started, the ship soon forced herself off the mud bank and reentered the Yangtze.[68]

4. No Chance of an Understanding

*A*METHYST's flash signal reporting that she was under fire and aground somewhere beyond Kiangyin was monitored by the British Embassy in Nanking and picked up off the Chinese coast by the 10,000-ton cruiser HMS *London* as she neared Shanghai with Vice-Admiral Madden on board.[1] One can imagine the look of astonishment on the faces of those receiving this startling and thoroughly unwelcome news, not the least because in stating *Amethyst's* position, her radio operator, without the benefit of a navigational chart, had contrived to place the vessel's latitude and longitude at a point some distance from either the Yangtze or any other river![2] Although this error introduced an inappropriate touch of the bizarre to the proceedings, the stark disclosure that the *Amethyst* had been fired upon and had suffered many casualties in this action alarmed the British naval authorities in China, and with good reason. Indeed, such was the tenor of the news that both Sir Ralph Stevenson, the British ambassador, and Vice-Admiral Madden, the flag officer second in command of the Far East Station, recognized from the outset that this latest incident on the Yangtze was likely to have an international rather than local significance. They were not mistaken.

Despite the seriousness of the situation, the British authorities faced an inevitable delay of several hours on that first day of the crisis before they could verify the alarming news that *Amethyst* had conveyed so unexpectedly that Wednesday morning. Nothing was known about the other parties involved in the incident, the exact casualty toll, or even the extent of the damage caused to the ship. Therefore, unless either the frigate came back on the air with more detailed information about her plight, or a rescue mission could reach the stranded vessel and relay a detailed message back to base, the British could do

61

nothing to improve their lack of knowledge about what had happened to their ship on the Yangtze.

Information was obviously badly needed, and without the benefit of aircraft, only one immediate option was available. HMS *Consort* was completing preparations for her intended departure downriver at lunchtime bound for Shanghai when the news about the *Amethyst* came through. She would be in the best position to discover what had happened that morning once she reached the spot where the *Amethyst* lay immobilized and could make contact with her. *Consort*'s crew could then radio the news direct to Nanking and Shanghai and stand by for further instructions. It was tacitly understood, however, that if Commander Ian Robertson, the captain of the destroyer, thought there was any chance of his vessel rendering direct help to the beleagured *Amethyst,* that opportunity would be taken.

As *London* neared Woosung at the end of her journey from Hong Kong, Madden wired the assistant naval attaché in Shanghai and asked whether it would be possible to send at least one tug upriver to try to refloat the stranded frigate.[3] He already knew that if all else failed, he had another frigate—HMS *Black Swan*—lying at anchor in Shanghai, which could be used to support his own cruiser during any future rescue mission that might be necessary.

At 10:53 A.M. Madden ordered *Consort* to proceed to the assistance of *Amethyst.*[4] It was expected that she would take three to three and a half hours to reach the ship. Robertson, however, asked for as much speed as possible on the passage down the Yangtze, so that *Consort*--steaming at between 27 and 29 knots and flying seven ensigns, one union flag, and two union jacks—made the journey in approximately two hours.[5]

Shortly after issuing his instructions to Commander Robertson, Madden informed the assistant naval attaché in Shanghai that although *Consort*'s task was to elicit as much information from *Amethyst* as possible, he thought that practical assistance was more likely to be rendered by *Black Swan,* with covering fire, if necessary, coming from *London.*[6] Such an idea suggested that direct help for *Amethyst* was still many hours away because *Black Swan* was not expected to reach her before 10:00 A.M. on the following morning (21 April).[7] In the meantime, attempts were being made by Robert Urquhart, the British consul general in Shanghai, to procure an aircraft that could be flown up the Yangtze to Nanking. He intended to send Howard Williams, a member of the British consular staff, with a pilot early in the afternoon, to try to establish contact with *Amethyst* by Aldis lamp and pass on any information they gleaned thereby to *Consort* using the same method of communication. Unfortunately, the plan had to be shelved because the aircraft he proposed to use for the flight could not be dispatched immediately.[8] This in turn meant that it would not reach the frigate before the destroyer did, which obviated the necessity for its journey in the first place.

As *Black Swan* and *London* forged their way upriver toward Kiangyin during Wednesday afternoon (20 April), Madden received what updated information was available from *Consort*.[9] He knew that despite wearing a vast array of imperial bunting, the 1,710-ton destroyer had come under heavy attack from the Communist field artillery on her way downriver. Despite this barrage, she had suffered only slight damage in reaching Rose Island, the place where *Amethyst* lay aground.[10] As the afternoon wore on, however, the news *Consort* relayed took on a more somber note, as reports were filed of serious casualties among her crew.[11] Whatever had triggered the original incident involving the *Amethyst*—whether it was a result of a dreadful misunderstanding or a deliberate act of provocation—the subsequent action involving *Consort* widened the scale of the Yangtze incident and complicated matters considerably.

For the time being, however, establishing the guilt or innocence of the parties to the dispute was of subordinate importance to getting aid to the wounded in these two naval engagements. Considering how *Consort*'s efforts had been beaten off with an unacceptably high casualty toll among her crew, no one could afford to underestimate the difficulty of launching a successful rescue bid for the *Amethyst,* particularly if she was still unable to refloat herself from the mud bank on which she was marooned.[12] Much, therefore, would ultimately depend upon the ability or otherwise of the frigate to help herself. If she could escape the cloying mud of Rose Island and become mobile again before the following morning when *Black Swan* and *London* were expected to reach her, arrangements could then be made to escort her back to Shanghai where better hospital and repair facilities existed than at Nanking, her original destination.[13]

Although Stevenson, the British ambassador, had acted swiftly to inform the Nationalist naval headquarters and its Ministry of Defence about the attack on the *Amethyst* and of Madden's decision to send rescue ships from Nanking and Shanghai to assist her, he knew from the outset that there was no guarantee his message would actually get through.[14] Lacking knowledge about the extent to which information could be passed speedily and effectively within the KMT and confidence in the discipline and competence of its troops in the field, the ambassador could only wait and hope for the best.

Unfortunately, there was a heightened sense of unease when addressing the same issue to the Communists. Apart from anything else, the impossibility of establishing direct contact with any units of the PLA from his embassy in Nanking meant that Stevenson had first had to inform the British consul in Peking about what had happened, and then rely on him to try to communicate with the military high command of the Communist forces. Thereafter, he could only hope that the PLA would issue a specific set of orders to its area commanders—or to those manning the batteries along the banks of the Yangtze—asking them to respect the rights of British ships to free movement on the river for humanitarian purposes.[15]

Despite having been informed about the *Amethyst* soon after she had gone aground, neither the Admiralty nor the Foreign Office in London tried to take over the handling of the crisis from their men on the spot.[16] Therefore, despite the gravity of the situation and the deep concern felt in British government circles over what had happened on the Yangtze, the ambassador and the flag officer were given virtually a free hand to devise a sensible and coherent policy for bringing this unfortunate incident to a timely end with a minimum loss of life. Far from being an abdication of responsibility on the part of the government, the practice of deferring to its men on the spot in an emergency was based on the principle that these individuals usually possessed far more current information and local knowledge, at least in the initial stages of a crisis, than did the relevant ministry in London. This did not mean that the Admiralty and Foreign Office merely sat back and waited for developments to take their course. On the contrary, because ministerial statements had to be prepared on the incident, both departments required as much detailed information as possible from their officials in the region, and this demand led to the exchange of a stream of telegrams with Stevenson and Madden in the next few hours.[17]

Some of the questions raised by the authorities in London contained implicit criticism of the decision made by the flag officer and the British ambassador to send *Amethyst* upriver to relieve *Consort*. In a wire sent in reply to Stevenson's cable reporting the attack on the frigate, the Foreign Office sent the following message:

> Naval Attache's signal 190417z/April to Flag Officer Second-in-Command Far East Station referred to a possible Communist crossing of the Yangtze on the 21st April and named the vicinity of Ku An as one of the two most likely crossing places below Nanking. I am not clear why Amethyst had to pass through danger zone so close to the possible zero hour and shall be grateful for immediate information as to precise circumstances in which Amethyst was proceeding to Nanking at this juncture.[18]

Although thrust on the defensive by this pointed query, Stevenson repeated all the advantages of maintaining a guard ship at Nanking, a policy decision to which the British government had not been opposed in the past.[19] Aware of this fact, he indicated that the local experts had believed that peace would prevail while the changeover was being made and that the two British vessels would have been outside the danger area before the ultimatum expired.[20]

At a Chiefs of Staff committee meeting held in London later that morning (20 April), Lord Fraser, the chief of naval staff, duly informed the other service chiefs of the few details known about the attack on the *Amethyst*. In his report, he reaffirmed Admiralty policy for the immediate future—which was to allow Madden to take whatever action he felt was necessary under the circumstances—but mentioned the Admiralty's intention of suspending all future passages by British ships up the Yangtze.[21] This statement looked like, and indeed was, a case of "Too little, too late" and must have stirred, in some of those present, memories of the familiar metaphor about shutting the stable door after the horse had bolted!

Later that same day, the China and South East Asia Committee met under the chairmanship of Clement Attlee, the prime minister. It was a small body charged with reviewing strategic policy, but it contained some of the most influential members of the government. Those present were Ernest Bevin, the foreign secretary; Sir Stafford Cripps, the chancellor of the exchequer; A. V. Alexander, the minister of defense; Hugh Dalton, the chancellor of the duchy of Lancaster; and George Isaacs, the minister of labor and national service. During the discussion that followed Alexander's opening remarks on the details of the incident, some doubts were expressed about the desirability of using a warship for carrying peaceful stores to the British Embassy.[22] According to the official report of the proceedings, which was couched in notoriously bland language and provided only a brief summary of the committee's conclusions, the ministers were careful not to make their criticism explicit; the minutes of the meeting do not mention any individuals by name and were confined, for the most part, to showing sympathy mixed with mild reproof for those who had allowed the *Amethyst* to sail upriver at this time without first obtaining a safe-conduct pass from both sides in the civil war.[23]

While the wheels of government were beginning to grind slowly in Britain, Madden's flagship, the cruiser *London*, was nearing the port of Kiangyin as the evening set in. Having been in frequent contact with the other ships under his command since the emergency began and recently learning of the plight of the *Consort*, the flag officer sent a secret cypher to the naval attaché in Nanking, in which he made the following suggestion:

> Request you will inform Ambassador that it may be necessary to bombard north shore of Yangtze to reduce opposition in vicinity of Amethyst before another attempt at rescue operations is made. Acknowledge.[24]

In contemplating such a grave option, Madden was keenly aware of the need to silence those batteries on the northern shore that had caused all the trouble. If they could be destroyed, the chances of staging a successful rescue bid for the *Amethyst* with the minimum number of casualties would increase considerably. There was no guarantee, of course, that either *Black Swan* or *London* could put these guns out of action, and if they did not, the whole operation would be imperiled. Nor could he fail to understand that sanctioning the use of fire-power against the Communists was bound to aggravate the existing diplomatic situation regardless of whether the *Amethyst* escaped or not. Therefore, any form of bombardment was likely to remain a last resort, unless used in self-defense. By the time an acknowledgment of this message was dispatched four hours later by Captain Vernon Donaldson, the naval attaché, far more information was at the disposal of those dealing with the crisis at the British Embassy in Nanking and at the center of naval operations on board *London* at anchor in Kiangyin than had been the case hitherto.[25]

At 8:00 P.M., the assistant naval attaché in Shanghai wired the flag officer with the news that the tug *Sea Eagle* would sail upriver from Shanghai in the morning and reach Kiangyin about 4:00 P.M. on 21 April. He also informed Madden that an additional tug was being recalled from Amoy for use on the Yangtze if required.[26] A tug would only be useful in certain well-defined contingencies, most notably if the frigate was severely disabled and could not proceed under her own steam. Even then, a tug could only venture north of Kiangyin into the danger area if a safe passage for it had been granted by the two belligerents in the civil war. If such an arrangement could not be devised, a tug's utility was strictly limited because it was unarmed and not designed to defend itself against hostile fire. Whether used or not, its presence as a support craft in the task force being assembled on the Yangtze represented in a small way, perhaps, the determination of the British to do everything in their power to bring the crisis surrounding the *Amethyst* to a swift and successful conclusion.

Just over a couple of hours later, Madden received even more encouraging news, this time from the commander of the British forces in Hong Kong to the effect that he had arranged for a Sunderland flying boat to make the trip up the Yangtze with medical supplies.

A.O.C. does not wish to land at Nanking unless it is safe and essential that Sunderland should do so. He requests exact dropping position and desires to make flight direct from Hong Kong to dropping position, make drop and return Hong Kong without landing.[27]

This supply drop would be a significant development, particularly if there was trouble in towing the *Amethyst* away from Rose Island and the mission had to be aborted, leaving the frigate still at the mercy of the Communist batteries. It was revealed in a later message that the flying boat would be carrying fresh supplies of water and about 400 pounds of provisions and would have a Royal Air Force (RAF) doctor on board. Whether he was to be transferred to the *Amethyst* or not was unclear. Although a transfer would appear to make the most sense, there was no definite commitment one way or the other at this stage.[28]

Shortly before news of the Sunderland first reached the flag officer, *Amethyst* put out a message at about 10:00 P.M. indicating that she was still aground on Rose Island, although efforts would be made to refloat her after repairs to vital equipment on board had been satisfactorily completed. In her message, *Amethyst* revealed that, as a result of the earlier attack by the Communists, approximately sixty of her crew, including four wounded ratings, were making their way to the nearest large town in Nationalist hands and that of those left behind on board, seventeen lay dead and twenty were seriously injured, one of whom was her captain Lieutenant-Commander Skinner.[29]

This information confirmed what *Consort* had already disclosed about her own voyage downriver, namely, that both ships were fired on only from the northern bank and that the firing zone extended about 12 miles from Rose Island to Low Island.[30] News of this nature, which specifically pinned the blame on the Communists for both incidents, was a matter of the highest importance and was quickly exchanged with the embassy in Nanking.[31] It increased Madden's natural anxiety for an agreement to be hammered out with the PLA, which would enable a vessel or vessels of the British Far East Station to recover the *Amethyst* and supervise her withdrawal from the Yangtze without further risk to life or limb. His agitation grew when Donaldson informed him that although everything had been done to pass messages concerning the *Amethyst* to the military high command in Peking, it was thought unlikely that any instructions from the Communist hierarchy could reach the frontline troops for several days.[32] Even then, no guarantee could be given that the PLA artillery troops assigned to the batteries on the Yangtze would be willing to respect these orders.

Shortly after midnight (21 April), *Amethyst* put out a wireless message for the naval authorities in Hong Kong, in which she asked the Far East Station to send all future messages to her in plain language because her confidential books and Typex cypher codes had been destroyed.[33] This request meant that secrecy had to be forsaken for clarity and that anyone monitoring the wavelength on which *Amethyst* was sending and receiving messages would now be able to read all the communications that passed between the ship and the shore or other British vessels without delay or difficulty.

Madden must have been relieved by the news that the frigate was back on the air again and that she was preparing to extricate herself from the mud bank on which she had lain for much of the previous day. He sent another message at 1:15 A.M. asking for a report on her present state and directing the frigate, once she had been refloated, to proceed approximately 10 miles upstream before anchoring and awaiting further orders.[34]

An hour later, *Amethyst* reported that she had managed to slip away from Rose Island and was now anchored in position 32 degrees, 16.5 minutes north and latitude 119 degrees, 42.5 minutes east. Besides several holes in her hull, the frigate's tiller flat had also received a direct hit on the waterline, but her steering gear and telegraph were operational.[35] Of the ship's company still on board, only four officers and fifty ratings could be said to be fully effective, but *Amethyst*'s acting captain still believed he had enough able-bodied men to steam the ship up or down the Yangtze as directed. He acknowledged, however, that matters were not quite that simple, as the frigate had lost the services of her two local pilots. She would also have to make do without the relevant chart of the river, which was yet another victim of the initial onslaught that morning. Moreover, there were still many other difficulties to be faced, not the least being the urgent need to treat the seriously wounded, eight of whom had thus far only received first aid for their injuries. Referring to the flight of the Sunderland, which was expected the next day, *Amethyst* requested urgent medical stores to add to the heavily depleted stock of morphia and dressings on board, but pointed out that she no longer possessed the means to collect even these essential supplies if they were dropped at some distance from the ship. Moreover, Weston warned the British authorities that the flying boat might be confronted with some small arms fire from the northern bank and the crew of the Sunderland ought to be prepared for this eventuality.[36]

Despite the enormity of the problems the *Amethyst* still faced, the fact that she had refloated herself and could make her own way on the river was most reassuring news for the British diplomatic and naval staff. It appeared to simplify the procedure for recovering the frigate, because it avoided both the need to take her in tow and the hazards associated with mounting such an operation. Madden's elation at this news was tempered by the recognition that the ship remained in a vulnerable spot and much still had to be done before the frigate could regain her freedom. After consulting his chart of the Yangtze, he recommended that she shift berth to what looked like a less-exposed and dangerous position at least 3 miles further west of her present location.[37]

This maneuver proved to be far more difficult than Madden had expected. *Amethyst* indicated the impossibility of following the flag officer's instructions in her next signal to HMS *London*.

Am anchored in position 010 Tai Wing Chow South West corner 7$^{1}/_{2}$ cables to keep maximum distance from fire from North Bank and according to remains of chart cannot shift three miles further West.[38]

Once again the realization that much remained to be done before this rescue operation could succeed came home to those on board the cruiser at Kiangyin. If the Communists were going to dispute the British request for permission to retrieve their frigate, the next few hours would witness a most dramatic confrontation on the Yangtze, putting at risk the professed claim of British neutrality in the civil war and any desire His Majesty's Government had to remain on reasonably good terms with the CCP and its military arm, the PLA. In such a situation, the British naval forces would need to be at their most disciplined and lucky if they were to emerge unscathed from what could well be a grim ordeal.

In preparation for this possible confrontation, the flag officer passed a message to Hong Kong at about 9:00 A.M. on Thursday morning (21 April) strongly recommending that the Sunderland flying boat should not land close to the *Amethyst*, but at a quiet spot on the river near Bate Point and close to where HMS *Black Swan* would be.[39] Alert to the unpredictable and potentially explosive nature of the morning's proceedings, Madden relayed his instructions to the commanding officers of the *Amethyst, Black Swan,* and *London* at 9:37 A.M., setting out the rescue plan in only the broadest outline.

As there seems to be no chance of an understanding with the opposition in the near future and as I consider Amethyst must have early assistance intend to take London up to her anchorage and escort her down river as soon as possible. Amethyst is to be under way in her present position with steam for maximum speed by 1100H.[40]

Immediately thereafter, Madden dispatched another signal to *Black Swan* ordering her to proceed independently of *London* and station herself south of Low Island at a distance that would enable her to provide indirect covering fire on that island—the point at which *Consort* had been fired on and badly damaged— should she be called upon to do so by *London*.[41] As the two British warships raced up the Yangtze and closed on their beleaguered target, the air of suspense and anticipation settled heavily over the men in each of the vessels. Now that the precautionary moves had been made, all that remained to be done was to await the outcome of the rescue mission and hope for the best, even if they were prepared for the worst.

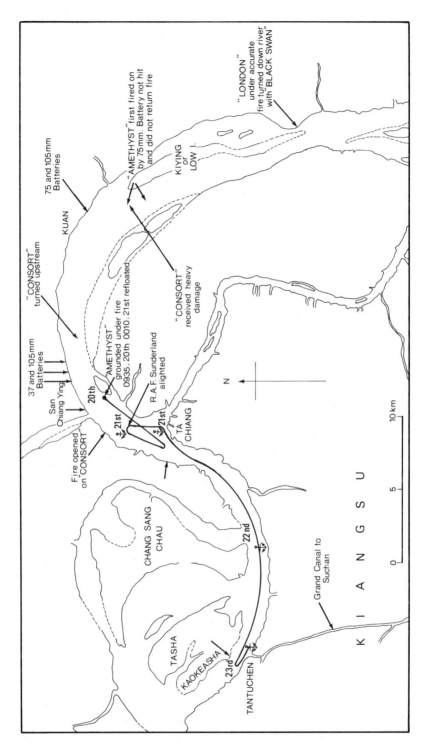

Map 3. Action on the Yangtze (20–23 April 1949)

5. Mounting a Rescue Attempt

SHORTLY after midnight on Thursday 21 April, HMS *Amethyst,* having at last broken free of the mud bank on which she had been trapped for much of the previous day, set course upstream at about 8 knots. Success was tinged with failure, however, for the jerking motion of the frigate as she clawed her way back into the river managed to detach the whaler boat from its position alongside and set it free to drift off with the current.[1] Apart from this mishap the first few minutes of the *Amethyst*'s journey were uneventful. Nonetheless, as she approached the Tan-tu Reach—a long sweeping bend in the river where the Yangtze narrows considerably—she encountered small arms fire from the northern bank. Without either an accurate chart or a local pilot who knew what hazards lay ahead, Weston decided to put about and return a couple of miles downriver to anchor for the night at a spot close to the southern shore opposite Ta-hsin-wei, not far from where the tributary of the Hsiao-ho joins the Yangtze and about 2 miles from her former unscheduled berth on Rose Island. Here the river widens so appreciably that by hugging the southern bank, the ship avoided being strafed by machine gun fire from the Communist positions on the northern shore. It was 1:30 A.M. by the time she hove to.[2]

After spending a relatively peaceful night, the ship's crew were going about their various tasks on the following morning when at about 9:15 A.M. a sampan was spotted with two men on board approaching the ship from the southern bank. As the first visitors to come alongside since the attack on the previous day, the two Nationalists aroused great interest among the ship's company. Lacking a trained interpreter and making do with the inexpert translation of those who had to be pressed into service for this purpose, Weston concluded that the two men had come to offer assistance to the wounded.[3]

This gesture presumably meant that the KMT was willing to make arrangements to evacuate the wounded by ship to hospitals behind the Nationalist lines. He refused their generous offer because he expected the Sunderland flying boat to airlift the injured later that same day out of the danger area to a British military hospital either in Shanghai or further south. Not discouraged by this negative reply, the Nationalists indicated that they would be prepared to send sampans to assist in transferring the wounded to the aircraft once it had landed on the Yangtze. After these messages had been exchanged, the two KMT soldiers withdrew, and the *Amethyst* was on her own once again.[4]

Within an hour, French, the telegraphist, received a signal from Madden instructing the acting captain to have steam up so that the frigate could achieve maximum speed at 11:00 A.M. when both *London* and *Black Swan* were expected to be on hand to assist her.[5] Weston informed the crew immediately. Jubilant about the prospects of an early rescue, the men returned to their duties with renewed vigor knowing that there was little time to be lost before the rendezvous would be made.

Meanwhile, two more Nationalist vessels drew alongside. At about 10:15 A.M., two army officers came on board extending offers of assistance similar to those made by their predecessors. Although Weston decided on this occasion to make certain provisional arrangements with them for landing the injured should the *Amethyst* fail to leave with HMS *London,* he otherwise politely declined their offer of immediate help.[6] About thirty minutes later, a junior officer commanding an LCM (landing craft mechanized) belonging to the Nationalist navy inquired whether he could be of any assistance, but his offer was also turned down owing to the imminence of *London*'s arrival on the scene.[7]

At 11:30 A.M. *Amethyst* weighed anchor and moved into the center of the river poised for action. As she circled slowly in the river, the Communists fired a few rounds at the ship from the San-chiang-ying batteries. Although she was not hit, the frigate moved back to her original position and dropped anchor again at 11:50 A.M. facing downriver. At once, the firing stopped.[8] By this time Weston and the men aboard the *Amethyst* were becoming anxious about the delay of *London,* particularly because they had heard an exchange of gunfire in the distance, which they assumed was the heavy cruiser encountering opposition from the Communist forces below Rose Island.[9]

Their assumption proved to be correct. *London,* festooned with eleven union flags and flying a large white flag, 16 feet square, had closed up for action stations at 10:26 A.M.[10] After weighing anchor, she followed *Black Swan* up river some 8 cables (1,600 yards) astern of the frigate. Within seven minutes, gunfire was spotted coming from a battery situated on the north bank of the river at Liu-wei-chiang, a short distance north of Bate Point Beacon.[11] *Black Swan* opened fire at it almost immediately. *London*, conscious of the need not to enflame matters further, was under general instructions not to fire except in self-defense. This commendable restraint almost certainly explains her failure to strike back instantly at the battery that had unleashed the first shots of the morning. Her apparent reluctance to engage the PLA artillery was not matched by a similar willingness to avoid aggravating matters on the part of the Communist gunners. A volley of 75-mm and 105-mm shells soon found their target on various parts of the cruiser. Once struck, *London* hesitated no longer; her full complement of guns swiftly beat out an uncompromising reply for three to four minutes before the battery fell silent. Neither British vessel could be certain of why the shelling stopped when it did, although the most likely reason was that the PLA battery had been knocked out by the concentrated fire of the two ships.[12]

After this somewhat unnerving experience, *London* increased her speed to 25 knots. At this rate, she swiftly overhauled and then forged ahead of her accompanying frigate. She had moved about 3 miles ahead of *Black Swan* and was passing the southern part of Beaver Island at 11:04 A.M. when a battery situated to the southeast of it suddenly opened fire upon her with startling success. At least one shell struck the bridge superstructure, hangar, and boat decks, scattering crew and shrapnel in various directions. Two minutes later another shell smashed into the bridge killing the Chinese pilot instantly, seriously injuring the navigating officer, and wounding two others, including Captain P. G. L. Cazelet. It also wrecked vital instruments and disrupted communications on the ship.[13] Cazelet estimated that *London* was still some 19 miles from the waiting *Amethyst* when Vice-Admiral Madden ordered him at 11:11 A.M. to give up the attempt to reach the frigate and turn back. There was scarcely any other decision that could have been reached under the circumstances, as the ship now had to be controlled from the emergency conning position abaft the funnels. This situation would have been bad enough without the added complication of having to contend with the unwelcome attentions of a hostile army able to make reasonably effective use of the 105-mm gun batteries, howitzers, and antitank weapons at its disposal. Despite *London*'s considerable attributes, she remained vulnerable to the high velocity 37-mm armor-piercing shells that the Communists possessed, for these were capable of penetrating even the supposedly extra-thick, protective steel walls of the turrets and gunhouses of the cruiser.[14]

Staging a withdrawal from her vulnerable position in the Yangtze proved to be quite a difficult maneuver for *London* because it involved executing a tight 180-degree turn in the navigable part of the river while under accurate and sustained bombardment from the shore, which lay less than a mile away. Unfortunately, her problems did not end there, as the downward passage proved to be far worse than anything experienced on the journey upriver. According to a report drawn up a few days later by Commander John Hodges, second in command to Cazelet, five batteries fired on both *London* and *Black Swan* as they made haste to reach the relative safety of Kiangyin. By 1:40 P.M., when the last of these batteries ceased firing, *London* had been subjected to forty-eight minutes of actual shelling spread over three and a quarter hours. During this period she had sustained twenty-four holes in her port side, as well as a large number of dents on other parts of the ship from shells that had struck the vessel but failed to explode on impact. In reply, *London*, although forced to operate for much of the time on local rather than centralized control, had still managed to fire a total of 449 rounds from her 4-inch guns and 155 rounds of high explosive shells from her 8-inch guns at the Communist battery positions on the banks of the Yangtze.[15] As Hodges revealed later,

> It is difficult to assess the damage and casualties inflicted on the opposition, but at least eight direct hits with 8" H.E. shell were obtained on the 4" batteries at an average range of less than 1500 yards. In addition 4" air bursts and close range direct fire must have caused many casualties in the target area.[16]

Black Swan limped back to Kiangyin, nursing four large holes that had been gouged out of her port side and with a $5^1/_2$ degree list to starboard, testimony to the accuracy of the Bate Point battery and another one established further east toward Kiangyin. Throughout the ordeal, *Black Swan* had been fortunate in only sustaining seven casualties among her crew, a figure that paled beside that of the grim toll inflicted on *London* in her vain attempt to rescue the *Amethyst*. *London* returned to Kiangyin with thirteen men killed, fourteen seriously wounded, and another forty injured.[17]

Such high losses bore witness to the view held earlier in the day by Madden and Cazelet that if the PLA was determined to thwart any naval mission to retrieve the *Amethyst*, it could do so regardless of what ships were sent to escort the frigate back to port. Sadly, both men had also believed that a rescue operation was likely to succeed against what was termed "light and sporadic opposition." There is also just the faintest suspicion that these naval officers— imbued with the confidence of the senior service and steeped in the traditions of its role in the past—may well have felt that a show of force by the Royal Navy was likely to make all the difference. If they thought that it would cow the

PLA gunners into an awed, if resentful, silence and thereby enable *Amethyst* to be escorted by *Black Swan* and *London* downriver toward Kiangyin and Shanghai, they were destined to be grievously disappointed. After concluding that the PLA would not oppose the British vessels on their errand of mercy, the flag officer had not shirked from proceeding upriver. Although this myth was quickly and effectively dispelled in the most violent way possible once the operation got under way, Madden still refused to abort the rescue mission until after his cruiser had suffered extensive damage at the hands of the PLA batteries on the northern shore of the Yangtze.[18] Madden's decision to go ahead with the rescue attempt was as understandable as it was admirable; his failure to react sooner to the dangerous conditions his ship faced on the river that Thursday morning, however, was a tragic and costly error, which compounded his original blunder of sending *Amethyst* up to Nanking two days previously.

At 12:15 P.M., more than an hour after Madden had decided to abandon the rescue operation, French received confirmation that *London* was withdrawing from the area. Her message simply read: "Am sorry we cannot help you today. We shall keep on trying."[19] This news was a crushing disappointment to the officers and men aboard the *Amethyst*. It appeared to rule out the possibility of a swift end to their confinement on the Yangtze and to jeopardize all escape plans that relied upon force rather than a negotiated settlement to eventually liberate the frigate. Although the men tried not to dwell on it, the realization that two British warships had been unable to silence the Communist batteries and move beyond their arc of fire was both highly significant and thoroughly depressing.[20]

Madden shared these pessimistic sentiments, as his message to Sir Patrick Brind, the commander in chief of the Far East Station, showed.

> Have had to order withdrawal of London and Black Swan. All sign of peaceful intent disregarded and heavy fire opened from batteries near Bates Point and on Southern end of Beaver Island this was effectively returned. Cleared (sic) impossible to bring Amethyst down as even at high speed casualties in London are not inconsiderable and we should lose more than we should gain by attempting it at present. It is considered that the most urgent steps on the highest level should be taken to try to expedite some agreement. N.A. Nanking is requested to keep me currently informed as to any possibility of getting Amethyst to Nanking. London, Black Swan are proceeding to Kiang Yin or Berowak it is though probable rebels are extending their mobile batteries to the East Ward.[21]

Besides the real danger posed by the Communists, there was also an unpredictable, trigger-happy element within the Nationalist forces on the Yangtze front with which the British would have to contend if they were to stage a successful rescue bid for the *Amethyst* in the near future. This additional complication to an already vexatious problem was extremely unwelcome, as Madden discovered firsthand on the return leg downriver to Kiangyin.[22]

In a report to Admiral Brind, his commander in chief, Madden noted that *London* had encountered brisk opposition to her presence on the Yangtze from a Nationalist battery opposite Kiangyin. In launching such a surprise attack, the battery had managed to inflict considerable damage upon the British cruiser. Although he indicated that this fire was returned, Madden made no mention of *Black Swan*'s whereabouts. After arriving in Shanghai, the officers of the two warships conferred and concluded that it was difficult to know whether errant units of the Nationalist army were to blame for this incident.[23] Nonetheless, as Madden subsequently disclosed in another message to his commander in chief,

> Some of the retaliatory fire from London fell in Nationalist territory which evoked signal from Gunboat YAT SEN "Those were ours." BLACK SWAN replied "I have only fired on battery which fired on London."[24]

In this confusion anything was possible, and with the Communists threatening to cross the Yangtze at any time, the likelihood of a rescue operation being mounted now by river seemed out of the question.

If *Amethyst* could not be moved and was destined to become a hostage to fortune, the British authorities would either have to begin making plans for a long stay on the Yangtze or be prepared to scuttle the frigate and airlift the officers and crew out of the area. These were, of course, weighty matters that would require deep and careful thought before any plan was executed. Before reaching any final decision, those coping with the crisis would have to consider the limited range of options available to them.

In the aftermath of the action on Thursday morning (21 April), the need to do something constructive to relieve the situation on board the *Amethyst* became imperative. Now that *London*'s plan to escort the frigate downstream had backfired, hopes rested once more on the flight of the Sunderland from Hong Kong, which was bringing medical help for the wounded. Just how successful this mission would be depended, however, on whether the flying boat would be allowed to land close to the ship so that it could transfer its supplies and the RAF doctor to the *Amethyst* and begin the process of removing the wounded from the vessel for the flight to Shanghai.

6. Kerans Enters the Picture

*E*VEN BEFORE *London* and *Black Swan* were foiled in their attempt to reach the *Amethyst*, steps had been taken by Captain Vernon Donaldson, the British naval attaché in Nanking, to send his mercurial Irish assistant Lieutenant-Commander John Simon Kerans, accompanied by Lieutenant-Colonel R. V. Dewar-Durie, the assistant military attaché, by jeep to Chinkiang in the hope of trying to establish contact with the ship or, failing that, at least with its evacuees.[1] Armed with a letter of authority from the commander in chief of the National-ist navy and supplies of morphia, two thousand cigarettes, a case of beer, and a Chinese Admiralty chart folio of the Yangtze, the two men set out at 10:00 A.M. on that Thursday morning on the tortuous 72-mile journey from Nank-ing. Although they had borrowed the Australian military attaché's jeep be-cause their own was thought to be too unreliable, the replacement managed to break down repeatedly enroute to Chinkiang. Eventually after motoring for about three and a half hours on a dusty, badly rutted road, Kerans and Dewar-Durie reached the Nationalist naval headquarters at Chinkiang.[2]

They had been instructed by Donaldson to ascertain what had happened to the twenty naval ratings from the *Amethyst*, which Reuters had reported as being in hospital in the town. For this purpose they were taken to see Captain Meh, the chief of staff, who told them that although there was no truth in the Reuters report, fifty-six men from the *Amethyst* had been evacuated by train that morning from Wutsin, a station 40 miles southeast of Chinkiang on the main railway line to Shanghai.[3] Captain Meh—who had traveled in Europe, spoke fluent English and French, and had been trained in the United States—was particularly helpful to Kerans and Dewar-Durie. Although they informed him of their desire to reach the frigate and hand over the supplies they had

Commander John Simon Kerans (courtesy of the National Portrait Gallery, London).

brought from Nanking, Meh advised the two men against approaching the *Amethyst* by river. He cited the obvious danger posed by the Communist batteries and explained that he did not have enough fast, serviceable craft to allow any of them to be used for making another attempt to reach the ship.[4]

While they were discussing the situation and wondering how best to overcome the problem of contacting the frigate, a sublieutenant in command of the LCM that had been alongside the *Amethyst* earlier that morning arrived in the building and was brought to meet Meh and the two British officers. He was unable to add much to what was already known about the warship, because his visit to the *Amethyst* and attempted dialogue with Weston had been marred by language difficulties and inadequate interpreting. Nonetheless, he was able to report the ship's latest position as being at the northwest corner of T'ai P'ing Island. Kerans and Dewar-Durie listened attentively as the sublieutenant went on to say he had been fired upon during his return passage to Chinkiang.[5]

His disclosure about the danger of the river passage appeared to confirm the impossibility, or at least questionable wisdom, of trying to reach the *Amethyst* by boat. It was scarcely surprising, therefore, that when Kerans telephoned Donaldson in Nanking with this news, he was told to return to the embassy because there was nothing else for him to do in Chinkiang. It was an unsatisfactory and depressing end to his trip, and the thought of making the difficult and exasperating return journey to Nanking on virtually an empty stomach did nothing to improve the mood of either assistant attaché.[6]

Meanwhile at the embassy, Donaldson was receiving the latest in a series of plaintive dispatches about the *Amethyst* from the flag officer. Madden had become most anxious that contact be established with the ship at the earliest possible moment regardless of whether or not the Sunderland was able to discharge its functions. He had been informed from Hong Kong that in addition to the flying boat that was already operational, another would be serviceable by 11:30 P.M. that evening and a third by 3:00 A.M. on the following day (Friday 22 April). Although the Dakota aircraft at Kaitak was inoperative for an indefinite period to come, a request had apparently been made for a replacement from Singapore, and it was expected to be ready for service within twenty-four hours.[7] In the event of a decision being reached to scuttle the *Amethyst*, sufficient aircraft would be available, at least in theory, to airlift what remained of the frigate's crew from the Yangtze. Although this was encouraging news, Madden did not have to be reminded that it was scarcely going to be as simple as that.

It was clear by now that the fate of the *Amethyst* actually rested in the hands of the Communists and that the British were probably no longer in a position to rescue both ship and crew if the PLA did not wish them to do so. Whatever happened ultimately, it was still likely to take some time before this problem could be solved one way or the other, and it was for this reason that Vice-Admiral Madden wanted Kerans to reach the *Amethyst* without delay. In the light of the action on the Yangtze that lunchtime (Thursday 21 April), the odds had increased considerably against a Sunderland being allowed to bring medical relief to the frigate and take the seriously wounded to a hospital. Therefore, the British assumed the worst and tried to make alternative arrangements for getting as much medical assistance to the ship as possible in the next few hours.

Not all of this assistance was to come from the British. Donaldson learned that the Americans were loaning them a U.S. naval doctor and his assistant, both of whom had set out by car from Nanking and were expected to arrive in Chinkiang in the middle of the afternoon.[8] Moreover, the Nationalists were sending one of their own doctors to the ship directly. In the light of these disclosures, Donaldson rapidly changed his mind and revoked the plan for Kerans and Dewar-Durie to return to Nanking. He called Chinkiang and told Kerans that his previous order had been cancelled and that he was now instructed to proceed overland, if necessary, to make personal contact with the *Amethyst* after dark.[9] Kerans's gloom, brought on by his previous conversation with the naval attaché, evaporated immediately; here was a challenge to be met and one that offered exciting possibilities. A brief look at the map convinced all concerned that *Amethyst* could be reached by a combination of motorized transport and ferry.

Shortly after the American doctor, Lieutenant-Commander Packard, and his assistant reached Chinkiang at 3:30 P.M., bearing medical chests and complaining bitterly about the state of the roads, two 1,500-weight trucks were procured by General Huang, the commanding officer of the Chinkiang area of the Fourth Army, for the journey to the coast and evacuation of the wounded once they had been brought ashore from the ship. Captain Meh, his chief of staff, joined the two Americans and the two British officers in the four-vehicle convoy that set out eastward at 4:15 P.M. toward T'ai P'ing Island where *Amethyst* had been at anchor earlier in the day.[10]

Meanwhile earlier in the afternoon, the *Amethyst* had received another visit from KMT personnel. At about 1:00 P.M., a sampan with two Nationalist soldiers had come alongside and asked whether one of the crew could return with them to the local garrison headquarters. Mr. E. Monaghan, the commissioned gunner, was deputed to go with them and make definite arrangements for sending medical assistance to the warship. While ashore he had a chance meeting with a Reuters correspondent from Chinkiang and used the opportunity to pass a written message in English for dispatch to the naval attaché in Nanking. His note stressed the deplorable situation on board the *Amethyst* and the urgent necessity for providing medical assistance to the wounded.[11]

When Monaghan returned at 3:30 P.M. he brought with him Lieutenant Chu Wei, a Chinese army doctor and two medical orderlies. This was the first time since Alderton and Baker had been killed the previous morning that expert medical assistance could be given to the wounded. While Chu was doing his rounds, Weston decided that the evacuation of the wounded should not be delayed much longer but ought to be accomplished under cover of darkness. Monaghan, who had favored an early evacuation from the outset, was instructed to take the sampan and make another trip to the local garrison headquarters to finalize these arrangements.[12]

As Monaghan was preparing to leave the frigate, the Sunderland emerged overhead, circled, and deftly touched down about 75 yards away from the *Amethyst* on the port side. Immediately, the sampan was commandeered by Monaghan. He ordered its crew of three Chinese laborers to row over to the flying boat. As they understood no English, Monaghan gesticulated excitedly in the direction of the aircraft, and they got the message with little difficulty. Before the sampan reached the Sunderland, however, the Communists had opened fire at the flying boat.[13]

What happened next has since been described by Flight-Lieutenant Michael Fearnley, the RAF doctor on board the Sunderland, as bearing all the hallmarks of first-class slapstick. Strangely enough in these dangerous and frightening circumstances, there was a comedy of errors more symptomatic perhaps of theatrical farce than real life drama played out on the Yangtze in the next few minutes. It began when Monaghan clambered out of the sampan and onto the flying boat to explain the current situation to the pilot and crew. After he had left the sampan, the three Chinese in it, knowing nothing of his intentions, hastened to put some distance between themselves and the aircraft, which was now the target of concentrated gunfire from the northern shore. Aware of the need for speed, Fearnley grabbed a haversack that he had stuffed with medical supplies on the flight from Shanghai and jumped out through the open door of the aircraft. He landed in the sampan, much to the surprise of its crew who had already pushed off from the Sunderland in a state of near hysteria. Their animated and uncoordinated attempts at getting out of harms way only succeeded in driving the sampan around in circles as the two men and the boy manning the oars pulled in different directions at the same time. Accompanied by the roar of shells landing close at hand, Fearnley shouted at the uncomprehending Chinese. He pointed at the *Amethyst*, indicating his destination, but they took no notice, preferring instead to head for the relative safety of the shore.

At this point—with the situation deteriorating rapidly and danger ever present—Fearnley decided that drastic action was required if he was to engage their attention. He promptly stood up in the sampan. It was a reckless act in choppy water and one accomplished much to the dismay of the Chinese laborers who were by now beside themselves with fear, threatened by shellfire on the one hand, and in danger of being capsized by a complete stranger on the other! They tried unsuccessfully to restrain him, but Fearnley, with strength and youth on his side, shrugged them off and continued to demand that they row him over to the *Amethyst*. Whether or not this demonstrative act would have been enough to convince the Chinese was never put to the test because he suddenly noticed a gun lying in the bottom of the sampan, presumably dropped there accidentally when Monaghan left the boat to clamber into the Sunderland only minutes before. A scuffle ensued as one of the Chinese men noticed the gun at virtually the same second and made a dive for it as well. Fearnley seized it first and made his intentions clear by waving it threateningly at the crew and then in the direction of the warship. Confronted now by superior force, the Chinese needed no second bidding, and the sampan was finally propelled, however reluctantly, in the direction of the *Amethyst*.[14]

Meanwhile, the Sunderland was coming under heavy fire from the Communist battery positions on the northern bank. Flight-Lieutenant Letford, the pilot of the flying boat, was left with no alternative but to get his plane airborne as quickly as possible in the hope of escaping undamaged from the Yangtze. Before Fearnley reached and boarded the frigate, the Sunderland had already turned, accelerated, and taken off from the river with Mr. Monaghan trapped on board and most of the medical supplies still in the aircraft.[15]

Unable to prevent the flying boat from leaving, the Communist gunners now took their revenge upon the *Amethyst* and began a short but bitter offensive against it. Shells struck the ship six times in the next few minutes, damaging the dynamo room and the number seven oil fuel tank in particular. Weston promptly ordered the ship upriver to a new, more-sheltered position over a mile away in a small creek at the confluence of the Hsiao-ho and Yangtze rivers. Although he would have liked to have taken the *Amethyst* some distance up the creek, the water proved to be too shallow to allow such a maneuver. Without the benefit of an Admiralty chart of the river, the first lieutenant wisely decided to drop anchor at the mouth of the creek and wait for darkness to fall before attempting to move again. Once more, the guns fell silent over the Yangtze.[16]

Fearnley immediately recognized from the state of the wounded on board ship that a speedy evacuation of the most seriously injured was vitally important if they were to be saved. After Fearnley met Lieutenant Chu on his rounds, the two doctors quickly agreed on the necessity for evacuating the stretcher cases to the shore and arranging their immediate transport by Nationalist troops to the nearest hospital. Chu offered to go ashore and sort things out, promising to return after dark with some sampans in order to begin the evacuation operation. He left the ship at about 6:00 P.M.[17]

At roughly the same time, the small four-vehicle convoy that had set out from Chinkiang bound for the coast and a rendezvous with the *Amethyst*, finally reached Tachiang, after a 23-mile journey eastward. Tachiang was a tiny, undistinguished farming village that now housed the headquarters of the regional district commander. By this point, the state of the roads had become so deplorable that the trucks had to be abandoned. This meant unloading their cargo of heavy medical chests and seeking alternative means of transportation to the ship. Fortunately, the regional commander was willing to use his influence with the local villagers, and soon six Chinese laborers and two large wheelbarrows were found for the purpose of taking medical supplies to the coast. The commander also agreed to provide a military escort for the group, which set out immediately.[18]

While Meh and the commander were arranging to send stretcher bearers to the ferry, Kerans was introduced to the same Reuters correspondent whom Monaghan had met earlier that afternoon. Kerans was shown the message the gunner had written to the naval attaché in Nanking and was, therefore, able to gauge just how intolerable conditions were on board the *Amethyst*. Kerans wrote out another message for transmission to Captain Donaldson and gave it to the journalist before rejoining the rest of his group as it prepared to embark once more on the latest leg of its journey to the river.[19]

Although the trucks had been ruled out, the jeep and the American saloon car, which had made the journey down from Nanking, were once more pressed back into service by Meh, Kerans, and company. Neither vehicle covered more than another 2 miles, however, before the track each had been following petered out altogether. After reluctantly abandoning the two vehicles, the group had no alternative but to go the rest of the way to the ferry terminus on foot. They set off in fading light, skirting south of an 850-foot hill on their enforced trek across country to the river.[20]

Back on board the *Amethyst*, the officers, and crew waited anxiously for Dr. Chu to return from the southern shore and for the evacuation of the injured to begin. Fearnley had worked nonstop to bring some relief to the seriously wounded and was evidently concerned about those like Weston and Berger who had somehow kept going throughout the ordeal despite their severe injuries, but whose condition was by now becoming more serious. On Fearnley's recommendation, a message was sent to Madden indicating that the evacuation was set for that evening and that only one executive officer, one engineer, one electrical officer, and forty ratings would remain on board after the operation had been accomplished. It was Fearnley's intention to land both the first lieutenant and the navigating officer after some means of transportation could be arranged by Dr. Chu.[21] Before this plan could be implemented, however, Weston woke up from a morphia-induced sleep and refused to sanction the scheme to put him ashore. He was in command and would remain so until relieved of his post by orders from a senior naval officer. This heroic obstinacy was an obstacle that proved impossible to circumvent, and so another message had to be sent to the flag officer correcting the earlier one.[22]

At about 9:30 P.M., Chu returned with a collection of sampans. Each sampan took at least two stretcher cases as well as a couple of the less seriously injured. As soon as a sampan had reached its complement of four or five, it moved off toward the Nationalist positions on the southern bank. Weston placed Able Seaman Raymond Calcott in charge of the party of wounded men, and Chu accompanied him both for liaison and medical purposes.[23]

While all this activity was going on around the *Amethyst*, Kerans and his group had safely negotiated their way through numerous paddy fields and finally reached the west bank of a creek where both the ferry and the frigate were supposed to be situated. Neither were to be seen; instead of being a hive of industry, the creek was home to a number of empty junks, a deserted military watchtower, and a solitary wood and mud hut that housed a couple of fishermen and their families who claimed they knew nothing about the frigate's existence. Upset at having made a mistake, Captain Meh decided there was no alternative but to return to the last village they had passed through and try to discover from some of the villagers what had happened to the ship and where the nearest ferry point was.[24]

Leaving Kerans, Packard, and his assistant in the fishermen's hut, Meh, Dewar-Durie, and two Chinese workers trudged wearily back along the narrow path through the paddy fields in crisp temperatures under an overcast sky. When they reached the village, Meh established that the creek they needed to find was north of the one they had mistakenly struck upon.[25] He sent the two laborers back to get the rest of the party and bring them to the village so everyone could set off together for the correct spot on the river. Once reunited, the group left the village and moved steadily northward. They passed through a couple of darkened hamlets and several military posts before reaching a spot about 1/2 mile from the main ferry terminus. Then with midnight approaching, as Dewar-Durie recalls, a most surprising development occurred.

> Suddenly out of the gloom appeared a party of 4 stretchers in charge of AB Calcutt(sic). He stated that 12 wounded had come in an earlier flight and been carried away; also that the frigate had moved and was now in the mouth of the creek.[26]

Apart from Calcott and the local stretcher bearers, the group consisted of a knot of Nationalist soldiers and Lieutenant Chu, the first grade surgeon who had been on board the *Amethyst* and arranged the evacuation procedure. From the vivid description given by Calcott and Chu to Kerans, Meh, and the others, it was obvious that relief was needed as soon as possible. There was no time to lose; the stretcher cases needed hospitalization, and Packard, his assistant, and Captain Meh resolved to return with them to Tachiang. Calcott revealed that there were still nine seriously wounded men on board the *Amethyst*. Kerans and Dewar-Durie indicated that they would go down to the river, make contact with the ship, and bring off the rest of the injured.[27]

Calcott, Dr. Chu, and the two British officers—accompanied as always by a number of Chinese laborers wheeling the medical chests—moved off in the direction of the river. At last the *Amethyst* became visible, a dark outline some distance offshore. Heartened by this discovery, the men were then forced to wait in growing frustration as efforts were made to persuade the local fishermen to release one of their boats so that Calcott, Chu, Dewar-Durie, and Kerans could be ferried out to the warship. Nearly forty minutes elapsed before a sampan could be requisitioned and made ready for the small expedition. It was therefore about 1:00 A.M. when the medical supplies had been stowed aboard and the four men jumped into the boat and cast off. Within minutes, however, misfortune once more played a hand in the proceedings. As their sampan moved across the calm waters of the river toward the silhouette of the frigate, the men saw a change in the outline of the *Amethyst*. Kerans watched in fascinated horror as the ship began to move upriver under its own steam and without the aid of navigational lights. Despite frantic signaling, the sampan was unable to establish contact with the retreating silhouette. Unable to prevent the warship from leaving her anchorage, the weary occupants of the sampan returned dejectedly to the shore where they were challenged by sentries alert to the possibility of Communist infiltration.[28]

Safely back on dry land, the four-man relief party decided to make for Lieutenant Chu's village where tea and cigarettes awaited them.[29] After discussing their predicament, the group reached the unanimous conclusion that there was no alternative but to return to Tachiang. Chu quickly arranged to provide another guide for the group and new carriers for the medical chests. They set off at 1:30 A.M. led by their guide who knew a shortcut over the saddle of the Ta Hung Shan peak, the ridge that dominates the area and around the southern part of which the group had slogged on their outward journey to the river. This route enabled them to reach the village of Tachiang at 3:45 A.M., whereupon they learned that sixteen severely wounded men from the *Amethyst* had just been brought in by stretcher parties. Dr. Packard was attending to them as best he could, but Lieutenant-Commander Skinner and Able Seaman Winter were beyond all medical help. Their deaths cast further gloom and despondency among those present.[30]

Before the injured men were moved into the waiting vehicles to begin what was bound to be an extremely cold and uncomfortable journey to Chinkiang, members of the local Nationalist regiment were ordered to cover the floorboards of the trucks with a fair amount of hay. This rudimentary mattress was designed to reduce the strength of the vibrations that would be felt once the trucks had set out, even at a low speed, along the uneven road surface in the direction of Chinkiang. Dr. Packard and his assistant accompanied the wounded, who were each still wrapped in their two ships blankets, on their journey back to the town. They left shortly after 5:00 A.M. and eventually reached their destination about three hours later. Not certain that all the wounded that were landed from the *Amethyst* had been accounted for and anxious to provide transport for them should they eventually reach the village, Kerans urged Meh to seek General Huang's approval for the delivery of two more trucks to Tachiang. Huang agreed, knowing that at least one truck was needed to take the bodies of Skinner and Winter to Chinkiang for burial. By the time the two extra trucks arrived in Tachiang later that morning, the main convoy had left the village.[31]

During the night as Kerans, Dewar-Durie, and their party were conducting their frustrating maneuvers through the Chinese countryside, life on board the quarry they were stalking was far from relaxed. After resisting all attempts to put him ashore with Berger, Wilkinson, and the last of the wounded men from the *Amethyst*, Weston found his own condition beginning to worsen, much as Fearnley had predicted it would. It became readily apparent that he could no longer stay awake and function adequately without regular doses of such pain-relieving drugs as morphia and benzedrine.[32] While the first lieutenant was battling gamely to stay on top of things, French received another message from the flag officer that increased the acting captain's resolve to remain at the helm.

> After landing your wounded you should have a shot at proceeding up river before moonrise tonight, which is at about 0300/22. Best water is midriver. You should proceed about ten miles then anchor. Only known enemy battery is about 3 miles up river from your present position and after 6 miles you should be safe.[33]

Following these instructions, Weston gave orders for the *Amethyst* to weigh anchor and move upriver toward Nanking. She left the creek where she had been for the last eight hours and began her passage at 1:10 A.M. just as Kerans, Meh, and the others were endeavoring vainly to reach her in the sampan.[34] Moving slowly and navigating by moonlight, the frigate made the journey without serious incident, even though she was occasionally the target for machine-gun fire from both banks. Dropping anchor close to the southern bank at about 2:30 A.M., the darkened ship—whose identity was unknown to those on shore—encountered small arms fire from the Nationalist positions.[35] Not wishing to take any unnecessary risks, Weston opted to illuminate the union jack on the port side of the vessel, in the expectation that this would help to mollify the KMT. On the contrary, this apparently sensible act somehow managed to antagonize them still further, and the firing intensified. Weston had little alternative but to weigh anchor once more and return about a mile downstream close to a canal outlet at Chen-pi. It proved to be a quiet spot, so the first lieutenant gave orders for the ship to hove to and drop anchor for the night. By this time, it was 3:00 A.M.[36]

While the crew settled down to a deserved sleep, French dispatched another message to Madden giving him an account of what had been happening on board, describing the river passage that had just been made, and stating the location of the vessel. The message also asked for information about the siting of the Communist batteries between Chen-pi and Nanking. This request made it clear that Weston was thinking of taking the *Amethyst* upriver the remaining 50 miles to Nanking. Nonetheless, it was frankly acknowledged that the success or failure of this scheme would largely depend upon the number and position of hostile batteries along the river.[37]

When Madden replied some four hours later, his message made no mention of Weston's request but dwelled instead on the need for the frigate to put some distance between her and the Communist battery at Pu-shun-wei, particularly because another Sunderland was expected to land next to the ship at midday, and he wished to avoid a recurrence of what had taken place on the previous day when the flying boat was driven off by artillery and small arms fire from the northern bank.[38] Madden's suggestion to move a few miles upriver was not acted upon because Weston seems to have preferred his existing anchorage to the possibilities upstream. Instead the first lieutenant, sick and weary from the drugs and loss of blood, gathered the crew together at 10:00 A.M. and told them of the impending flight of the Sunderland, which would be carrying an engineering officer, some shipwrights, and a padre, all of whom would be transferred to the ship as expeditiously as possible. In the meantime, the crew were instructed to clean up the ship as best they could and finish preparing the dead for sea burial.[39]

Earlier that Friday morning (22 April), Kerans and Dewar-Durie had reached Chinkiang in their jeep at 7:15 A.M. Their first task was to confirm that arrangements had been made for a hospital to prepare hot drinks and light food for the injured men upon their arrival in town and before they could be shifted onto the train for Shanghai later that morning. Satisfied that the staff of the Christian missionary hospital was expecting the men, the two attachés went off in search of the naval duty officer responsible for the train service out of Chinkiang. Brandishing his letter of authority from Admiral Kwei Yung Ching, the commander in chief of the Nationalist navy in Nanking, Kerans was able to get a first-class sleeper coach added to the Shanghai-bound train, which was due to leave at 10:30 A.M.[40]

While the depleted crew of the *Amethyst* received their instructions from Lieutenant Weston in midmorning, their injured shipmates were being loaded aboard the Shanghai train in Chinkiang station. It took much longer than Kerans anticipated to deal with the wounded when they arrived from Tachiang shortly after 8:00 A.M. To begin with all those in serious condition had to be lifted carefully out of the trucks and brought to the end of the railway station platform, where they were given some nourishment by the nurses from the American hospital and further drugs or transfusions by Dr. Packard. Only when he had finished his rounds could the stretchers be loaded aboard the east-bound train.[41]

Moving men in such a critical condition was bound to be a slow job, as Dewar-Durie acknowledged later, but the entire operation was hindered by the unexpectedly large crowds of local people milling around the station. Apparently they had heard rumors that the Communists were in the process of fulfilling their promise to cross the Yangtze, and some may well have learned that there was some substance to these stories. Kerans was told in confidence that the crossings had already begun and that units of the PLA had managed to get ashore on the southern bank to the west of Kiangyin. This news suggested that in all probability, it would only be a few hours before these troops would cut the railway line to Shanghai. It was hardly surprising then that vast crowds now thronged the station in hope of getting away on what was likely to be the last train to leave Chinkiang for the provincial capital before the Communists arrived in the city.[42]

Aware of this rapidly worsening situation and yet undaunted by it, Kerans prevailed upon the station master to delay the train until all the stretcher cases had been carried into the lower bunks of the compartments assigned to them or placed along the corridors of the rear coach. While the injured were being transferred in this way, another truck arrived at about 11:00 A.M. from Ta-chiang containing four men from the *Amethyst*, three of whom were in a serious condition. They were seen by Packard, given immediate treatment, and put aboard the train with the other survivors. Such was the plight of the men that it was essential that the American doctor went with them to Shang-hai to oversee their transfer to a hospital in that city.[43] Kerans used the further delay to try to establish the whereabouts of the other truck containing the bodies of Skinner and Winter, but his telephone calls to every hospital in Chinkiang were to no avail. Just as the train was leaving the station, however, the truck arrived with its sad cargo. The train jolted to a halt, and the bodies were lifted aboard and placed at one end of the coach. Eventually—about an hour and forty minutes late—the train steamed out of the station and reached Shanghai safely some hours later.[44]

After seeing the train out of the station, Kerans and Dewar-Durie returned to the Nationalist naval headquarters in the town and telephoned Donaldson in Nanking with the latest news about the *Amethyst*. Although Kerans did not know her exact location, he guessed from conversations he had had with members of the KMT naval staff that she must be anchored somewhere below Chinkiang. Aware of Weston's condition and the need to relieve him at the earliest opportunity, the assistant naval attaché proposed that he would go onboard, assume command, and put Weston ashore for hospital treatment. When this had been accomplished, he could then try to take the frigate up to Nanking, leaving Dewar-Durie in Chinkiang in case he was needed there in the event of further trouble occurring upriver. This plan received the immediate endorsement of Sir Ralph Stevenson, who saw it as the best practical solution to the current difficulties surrounding the *Amethyst*. Kerans was, therefore, encouraged to implement his plan of action as quickly as possible.[45]

Kerans needed no second bidding, but his enthusiasm to embark upon this expedition was not matched by the senior officers in the Nationalist navy, whose permission he needed before a boat could be released to take him out to the frigate, wherever she was downriver. Much of their reluctance stemmed from the realization that the period of ceasefire and stalling between the KMT and PLA was now over and that the Communists had begun a concerted move against Nationalist positions along the Yangtze front. Nonetheless, armed with his letter of authorization from Admiral Kwei, Kerans was able to overcome the resistance of the KMT officers and procure an assault craft, which he boarded at 2:00 P.M., taking his medical supplies and navigation charts with him.[46]

Meanwhile downriver, a RAF Sunderland, which had been sent up from Shanghai with Mr. Monaghan and a party of officers and ratings on board, was circling the *Amethyst* and signaling to her with lights. Unfortunately, no one on board ship could read the flying boat's messages, not even the indispensable but weary French, whose telegraphic skills had been much in evidence and upon whom so much work had fallen in the last two days.[47] After ten or fifteen minutes spent in the vicinity of the ship, the Sunderland was encouraged by French to come in to land between the frigate and the southern bank of the Yangtze.[48] Weston's account reveals what happened next.

> Almost the same sequence of events occurred as before. Hitherto undisclosed batteries opened immediate and accurate fire, and the flying boat was forced to take off before anyone could be transferred. Its dinghy was swept away by the tide.[49]

Weston immediately ordered the ship to weigh anchor and move upstream. As soon as the *Amethyst* got under way, the firing stopped. She went about 3 miles before anchoring just to the south of a possible battery site on Ta-Sha Island at a point approximately 5 miles from Chinkiang.[50]

By this time it was 2:00 P.M., and already Kerans's assault craft was seen closing on the frigate from upstream. Although it was a Nationalist vessel, no one on board the *Amethyst* was prepared to take any chances, so a bren gun was set up to cover the slow-moving craft as it came alongside. As the distance between the large LST (landing ship tank) and the British warship narrowed, so Kerans, anxious to defuse any tension that might have been engendered by the appearance of an armed landing craft on the river, stood up in the bow of the KMT vessel waving his Admiralty charts at those on board the *Amethyst* in what he hoped would be an unmistakable gesture of friendship. His action was a sensible precaution and it achieved its objective, for instead of opening fire on the landing craft as it approached, the crew of the British frigate welcomed it and its passenger warmly.[51]

Kerans finally stepped on board the much-battered warship at 3:00 P.M. on Friday 22 April. He immediately went to meet Weston who was sitting in the wireless office obviously in some considerable discomfort. Although there could have been no doubt that the first lieutenant would have to be evacuated ashore, Kerans still asked Dr. Fearnley for his professional opinion of Weston's capacity and fitness to remain on board ship as acting captain. Fearnley made it plain that this was most undesirable as Weston needed hospital treatment promptly if he wished to remain alive much longer. Whatever arguments Weston could put forward were rendered useless by this devastating medical report. Knowing that there was nothing to be gained from a long discussion of the case, Kerans asked Weston to leave the ship and return in the landing craft to Chinkiang, where Dewar-Durie would be on hand to receive him and make arrangements for his journey to the hospital. Stubborn to the last, Weston objected somewhat halfheartedly, conjuring up a range of specious excuses, none of which won him a reprieve. Kerans remained unmoved; if Weston would not leave of his own volition, the assistant naval attaché was prepared to order him off the *Amethyst*. There was no more to be said; the first lieutenant recognized *force majeure* when he saw it and quietly left the ship as cheerful as he could under the circumstances.[52]

Within a half hour of Weston's departure, Kerans sent a radio message to Vice-Admiral Madden indicating that he had sent the first lieutenant ashore and that he remained committed to taking the frigate up to Nanking if this was still possible. His intention was to weigh anchor opposite Chin-chia-shan at 6:30 P.M. and head upriver hoping to pass Chinkiang before the expected Communist bombardment of the town began that evening. Kerans hoped that by going at dusk and in a darkened ship, he might be able to slip past the batteries at Shuang-shih-wu-wei and Kua-chow-chen and reach a point of the river just to the south of Deer Island, which reputedly was still in Nationalist hands.[53]

Almost immediately thereafter, Madden sent Kerans a call authorizing him to assume command of the *Amethyst* forthwith and giving him discretion to act as he thought fit in the light of the prevailing situation on the Yangtze. Even so, this discretionary power was limited by the need both to avoid casualties and to respect standing orders; that is, the ship would be destroyed or sunk if there was no alternative to a complete evacuation of her.[54]

Before Kerans could embark upon his plan to take the frigate past Chinkiang, he had to finalize the arrangements for burying the seventeen dead men remaining aboard the *Amethyst*. Each body was sewn into a hammock into which two 4-inch live shells were added to increase the weight of the shroud and ensure that it would sink 12 fathoms to the bottom of the river when it was cast over the side of the ship. Two short funeral services were performed for the Anglican and Roman Catholic dead, with Kerans reading the committal service for the former and Petty Officer Jeremiah Murphy, the senior Roman Catholic rating, conducting the same rites for the latter. Once this had been completed, all seventeen bodies were piped overboard, and they sank from view into the murky waters of the Yangtze.[55]

Whatever optimistic notions Kerans still entertained about getting through to Nanking, Donaldson and Stevenson did not share them and passed on their fears to Madden. According to the latest intelligence reports monitored at the embassy, the Communists were making inroads into the Nationalist positions in the area. If true, the situation would seriously imperil the lives of those onboard the *Amethyst* should they try to force their way through to Nanking.[56] As the afternoon wore on, confirmation of this news was received in Nanking and passed on to Shanghai. Madden delayed no longer. Just before 6:00 P.M. he radioed the frigate with the following message:

> Latest news just received by Telephone from Nanking indicates that Communists have crossed in some strength 15 miles east of Nanking and situation is expected to deteriorate quickly. You are therefore not repetition not to proceed to Nanking.[57]

While Kerans waited anxiously for further orders, Madden was steadily coming to the conclusion that the *Amethyst* was stuck and incapable of reaching safety without serious disablement if she tried to run the gauntlet of the PLA either up- or downriver from her present position. He informed his superior officer Sir Patrick Brind, who was still in London, that there seemed no alternative but to evacuate and sink the frigate in order that the officers and crew could reach the railway line to Shanghai before it was too late.[58] He also sent an urgent radio message to the *Amethyst* shortly before 8:00 P.M., which stipulated that the safety of the ship's company should be Kerans's first consideration and that he was to begin preparations to evacuate his vessel and sink her. Kerans was further charged with reporting to the flag officer when these arrangements were complete.[59]

It did not take the acting captain long to realize that sinking the *Amethyst* in the Yangtze posed numerous problems, not least because there were no boats in which the exhausted ship's company could row ashore. Fearing that many of the crew would not be able to swim the short distance to shore, Kerans replied to Madden with an alternative proposal for beaching the ship, opening the seacocks, and destroying what he could of her. He added resolutely that he intended to keep the ensign flying while his ship met her final fate.[60]

While waiting for the flag officer's response to this idea, Kerans supervised the division of the crew into three parties, each headed by an officer—namely Fearnley, Hett, and Strain—all of whom had certain tasks allotted to them in preparation for abandoning and immobilizing the ship.[61] Kerans's official report of the incident continues the story:

> It was not intended to set fire to the ship on beaching as this would only have caused embarassement[sic] to the Nationalist soldiers entrenched in the vicinity and may have jeopardised our safety when we reached the shore. The possibility of the shore being mined was not overlooked. Demolition charges had unfortunately all been destroyed when the depth charge store was hit and set on fire, on the 20th April, but detonators were available.[62]

Small rations of chocolate and food were issued to all the men on board ship, and Kerans gave evacuation instructions for everyone to follow should the order to abandon the *Amethyst* be given by Vice-Admiral Madden. In the event of evacuation, the men were expected to wait together on shore for Kerans to join them after he set off an explosion that would cripple the frigate. His escape plan was for the ship's company to walk the short distance from where the *Amethyst* would be beached to Tan-ta-chen, where the Grand Canal to Soochow joins the Yangtze. There they would strike due south along the banks of the canal, as it proceeds on its 250-mile journey through Soochow to Shanghai.[63]

As the men braced themselves for the coming ordeal, another message was received from Madden. It stated simply, without explanation, that the order to abandon ship would probably not be given that night, and under no circumstances were they to immobilize the ship.[64] What this surprising development meant was far from clear. Without being informed of the reason for the change of plan, Kerans could not tell whether it was just a postponement or indeed a cancellation of the decision to evacuate the ship. At this stage, however, puzzling over Madden's decision was unlikely to keep either Kerans or his men awake long that evening. Exhausted, the men wearily and gratefully took to their bunks or settled down on the deck and went to sleep.[65]

As they did so, the Nationalist naval headquarters at Chinkiang was the scene of frenetic activity as men rushed hither and thither packing files and personal belongings so they could evacuate the premises at short notice. By the early hours of the morning, they had left.[66] *Amethyst* was alone.

7. Youde's Mission

*B*RITISH efforts to seek a diplomatic solution to the *Amethyst* crisis were frustrated in the immediate aftermath of the shelling on the Yangtze. By refusing to accept any official communications from the British consul in Peking, the Communist authorities in the city effectively nullified all attempts to bring the issue to an early close.[1] Ambassador Stevenson in Nanking had hoped this approach might result in immediate orders being sent to local PLA commanders in the Chinkiang area of the Yangtze front instructing them to refrain from any further military activity against the stricken frigate.[2] Instead, British diplomacy was denied a role in the affair.

In rejecting any overtures from the British as they had done consistently throughout the previous winter, the Communist officials in Peking underlined their contempt for the Attlee administration's position on China. Although officially proclaiming to be neutral in the civil war, the British were perceived as being biased in favor of the Nationalists. For this reason, neither the CCP nor the PLA were eager to assist an ideological foe and one that had now shown its true colors by aiding and abetting the Nationalists in their attempt to prevent the Communists from crossing the Yangtze.[3]

After the abject failure of these initial efforts to contact the leaders of the Communist movement, the British ambassador, together with his senior embassy staff, was obliged to reflect on the serious nature of this continuing rupture in relations with Mao Tse-tung's party and military forces. At their meeting on the morning of Thursday 21 April, none of the diplomats present doubted the need to establish contact with the Communists. All agreed that without meeting them, it was nearly impossible for the British to scotch the misunderstandings that obviously had arisen over their policy toward China in general and their continued insistence on using the Yangtze as an international waterway in particular.

Clearly the problem that needed to be resolved first was the kind of approach the British should take to get their message of friendship across to the relevant authorities. Only then could the oft-repeated explanations about the peaceful, humanitarian nature of the *Amethyst*'s journey up the Yangtze on 19–20 April be given additional emphasis and stand a better chance of being believed. This goal was fine in theory, but a major practical difficulty remained, namely, deciding where and to whom the British should address their remarks in the first instance. Peking appeared to be a nonstarter. Moreover, even in the unlikely event that a new initiative in that city was successful and the Communists agreed to pass a message of restraint to their frontline forces on the Yangtze, there was still bound to be an indefinite delay before such an order could get through and be acted upon. For this reason, Stevenson and his advisors resolved that the time had come for a direct approach to the local Communist command headquarters, which was thought to be situated at Yangchow opposite Chinkiang and to be responsible for the artillery batteries that had opened fire upon the *Amethyst* and *Consort* on the previous day.[4]

Edward Youde—twenty-four years old, a third secretary at the embassy, and a fluent speaker of Mandarin—volunteered to try to get behind the Communist lines in hope that, as a diplomat, he might be allowed to make a personal approach to the senior military officer of the PLA at Yangchow.[5] His aim was essentially narrowly based and amounted to an appeal for a safe-conduct pass for the *Amethyst* so that she could sail unmolested to either Nanking or Shanghai to land her dead and wounded. This plan was obviously an unconventional and rather daring one in which the risks for Youde were obvious and his personal safety could not be guaranteed. Nonetheless, because he was willing to give it a try and in the light of the negative response of the Communists to the British consul's earlier initiative in Peking, it was probably the only realistic option left to the British at this time. Even so, it was essentially a gamble, and the odds were stacked against its success. Despite the likelihood that the mission would fail, the ambassador and his advisers trusted the plausibility of the old adage "Nothing ventured, nothing gained" and therefore granted permission for the third secretary to embark upon his mission later that day.[6]

Before he could do so, however, much remained to be done. Youde first had to obtain a permit to cross the Nationalist lines from the KMT forces who held the Pukow bridgehead. For this purpose, he made contact with units of the KMT's Thirty-eighth Army at their headquarters in the Nanking garrison, and to his intense surprise and relief, the relevant pass was speedily issued by the Nationalist officials without the usual delay that accompanied most requests made of the military bureaucracy. After obtaining his permit and with an additional letter addressed to the commander of the Thirty-eighth Army, Youde returned to his quarters in the embassy compound and stuffed a few rough-and-ready items of clothing into a haversack for the journey. Exciting though this adventure promised to be, it was also more than a little unnerving. At the outset, Youde had no idea how long the trip would take or what sort of reception he would get from the frontline troops on either side. He also took the precaution of providing himself with fifty silver dollars, which could be used for payment of food or for bribery, if need be, of local officials.[7]

Interestingly, the only documents of identification Youde carried with him on his mission behind the Communist lines were those issued by the Nationalist government and signed by members of the KMT military, all of whom the PLA would later rank as "war criminals"! It seems odd, to say the least, that he did not take with him any document of authorization or identity bearing the imprimatur of his ambassador Sir Ralph Stevenson. In the official report he wrote later, a not entirely convincing case was made for this apparently inexplicable omission. Youde indicated that the decision not to issue him any embassy identification had been based on the assumption that since the Communist authorities had refused to accept any official document from British representatives in the past, there appeared to be no reason why they should accept his.[8] Although this assumption might indeed have been the case, it seems most improbable that his mission would have been hampered by such a letter, particularly as he made no attempt to conceal that he was a British diplomat charged with seeking a safe-conduct pass for the frigate HMS *Amethyst*.

Youde set off across the Yangtze in a naval launch belonging to the Nationalists just as the Thursday evening twilight ended. He gained the bank on the other side of the river without difficulty and found the local headquarters of the Thirty-eighth Army. He was not surprised to learn that no one was expecting him, least of all the general in command who seemed to regard this diplomat's presence in his midst as an unnecessary complication to an already taxing task. Despite Youde's permit and letter explaining his mission, the general was far from keen on assisting him, pointing out the impossibility of crossing the lines and the fact that the two armies were too close and already locked in combat. Youde had to work hard to save the situation, and only after a good deal of earnest negotiation was he able to extract a promise from the general to review the situation in the morning.[9]

In the meantime, the general asked his adjutant to look after the British diplomat and make arrangements for him to have some food and a bed for the night. During the evening—which he spent with the adjutant and his friend, the ordnance officer—the young third secretary was made to feel that his personal initiative would almost certainly end in violent, abject defeat. Both Nationalists appeared convinced that even if he somehow managed to avoid falling victim to plainclothes bandits who preyed on those rash enough to be caught in no-man's-land between the two front lines, none of the Communist officials with whom he might eventually make contact would bother to listen to reason and nothing would be done to extricate the *Amethyst* from her present predicament. If Youde was bothered by this talk of the hopelessness of his situation, he did not let it show. Eventually the discussion petered out, and he went to bed.[10]

After breakfasting at dawn on Friday 22 April, Youde went to see the general who had been so discouraging the night before. On this occasion, the commanding officer was more positive and ready to help the diplomat. He told Youde of a place in the front where a person might be able to cross over into the Communist lines without facing insuperable odds. A young soldier was deputed to take Youde to the area in question, a Nationalist outpost to the northeast of their present location.[11]

After gratefully accepting a couple of packets of army biscuits as iron rations, the diplomat and his young guide set out by foot almost immediately. Although a slight drizzle was falling at the time, it failed to dampen Youde's spirits or his enthusiasm for what lay in store for him. He and the soldier walked along the riverbank for about ninety minutes until the KMT outpost was reached. Stationed there—as Youde was later to describe—were six very sleepy soldiers and two extremely active mongrels. This outpost was the point at which Youde was left to fend for himself. His former guide indicated the route he ought to take in order to reach the next town, where contact could be sought with the magistrate, and ended by reiterating the warning that he was about to proceed through bandit country. Youde was left in no doubt that if he was caught by the bandits, which seemed virtually certain, it would be safer to cooperate and not argue with them.[12]

Contrary to popular belief, the young diplomat was neither attacked, robbed, nor physically abused after he had left the Nationalist lines. In fact, he walked for about two hours with no problems at all. His presence was naturally a talking point with the large groups of peasants whom he passed on the road, and he derived great amusement and satisfaction from the spectacle that he, a foreigner, must have created in this slightly unworldly setting. None of the peasants claimed to have seen the Communists, nor were they much concerned about the bandits that were supposed to operate freely in the area. What this situation revealed about Nationalist intelligence was not lost on the third secretary.[13]

> My reveries en route were rudely interrupted on the outskirts of Hsiehchiatien, where I was to contact the magistrate. As a single rifle shot winged past me I made a dive for cover, but since no more shots came my way I emerged from my rabbit hole and walked on. It was an unpropitious moment because a machine gunner, seemingly mistaking the stick I carried for a rifle, tested his sights on me. A spirited exchange then developed between a Nationalist gunner on an island in the river and my assailant just over my head (which by this time was as low as it could get in a nearby brick kiln in company with the heads of a few local peasants). When chips began to fly off the edge of the kiln we moved our abode to a Chinese grave yard and there discussed the situation.[14]

Youde quickly discovered that Hsiehchiatien was in turmoil and that the magistrate, whom he had been hoping to meet, had left the area before the Communists had begun entering the town the previous evening. According to the peasants, a Communist battalion had already occupied the large Yung Li chemical factory and were consolidating their hold on the town as the hours went by. If this information could be trusted, and there was no reason to disbelieve it, Youde was within a short distance of the Communist front line. He asked for a volunteer to take him to the factory premises, but no one could be persuaded to come forward and offer their services to this apparently eccentric foreigner with his odd desire to become personally acquainted with the forward troops of the PLA.[15]

As he sat huddled with the peasants behind their defensive shield of grave-stones, Youde's optimism deserted him temporarily. Pinned down by hostile fire, it was easy to begin doubting the wisdom of going it alone. He began to convince himself that it was unrealistic to try to make contact with the local commander of the PLA in the town unless he could count on receiving some local assistance along the way.

> Just at this moment, when I was resigning myself to sitting in the grave yard until someone found me, a Communist patrol came over the hill. Fortunately I saw them first and walked towards them with my hands up. Their surprise did not affect their discipline. In a trice the patrol had dispersed into the surrounding paddy fields and had me covered from all sides. The patrol commander listened to the explanation of my mission and without hesitation told off two men to escort me back to headquarters.[16]

When Youde and his two escorts arrived at what he presumed was company headquarters, the two Communist soldiers were relieved and replaced by a hearty individual who, despite being burdened down with a pack, private rice supply, five hand grenades, a pistol, and a rifle, still managed to walk at a brisk 5 miles an hour. Dressed in civilian clothes and wearing a hat that looked like a bowler without a rim, Youde's new guide made light work of the load he carried and the route he followed. Young though he was, the British diplomat found it difficult to keep up with this relatively new recruit into the army. While they were on their own the pace never slackened, and the diplomat was immensely grateful when after about an hour's walking they caught up with and joined a small group of former officials of the Yung Li factory and KMT personnel who were being sent back under escort to the area headquarters of the PLA. This group of prisoners was moving at a more sedate pace, which was easier for Youde to maintain. During their journey, the group was allowed frequent rest periods and given the opportunity to drink hot water and buy food from the peasantry.

> We reached a higher headquarters at about four in the afternoon. Parties of Kuomintang police, prisoners of war and small officials were being assembled in the village at the time of my arrival and my companions were led off to be fed and registered. I was taken in to see the commanding officer who was seated with two others in a small room in a farm house. I was surprised to see that the rightful occupants had not been turned out but went about their business quite normally even during our talks. I again explained my mission and after some discussion on the subject of why our ships had entered territorial waters, why they had fired on Communist batteries, etc. I was told that the matter could not be settled at that level but that since time was short they would send me up the same evening to a superior headquarters who would be in radio contact with "the superior organ" and would be able to give me an answer.[17]

In the meantime, Youde was expected to discuss a number of current issues in international affairs with three Communist officials and defend the British government's stand on such matters as the Berlin Blockade, NATO, the United Nations, and the Chinese civil war. In addition, he was expected to provide detailed information on the British welfare state and the rationing system. Although the debate with these Communist officials was essentially good-natured, it lapsed into that frustratingly recursive way it often does when people do not agree with one another. While this dialectic was proceeding, a welcome and tasty meal of rice and chopped vegetables was prepared for the diplomat by the farmer's wife. By the time he had eaten it, the debate had fizzled out inconclusively.[18]

Shortly before Youde left the farmhouse on the next stage of his journey, he was told by the commanding officer that because of the shortage of manpower in his unit, no one could be spared for escort duty at this time. To avoid delay, the young Briton would have to join a party of prisoners who were going to a reeducation or training camp in the same general direction as his particular destination. As he waited for the prisoners to march off, Youde listened as a PLA officer told the group that everyone would be well treated, provided they behaved themselves and obeyed orders. If any trouble was caused, however, the escort guards might have to take retaliatory action.[19]

Eventually the prisoners were marched off with a peasant as their guide, followed by the corporal of the guard and Youde at the head of the column. As the trek continued the group was allowed a rest period about every ninety minutes, at which time the guide was changed. As darkness closed in on the prisoners and the rough terrain began to take its toll on the slightly wounded or unfit members of the party, more frequent stops were made. Youde, who had been walking practically all day long without much food or rest, was physically exhausted and therefore especially grateful for the chance to sit down and relax for a few minutes.[20]

It was after 9:00 P.M. when the group reached what was supposed to be their final destination. Unfortunately, their luck was out; the camp had been moved elsewhere, and they were forced to march on to another place a few miles away, which they reached at about 10:30 P.M. Once there, arrangements were made between the corporal and the head of the village to provide some shelter for the prisoners, and a price was agreed upon for the purchase of some rice with which to feed them. Youde noticed with some surprise that the prisoners were fed before the escorts had their rice and only after everyone else had eaten did the corporal begin to eat his own bowl of rice. Afterward, Youde was given a quilt, and he went to sleep on the straw-covered floor of the farmhouse where he was billeted with one of the escorts.[21]

They began walking again at 5:00 A.M. It took them just over four hours to reach the new camp, where Youde and the others parted company. While the prisoners waited to be interned, Youde was sent on to the village where the forward headquarters of the PLA was supposedly situated. He soon learned that the headquarters had been shifted in the night to the recently captured town of Puchen some 35 li, or nearly 12 miles, away. This discovery frustrated Youde even more because Puchen lay only 4 miles west of the Nationalist bridgehead from which he had begun his mission a day and half before.[22]

Faced by the prospect of another long walk and no guarantee that when he reached Puchen the forward headquarters would still be there, Youde began to despair. He asked to be sent back in some form of motorized transport to Yangchow, the site of the rear headquarters. As neither a vehicle nor a horse could be spared for such a journey, the diplomat was left with the unappealing prospect of a two-day walk back to Yangchow or a further march up to the front line. He chose the latter and moved off with a unit in that direction shortly afterward.[23]

They stopped for a meal at noon and rested for two hours while they waited for information about the location of the forward headquarters. This unit, like many others, had no radio equipment and relied on a well-organized system of runners to carry orders and relay intelligence. After the instructions had been received from one of these runners, the unit continued its progress. Soon the soldiers came across another obstacle, an antipersonnel minefield, which the Nationalists had presumably sown before pulling out of the area. A further delay occurred, as it took about thirty minutes for the unit's engineers to remove some of the mines. They had not completed their task before the commanding officer decided he could not afford to wait any longer and issued orders for the men to line up in single file before proceeding cautiously through the minefield. Led by their commander with his deputy behind him, the troops and the British diplomat followed. As soon as a mine was spotted, information about its position was relayed back down the line. Displaying both vigilance and care, the unit passed through the minefield safely and continued on its march toward Puchen. The group soon arrived on the outskirts of Puchen, but once there, the men learned that the town was littered with Nationalist mines. Fortunately these mines had already been detected and marked with chalk and vegetation, so the unit was able to pass through the area with no difficulty.[24]

This experience seemed to illustrate the marked difference between the rival armies in the civil war. Whereas the Nationalists appeared rather woebegone, lacking in morale and ideas, the Communists tackled problems sensibly, coolly, and efficiently. Indeed throughout his mission, Youde had been impressed by the esprit de corps displayed by both the officers and troops of the PLA; relations between them appeared to be good, discipline was excellent, orders were carried out promptly, and everyone with whom he met and talked seemed to know the importance of the cause for which they were fighting.[25] In his report he noted:

> Their morale was outstanding. As we marched over the hill near Puchen which brought us into sight of Nanking a spontaneous shout went up as soon as they had confirmed from me that it really was the capital. I was then asked where the road to Shanghai was. They were going there next.[26]

After his short but eventful experience in the company of the PLA troops, Youde had seen enough to convince him of the vitality of this military-politico force and the dangers of underestimating its part in shaping the future of China. Although the military force had made a wholly favorable impression upon him, the political indoctrination of the PLA was so thorough that it made successful negotiation on contentious issues a futile exercise. Arguments on any number of themes that Youde had had with both officers and men were subject to familiar criticisms and foundered on an almost total lack of common ground between the two sides.[27]

One such meeting occurred at 6:00 P.M. on Saturday 23 April at the forward headquarters of the PLA in Puchen, when Youde at last came face to face with the military officer whom he had been tracking for the past two days. Having finally caught up with him, Youde had to try to persuade the commander to allow the *Amethyst* to proceed unmolested to either Shanghai or Nanking. Whatever his optimism at the outset, Youde's spirits had become subdued and his expectation of success reduced after the rich and yet often exasperating experience of the past forty-eight hours. Although he was politely received and listened to, the diplomat's worst fears were quickly confirmed. His appeals for immunity and a safe-conduct pass for the *Amethyst* met the kind of fate that the old China hands in Nanking and London could have predicted had they been asked. Unwilling to make any decision on such a grave matter on his own, the commander explained that he would have to refer Youde's request to a higher authority.[28] This statement was not a stalling device, for the answer was promptly received. Unfortunately, the Communist terms for granting Youde's request, which amounted to a demand that the *Amethyst* provide assistance for the PLA troops in crossing the Yangtze, were simply unacceptable. When Youde rejected this proposal, he was told bluntly that the British would have to find the solution to the problem by themselves.[29]

The Communists believed that the blame for the *Amethyst* crisis lay solely with the British. It was pointed out most forcefully to Youde that none of the British warships using the Yangtze and entering the war zone had received any clearance from the PLA to do so. Far from being surprised by this line of argument, Youde tried to counter it by stating that it would have been impossible for the British to obtain such a permit prior to the voyage of the *Amethyst*, simply because the Communist authorities in Peking had, for months past, steadfastly refused to accept any communication from Mr. Buxton, His Majesty's consul, in the city. To this rejoinder the commander gave no reply, but switched the discussion immediately to another area of complaint, namely, the heavy casualties incurred by the Communist troops as a result of the naval bombardment of the Yangtze shore defenses by the British warships. When Youde attempted to argue that the ships had a right to defend themselves, the commander refused without further elaboration to accept his claim. At this point of impasse, Youde's mission came to an abrupt end.[30]

Although his initiative had failed to secure the *Amethyst*'s freedom, the third secretary had no method of passing this information on to the British government until he could return to Nanking and report personally to Sir Ralph Stevenson. By Saturday evening, this stage of the journey looked as though it might present the young, disappointed diplomat with more difficulties than he had originally anticipated. Apart from any other considerations, the PLA commander had refused to recognize him as the official representative of the British embassy, despite Youde's insistence that he was. As a result, he would be protected and assisted by the PLA as an ordinary foreign national but not accorded any diplomatic privileges, such as the granting of a special travel pass, which would have eased his return to Nanking considerably.[31]

In the wake of the Communist attacks of the last few days, Youde's original plan of crossing into one of the Nationalist bridgeheads lay in ruins. Pukow, for instance, had fallen the morning before, and hundreds of miles now separated him from other Nationalist positions on the northern side of the river. His dilemma was obvious: he needed to get back to Nanking speedily. As Pukow had fallen, however, there now seemed few alternatives to the unenviable and laborious task of walking to Wuhu, which was likely to take him an additional three days before he could cross the Yangtze in safety and then double back along the railway line to Nanking. It was a sobering thought and one that weighed heavily upon him that Saturday evening as he wandered the streets looking for an inn in which to spend the night. Eventually he was directed by a small boy to a *peng* hut, a rudimentary dwelling where he found a straw mattress to sleep on for the night.[32]

He got up at dawn the next morning, motivated again and ready to support his belief that despite all signs to the contrary, the place to make for was Pukow. His confidence was rewarded. As he reached the town and walked along the riverbank, he saw a steam ferry approaching from the direction of Nanking. He discovered that the Nationalists had left Nanking on Saturday morning and that the PLA was now entering it unopposed. This fact accounted for the presence of the ferry, which was being used to carry Communist troops across the river to the former KMT capital. Youde had no difficulty boarding the next ferry for Nanking. When he arrived, he walked the short distance from the jetty to the embassy compound, arriving at about 7:30 A.M. on Sunday 24 April.[33] Although his gallant personal mission had ended, as expected, in failure, nothing substantial had been lost by embarking upon it in the first place. Now, however, the attention would shift to more conventional diplomatic initiatives. Only time would tell whether these new efforts to bring the Yangtze incident to a negotiated end would be any more successful than Youde's brave, individual, and ultimately frustrated attempt to solve this latest crisis in Anglo-Chinese relations.

8. Exploring Other Possibilities

WELL BEFORE Kerans had assumed command of the *Amethyst* and Youde had penetrated far into Communist territory, the grave implications of the Yangtze incident for Britain's relations with the Chinese Communists were evident. Ambassador Stevenson did not need reminding that because a military solution was now out of the question, the British could only bring the affair to a successful conclusion by a great deal of careful diplomacy and a large slice of luck. Much depended upon the Communist authorities, for if they refused to negotiate on satisfactory terms, the possibilities of achieving an acceptable settlement of the Yangtze affair appeared to be remote and perhaps even nonexistent.

Aware of the sensitive nature of this crisis in Anglo-Chinese relations, Stevenson knew he must be swift in defending the peaceful nature of the *Amethyst*'s voyage up the Yangtze. An explanatory message, stressing the nonmilitary, impartial attitude of the British toward the civil war, was conveyed to the Communist authorities not only in diplomatic communications, but also in a series of press releases, which he began issuing in the hours after the frigate's first engagement with the Communist shore batteries on Wednesday 20 April.[1] These press statements were intended to alert the PLA to the measures the British were going to take—or sought to explain those actions already taken—in connection with the *Amethyst* dispute. Stevenson thought that using the media was necessary because normal methods of diplomacy could be virtually discounted as having any influence with the Communists after their persistent refusal to accept any communication from the British in the recent past.[2] Therefore, he intended to use newspapers and the radio as forums for proclaiming the innocence of the *Amethyst* in the river war that had broken out on the Yangtze, while vigorously defending subsequent British naval action as an understandable response to what had taken place on that fateful Wednesday morning in the vicinity of Rose Island.

In a situation like this one, however, Stevenson should have been judicious in his choice of words and cautious not to apportion blame unwisely or appear to be jingoistic. His press briefings were hardly models of circumspection in these areas; he gave the impression that the Communists were entirely to blame for the original incident and all the conflict that followed.[3] His stridency about the iniquitous way the PLA had behaved toward the British on the Yangtze undoubtedly reflected the ambassador's own personal distaste for the Chinese Communists, a feeling he had not failed to express in the past. One might consider, therefore, that Stevenson's diplomatic efforts to solve the crisis, if not fatally compromised by his well-known hostility to Communism, were likely to be as unsuccessful as Youde's had been.

Not surprisingly, perhaps, the Communists' own interpretation of the events on the Yangtze differed fundamentally from the official British version. In a vigorous statement denouncing British naval policy issued by the New China News Agency on 22 April, the action on the river during the previous two days was described as a joint attack mounted by both the KMT and the Royal Navy against the PLA.

> Public opinion here points out that the British Imperialist Navy has joined hands with the K.M.T. reactionaries to challenge the P.L.A. and directly participated [in] China's war by firing on P.L.A. positions. The British Imperialist Government should be fully responsible for the losses suffered by the P.L.A. The K.M.T. reactionaries who started the civil war in collaboration with American imperialism have now committed another traitorous act by working in collusion with British Imperialist Naval vessels which sailed far up the Yangtse to hinder the crossing of the P.L.A.[4]

This aspect of alleged collusion between the KMT and the British, although adding a new and dangerous element to the story, nonetheless failed to arouse the British ambassador's ire. He appears to have dismissed it as being an exaggerated piece of propaganda and unworthy of a reply, because he failed to answer the accusation directly. He merely repeated the nature of the *Amethyst*'s business on the Yangtze and the humanitarian and peaceful role that the other British warships were undertaking when they too were attacked by Communist artillery fire on 20–21 April.[5]

In its statement of 22 April, the New China News Agency had also alleged that the *Amethyst* had fired on the PLA positions first and that the Communist forces had only retaliated in self defense.[6] In the *People's Daily* of 24 April, this allegation was repeated, and a more detailed account of the story was provided.

> Our PLA army was attacking the Nationalist bridgeheads on the north bank of the Yangtze river on April 20 as a preparation for the 'general crossing' when two enemy warships from the east opened fire on PLA positions in Kou An so as to halt the crossing.
>
> Our artillery men returned the fire hitting one of the vessels which subsequently sank. The other vessel steamed westwards and was half sunk near Chinkiang.[7]

This report went on to claim that several other vessels nearby also participated in a minor capacity in the subsequent ship-to-shore encounters that occurred between several of these unidentified warships and the PLA in the next twenty-four hours. According to the newspaper report, from the outset the PLA had mistakenly believed that all these vessels belonged to the Nationalist navy, and they were only disabused of this notion on Friday 22 April when they finally learned from various sources that four of the warships had in fact been British.[8]

Here then was the substance of the indictment that the Communists would use in all future negotiations with the British over the responsibility for the *Amethyst* crisis. That any of these claims would be difficult to substantiate in an international court of law did not concern the PLA, because the matter would not be thrashed out in such a judicial setting. Even so, the nature of the charges were such that they could not be easily disproved either. Lack of satisfactory evidence to prove their innocence would naturally handicap the British when it was time to negotiate a satisfactory settlement to the affair. All they could do under the circumstances was to reject point by point all the charges of guilt and complicity leveled against them by the Communists and instead accuse the PLA of provoking the incident by maintaining that its troops opened fire on the *Amethyst* first.

Meanwhile, the case for seeking a political solution to the crisis encountered further resistance from the Communist bureaucracy in Peking. On 20 April, shortly after news of the attack on the *Amethyst* had filtered through, M. P. Buxton, the British consul, approached the local authorities in Peking with an appeal for restraint from his ambassador. Failing to get that support, he decided to write a personal letter to General Chu Teh, the military supremo of the PLA. Having drafted it, he approached Chen, an official of the Aliens Affairs Bureau, and requested that he accept the letter and forward it to the headquarters of the PLA. This request was politely refused on the grounds that the bureau's authority was limited only to the Peking area. Chen advised the consul to ask the post office to deliver the letter by express mail through the regular channels, and he offered to have a word with the postal authorities so that they would give the letter special priority. He declined, however, to give the consul the specific military address of Chu Teh. Although Buxton had a long and reasonably satisfactory conversation with Chen about the mission of the *Amethyst,* his additional request for a meeting with a senior official of the municipal council was denied.[9] Once again Buxton had achieved disconcertingly little through no fault of his own, but this lack of success augured badly for the establishment of any diplomatic machinery to resolve the Yangtze crisis in the near future and was suggestive, perhaps, of a lack of real urgency on the part of the Communists concerning this matter.

Buxton's letter was duly dispatched, but when there was no immediate acknowledgment that his message had reached Chu Teh, the consul interpreted the silence to mean that his latest initiative had probably come to naught. At this point he turned somewhat despairingly to Stevenson, reiterating the problems he faced in representing the British in a city where the Communist officials remained unwilling to recognize him as a bona fide diplomat or accord him any useful channel of approach to the higher organs of the party or military. In his opinion, an approach to Chu Teh was still a good idea, for if he could be persuaded to support the call for a cease-fire against the British frigate, it would be an important breakthrough.[10]

His suggestion that Stevenson should issue a fresh appeal to Chu Teh was not one that the British ambassador endorsed, as his telegram to the Foreign Office on 22 April makes clear.

> My own view is that by doing so we might risk prematurely compromising our position with regard to recognition of the Chinese Communist administration without real hope of obtaining action desired. As a result of Communist authorities having obstinately ignored our previous communications I fear it is now in any case too late even to ensure immunity of Amethyst from continued deliberate attacks which must be known by now to the Communists Supreme Command who could have taken active steps to prevent them.[11]

Stevenson felt that the outcome of an appeal such as this would be to expose the British to the charge that they had been prepared to do deals with the Communists while still officially recognizing the Nationalists as the government of the country.[12] His reservations about the plan were also held by the Foreign Office in London, which registered its disapproval in a cable on 23 April, indicating that a direct approach to Chu Teh was ruled out for the time being.[13]

As Buxton labored vainly to make an impression upon the impassive face of the Communist bureaucracy in Peking, his ambassador maintained an active and altogether more successful link with the Nationalist ministers who remained behind in Nanking. Stevenson had access to the highest ministers and their officials and used this opportunity to gauge what was going on along the war front and to discover what KMT policy was likely to be if the PLA crossed the Yangtze and captured the southern bank of the river. From information already published in the international press, together with what he could glean from his own sources—including a talk he had had with Hang Li-wu, the minister of education—Stevenson was sure that the long-awaited Communist offensive was proving to be an unstoppable drive that threatened to engulf the KMT troops and its political leaders unless they staged a strategic withdrawal from the scene.[14]

If the Nationalists wished to live to fight another day, they appeared to have no alternative but to abandon the Yangtze region as quickly as possible and move further south. This strategic notion and much more was confirmed by George Yeh, the acting minister for foreign affairs, in an interview he had with Stevenson early in the morning of Friday 22 April. Admitting that Li Tsung-jen and his cabinet were leaving shortly for Canton where the seat of government had already been formally established, Yeh advised Stevenson that rather than continue to stay in a city that was about to fall to the Communists, he ought to leave for Shanghai while he still could.[15]

Stevenson had no intention of leaving his embassy or the city in which he had spent much of the previous three years. Such a retreat would run counter to official British policy in China. Moreover, the Communist takeover seemed to provide a splendid opportunity for his staff to meet and get to know the officials who would be wielding power in Nanking after the KMT abandoned its former capital. In the meantime before the Communists arrived, he was on hand to describe the upheaval that convulsed the city in the last few hours before the Nationalist leaders, military, and police finally departed, leaving the civilian population to fend for themselves and await the day of "liberation" at the hands of the PLA.[16]

Although a military defeat for the KMT in the Yangtze valley had long been predicted, it was the abject manner in which the Nationalists accepted the situation that was perhaps the most surprising feature of the renewed campaign. On Thursday (21 April), a few hours after the Communist ultimatum to the Nationalist government had expired and the day on which Youde had crossed the Yangtze, the PLA had begun the first of its own military excursions in the opposite direction. By mounting an offensive southwest of Nanking, forward units of the Communist military had been able to cross the river in force near Wuhu some 60 miles up the Yangtze from the former KMT capital. According to the intelligence reports obtained by the military and naval attachés in Nanking and from other diplomatic personnel elsewhere in China, resistance to the drive had appeared to be negligible. On the following day (22 April), the PLA had launched a series of successful river crossings over a 250-mile front. The Communist capture of the forts around the naval base at Kiangyin and the rapidity of their advance persuaded the Nationalists to evacuate Chinkiang on the same day and its former capital, Nanking, a day later.[17]

By deciding not to defend this historic city in favor of beating a strategic retreat from the area, the KMT had in a matter of a few hours rendered obsolete the British policy of stationing a guardship at Nanking, which they had steadfastly maintained since the previous November. In truth, however, this retreat merely formalized the destruction of something that had already been severely compromised, if not entirely wrecked by the *Amethyst* incident and the events of 20–21 April. From Saturday 23 April onward—the day when the last of the Nationalist groups left Nanking—the case for having a warship at the port could no longer be made with the same conviction as before by either Attlee's government in London or any of its diplomatic, military, economic, or commercial advisers. Stevenson knew this as well as anyone else, and he wrote in this sense to the Foreign Office shortly after Youde had returned empty-handed early on Sunday morning from his foray behind the Communist lines.[18]

It had now become impossible for the British to maintain the fiction any longer that the Yangtze was an international waterway on which their ships had inalienable rights of passage, which they would use to provide continuing support for all Commonwealth embassies and nationals living in the area. As a result of the Communists' growing strength in recent months, together with the disintegration and collapse of the KMT position south of the Yangtze, it had become an established fact that the PLA now controlled much of the river from Woosung to Nanking and that all ships would in the future require its permission before venturing further on this vital waterway. Like it or not, the British could do very little to arrest this development in the short term; they would have to accept that for all intents and purposes, the Yangtze was out-of-bounds to any of their warships for the foreseeable future.

In London the Chiefs of Staff (COS) had already come to that conclusion as early as 20 April.[19] Thereafter their main concern was to limit the harm that the *Amethyst* incident might do to British interests in China. When the matter was raised again at their next meeting on Friday 22 April and the members began exploring what few nondiplomatic solutions existed for bringing the crisis to a timely end, Admiral Sir John Edelsten, the vice chief of the naval staff, ruled out any possibility of the *Amethyst* being able to save herself. He mentioned that although the frigate could probably do 17 knots at full speed, it was simply out of the question for anyone to expect her to run the Communist gauntlet down the Yangtze for more than 100 miles in order to reach the safety of the open sea. When this gloomy assessment was added to the recognition that external force could no longer be used against the Communist artillery positions on the banks of the Yangtze, the COS were left wondering whether an acceptable military option was possible under the circumstances.[20]

Madden's alternative suggestion—made in a telegram dispatched to the Admiralty on Friday morning (22 April)—of scuttling the frigate and airlifting her crew from the river by flying boat did not appeal to the first sea lord or to either of his two service colleagues on the COS when they met later that day.[21] Lord Fraser, the chief of naval staff, thought it far too premature for such a drastic and irreversible step as this to be taken, especially in light of what Youde's mission might be able to achieve and of Madden's own admission that the ship was in a fairly good position and could sustain herself for at least a few days providing there was no concerted attempt by the Communists to threaten her existence. Fraser echoed these sentiments in an urgent wire to the flag officer, which was sent off in the early afternoon. Ironically, given what Edelsten thought about the inability of the *Amethyst* to escape on her own, Fraser had added a hopeful note suggesting that her chances of escaping might improve after the Communist troops had crossed the Yangtze.[22]

Alive to the concern expressed by Lord Fraser, Madden replied cautiously, "I shall certainly not order abandonment until I am convinced that other course offers a reasonable chance of escape without high percentage of casualties."[23] In fact, he had already decided not to go ahead with the order to immobilize the ship before he received Fraser's anxious telegram counseling such restraint. This exchange underlines once more the strength of the regional expert. In the end it would be up to Madden and not his superiors in the Admiralty to judge what to do for the best. Although the Admiralty could indeed play an advisory role and did expect to be consulted on all matters, ultimately it was Madden's responsibility to make decisions based on all the information at his disposal. It was a responsibility that all serving officers would recognize and jealously guard as being their right under the circumstances.

Madden received an update on *Amethyst's* position some six hours after

Kerans had been informed that evacuation would not be ordered that evening. It simply confirmed that as long as she was left alone by the Communists all would be well for some time to come.

> Fuel 260 tons approx. Feed water and steering o.k. Provisions 2 months basic items. Evaporators o.k. Can fight with one four inch or secondary armament one side.[24]

These signs were healthy and took the pressure off the flag officer because they allowed him more time to maneuver. He could defer a decision on what to do for some time to allow the situation on the Yangtze to settle down. By dawn on Saturday 23 April, the Communist troops were in a position to have boarded and overrun the *Amethyst* if they had wished to; the fact that they had not done so was, perhaps, an indication that the British warship did not rank high on their list of priorities at this time. Madden's apparently odd decision of the previous evening to postpone the evacuation procedure, which he had ordered Kerans to arrange only a few hours before, seems to have been influenced by this reluctance on the part of the PLA to interfere with the frigate. As long as they continued to leave the *Amethyst* alone, Madden would not need to order Kerans to destroy the ship.[25]

Whether or not Fraser's reading of the situation on the river influenced the flag officer's subsequent conduct is unclear, but it certainly did not take Madden long to make a wholly fresh suggestion to Kerans, as the following telegram shows: "If I judged prospect of making a downstream passage reasonably promising would you feel it practicable navigationally by night?"[26] Kerans replied virtually immediately.

> Yes I feel navigation by night feasible at slow speed and presume that risk of grounding must in circumstances be acceptable. Have no radar or gyro and doubtful magnetic compass, main steering however is alright.[27]

Kerans's willingness to accept the risks of trying to take the *Amethyst* on a nighttime passage to freedom had never been doubted; reaffirming his attitude in this way, however, opened up another possible option for ending the crisis and one that had become all but discounted after the renewed Communist offensive in the Yangtze area.

A stay of execution for the frigate seemed particularly appropriate on that Saturday morning. A thick fog enveloped the ship, and an eerie stillness settled over the river. This uneasy calm was punctuated twice by the sound of aircraft engines as first a Sunderland and then a Dakota flew directly overhead without trying to circle the ship or land nearby. Nothing stirred on the river except the sounds of activity on board the *Amethyst* as the crew rose, breakfasted, and then got on with their various tasks of preparation and repair work throughout the ship. Even after the bank of fog had lifted by 9:00 A.M., the river remained quiet, and no activity could be detected on either shore.[28] At this point Kerans decided to ask the flag officer whether he thought it worthwhile for the frigate to use this apparent lull in the fighting to move cautiously downstream.[29] Madden was not convinced that this was a sound move. He made it clear that he much preferred to await the air reconnaissance report—which the crew of the Sunderland would compile once they had reached Shanghai—before deciding what crucial steps the *Amethyst* should take next to extricate herself from her present predicament.[30]

All that morning, the unusual calm on the Yangtze and in the immediate vicinity of the boat continued. Then shortly after midday, some Chinese troops—which the lookouts on the *Amethyst* presumed were from the PLA— were spotted on Ta-Sha Island on the northern bank of the river.[31] Kerans rapidly came to the conclusion that they were probably establishing a battery there in order to provide covering fire for a crossing of the river in that area. His report of the incident continues.

> I therefore decided it advisable to shift berth a short distance down river and anchor opposite land with no natural cover off the southern edge of TASHA Island. This at any rate, I had hoped, would have made sniping more difficult. As I was about to anchor, accurate artillery fire was opened on the ship by the battery probably situated on YU-LUNG-CHOW or PU-SHUN-WEI. Immediately turned back at full speed and anchored close to the south bank in twelve fathoms mid-way between the villages of TAN-TA-CHEN and CHEN-PI CHEN-KOU. Firing ceased and no hits were sustained.[32]

This sobering experience, which had taken less than forty-five minutes to enact, was enough to convince Kerans that the Communists were assembled in such strength along the river that it would have been impossible for the *Amethyst* to attempt an escape in daylight hours, and even in the dark the prospect was one that filled him with foreboding. Depressed by what he had seen and certain that his ships was trapped between several batteries, Kerans began to consider the few options that appeared to be left to him and his crew. After listening to the BBC World Service news broadcast at 1:00 P.M., in which the prospect of a ceasefire, safe-conduct pass, or both for the frigate was mentioned, he wired Madden shortly afterward with the following request:

> Is there any hope of SAFE CONDUCT which I can pass (onto) ships company who are behaving splendidly but nearing breaking point. Have not been fired at

again. If I come under fire before dark intend to beach, sink, destroy and reach Shanghai. Am ready to do this now.[33]

Madden's reply gave him the authority to act as he thought fit if he was fired on again or if he felt there was no other satisfactory alternative to scuttling his vessel.[34]

During Saturday afternoon (23 April), the Communists crossed the Yangtze in considerable strength both ahead and astern of where the *Amethyst* lay at anchor. One of the two busiest crossing points from the northern bank lay just over 1 nautical mile to the west of the frigate at Tan-ta-chen at the junction of the Grand Canal and the Yangtze. By using this route for the landings, the PLA had unintentionally provided full justification for Kerans's earlier decision to move his ship to a new location at Ma-chia-shaw. If he had failed to do so, his morning's anchorage opposite Chan-chia-shan would have lain directly in the path of the flotilla of Communist vessels ferrying troops to the southern bank of the river.[35] Under those circumstances, the chances of the British frigate being involved in some further diplomatic or military incident with the PLA would have been considerable. In her new location, however, the *Amethyst* remained unaffected by the landings. The Communists made no effort to approach the ship or to require any response from those on board. By the late afternoon, the crew were able to relax a little and become interested spectators, rather than anxious observers, of what was taking place all around them. Few doubted, though, that the only rational way to regain their freedom would be for a diplomatic settlement to be made at the highest level. A naval solution seemed totally out of the question.

As evening fell, the fevered activity of the afternoon ceased, and a calm returned to the river. Kerans darkened the ship, and the crew settled down for another night on the Yangtze. At about 10:00 P.M. several Nationalist ships began passing the *Amethyst* on their way downriver from Nanking toward Shanghai. Kerans describes what happened next.

> The fourth of these Units suddenly opened fire in the direction of Tasha Island above five cables astern of us. This was the signal for everything to open fire and a fairly heavy engagement took place which finally ceased about an hour later. No Nationalist ships appeared to be hit but two large fires were seen in the direction of the PU-SHUN-WEI battery.[36]

By 11:15 P.M. the firing stopped. Except for this spectacle, the rest of the night was uneventful, and Kerans's understandable anxiety that his ship might have been illuminated in the barrage and mistaken for a Nationalist vessel, with dire consequences for everyone on board, did not materialize.[37]

At 7:00 A.M. the next morning (Sunday 24 April), the *Amethyst* suddenly developed a severe list to starboard. An immediate investigation revealed that the wardroom was partially flooded. A number of plates had been weakened, and a hole on the waterline had done the rest. Emergency measures to patch up the ship began immediately. While some hands worked the pumps and began baling out the wardroom, others were on deck throwing overboard weighty articles that were considered surplus to requirements. This dual approach brought the ship back on an even keel by 10:00 A.M. Afterward the crew was ordered to continue reducing fire risks throughout the ship by clearing up as much of the debris of the past few days' artillery damage as possible. In addition, work that had begun the previous day on sandbagging some of the essential parts of the frigate to provide some cover against sniper fire or artillery barrage went on apace.[38]

After the rigors of the morning, the frigate rode gently at anchor during the afternoon—an idle observer of the rapidly changing scene all around her—as junks and vessels of all descriptions and sizes plied the river accompanied by the roar of fighter aircraft overhead.[39] Watching these developments, Kerans wondered whether he ought to try to join some of the civilian traffic on its course upriver toward Chinkiang. On hearing this latest suggestion, Madden advised Kerans against doing anything that could complicate matters still further. *Amethyst,* therefore, remained where she was, technically free but effectively unable to exercise that liberty in any direction without Communist approval.[40]

In this situation both Stevenson and Madden came to the conclusion that it would be tactful for the British to recognize Communist superiority in the Yangtze region and do nothing that might appear to dispute that command, obstruct their progress, or otherwise irritate them. Stevenson wrote in this sense to the Foreign Office on 24 April.

> As it is clear that, under the conditions prevailing at present on the Yangtse, it is no longer practical to attempt to provide succour to Commonwealth embassies and nationals in Nanking through the presence here of one of His Majesty's ships, His Majesty's Ambassador withdraws the request originally stated in Nanking telegram No. 261 dated November 9th, 1948 D.T.C. 090343Z November.[41]

In reality, of course, he was merely acknowledging an undisputed fact: with the fall of Nanking and the elimination of Nationalist power in the region, the eastern stretch of the Yangtze was now in Communist hands, and all movement by foreign vessels on the river was forbidden unless prior approval had been granted by the PLA.

Madden took this attitude a stage further in a message he addressed to the Admiralty in the early hours of Monday 25 April.

> It seems that the presence of warships at Shanghai can only be an irritant to the Communists when they arrive and that they may constitute a positive disadvantage to the British community. I therefore intend to reduce the number of warships at Shanghai immediately by sailing *SHOALHAVEN* for Kure tomorrow Monday and *CONSTANCE* for the Chusan Archipelago on the following day.[42]

He went on to reveal that arrangements would also be made for the dispatch of *London* and *Black Swan* as circumstances permitted in the near future.

Ambassador Stevenson was more reluctant than Madden to see these ships withdrawn, lest the decision intensify the feeling of vulnerability on the part of the local community and undermine the British claim that their vessels were stationed in Chinese waters for purely peaceful and humanitarian purposes.[43] Stevenson's concerns were discussed at a select meeting of the Nanking diplomatic corps on 25 April. It was unanimously agreed that for safety reasons all foreign warships ought to be removed from the Whangpoo River.[44] Robert Urquhart, the British consul general in Shanghai, wondered aloud whether it was possible to improve relations with the Communists by telling them of Britain's desire to avoid running the risk of any further confrontation between them: "If it were desired to go further we might offer to leave our ships here until the change-over was complete, in the general interest of Shanghai and then withdraw them."[45]

Some of these suggestions by British officials in China were discussed by the COS at their meeting in London on Monday 25 April with A. V. Alexander, the minister of defense and Sir Patrick Brind, the commander in chief of the Far East Station. Although they did not overrule the decisions of either Stevenson or Madden, the COS did not feel that it was absolutely necessary to take quite such an ingratiating attitude toward the PLA as both the British consul and flag officer had done. In fact, they went on record as suggesting that the effects of the *Amethyst* incident were only likely to be felt locally and that the naval clash on the Yangtze would not prejudice the conduct of the Communists toward the British community in Shanghai.[46]

> Nevertheless it must be recognised that if the Communists wished to stop foreign ships going up the River Whangpoo to Shanghai, they could very quickly do so by establishing artillery at the entrance. They might be in a position to do so within the next day or two. The meeting considered the possibility of attacking these batteries with aircraft but the Chiefs of Staff did not consider such an operation would be worthwhile.[47]

Although it remained official policy for British nationals to remain in Shanghai, an emergency evacuation plan had been drawn up by the government in case there was a total breakdown in services during the hiatus between the Nationalist withdrawal and Communist occupation of the city. As part of the plan, the cruiser HMS *Belfast* remained on standby in Hong Kong, ready to take two companies of infantry to Shanghai to assist in the evacuation operation if it was deemed essential by the COS.[48] Deciding not to implement these plans for the time being, the COS thought they might have little practical value in any case because the Communists were likely to insist upon the withdrawal of all foreign warships from the city in the near future.[49] Even so, the COS were anxious to release a public statement that would help explain British policy in the best and most reasonable light. They hit upon the following text:

> H.M. ships have been at Nanking and are at Shanghai solely to provide a refuge for Commonwealth Nationals in case of disorder during any change over from one government to another. As soon as it is clear that law and order are assured it is intended to withdraw British warships and to continue normal procedure with regard to visits to foreign ports.[50]

What this statement was intended to achieve was never made clear. If, on one hand, it was designed to impress the Communists with the idea that the British had acted throughout in good faith and had merely been misunderstood, it failed singularly in its objective.[51] If, on the other hand, it was intended for purely domestic consumption—that is, the kind of statement ministers could use to defend their policy in China from attack by parliamentary opponents— the impact was probably small and indecisive. Whatever the purpose, the statement was but one further inadequate explanation of a policy that ought to have been scrapped long before it failed so disastrously on Wednesday 20 April.

9. A Political Storm Is Brewing

*O*N TUESDAY afternoon (26 April), less than a week after the initial attack had been launched on the *Amethyst,* Winston Churchill, the leader of the opposition, rose from his seat opposite the dispatch box in the House of Commons to ask the prime minister for a statement about the crisis on the Yangtze.

Attlee began his answer by explaining what the British policy of noninterventionism in the Chinese civil war had meant in practice and why the government had made the decision to remain behind in Nanking after the Nationalist government signaled its intention to move its capital south to Canton in February 1949.[1] It was a model civil service answer, designed to be strong on the uncontentious details while being plausible and yet ambiguous on the weak points of the case.

In referring to the British failure to notify the Communists about the *Amethyst*'s movements on 19–20 April, the prime minister repeated the old argument about the inability of the consular officials in China to make contact with the Communist authorities in those cities or areas that they now controlled. Despite these problems, however, he stressed that his government had never failed to inform the Nationalist authorities about the movements of British warships on the Yangtze and that these had always taken place with the full knowledge and consent of the KMT.[2]

After describing to the packed chamber the events that had taken place on the river up to the end of the Youde mission on 24 April, Attlee deftly shifted his ground and sought to rebut criticism in advance about the high casualty rate and extensive damage inflicted upon the British vessels on the Yangtze by the PLA on 20–21 April. His defense was eminently reasonable, stressing the unwillingness of the British to engage in any punitive expedition against the

118

Communists and the fact that warships were never intended to conduct artillery exchanges in such confined spaces as the narrow reaches of the Yangtze against well-supplied, enemy forces sheltered by reeds and mud flats.[3]

Turning to other matters, the prime minister dealt with the allegation made in a Communist broadcast that the *Amethyst* and the other British warships, none of which had been identified at the time, had opened fire on the PLA positions to prevent the Communists from crossing the Yangtze. This act of aggression, which had caused 252 casualties among the PLA troops, had been denounced by the Communists in their news bulletin. They claimed that by sanctioning the use of violence against them, the British government had shed its supposed neutrality in favor of participating in the civil war on the Nationalist side.[4] He dismissed these accusations peremptorily.

These claims are, of course, so far as they relate to His Majesty's Government or the Royal Navy, as fantastic as they are unfounded. If there was any initial misunderstanding as to the nationality of H.M.S. "*Amethyst*" this would have been speedily resolved had the authorities in Peking acted on H.M. Ambassador's message. Moreover, had the Communist authorities objected in the past to the movement of British ships on the Yangtse it was always open to them to raise these through our consular authorities in North China. It is the fact that for reasons best known to themselves the Communists have failed to notify any foreign authority present in areas which they have occupied of the channels through which contact can be maintained and that they have rejected all communications made to them. In these circumstances His Majesty's Government can only reserve their position.[5]

After specially commending to the Commons the brave exploits of Skinner, Weston, and French on board the *Amethyst* and the skill and daring of Letford, the pilot of the Sunderland, Attlee also applauded Youde for his initiative and remarked on the courage and fortitude shown by the rest of the British sailors involved in the crisis. He concluded by specifically mentioning the assistance provided by the American naval authorities and the British community in Shanghai, as well as the Chinese Nationalist forces in the Chinkiang area, who had provided medical aid and stores when he felt they could ill afford to do so.[6]

It was more of a factual report than a flowing oratory, a typically restrained speech that fitted the prime minister's mood at the time, rather than the fulminating, jingoistic rhetoric others might have resorted to under the circumstances.[7] Attlee presented his material, as always, in a logical, concise fashion, unencumbered by emotion and devoid of the ostentatiousness that other politicians were inclined to use if given the slightest encouragement or provocation. That his statement did not satisfy the Commons is hardly surprising. Indeed it is doubtful whether any such statement could have done so. It would take more than the prime minister's initial explanation for members to begin to understand why and how this crisis in Anglo-Chinese relations had arisen at this time and what the likely repercussions were to be in the future.

Winston Churchill was not convinced that the prime minister had been forthright about the background to the case. He suggested that the government was largely responsible for creating the circumstances of the crisis into which the *Amethyst* had innocently stumbled on the morning of 20 April. It was his contention that the crisis was avoidable and need never have arisen if the government had exercised vigilance in the matter as it ought to have done. Addressing the prime minister directly, the leader of the Conservative party began to revel in his cross-examination of his political rival.

> May I ask whether he does not think that there is a certain resemblance—a coincidental resemblance—between this episode, where a vessel goes on a routine cruise or journey up the river on the very eve of a battle—a civil war battle—and the sending out of aeroplanes some weeks ago in Egypt into a battle area within a few hours of a truce being declared? Does this not require very careful attention from the point of view of not putting our airmen and sailors into unnecessary dangers?[8]

Churchill clearly thought that it did. His dissatisfaction with the inadequacy of Attlee's explanation was reflected in his desire for a further statement from the government on the incident. Before ending, he posed a provocative question, which by implication attacked Labour's defense policy.

> How is it that at this time we have not got in Chinese waters one aircraft carrier, if not two, capable of affording protection to our nationals who may be increasingly involved in peril and misfortune, and capable of affording that protection in the only way which is understood by those who are attacking us, murdering us and insulting us, namely, by effective power of retaliation?[9]

Attlee did not respond to Churchill's provocative question by divulging any information about the deployment of aircraft carriers in Chinese waters. He preferred to deflect the opposition leader's criticisms by pointing out that the civil war in China had lasted a long time already and that once it was considered wise to maintain a guardship at Nanking, the question of relief became a matter for the senior British officials in the region to decide upon.

> If it is put off all the time, because of a possible danger—and it is very difficult when there are irregular forces on one side—we should never get that relief, and so I think a decision had to be come to. The right hon. Gentleman would notice

that there was talk of an armistice, and the armistice expired but hostilities were not opened. A period of waiting then ensued to consider the position. Then, when there was an ultimatum, it was decided to relieve this ship in time before the ultimatum expired. In our view, the commanding officer there on the spot exercised a right judgment.[10]

Churchill returned to the fray with a pointed rejoinder that whoever was responsible for deciding upon relief for the British warship at Nanking managed to send the *Amethyst* upriver almost exactly at zero hour. He was not put off in the slightest by Attlee's erroneous retort that the voyage would have been completed twenty-four hours before the expiry of the ultimatum. Indeed it merely enabled him to draw breath before launching into a further bout of questioning. This time Churchill concentrated not on the details of the incident but on what the government's reaction was likely to be in dealing with this matter. He indicated that although he expected little more in the way of explanation on this occasion, he would require another opportunity for parliament to debate this issue further.[11]

As soon as Churchill sat down, other members began waving order papers in an attempt to catch the Speaker's eye and weigh in with questions of their own. Clement Davies, the leader of the Liberal party and MP (member of parliament) for Montgomeryshire, opened the exchange with the prime minister by asking exactly when the warning about foreign warships on the Yangtze was issued by the Nationalist government before it moved to Canton. He wished to know the substance of the message, to whom it was given, and why the British government had decided not to heed the warning regardless of what happened subsequently.[12]

Attlee replied with some general and rather unsatisfactory remarks, indicating that although he did not know the exact date of the warning, it was evidently a long time ago. His failure to give any specific information on this score, however, seemed to prompt him to repeat what he had said formerly about the passage of British vessels up the Yangtze: that the KMT were notified each time a journey had been made and that no objection had ever been received from the Nationalists and authorities to any of these naval activities.[13]

Davies was not deflected by this tangential reply and probed further:

> If the right hon. Gentleman was disregarding that serious warning, in view of the steady advance made by the Communist armies, if no guarantee could be obtained from both sides before the ship was sent up, would it not have been better to withdraw our nationals and protect them at that particular moment?[14]

Attlee had no difficulty squashing this query, reiterating that the government's policy of not withdrawing from China had been announced months before in the Commons. His point clearly was that this policy had been accepted by the house in the past, and it was too late now to complain about the questionable wisdom of this decision.[15]

If Davies had been temporarily silenced, the Tory MP Colonel Dower was not content to receive answers that lacked specific information. He roundly criticized those responsible for their gross error of judgment in sending the *Amethyst* upriver at a time when the situation on the Yangtze was so critical and for making matters worse by not providing the frigate with air cover.[16] Attlee avoided making any reference to the reasons why no aircraft were deployed to assist the *Amethyst* on its voyage to Nanking and resorted instead to a defense of why the relief operation had gone ahead during an extension of the armistice. Commander Noble, another Conservative member, did not think this explanation made much sense because the armistice was not indefinite, and a safe guarantee had not been obtained from both the Communists and the Nationalists before the *Amethyst* embarked upon her fateful journey upriver.[17]

Attlee's patience with this line of questioning and what he perceived to be a deliberate distortion of his words began to wear thin. He showed his exasperation by curtly replying that *Consort* had to be relieved and *Amethyst*'s supplies had to get through. In this situation, the commander on the spot had to decide when it ought to be done.

> I have been through the dates very often, but this was the time selected as, otherwise, he might not have been able to reach them at all. He considered— and I think he was right in thinking that, in view of the evidence available and actions of the past—that the relief could be effected during this pause.[18]

Not all the members were hostile though, and a few of the party faithful came to the prime minister's assistance, asking friendly, uncomplicated questions, which Attlee answered with clinical proficiency. Most of the time, however, the pressure on him was maintained at an uncomfortably high level.

William Gallacher, the Communist MP for West Fife, opened up a new avenue of criticism when he revealed that the embassy in Nanking could have been supplied during the period of the truce by both road and rail, and therefore, a river passage was both superfluous and dangerous.[19] Had he restricted his remarks to this one point, Gallacher would have revealed a weakness in the government's case that could have tested Attlee's mettle in providing an effective answer. Instead, the prime minister was spared the effort of having to explain his way out of a potentially tricky situation by Gallacher's inability to resist making a wild lunge at those persons who he felt were responsible for creating the crisis in the first place. By delivering a waspish reply to this criticism, Attlee subdued his impetuous opponent for what remained of Question Time on that day.[20]

Attlee's debating skill won him only a temporary reprieve, however, before several former military officers from the Conservative side of the house raised the issue of why there was no air cover for the *Amethyst* on her voyage upriver or, perhaps more pertinently, for the subsequent rescue attempts that were launched by *Consort, London,* and *Black Swan* on 20–21 April. In reply, Attlee easily dismissed the suggestion that the *Amethyst* ought to have had bomber support on her peaceful voyage up the Yangtze, but soon found himself retreating when forced to defend Madden's policy of providing no air cover for all rescue operations mounted after the initial attack had been made on the frigate. After being harried on the subject, he finally admitted that the only shore-based aircraft available in the region were at Hong Kong and that these had not been ordered by the local commander to assist the warships in their rescue mission. This answer did not appease the Tories; neither did Attlee's admission that no advice or instructions were sought by the flag officer from either the Admiralty or the government before the *Amethyst* had been dispatched upriver on 19 April.[21]

Belated candor did not disarm the critics of the government's China policy, and several opposition members—Churchill prominent among them—rose in turn to harry the prime minister on various matters that had not been adequately explained thus far. Attlee's answers began to lose their crispness as Question Time continued; too frequently, he used stalling tactics, mentioning that more detailed answers could be given on another occasion. In the end the Speaker intervened to bring the exchanges to a close and save the prime minister from further punishment.[22] It had proved to be an uncomfortable experience for him, perhaps a good deal worse than he had envisaged. Apparently, he had not been prepared to field some of the questions thrown at him during the hour-long session, and his general response to other questions added little to what was already known about the incident from newspaper sources. This first parliamentary inquiry into the incident had revealed that the prime minister apparently knew little more about events on the Yangtze than did anyone else in the United Kingdom. Attlee did not need to cover up the government's role in the crisis, for the alarming fact was that it had performed no function at all. As a result, his task had been to defend as best he could what others would describe as an excessive delegation of authority to Madden, the acting local commander on the spot, and to support the Yangtze policy decisions that had been made by the flag officer.

Although he had done what was expected of him, the prime minister had been placed in a weak position and one from which it was difficult to argue convincingly. His answers had revealed just how vulnerable the government's position on this crisis was. Moreover, any further probing into the *Amethyst* crisis was bound to raise other issues of far wider significance for critical review, namely, the whole thrust of the Cabinet's defense strategy and foreign policy. Both Churchill and Boyd-Carpenter had already linked the Yangtze incident to British policy in China as a whole by asking why there were no aircraft carriers on the China station in view of the deteriorating situation in the country.[23] In fact, Boyd-Carpenter had pointed out that there had been two aircraft carriers there until 1947, at which time the government withdrew them as part of its program to reduce its presence east of Suez and trim the defense budget in view of the parlous state of the British economy.[24]

By granting the opposition a full-scale debate on the subject of the *Amethyst* crisis in the next few days, the government recognized that it would have to brace itself for a sustained attack on its foreign and defense policy by those who saw in the Yangtze episode the result of economizing on strategic services. They would claim that the decision to do so had reduced the value of deterrence and led ultimately to a loss of British influence in the region.

If Attlee had found Question Time a little uncomfortable, particularly toward the end of the session, Viscount Hall, the first lord of the Admiralty, had to endure a far more gruelling experience in the upper chamber at the hands of Viscount Swinton, a former secretary of state for air and currently the leader of the Conservative peers in the House of Lords. Swinton, from the outset, unerringly alighted upon the real weaknesses in the government's prepared statement about the Yangtze incident, namely, the lack of ministerial and departmental advice on what to do and when to do it in China, the mistakes made by its local officials, and the sad consequences of these grave errors of judgment. His perceptive and analytical probing of the weak spots in the government's case did nothing to endear him to his parliamentary opponents sitting on the Labour benches.

Lord Strabolgi, a former lieutenant commander and Labour MP, took up the cudgels on the government's behalf. Describing Swinton's performance as "not only out of order but thoroughly mischevious," Strabolgi pointed out that detailed answers should not be expected of his ministerial colleagues until such time that the government possessed all the facts of the case. Viscount Hall followed his diversionary lead, grumbling about Swinton's abuse of parliamentary procedure and reproaching him for trying to make political capital out of a difficult and fluid situation.[25]

Although the critics of the government's policy in China had been outmaneuvered in both houses on this occasion, neither the prime minister nor his first lord were entitled to feel that their opponents had been conclusively worsted. Both were experienced enough to realize that other opportunities would soon arise when their parliamentary foes would mass once again for a full frontal attack. Moreover, it was possible in the future as more evidence leaked out about naval policy in the Far East that criticism of it was unlikely to be confined to those imperial grandees—the saber-rattling Tory right wingers. There were also a number of politicians on the government's own benches who regarded British policy in China as being either inept or inappropriate and who would express these views in the debate on 5 May.

In the meantime, however, the *Amethyst* crisis remained good copy for the British newspapers. On the whole, the Far Eastern Department of the Foreign Office thought that press coverage of the incident was favorable to the government, although even the friendly organs had wondered aloud whether the *Amethyst*'s journey upriver was really necessary.[26] Commenting on the affair in early May, the News Department agreed that the government had received a good press and ascribed the lack of critical comment to the anger felt by the British people toward the Communists for opening fire upon the *Amethyst* without warning.[27] Instead of attacking the government, the daily newspapers looked sympathetically upon it, especially after Attlee's performance at Question Time in the Commons. Most editorials thereafter proclaimed that the original relief journey had been necessary and that all reasonable precautions had been taken to ensure the safety of the *Amethyst* on its voyage up to Nanking.[28] Attlee could not have asked for more. Indeed it is most surprising, given the background to the incident, that the dailies gave the government the benefit of the doubt, rather than heaping severe criticism and scorn upon it for failing to prevent an avoidable accident in the first place.

Interestingly, weekly periodicals such as the *Economist* and the *Spectator* took a much more measured view of the entire situation, refusing to join in the chorus of support for the government and pointing to the inadequacy and even delinquency of its policy. Describing the blow to British prestige in Asia as being "incalculable," the *Economist,* in its issue of 30 April, continued:

> The real question is why the danger of Communist attack was not taken more seriously in view of the rabid incitements against the "imperialist bloc" continually pouring forth from the Chinese Communists. Mr. Attlee told the House of Commons—as if it were a justification of the decision to send British warships up and down the Yangtze—that "warships are not designed to operate in rivers against massed artillery and infantry sheltered by reeds and mudbanks." As this limitation of sea-power was perfectly well known to the naval

authorities, it would have been madness for them to send a frigate to Nanking if they had been sufficiently warned that the Communists were likely to attack it.[29]

In ascribing blame for the incident, the *Economist* took the Foreign Office and the diplomatic corps to task. Accusing them of spreading optimism, creating illusions, and preferring wishful thinking to sobering reality, the journal went on to attack the unwillingness of the government to accept the fact that the Communists might not always act in a moderate, restrained way with international powers whom they despised.

> It appears to be a neo-British characteristic not to give credence to anybody who openly declares hostile intentions. In Aesop's time it was thought a clever trick for a wolf to go about in sheep's clothing. Nowadays the wolf does much better to go about in his own clothing, as all sensible people are then convinced that he is really a sheep.[30]

The *Spectator* produced an even more damning indictment of the "disaster" that had occurred on the Yangtze. Although sympathetic to the original plan to station a gunboat at Nanking, the journal rapidly distanced itself from the decision to continue this practice after the orderly liberation of both Peking and Tientsin by the PLA.[31]

While the British press responded more positively than many in the government had a right to expect, hostility from the Chinese Communist-controlled media was as intense as it could be. On 30 April, the New China News Agency in Peking broadcast a statement drafted by Mao Tse-tung and delivered by General Li Tao, a spokesman for the PLA headquarters.[32] It pulled no punches.

> We denounce the preposterous statement of the warmonger Churchill. In the British House of Commons on April 26, Churchill demanded that the British government should send two aircraft carriers to the Far East for "effective power of retaliation." What are you "retaliating" for, Mr. Churchill? British warships together with Kuomintang warships intruded into the defence area of the Chinese People's Liberation Army, causing no less than 252 casualties among our loyal and gallant fighters. Since the British have trespassed on Chinese territory and committed so great a crime, the People's Liberation Army has good reason to demand that the British government admit its wrongdoing, apologize and make compensation. Isn't this what you should do, instead of dispatching forces to China to "retaliate" against the Chinese People's Liberation Army?[33]

General Li then addressed Attlee's claim that the British were within their rights to send warships up the Yangtze. Li had little time for such posturing.

He pointedly described the river as a Chinese inland waterway and rejected the interpretation that foreign powers had any rights whatsoever to sail on it without seeking permission from the Chinese themselves, who would reject such an encroachment on their territorial and sovereign possessions. He continued:

> Attlee said that the People's Liberation Army "would be prepared to allow the ship (Amethyst) to proceed to Nanking but only on condition that she should assist the People's Liberation Army to cross the Yangtse." Attlee lied. The People's Liberation Army gave no permission to the *Amethyst* to proceed to Nanking. The People's Liberation Army does not want the armed forces of any foreign country to help it across the Yangtse or to do anything else. On the contrary, the People's Liberation Army demands that Britain, the United States and France quickly withdraw their armed forces—their warships, military aircraft and marines stationed in the Yangtse and Whangpoo Rivers and other parts of China—from China's territorial inland waters, seas, land and air and that they refrain from helping the enemy of the Chinese people to wage civil war.[34]

Li then proceeded to lay down the Communist terms for establishing diplomatic relations with foreign governments in the future. He stressed that recognition could only be accorded to such countries on the basis of equality, mutual benefit, and respect for sovereignty and territorial integrity. Above all, the powers concerned must refuse to assist the KMT in the civil war. His conditions did not end there. He required that any foreign nation wishing to establish diplomatic relations with the Communist government had to first sever its ties with the Nationalists and withdraw its armed forces from China. He ended by addressing the British once more.

> Attlee complained that the Communist Party of China, having no diplomatic relations with foreign countries, was unwilling to have contacts with the old diplomatic personnel of foreign governments (consuls recognised by the Kuomintang). Such complaints are groundless. In the past few years, the governments of the United States, Britain, Canada, etc. have helped the Kuomintang to oppose us. Can Mr. Attlee have forgotten this? Can it also be that Mr. Attlee does not know which country gave the Kuomintang the Chungking, the heavy cruiser which was recently sunk?[35]

Clement Attlee recognized that, aside from the exaggerated rhetoric of the Communist polemic, the attack had some substance and could not, therefore, be safely ignored as mere propaganda. An opportunity for a detailed rebuttal of the Communist case would be afforded to the government when parliament came to debate the question of British policy in China on 5 May, but in the interim, Ambassador Stevenson issued a public statement from Nanking that sought to clarify Britain's position on the emotive subject of extraterritorial rights raised in Li's speech.

> His Majesty's Government do not (repeat not) claim the right of their naval vessels to move freely in the territorial waters of other nations, subject to the generally admitted exceptions of refuge from storm danger, and of saving lives. On the contrary, His Majesty's Government have voluntarily abandoned any specific privileges in this respect existing under previous treaties by virtue of the provisions of the 1943 Sino-British Treaty.[36]

Stevenson also revealed that because the British government was aware of PLA sensitivities on this point, it had decided not to send ships into Chinese waters controlled by the Communists and was withdrawing its naval units from Shanghai in anticipation of an extension of the PLA's hold over the lower Yangtze region.[37]

By the time the British ambassador had attempted to answer the broadside directed at his government's policy in China, attention had switched back to the House of Commons. There, on 2 May, the prime minister was due to answer further questions about the absence of air support for the *Amethyst* and the ships that had tried in vain to rescue her on 20–21 April. Attlee was well briefed on this occasion by the Admiralty and responded vigorously to the oral questions raised by his Tory opponents.[38] He rejected the idea of providing air support for the *Amethyst* on 19–20 April on the grounds that she was making a normal peacetime passage upriver and had never intended or was expected to force her way through armed defenses to reach Nanking.

> When our ships had been attacked, Sunderlands were sent up from Hong Kong. One of these reached Shanghai on 21st April and a second on 23rd April. In addition, a Dakota with supply dropping gear was ordered to Hong Kong. The nearest R.A.F. fighter aircraft were in Malaya, some 2,000 miles away. It was the decision of the Flag Officer, which I support, not to call upon them.[39]

Attlee had been informed by the Admiralty that rocket-firing Beaufighters, which were stationed at Singapore, were the only type of aircraft that could have been used with any success on the Yangtze against massed artillery. Even then, they were between thirty-six and forty-eight hours transit time away from the scene of the action and would have had to operate from a Nationalist airfield in the area rather than from a distant one in Shanghai. This tactic in turn would have compromised Britain's desire to remain neutral in the civil war. Moreover, to have been fully effective, the aircraft would have had to give support to the warships for at least eight hours against a large number of batteries deployed in numerous unknown locations over a distance of at least 60 miles. If such a situation had occurred in conjunction with the attempt made by *London* and *Black Swan* to rescue the *Amethyst,* the Admiralty felt that it would have been tantamount to and construed as a clear act of war against the Communists. Although he was not asked about the role of the nonexistent aircraft carriers, Attlee knew from his brief that even if one or two had been available, they would have faced the same disadvantages as the shore-based planes in confronting a hidden enemy operating in strength over a large area.[40] Taken as a whole, therefore, these points established a fairly persuasive argument in favor of why aircraft were not used in the aftermath of the *Amethyst* incident, even if Attlee had not tackled and eliminated criticism about Britain's failure to provide a credible system of support for its warships in China before the frigate was attacked.

Despite the fact that Question Time on 2 May had posed no major problems for the government, the same was unlikely to be true of the full-dressed debate three days later. On this occasion the entire issue of British policy in China was to be thrashed out in excrutiating detail, providing a public forum for the most vehement critics of Labour's foreign and defense policy to hold the stage and to proclaim the incompetence of the government at every turn. In this debate, it would be difficult for the government to do well. After all, the *Amethyst* crisis had hardly been a triumphant piece of naval or political diplomacy, and few on the Labour benches or with Far Eastern responsibilities in the Admiralty and Foreign Office could hardly have relished the prospect of an even closer investigation of their policy making or lack of it in China than they had been subject to already by parliament and the press.

Lord Fraser, the chief of naval staff, was typical of those who anticipated trouble. He told his colleagues at the COS meeting on 4 May that he expected the Admiralty to be criticized on the grounds that it had not provided sufficient support and guidance from London for the local naval authorities in China.[41] He naturally thought this would be unfair and hoped that A. V. Alexander, the minister of defense and the man slated to lead the government's side in the debate, would pass the buck to the British Defence Co-ordination Committee, Far East, a mixed service and political body that had been established to give advice to the government on the region and had responsibility for overseeing naval policy in China.[42] Fraser need not have worried, because Alexander had long been adept in attacking those who criticized him. If criticism was directed at the Admiralty, he was the man to deflect it elsewhere.

As the machinery of government geared itself up for the debate with requests for information from its local and regional experts, the officials on the spot were concerned that nothing be said in the Commons that would further harm Sino-British relations and jeopardize the release of the *Amethyst* and her crew. Ambassador Stevenson was most anxious on this score and hoped fervently for a parliamentary discussion that was moderate and not inflammatory or jingoistic in tone.[43] He was also worried by some of the articles that were beginning to appear in a few British journals, which suggested that the government was keeping its warships in Chinese waters to protect British subjects against the PLA.[44] In his cable to the Foreign Office on 3 May, the ambassador commented:

> Such assertions are as dangerous as they are incorrect. I would therefore urge the desirability of stressing in the debate and also in any other public statements, the fact that H.M. ships were standing by to give aid and support to local British and other communities in the event of a breakdown of law and order during the interim period . . . and that our intention was to withdraw them afterwards as soon as effective administration should be restored.[45]

Evidently, the ambassador feared that an anti-Communist tone might be creeping into press coverage of the situation in China and wished, if possible, to stop it before it caused serious damage to British interests in the country, particularly as these interests were becoming increasingly dependent upon the Communists for their continued existence.[46]

Besides Stevenson, who was at pains to point out the need for both the media and politicians to avoid taking a provocative anti-Communist stance when dealing with the Yangtze crisis and the civil war, Madden also seemed to go out of his way to express the accidental rather than the deliberate nature of the *Amethyst* affair. He cabled the Admiralty on 1 May with a message indicating that there was no evidence to support the theory that the *Amethyst* had been the subject of a planned attack by the Communist high command. In fact, he preferred to see it as a case of bad firing discipline on behalf of one of the PLA batteries rather than an orchestrated campaign against the British warship.[47] He followed this wire with another one two days later supporting the same theory: "My appreciation is that at time of *Amethyst* incident, Communist orders to their batteries were that they were not, repetition not, to fire on British ships."[48] Unfortunately, even if Madden was right and it had been just an isolated case of indiscipline among a few artillery troops drawn up on the northern bank of the Yangtze, the sad fact was that ultimate responsibility for the initial attack was unlikely to be admitted by those who were actually culpable. It had already become too serious a business for the truth to be told and candor to prevail.

10. Opening Negotiations on the Yangtze

WHILE THE British government and opposition were gearing themselves up for a parliamentary confrontation over the Yangtze incident, life on board the *Amethyst* began to assume a wearisome routine that consisted mostly of reducing fire hazards and cleaning up the mess of the previous week's action.[1] In contrast to the rigors and excitement of the past few days, Monday 25 April proved to be a peaceful, rather boring anticlimax with nothing untoward happening on the vessel. As the men of the *Amethyst* got on with their allotted tasks, further Communist troop movements could be spotted on the southern bank of the river. Therefore, it could now be safely assumed that the PLA was in control of the immediate area on both sides of the Yangtze.[2]

Despite their commanding presence in the region, the Communists had made no attempt thus far to interfere or make contact with the crew of the frigate that was so obviously stranded in their midst. This fact was soon to change, however, for in the early afternoon of Tuesday 26 April, three PLA soldiers accompanied by a small number of civilians came to a halt on the southern bank near where the *Amethyst* rode at anchor and began gesticulating to the crew. Although their collective shouts were drowned out in the high wind that had blown up along the river, it was clear from their behavior that this was something more than just an accidental meeting. It seemed apparent from their general demeanor and the gestures they were making that they expected or hoped the *Amethyst* would send a boat to the shore to meet them. On this occasion, however, they were foiled by the weather, which was whipping up a heavy swell on the river and rendering long-distance dialogue inaudible. After several minutes of fruitless shouting and waving, the small group of Communists withdrew only to reappear—without the civilians—a little later in the afternoon when the wind had died down and the Yangtze had become calm once again.[3]

At 2:40 P.M. the three soldiers returned to the river's edge brandishing what appeared to be a letter. They resumed their previous antics in a bid to attract attention and were finally rewarded when their shouts were heard and translated by But Sai Tin, a Chinese member of the crew from Wei-hai-wei and the steward of Lieutenant-Commander Kerans. Their message indicated that they wished to meet someone in authority from the *Amethyst* immediately, either on board the frigate or ashore. Kerans agreed to risk sending his only boat, the badly damaged and patched-up whaler, but did not think it justifiable to send a senior officer to meet the group of Communist soldiers. Instead he asked for a petty officer to assume the role on his behalf. It was decided that the person chosen for this task would be rowed to the southern bank of the river in the battered whaler by a group of volunteers drawn from among the crew of the *Amethyst*. Such was the state of the decrepit, small boat that Kerans insisted that only strong swimmers could take the oars for fear that the boat might sink en route to or from the shore.[4]

Henry Freeman grasped the chance to do something out of the ordinary and offered to go ashore and meet the Communists on Kerans's behalf. His enthusiastic response was appreciated by the captain and readily agreed to. Besides insisting that But Sai Tin go along to act as the petty officer's interpreter, Kerans asked Freeman to change into the uniform of Lieutenant Strain before leaving for the rendezvous with the PLA deputation. Masquerading as a senior officer in a bid to impress the Communists, Freeman joined But and the other volunteer rowers in the whaler and pushed off for the shore at 3:30 P.M.[5]

After the boat reached the southern bank, the three Communist soldiers escorted Freeman and But to a peasant's cottage in a village some 12 miles inland. After about an hour's wait, a PLA officer arrived claiming to be Major Kung, the battery commander from San-chiang ying, the unit responsible for inflicting the initial damage upon the *Amethyst* and forcing her aground on the previous Wednesday morning.[6]

Kung began the discussion by stating categorically that the *Amethyst* had been responsible for creating the original incident on the Yangtze by opening fire upon the Communist positions on the northern shore. He insisted that the PLA had recognized the *Amethyst* as a British vessel from the outset but had not planned to attack it until the frigate began bombarding the shore batteries. Kung's claim that his own artillery had not initiated anything and only returned the frigate's fire was strongly rejected by Freeman. He presented a radically different version of the events that had taken place on the morning of

20 April. Freeman made it plain that the PLA artillery troops and not the *Amethyst* were guilty of firing the first shots in the affair.[7]

It became apparent that any further arguing on this issue was pointless at this time because neither side seemed prepared to admit a mistake had been made and that they had been the ones to make it. Aware of the cyclical nature of this problem, Freeman tried steering the conversation away from who was to blame and on to the somewhat less emotionally charged question of whether the PLA would allow the *Amethyst* a safe passage downriver to Shanghai. Kung said he was not empowered to grant such a request and that only the authorities in Nanking could make a decision on this matter. He did indicate, however, that as long as the ship did not try to leave the area without permission or cause any further trouble (whatever that meant), the Communists would not need to attack or interfere with her in any way. Freeman was certain, however, that if the *Amethyst* did attempt to escape she would be fired upon.[8]

As if to reemphasize his point more forcibly, Kung indicated that the Sunderland flying boat had been fired upon when it tried to establish contact with the *Amethyst* on 21–22 April because it had not sought permission of the Communist authorities before making its journey. Despite Freeman's protest that the aircraft was engaged on a mission of mercy, providing urgent medical assistance to the seriously wounded on board the frigate, the battery commander rejected the claim and remarked that had the Communists been asked, they would have tended to the injured. Freeman kept his temper and was not provoked into pursuing this matter any further, although he found Kung's explanation thoroughly unsatisfactory.[9]

Before completing his indictment of the British, Kung informed Freeman that their four warships had together caused about 250 casualties among the Communist troops and peasantry who had been in the vicinity of San-chiang-ying on 20–21 April when the artillery exchanges had occurred. This news surprised even the stoical Freeman, who knew in rough terms the scale of British loss and injury aboard the vessels and recognized that it was significantly lighter than that apparently inflicted upon the PLA troops and civilian population by the *Amethyst, Consort, London,* and *Black Swan.*[10]

Although relations between the two men had been cordial thus far—as shown by the willingness of the battery commander to provide a sampan and a crew for use by those on board the frigate in the absence of a reliable boat of their own—the fact remained that Kung and Freeman held such fundamentally different opinions on how this crisis had begun that a mutually satisfactory settlement was unlikely to be arranged in the near future. Even so, Kung tried his best to bring the interview to an end on a slightly more positive note by addressing the petty officer directly in English and in such a way as to suggest to Freeman that he regretted how the previous good state of Anglo-Chinese relations had been impaired by this particular incident. At the conclusion of their talk, Kung bowed formally and withdrew, leaving the two-man delegation from the *Amethyst* to make their own way back to rejoin their colleagues in the whaler and subsequently to the frigate, which they reached in the early evening.[11]

After debriefing the petty officer, Kerans concluded that Kung—who seemed anxious that hostile foreign reaction toward the PLA might result from the *Amethyst* incident—may have adopted the stance he had assumed during the interview to the effect that the British had fired first so as to vindicate his own conduct or that of the men for whom he was technically and directly responsible. Kerans duly informed Madden about the substance of the interview and awaited the next overture, which was expected to be an orchestrated campaign by the Communists to bring diplomatic pressure to bear upon the officers and crew of the *Amethyst* to admit their guilt in causing the original incident.[12]

This campaign was not long in coming. At about midday on Wednesday 27 April, a junk bearing a number of PLA soldiers came alongside the *Amethyst* and a message was passed to Kerans in Chinese asking that he go ashore for a meeting with Kung, the battery commander. Unwilling to leave the ship at this stage for any reason, Kerans refused to comply with the request. Nonetheless, because he did not wish to appear intransigent, he ordered Lieutenant Keir Hett, the director-control officer, to deputize for him ashore in talks with the PLA official.[13]

Before leaving the *Amethyst,* Hett was given an aide-mémoire by Kerans for delivery to the senior military commander of the PLA in the Chinkiang area requesting information about three British naval ratings who had been evacuated from the frigate on 20 April and whose present whereabouts were unknown. Two of these men had last been reported to be undergoing treatment in the Stevenson Mission Hospital in Wutsin on 21 April, but the third missing crew member, a stoker mechanic, had not been heard of or seen since he had set out to swim ashore. In polite and restrained language, the aide-mémoire ended by suggesting that, if the Communist authorities were agreeable, the two men who had been hospitalized could be repatriated to their ship. No such request was made on behalf of the third man, who it was feared had almost certainly drowned while trying to swim ashore.[14]

Hett and Butt boarded the junk and sailed the short distance ashore to keep the appointment with Kung. According to the official report, the interview began on an unpromising note and continued in that vein throughout. Kung began the procedings, as he had done on the first occasion, by alleging that the *Amethyst* had fired the first shell and that the shore defenses had only opened up against her in self defense. Hett naturally contested this claim and indicated that the responsibility for opening fire rested solely with the PLA artillery troops. Deadlock was rapidly reached as neither side was prepared to give way an inch or invoke a spirit of compromise to avoid the impasse that had been reached.[15]

> The impression was gained during the interview that the Battery Commander was confused as to exactly where the "CONSORT" fitted into the incident. He was not aware that fire had been opened at *Amethyst* earlier on that day. It seemed evident to Lieutenant Hett that the Battery Commander had been present all the time at San Chiang Ying and that it was not hasty errors on the part of his subordinates.[16]

Eventually after various charges had been hurled at one another and with no agreement in sight, Kung raised the question of the immediate future of the *Amethyst* once more. He assured Hett that the ship's crew would be perfectly safe provided the frigate remained where she was. He also reaffirmed the fact that he was not empowered to give the vessel a safe-conduct pass. Kung stressed that this pass could only be granted by the Communist authorities in Nanking, and so he advised Hett that another request for such a permit be made by the British ambassador who was resident in the city.[17]

Kung also mentioned that the local Chinese community was afraid of the presence of the *Amethyst* in its midst and suggested that an officer together with four ratings be kept ashore to liaise with members of the local population.[18] Although intending to serve as a guarantee of safety—because the ship could hardly be expected to bombard the shore if some of her crew were living in the village—the proposal looked to be an ingenious device for keeping the ship's company apart rather than for settling public disquiet, even if it had been expressed by civilians who lived in the area. Therefore, as doubt was cast on the authenticity of the allegation, the recommendation was never seriously entertained by the captain of the *Amethyst* either at this stage or at any other of what would become a protracted series of negotiations.

In closing, Kung indicated that the eight Chinese sailors who were crew members of the *Amethyst* were welcome to go ashore if they wished and that the Communist authorities would provide any medical assistance required on board the frigate if it were requested by the captain of the vessel. He also agreed to forward the aide-mémoire on this subject to a higher authority. Just before the interview finally ended, Kung mentioned a future interview with the General Office Commanding (GOC) of the Chinkiang area and hinted darkly that the *Amethyst* would likely have to remain on the Yangtze until the end of the civil war.[19] At this rather unfortunate juncture, the formalities were concluded, and the various parties withdrew.

Kerans seems to have been convinced that Kung now realized his initial mistake in opening fire upon the *Amethyst* but had decided to construct a story for his superiors within the PLA that would justify his use of force against the ship.

> There is no shadow of doubt that Major Kung could have been under no misapprehension regarding the identity of "*Amethyst.*" The number of direct hits on the starboard beam, including the bridge, indicated that there was adequate time to indentify [sic] the ship. *He could NOT have genuinely thought* that "*Amethyst*" fired first and I came to the conclusion that he was adopting a policy of vacillation to suit his own ends.[20]

Besides these comments, Kerans informed the flag officer that he had formed the impression that Kung had been present throughout the original incident at Rose Island. It was an opinion that was not corroborated by any factual evidence either at the time or subsequently.[21]

While Kerans and his crew embarked upon their second week in virtual captivity, moves to free them were being contemplated elsewhere. Ambassador Stevenson would have liked to have made contact with the Communist military or municipal authority in Nanking, if one had been established, but in the early days after its capture the center of the city remained in the hands of an interim citizen's self-protection committee which was unlikely to be of any help in putting pressure on the PLA to release the *Amethyst.* Faced by this peculiar vacuum in power in Nanking and aware that the Communists still refused to recognize either of the British consuls in Peking or Tientsin or to receive any messages from them, Stevenson cast around forlornly for some other possibility.[22]

His search soon yielded the name of a Mr. Harmon, who was recommended highly by the governor of Hong Kong and known to have built up friendly relations with the highest Communist leaders. Stevenson readily agreed to use Harmon as an intermediary to convey a message to the Communist headquarters at Peking asking for a safe-conduct pass for the *Amethyst.*[23]

Not all who found out about the proposal were enthusiastic about it, however. In a minute drawn up in the Foreign Office on 27 April, P. D. Coates penciled in the frustration felt by many British officials who could do nothing effectively to assist the crew of the beleagured frigate.

> Events now face the use of channels which it had previously been thought inadvisable to use. Probably nothing will be gained by their use & we may possibly be snubbed; but obviously in present circumstances every expedient must be tried.[24]

Coates was proved right on both counts.

No further contact was made between the Communists and the *Amethyst* for several days after Hett's interview with Kung, and life on board the frigate became more and more tedious as the days passed. Kerans tried his best to combat the boredom by ensuring that the officers and crew undertook their normal duties, but after these had been discharged, there was precious little for them to do in their spare time except speculate on what was going to happen to them and how much longer they were likely to remain cooped up at anchor on the Yangtze before the Communists would let them go. Under such circumstances, wishful thinking and rumormongering were almost bound to affect the crew and mislead even the most levelheaded of men. In this way, throughout their lengthy and enforced sojourn on the Yangtze, hopes were periodically raised and then dashed as time and opportunity passed with little or no material change occurring in their lives. If frustration with their situation was to be expected, so was the likelihood that it would increase as time wore on. Kerans and his fellow officers were alive to this danger in their men, but recognizing this probability did not necessarily mean they would be able to cope with it much better themselves.

As the days passed and the month drew to a close, the only untoward event that happened on the river to raise the pulse rate of those on board the *Amethyst*—and that only momentarily—was the discovery early on the morning of Thursday 28 April that the frigate had suddenly developed a $7^{1}/_{2}$-degree list causing the ship to swing on her anchor from north 50 degrees west to north.[25] Thereafter, according to the handwritten log, the days appeared to be almost entirely incident free. No contact was made with the military, and the only log entry concerned the occurrence for a time of a strong cross wind that accentuated the swinging motion of the *Amethyst* as she slewed on her anchor chain during the early hours of Saturday 30 April.[26]

On May Day the clocks in the Yangtze region of China advanced one hour in order to benefit from the extra daylight saving for the summer period. This particular Sunday was busier than for many days past, as the log entries reveal, with mention made of a Liberator aircraft passing overhead, junks moving along the river, soldiers seen on patrol on the southern bank, and two sampans coming alongside the *Amethyst*. One of these sampans was to become a familiar visitor to the ship in the coming weeks. Although the log does not identify the crew, it was almost certainly composed of two young Chinese women and an elderly Chinese matriarch who sensed that the ship's galley would contain more food and drink than what was available to them on shore. They began what became a series of frequent visits by requesting water. After it had been granted, they left the port side of the ship and returned to the shore.[27]

A day passed before further contact was made with the Communists. In the late afternoon of Monday 2 May, a sampan drew alongside the *Amethyst* with the local PLA garrison commander and two soldiers on board. They indicated their wish to see Kerans, and a meeting was swiftly convened in his cabin with Hett and Butt present. According to the official report, the interview was conducted without any of the rancor or acrimony that had attended the first two negotiating sessions on shore when allegations had been traded over responsibility for firing the first shot on 20 April.[28] On this occasion, Captain Tai Kuo-liang avoided the controversial subject altogether. Kerans recorded the event.

> It appeared that he had been sent onboard to give me a message from General Liu Po-Cheng in Nanking that agreement for a safe passage for *"Amethyst"* may be given "in a short time." He was unable, or would not elaborate or elucidate further except to add the usual remark that "the General was very busy." He stated that we should be perfectly safe here provided that we did not move; he asked me to confirm in writing exactly where we were anchored and that we would not move until the safe passage agreement had been given to us. I complied with this, and added a paragraph asking that our two ratings in the Mission Hospital at Changchow might be returned to *"Amethyst"* if possible and whether they could give us any information about them. Tai Kuo-liang added during this conversation that other shipping may be fired on, and especially referred to United States Ships, and the Chinese Navy. I made no comment on this, and can only conclude that Communist dislike for anything American has been well indoctrinated into their military forces.[29]

Kerans clearly felt that progress was at last being made in these talks. He was relieved that the adversarial nature of the proceedings had changed for the better, and he wired Madden to this effect later in the evening.[30]

During the next couple of days, the Communists established a battery on the southern bank of the Yangtze about half a mile from where the *Amethyst* rode uneasily at anchor. It soon became evident that the purpose of the gun emplacement was to control river traffic. Any vessels without the necessary clearance from the PLA authorities were fired upon, intercepted, and ordered to put in to the southern bank for questioning and inspection.[31] Most of those craft flying a red flag were, however, allowed to proceed without any interruption, but occasionally even that sign of political solidarity did not save a ship from being shelled by the battery for one reason or another.[32]

While the tempo of river traffic appeared to be increasing, there was also continuing activity in the sky above the Chinkiang area where Nationalist planes, usually Mitchells, could still be seen operating alone without aerial opposition from the Communist forces or antiaircraft guns to combat them. Occasionally a plane would drop a bomb in this sector of the front, but seldom with much effect, although on one occasion on army oil dump near Chinkiang actually received a direct hit and blazed uncontrollably for a number of hours. Despite their rather mediocre record, the KMT planes still managed to cause a mixture of blind panic and understandable anxiety among local boatmen whose vessels were plying up and down the river either on cargo runs or ferrying troops to and from various parts of the front. Most ships and other naval vessels sought protection by camouflaging themselves and sailing close to the shoreline in the hope of avoiding an aerial assault of any kind. Sometimes the element of caution could be overdone and result in farcical situations, such as that experienced by the slow ferry the *Tai Tung,* which ran aground immediately when its helmsman caught sight of a KMT plane in the distance.[33]

During Thursday morning (5 May), a local merchant came alongside with 65 pounds of fresh potatoes to sell or barter and with a strange message from the local garrison commander inviting the Cantonese crew members of the *Amethyst* to pay a courtesy call on the Chinkiang area commander.[34] Kerans's suspicion that the Communists might appeal to the Chinese members of the crew to jump ship or alternatively to spy on those who remained on board may not necessarily have been a symptom of paranoia on his part. Subtle political indoctrination could not be discounted now that the military dominance of the PLA had become firmly established throughout northern and central China, increasing the momentum of the Communist revolution and making its ultimate success against the KMT appear increasingly assured.[35] Moreover, the leading steward and sole interpreter to date—But Sai Tin—was regarded by both Hett and Kerans as being politically unreliable and more sympathetic to the Communist cause than they thought was advisable under the circumstances. Gauging whether But could be trusted to fulfill his duties correctly would have been difficult enough without the added complication of knowing that the other Chinese ratings on board the *Amethyst* looked to him for leadership.[36]

This delicate matter had not been resolved by the time Captain Tai Kuo-liang called on Kerans just after 9:00 A.M. on the following Sunday (8 May) and presented an invitation to the eight Chinese members of the crew to go ashore and attend a party to be given by the Chinkiang area commander the next day. When Kerans tactfully refused the invitation, citing difficulties that their withdrawal would create for the rest of the crew, he was told that if he persisted in his refusal all the Chinese would be withdrawn from the ship permanently. Faced with this possibility, Kerans proposed a compromise solution, which was accepted by Tai and entailed allowing six of the eight Chinese to go ashore.[37]

A tugboat with two officers on board came alongside at 11:45 A.M. on the following day (Monday 9 May), collected the six stewards, and departed for the shore. Kerans was later informed by But that the Communists had made no attempt to use the occasion to score political points or lure the members of his group into the Communist fold. Instead of any subtle or brazen attempt at instant indoctrination, the group was taken to a Chinese temple on the island of Chiaoshan where a burial service was held for those Chinese who had been killed on board the *Amethyst* or had died as a result of their wounds during evacuation from the ship. After the service ended, the six crew members were sent back to the frigate, arriving on board shortly before 7:00 P.M.[38] This incident hardly marked the start of a campaign to wean the Chinese crew members away from dependence upon the *Amethyst;* the Communists never issued another invitation to them to go ashore again.

While Kerans was worrying about the likelihood of external efforts being made to create divisions in his crew, the question of securing a safe-conduct pass for the *Amethyst* to pass unmolested downriver to Shanghai remained unresolved. If such a pass could be obtained, no one seemed to know how long it would be before it would be issued. Captain Tai had developed the habit of suggesting a date several days in advance to forestall further questioning. When this deadline passed, another would be suggested, and so on. By Friday 13 May, Kerans's annoyance at not hearing any news about an agreement to let the *Amethyst* go was such that he sent Hett ashore once again to badger Tai with further queries and requests on this score. Hett quickly discovered that no such agreement had come from Nanking, and that despite Communist assurances that they were doing all they could to expedite matters, no date could be confidently predicted when this essential clearance would be given by the PLA.[39]

In these singularly depressing circumstances and with no immediate prospect of a release being granted to the *Amethyst,* Kerans decided to try his luck with the local authorities in an effort to get authorization to move downriver to the limit of the Chinkiang area. He had already begun to think that an escape might be the only way of breaking the deadlock on the Yangtze, so that any ruse that would shorten the distance involved in a run for freedom was welcome. Although a move to Kiangyin remained a theoretical possibility, Kerans was unable to convince Tai or anyone else at the local level to agree to this proposal. As a result, hope for an early release still rested on the possibility of obtaining a safe-conduct pass from the Communist authorities in Nanking. These hopes were raised temporarily by Tai's arrival on board ship late in the afternoon of Tuesday 17 May but were dashed soon afterward by his admission that the necessary clearance papers for the ship might be delayed until after the fall of Shanghai.[40]

Disappointed and frustrated at his own total inability to improve the situation thus far, Kerans pinned what hopes he had left on a meeting with the area commander. He hoped that a sympathetic portrayal of the case might result in General Yuan Chung-hsien being more favorably disposed to the plight of the *Amethyst*'s crew than he might otherwise have been. Although neither his remonstrances to Tai nor Hett's appeal of the following day had the desired effect, the Communist authorities soon responded by raising the tempo of the political exchanges.

At about 3:25 P.M. on 18 May, the *Amethyst* was hailed by a Communist soldier on the beach. Shortly afterward a sampan pushed off from the shore and came alongside the ship. Three PLA officers presented Kerans with an uncompromising reply to his last three aide-mémoires. Their note spelled out in unmistakably trenchant terms just how difficult it would probably be for the British to settle the Yangtze incident to the satisfaction of both sides in the dispute.

> The Chinese People's Liberation Army Command Post on the Chenkiang Front is [sic] decided to solve through negotiations (all problems) arising from the atrocious action of British Navy's warships in their invasion of Chinese People's Liberation Army front and their incumbent responsibility.[41]

These discussions would henceforth be held between Colonel Kang Mao-chao, the personal representative of General Yuan, the area commander, and either Kerans or another naval officer who would represent the Royal Navy. In the course of what became an extremely disagreeable interview, Kerans was informed that his meeting with Kang, the political commissioner of the Third Artillery Regiment, would not take place until a written reply had been received and his credentials as a representative were agreed upon. He was also informed that there would be no discussion about a safe-conduct pass for the *Amethyst* until after the meeting with Kang was held and all outstanding matters were settled to the PLA's satisfaction. In the meantime, he was warned against making any attempt to move the ship, as this would result in it being fired upon by the Communist gunners. Not surprisingly, the meeting closed on an unpromising note with Kerans suspecting that his ship was likely to remain marooned in the Yangtze for a long time to come.[42]

After relaying this information to Admiral Madden in a series of signals, Kerans was left to consider the *Amethyst*'s uncertain future. Knowing the physical and mental state of his crew, who were sorely taxed by their ordeal in the unrelenting heat and humidity of a typical Yangtze summer, he was also worried that the onset of the typhoon season would pose further strains upon both his men and his ship. Unless something drastic was done to remedy the situation, the *Amethyst* was in grave danger of running out of fuel by mid-June. He concluded that without access to further stocks of fuel, severe economies designed to cut the daily rate of consumption would have to be enforced immediately in order to give the ship a few extra days of grace before the inevitable happened. As a result, Kerans ordered that all power was to be shut down throughout the ship at night, and more use was to be made of diesel and heavy minerals. Kerans knew, however, that these measures could only be achieved at great personal cost to his men and particularly to the wounded who remained on board.[43]

By this time it had become clear to the British authorities both in China and in London that the next few weeks were likely to be as exacting diplomatically as they would undoubtedly become physically for the crew of the *Amethyst*. It already looked as though the Communists were using delaying tactics as a means of applying psychological pressure to the ship's company. Anyone chosen to represent the Royal Navy in the forthcoming negotiations with the Communists over the Yangtze incident was almost certain to need a high degree of forebearance and tact.

11. More Questions Than Answers

WHILE THE CREW of the *Amethyst* were languishing some 10,000 miles away on the Yangtze, an eagerly awaited debate began in the British Parliament on Thursday 5 May over the government's policy in China. Harold Macmillan, the Conservative MP for Bromley, opened the proceedings in the House of Commons, and by the time the prime minister wound up the debate six and a quarter hours later, 125 columns of Hansard had been filled with speeches devoted more or less to this issue. As a result of the ambiguous wording of the motion before them, members were able to concentrate upon more than just a detailed reexamination of the *Amethyst* crisis, and the debate became a wide-ranging affair that went far beyond the confines of the Yangtze to embrace future policy goals both within China and throughout the Far East region.

Macmillan's growing reputation as a fluent and witty debater was confirmed by his performance on this occasion, as he methodically built a strong case against the government in his vigorous speech. He began by describing how the *Amethyst* crisis had unfortunately led to a worsening of Britain's relations with the Communists in China.[1] Although he did not subscribe to the theory that the original attack on the frigate had been deliberately planned by the PLA high command—preferring instead to see it as a foolish error made by a local artillery commander—the fact was that the Communists had now shown themselves to be fully supportive of those responsible for the outrage. This stance, he felt, could only have serious consequences for the British in a country where prestige was all important and loss of face a matter of the deepest shame.[2] Macmillan's thesis was that the *Amethyst* crisis should never have occurred in the first place.

143

It is really not good enough to talk about the decision of the man on the spot and about full support to the officer commanding. Whatever criticisms there may be of some of the decisions made, often at short notice and under great stress, all the trouble springs from certain initial mistakes and confusions, and indeed contradictions, of policy. For this His Majesty's Government, and His Majesty's Government alone, are responsible. It is from their faulty appreciation of the situation and from their mistakes of judgment and action that this grave disaster stems.[3]

Macmillan clearly had little sympathy for the plan to relieve *Consort* or for the fact that relief could only be effected a few hours before the expiry of the Communist ultimatum at midnight on 20 April. He wondered whether the decision had been referred to the Admiralty and the first lord for approval before it was implemented.[4] He also raised the question of the nonavailability of air cover for the rescue missions that were mounted in the period after the *Amethyst* had been attacked. This question brought him to the theme of the loss of the two light aircraft carriers *Theseus* and *Glory*, which had been withdrawn by the minister of defense from the China Station in October 1947. Macmillan attacked the decision and the failure of the minister to do anything to add to British naval strength in the Far East since then.[5]

I come back to the main question, "Air support or no air support?" The root of all these troubles lies in the decision to keep a naval vessel at Nanking. More prudently and, I think, more wisely, the Americans withdrew their own. I have no doubt that in the early stages of this affair, before the Communist armies had reached the Yangtse in force and before they were known to be about to effect the crossing, a destroyer or a gunboat may have been of some moral and practical assistance to British interests in Nanking, although I am bound to say that the "gunboat" mentality seems to be rather out of date.[6]

Macmillan pointed out that the government must have realized after Nanking was taken by the Communists that the value of having a British warship in port would be lost altogether, because from that time onward PLA approval would be required for any journey a ship might wish to undertake downriver. Besides wondering whose decision it had been to keep a ship at Nanking, he wanted to know why supplies could not have been made by road, rail, or air, as all such routes were still open on 20 April.[7]

After commenting wryly on the plan to bring relief to *Consort* by using the river route to Nanking—a method that, in his opinion, was the most dangerous one that could have been contemplated under the circumstances—Macmillan summed up his feelings about the entire episode in a few well chosen words.

In spite of the agility of the Prime Minister in his statement the other day in skating over some very thin ice, if one takes this story as a whole in all its aspects, and all the responsibilities connected with it, it seems to me that it is an absolute gem, a little cameo of incompetence, a miniature masterpiece of mismanagement, a classical illustration, which I have no doubt will long be studied by the staff colleges of the world, of exactly how not to do it.[8]

Thereafter, as if to reinforce this assessment of the situation, Macmillan queried the British government's decision to retain an ambassador as opposed to a mere chargé d'affaires in China, raised once more the inevitable question of whether relief was strictly necessary for *Consort,* and argued succinctly that, even if it was, it should never have been effected on the particular day it was attempted.[9]

If members thought that Macmillan had finished for the day, they were very much mistaken for he then turned to deal with some of the outstanding problems aggravated by the Yangtze incident. It was a depressing catalog of potential future crises that was not restricted to China alone but took in the entire Southeast Asian region. He wondered aloud what the British government's policy was on such matters as the future of Hong Kong and Shanghai, how it intended upholding British interests in a hostile environment, and what future role it sought to play in encouraging diplomacy between other powers and developing links with them in the fight to contain the burgeoning strength of international communism.[10]

As Macmillan resumed his seat on the other side of the house to warm approval from his party colleagues, the minister of defense took his place at the dispatch box. A. V. Alexander was a curious mixture of socialist and imperialist and a man who had a great wealth of parliamentary and ministerial experience. He was hardly likely to be seriously inconvenienced by having to defend himself and his government in the Commons against the charges of incompetence leveled at them by a political opponent, no matter how eloquent that opponent might be. He behaved, as one might have expected him to, in a matter-of-fact way, rebutting criticism when it was easy to do so, clarifying some issues, and making as reasonable a defense on others as he could under the circumstances.

In essence, Alexander's case rested upon the same foundations that the prime minister had revealed a week earlier in the house. What he had to say, therefore, came as no surprise to the packed chamber, but it was presented with slightly more elaboration and panache than Attlee had managed at Question Time on 26 April. Essentially, therefore, the theme that was repeatedly stressed was that the *Amethyst* incident arose out of an unfortunate accident that had occurred despite strenuous efforts by British representatives to ensure that the relief operation went ahead smoothly.[11] In the submission of the defense minister, however, the enviable hindsight displayed by members of the opposition subsequent to the emergence of that crisis was too obviously opportunistic and partisan in tone for the government to be embarrassed by it. According to Alexander, before the *Amethyst* crisis occurred, there had been a general acceptance from all quarters that a British naval presence in Nanking was entirely beneficial, that it exerted a steadying influence upon the two sides in the civil war and contributed to the maintenance of law and order in China.[12]

> The periodical relief of ships and passage up and down the river, in those long weeks and months when the Communist forces were gathered to the North of the Yangtse, seemed to have had the desired effect. That must be remembered. The ship was also required to provide wireless communication for the Embassy as well as certain stores and supplies. There was no reason to expect a deliberate and organised resistance to the movement of His Majesty's ships so long as they did not enter a battle area. We submit that this was not a battle area when the "*Amethyst*" was on passage, any more than it had been in the weeks and months before when this regular process had been going on with the troops still there. . . .[13]

It was Alexander's contention that a ship could provide a better, more comprehensive range of services than any transport aircraft could have done at Nanking. He felt that despite opposition claims that other methods of relief were available to the British and ought to have been used in preference to the river route, none of these alternative forms were free of major disadvantages.[14]

Such a statement was bound to provoke comment and further questions from the opposition benches, and a number of Conservative politicians rose to take issue with him on some of these points. Alexander glossed over the use of the guard ship at Nanking as a wireless communications post for the embassy, reiterated his stand that the river was not yet a battle area, and defended stoutly the lack of air cover for the *Amethyst*'s voyage and those subsequently of *Consort, London,* and *Black Swan.*[15] Alexander had, in fact, little difficulty in outlining why it would have been impractical for air cover to have been provided for the rescue operations on the Yangtze. His cogent arguments were much in line with Lord Fraser's memo that Attlee had used when answering questions in the house on 2 May.[16]

On the issue of whether the government delegated too much responsibility to the flag officer and the British ambassador in implementing its policy in China, Alexander set out the rationale for allowing decision making by responsible officials in the region who were conversant with the latest information about local conditions.

> It is only too easy in the present case to say, in the light of events, that the Government should have stepped in and stopped the sailing of the *"Amethyst,"* but that kind of wisdom after the event gets us nowhere. It was the judgment of Admiral Madden that, balancing one risk against the other, and in full regard of the local circumstances as they were known to him, the relief of the "Consort" by the *"Amethyst"* should take place 24 hours before the expiration of the second ultimatum. I am not prepared to say, and nor is anyone else from the remote comfort of London entitled to say, that that decision was wrong at the time he took it.[17]

If Alexander hoped that this would somehow silence the opposition's demand for an even closer in-depth study of the decision-making process at the time of the *Amethyst* incident, he was to be sadly mistaken. Although he went on to outline the situation in China generally and problems surrounding Shanghai and Hong Kong specifically, including the provision of substantial reinforcements for the garrison in the crown colony, members refrained from being diverted to another subject and remained insistent upon having chapter and verse spelled out for them as far as the Yangtze incident was concerned.

Wilfrid Roberts, the Liberal MP for Cumberland, Northern, was the first to take up the cudgels and attack what he saw as a deplorable decision to send the *Amethyst* upriver to Nanking on 19 April. He alleged that Peking radio had reported naval action on the Yangtze involving Nationalist warships the day before the frigate left Shanghai on her way to relieve *Consort*.[18] Moreover, he contended that there had not been a fixed time limit on the Communist ultimatum to the Nationalists and that the vague way in which the warning to the KMT had been couched ought further to have deterred the local officers from making the decision to send *Amethyst* upriver at this time.

> I do not know a great deal about China but I should not have thought that the going up and down the Yangtse by two warships, within a few hours of a major operation involving the crossing of the Yangtse, which was regarded as the frontier to hold the Communists back, would have been sanctioned.[19]

In Roberts's opinion, the unacceptably high risks involved in mounting a relief operation ought to have been recognized by all those concerned in planning it. He felt that the mission should never have been attempted until matters had become more stable along the Yangtze basin.[20]

Roberts believed that part of the problem stemmed from the British failure to work closely with the Communists. He suggested that if the British government had officially recognized the CCP as constituting the de facto government in China, the *Amethyst* affair would never have occurred.[21] Like all hypothetical comments, however, this statement is unsatisfactory because it cannot be conclusively proved or disproved—a feature that has certain attractions to a politician with a particular thesis in mind. In this case, the Liberal MP felt that an opportunity probably existed for establishing an enduring special relationship with the Chinese Communists, providing the British agreed to withdraw militarily from China's territorial waters and no longer recognize the Nationalist government.[22]

> The time will come—indeed, I believe it has come—when that offer could be a basis for opening negotiations for proper representation. In fact, we have an Ambassador in a capital which is not held by the Government to whom he is accredited. What exactly that means at present I do not know. The Nationalist Government are scattered; some of them are in Canton and some of them have apparently gone to the island of Formosa. The position is totally illogical so far as our Ambassador and our relations with China are concerned.[23]

Roberts's argument had some validity, as anyone monitoring the situation in China would have readily acknowledged off the record. He ended on an uncontentious note, wishing that the British government would seek to build a constructive relationship between itself and the Chinese Communists in order that cooperation rather than hostility would prevail in the future. Such a relationship would provide a safeguard against excess and reduce the likelihood of a challenge being mounted to British interests in the country.[24]

This peculiar contrast between upbeat optimism and bleak pessimism hinted at by Roberts was captured beautifully by the next speaker, the Labour MP Woodrow Wyatt. He pulled no punches and stated categorically that he could not imagine anything other than a Communist victory in China.[25] For this reason he saw no alternative other than adopting as friendly a policy toward the PLA as possible, with the proviso that the government should be prepared to stand up for British rights if the occasion demanded it. According to Wyatt, if Attlee's administration failed to grasp the initiative and act in a friendly manner toward the Communists, the two sides would be on a collision course that would cause irreparable damage to British interests in China, putting at risk trade and investment, threatening the very existence of Hong Kong, and conjuring up the specter of defeat at the hands of the Communists both there and ultimately in Malaya too.[26]

Wyatt managed to devote his entire speech to this theme and to giving an assessment of the burgeoning Chinese Communist party, never once mentioning the *Amethyst* crisis in the twenty minutes he was on his feet in the packed chamber. Rehashing the Yangtze story was not for him, but his natural reluctance at delving once more into those murky waters was not shared by his political opponents.

Walter Fletcher, the Conservative MP for Bury, had no such qualms about reinvestigating the background to the Yangtze crisis and began by attacking the lame excuses offered by both Attlee and Alexander in defending the decision to send the frigate to Nanking.

> Everybody with the slightest knowledge, either by radio from Pekin [sic] or from any other source, knew perfectly well, weeks beforehand, that a heavily-armed force, about to cross the Yangtse from the north bank, was sitting on the north bank waiting for the moment to cross. There never was a justification for sending that gunboat up the Yangtse. During the war I was in Chungking. Extremely heavy wireless traffic was carried, with no gunboat within 500 miles. It was perfectly possible to carry an enormous number of messages for the whole campaign in China. It was equally possible to do that in Nanking on this occasion. . . .[27]

Despite opening with this critique, Fletcher did not sustain his attack, preferring instead to lecture the government on the dire need to defend Hong Kong resolutely against all comers and to follow policies on the mainland that would undermine the Communist hold over the Chinese people. By advocating an aggressive approach to this question, Fletcher showed that he had little sympathy with the impressionistic and encouraging descriptions of Mao and his Communist followers that Wyatt and Roberts had presented that afternoon.[28]

Sir Arthur Salter, the Independent MP for Oxford University, was also not convinced that the Communists were merely misunderstood and actually meant well. He took issue with the idea, accepted somewhat complacently by both Macmillan and Alexander, that the attack upon the *Amethyst* was really the result of an unfortunate accident.[29]

> That may be so as to the first shots, but if we consider the incident as a whole, not only the first stage but what happened afterwards and the treatment of our efforts to get into some sort of relationship with the Communist forces, the time that has elapsed and the developments that have taken place since, it is I think the reasonable view that the attack reflects quite definitely a deliberately hostile attitude by the Communist leaders towards us and our ships. I should myself think, taking the incident as a whole, that it is properly to be regarded as a deliberate attack and a deliberate attempt to put us into a weak, bargaining position through the fact of the marooning of the *"Amethyst,"* rather than a mere unintended incident in the struggle taking place between the two rival forces on the Yangtse River.[30]

Salter's jaundiced view of the Communists contradicted the wishful thinking of those who were disposed to seeing the promise of a new dawn breaking in Anglo-Chinese relations. He failed to be that charitable and warned the Labour administration at length about the perils associated with a premature recognition of the People's government.[31] He also thought it undesirable for the British to retain an ambassador in China, when it was now palpably clear that the KMT government to which the ambassador was accredited was in real danger of losing the civil war within a matter of months or weeks.[32]

John Paton, the Labour MP for Norwich, disagreed with both the two previous speakers in the debate and considered most of Wyatt's earlier sanguine remarks about the state of the Chinese Communist party to be based more on illusion than on reality.[33]

> I do not believe that we can expect friendship from the Communist leaders in China because they detest our policies and nourish very bitter memories of the history of the relations between Britain and China over the last century.[34]

Paton did not mean that the British should not seek to establish and develop commercial and financial links with the Communists, but he thought it might be easier said than done. Despite the practical problems involved, he believed every effort should be made to preserve and extend British interests in China, a policy that inevitably would mean giving de facto recognition to Mao's government.[35]

By the time Mr. Gammans, the Unionist MP for Hornsey, rose to deliver another broadside at the Labour government, the debate had been in session for over three hours and twenty minutes, and it was difficult to see how any further contribution to the motion before the house could be original or valuable. Gammans appeared unconcerned by such considerations and without any diffidence whatsoever sailed straight into an attack on Paton, Wyatt, and Alexander, all of whom had irritated him with a combination of what he perceived as feeble opinions, wishful thinking, and an inability to answer specific questions directly.[36] He focused on the matter of wireless and telegraphic communications particularly and totally dismissed the defense minister's statement that a warship was needed for this purpose in Nanking. Describing the excuse proffered by Alexander as a fantastic story, Gammans wondered aloud whether it had been suggested to him by the Admiralty or it was something he had personally made up on the spot to explain the case for having a ship at Nanking in the first place.[37]

> Does he really suggest that the British Embassy in Nanking had no wireless? Is there any reason why it should not have had it? If it was without wireless before

the trouble started, why should not a temporary field set have been put into operation? The suggestion that one of His Majesty's ships must be kept under dangerous and difficult circumstances to provide wireless, is utter nonsense. Incidentally, what happened when H.M.S. "Consort" left Nanking; how did the Embassy fare then for wireless?[38]

Gammans's dissatisfaction on this score and with other aspects of the *Amethyst* affair—which had already been commented upon in some detail—merely served as the preface for the critical remarks he wished to make about what he saw as the government's inadequate defense policy on Hong Kong.[39]

Thereafter the speeches began to lose their crispness and vitality, and the debate degenerated into a general free-for-all on what was the best policy to pursue in dealing with the Communists in China.[40] For well over an hour, the house heard only passing references to the *Amethyst* crisis, as members indulged themselves in a desultory and often elusive search for ideas and arguments that would make a genuine contribution to the debate. Even when the issue was addressed directly by Commander Maitland, the Conservative MP for Horncastle, it was only to ask for further information from the prime minister on a number of questions that he felt had been inadequately answered in the debate hitherto.[41]

Eventually the *Amethyst* crisis resurfaced in a rambling speech made by William Teeling, the Conservative MP for Brighton, who complained bitterly about the quality of foresight, planning, and advice of those responsible for making decisions affecting British interests in China in the recent past. Although the latter part of his speech lunged off into a curious diatribe about communism generally and is perhaps best forgotten, he did make a positive contribution to the debate in his early remarks by raising the question of whether it was absolutely necessary to relieve *Consort* on 20 April. It became clear from his comments that he did not think a relief operation was vital at that time.

> The Minister has told us that there was a lack of fuel—whatever that means, for, after all, the ship was already up the Yangtse. He also said that the men were tired, and that there was also possibly a shortage of materials on board ship. Surely, however, everbody knew that this would be the case. Why, then, did not the "Consort" go down river a week or so before?[42]

Teeling went on to attack the lack of interest and control exercised by the government ministeries over what their representatives were doing in China and mentioned, without further elaboration, the British ambassador's role in the affair as a case in point.[43] Thereafter his speech became vague and seemed to tail off into a general and diffuse monologue on China, which though lacking inspiration, was at least mercifully short.[44]

As Teeling resumed his seat on the Tory benches to the immense relief of most members, Aidan Crawley, the Labour MP for Buckingham, rose to defend the government for keeping warships on the Yangtze as a means of providing a refuge for the British community in Nanking. Crawley pointed to the historical precedents for this kind of policy.

> In nearly all the major troubles that have taken place in China and on the Yangtse, gunboats and warships have been able to act as refuges in one form or another, and that notwithstanding the fact that at any time during the troubles the guns on the banks of the Yangtse could undoubtedly have blown these ships out of the water. This is as true of the Boxer Rebellion as it is today.[45]

Teeling evidently believed in the moral support these ships could provide for the expatriate community in China, a claim the Labour government had consistently made in defending its decision to station a guardship permanently at Nanking. He also tried to indicate the practical necessity for delegating authority and responsibility for decision making to the government's representatives in the field.

> The suggestion that if we left the ships on the Yangtse a Government in Whitehall could say when a particular ship on any reach of the river was to be relieved is fantastic, because no Government could possibly have taken that point of view.[46]

Not content with showing his solidarity with the government, Crawley went on to attack those in the opposition ranks who had earlier attempted to exploit the decision not to use air cover for the rescue operations on the river. His tactics were eminently successful, but since the latter point had been disposed of at Question Time on 2 May, the data that he used to elaborate the impracticality of aerial support could best be described as interestingly tangential to what had been discussed in the debate on this occasion.[47]

It was 9:10 P.M. when R. A. Butler, the Conservative MP for Saffron Walden, began his summing up of the opposition's case against the government over the Yangtze incident. His contention was that through a lack of appreciation of the current situation in China, the British government had become involved in hostilities with the Communists, even though its policy hitherto had been to chart a course of nonintervention in the civil war and favor neither side in this protracted struggle.[48]

In considering the government's explanation of how the crisis developed, Butler indicated that his colleagues in the Conservative party were not convinced that either the passage of the *Amethyst* was necessary or that *Consort* needed relieving.[49] He intimated that few among the opposition could accept the idea that a warship was required in Nanking to provide supplementary wireless and telegraphic assistance to the British embassy.[50]

> I am informed that the British Embassy's wireless was quite sufficient to communicate locally, at any rate with the Fleet at Shanghai, and that it would have been possible all along for the British Embassy to have kept in touch with the Commander-in-Chief. I do not believe—and it was one of the four main reasons for this voyage which were given by the Minister of Defence—that the provision of extra wireless in the "Amethyst" was necessary. The "Consort" could have stayed there longer. Those reasons, in our view, are not sufficient, therefore, to justify the course of this voyage.[51]

Butler spent the rest of his twenty-five-minute speech appealing for reinforcements in the Far East, such as an aircraft carrier, and for efforts to be made to construct a Pacific pact with other democratic nations that were determined to prevent communism from spreading throughout the region and endangering the independence and integrity of those Asian countries that had not yet yielded to Marxism-Leninism.[52]

Winding up for the government, Clement Attlee adopted a restrained and moderate tone, pointing out the risks involved in protecting British nationals living and working abroad in hostile environments and the concern felt by the cabinet for those people caught up in the dramatic events on the Yangtze.[53] His speech aimed to demonstrate that far from being incompetent or slothful in dealing with the situation in China, his government had behaved in a reasonable manner, relying upon the experience and sound judgment of its local representatives for day-to-day administrative control of British interests in the country.[54]

Referring to the voyage of the *Amethyst,* which had precipitated the crisis, Attlee continued:

> This vessel was not sent up to take part in war; it was sent up because, in what has been described by a great many hon. Members as a fluid situation, there was a danger of an interregnum, and our experience has been that it is precisely in these conditions that it is valuable to have a vessel on the spot. Now the question arises as to why, if we had the "Consort" there, she should have been relieved. She had been there a considerable time; a great deal of her stores had been consumed; and it was thought and judged that she should be relieved.[55]

Although Attlee admitted that *Consort* could have remained longer at Nanking, he agreed with the decision of the local commander not to postpone her relief indefinitely but to make arrangements for her replacement before the expiry of the latest Communist ultimatum to the KMT at midnight on 20 April.[56] He acknowledged that there was a risk involved in sending foreign vessels up the Yangtze at this time, but the fact that several warships had made this same journey for months past without being involved in any incident had been an important factor in persuading the local officials to press on with the relief of the destroyer.[57] Despite the tragic cost of this mistake, Attlee could nonetheless understand and sympathize with those who had made the original decision to send the *Amethyst* upriver. In his view, the decision had been a rational one for the flag officer and the British ambassador to have made, based as it was on information available to them at that time. His overall position on the crisis was that the initial firing upon the *Amethyst* had been an unfortunate accident that could not have been predicted in advance.[58] Nevertheless, the government accepted full responsibility for the mishap and would continue to monitor events on the Yangtze with the closest vigilance until a satisfactory solution could be reached that would allow the *Amethyst* and her crew to be repatriated to British territory.[59]

In addressing other matters raised in the debate, Attlee expressed surprise that the focus of the discussion had moved away from the *Amethyst* crisis to embrace the wider issue of British foreign policy in the Far East.[60] Although he did not admit it, the suspicion exists that the government probably viewed this broader discussion as an entirely welcome development, because it was definitely easier to fudge regional considerations than to answer highly specific questions relating to the Yangtze incident. Attlee certainly seemed more comfortable in dealing with this kind of enquiry than one of a more restricted nature. He exuded a steady calmness, which was demonstrated in his refusal to be rushed into hasty and ill-considered action against the Communists, and reserved his position on naval reinforcements for the Far East and diplomatic accreditation with the People's government pending further evaluation of the problem at cabinet level.[61] The note of quiet confidence he struck in ending the debate was best shown in his assessment of what damage, if any, the *Amethyst* crisis had had upon British prestige in the east.

> I know that an incident of this kind is bound to have its effect; but I do not believe that British prestige is low in the East. On the contrary, the evidence I have had from people who have been there recently is that our prestige is high in the East, because they believe that we stand for certain definite principles, and that we have been putting those principles into effect. I think it will be found that in Eastern countries there is a great deal of confidence in Britain; and despite an incident of this kind—an incident which we all deplore but an incident such as may happen from time to time if we look after, as we must, the interests of

our nationals in these disturbed countries—I do not believe that there has been a lowering of our influence in the East.[62]

As far as Attlee was concerned, the damage wrought by the *Amethyst* crisis had thus far been contained. He did not speculate about the future and with good reason, as time and future developments would soon testify.

12. The Limitations of Naval Diplomacy

*D*ESPITE his concern for what was going on between the *Amethyst* and the local Communist authorities in the Chinkiang area, Sir Ralph Stevenson had few options in seeking a satisfactory settlement of the Yangtze incident. Although he used what diplomatic leverage he could to try to effect a breakthrough with the Foreign National Affairs Department in Nanking, he was under no illusions about the difficulty of achieving anything by this method. An aide-mémoire was duly dispatched by him to this new Communist department on 14 May, but because it merely repeated what had been said in the past, there was little reason to suspect that it would be any more successful than the other previous appeals that were issued since the crisis had begun over three weeks before.[1]

While Stevenson waited more in hope than confidence for a positive reply from the Communists, Sir Patrick Brind, the commander in chief of the Far East Station, began to assert himself for the first time in the crisis.[2] In a message to Captain Donaldson in Nanking, Brind cautioned the naval attaché about the dangers of relaying uncoded messages on sensitive matters to the *Amethyst* when the Communists could monitor the radio traffic and thereby easily discover what the British stand was on these issues. Aware of the dangers of conducting negotiations under intense pressure, Brind insisted that Kerans must avoid local discussions with the Communists on the question of who was ultimately responsible for firing the first shot on the Yangtze on 20 April. He felt—and incidentally it was an opinion shared by the Admiralty in London—that the British should insist that all controversial questions such as this one be discussed at the highest diplomatic level and not left in the hands of local and subordinate personnel.[3]

Admiral Sir Patrick Brind (courtesy of the National Portrait Gallery, London).

Learning from Kerans that *Amethyst*'s fuel stocks were down to 170 tons and that economies were being put in hand to lengthen the period before her fuel ran out, Brind proposed a dramatic solution to resolve the impasse.

> If meeting referred to in *Amethyst*'s 180814 becomes essential & if Admiralty have no objection, I am considering flying to *Amethyst*, hoisting my Flag in her and attending meeting personally. This offers far the best chance to release *Amethyst* and possibility of British Warships being impounded is serious enough to justify risks involved. If my negotiations fail I should declare my intention to sail down river on stated date and time and I should do so. If Woosung is still a battle area I should anchor before reaching it. It is most unlikely that Communists would fire in the circumstances, particularly if we take every possible step by broadcasting and other means to tell Communist Government.[4]

Brind believed that the risks of launching such an initiative were small and worth incurring if the likelihood of success was good.[5]

Such dramatic initiatives are rarely welcomed or sanctioned by government departments, and this was no exception. Brind was told by the Admiralty that it did not share his enthusiasm for this adventure or his belief in its likely success. Ordering him not to undertake his mission, the Admiralty emphasized the risk of failure in the enterprise, which would then inevitably raise other problems such as prestige, national honor, and the further estrangement in relations between the Communists and the British government—which was about the last thing it needed at this particular time. Adopting a pragmatic tone, the Admiralty message put forward the idea currently being floated in ministerial circles in London that perhaps the most sensible course to follow was to wait until after the city of Shanghai had fallen to the Communists before making another major effort at resolving the crisis.[6]

Thwarted on this front and recognizing the probability that the Communists would insist upon negotiating with the British at the local level, Brind drew up a personal message for General Yuan Chung-hsien, the PLA commander in chief of the Chinkiang area. In it, Brind attempted vainly to torpedo the plan for local talks before they began to reach a decisive stage. Besides objecting to any negotiations involving the captain of the *Amethyst* and the PLA over the responsibility for the Yangtze incident, Brind pointed out that because the Royal Navy had maintained a strictly neutral position in the civil war from the outset, the Communists ought to show just cause for denying the *Amethyst* a safe-conduct pass downriver to Shanghai. In requesting approval for this journey, Brind was ever mindful of the fact that the frigate, which had been up the Yangtze for more than a month, still had a number of injured men on board who needed hospital treatment as soon as possible.[7]

Before this note had even been written, the British ambassador had urged the Foreign Office not to allow the government to submit to what he described as virtual blackmail by the Communists. Despite his prompting, Stevenson admitted that he did not believe the PLA would allow the *Amethyst* to go free until the British admitted responsibility for the Yangtze incident. Such an admission would presumably mean the payment by the British of an as yet undisclosed figure in compensation to the Chinese authorities. Although it was obvious that Stevenson was opposed to the idea of his government admitting liability in order to bring the case to an end, he was well aware of the difficulties that a continued refusal to accept any wrongdoing would cause for the men of the *Amethyst*. Their detention on the Yangtze was, therefore, likely to last a good deal longer than either they or the British government would have wished.[8]

Stevenson's message underlined the limited diplomatic options available to his government. If the Communists were not prepared to discuss this case at the national level, there was little that Attlee's cabinet could do about it. A naval demonstration was out of the question, and a rescue mission had already been tried and had failed. If talks had to take place at the local level, therefore, the British representative would almost certainly have to endure a protracted series of meetings and a fair amount of frustration before any settlement was possible. Working on the basis that reason and logic would not sway the local PLA officials, Stevenson suggested the best arrangement would be for Brind to circumvent this obstacle by going personally to Nanking, or to the *Amethyst*, so that he might be able to discuss the crisis with an officer of similar standing to himself within the PLA. If this tactic should prove to be impossible for any reason and the British were forced instead to reply on purely local contacts, the ambassador urged that these discussions should be limited from the outset. He felt that Kerans ought not to be asked to defend the principle of British naval policy in China or the individual action of any of His Majesty's ships in the region. Instead, he should be told to restrict any future discussions he might have with the PLA to technical arrangements for taking his ship downriver under a safe-conduct pass. Obviously this suggestion could only be used as a holding operation and was hardly likely to be acceptable to the PLA in the long term.[9]

Judging from the difficulties encountered up to this point and being acutely aware of the Admiralty's warning that the *Amethyst* would not have sufficient fuel to make the journey downriver to Shanghai after 9 June, the Foreign Office let Stevenson know that it was anxious to explore every possible approach to the Communists in an effort to get a safe-conduct pass for the ship before the end of the month.[10] Prompted by this telegram, the ambassador proposed that the best interests of the British would be served by seeking some method of establishing direct contact with the regional or national officials of the PLA, in the hope that they might be able to influence the local officers at the Chinkiang front whose task it was to settle the Yangtze incident. He suggested that an appeal from his embassy should be lodged in the first instance with Liu Po-cheng, the mayor of Nanking and chairman of the city's military control committee. If this appeal did not work, Brind could be asked to send a personal telegram to Chu Teh, the commander in chief of the PLA, requesting a safe-conduct pass for the *Amethyst*. As a long shot, the ambassador thought that the Foreign Office might be able to trace and persuade General Adrian Carton de Wiart to send a message to his old friend Chou En-lai asking him to intercede in the dispute and arrange for the release of the frigate in the interests of improving ties between China and the United Kingdom.[11]

By this time, however, with the PLA at the gates of Shanghai and its confidence in achieving total victory in the civil war at a high level, there was little that the British could do to make the Communists more amenable to their wishes. Robert Urquhart, the British consul, revealed the pointlessness of registering any form of protest with the Communist military about the occupation of British property in the Shanghai area, because the PLA saw it as compensation for the damage and destruction caused on the banks of the Yangtze to Chinese lives and property by vessels of the Royal Navy on 20–21 April.[12] Exasperated though the British may have been, there was nothing to be gained by trying to stand in the way of the PLA, for it would only aggravate the situation. For this reason, Stevenson became anxious lest the commandeering of British-flagged merchant vessels by the Nationalists would be seen as further evidence of collusion between the two former allies.[13]

As commander in chief, Brind was anxious to maintain morale among the crew of the *Amethyst* and not allow those on board to feel they had been forgotten by the British authorities. Even so, he refrained from exaggerating the prospects of success at the diplomatic level and openly admitted in a message to the ship on 21 May that he could not promise an early end to their enforced stay on the Yangtze.[14] Kerans took a positive view of this latest explanatory note, as the following comments suggest.

> This is what I have always suspected, namely that the overall question of responsibility has been taken up on the very highest of levels by the British Government and the Chinese Communist Party in Peking, through our Ambassador in Nanking. It inevitably involves partial recognition of the Communist regime which will, of course, affect the occidental powers in Europe. As we have no codes or cyphers there is little that we can be told. I am confident that a satisfactorily agreed conclusion will eventuate. The fine "teamwork" displayed by everyone in the past few weeks is an added pointer to success.[15]

Brind's message for General Yuan was received by Kerans on Sunday 22 May. Knowing the importance of it and wishing to deliver the note personally, he contacted Colonel Kang Mao-chao on the following day asking for an interview with Yuan as soon as possible.[16] It was arranged for the afternoon of Tuesday 24 May. Shortly after 2:30 P.M. on the appointed day, a sampan with a Communist soldier on board arrived alongside the *Amethyst* to take Kerans to the shore. No one else from the crew accompanied him on this occasion.

After reaching the southern bank, he was taken to the local garrison headquarters in a nearby village where he was greeted by Captain Tai Kuo-liang whom he had met earlier in the month on board ship. Tai led him along a path that eventually joined the main road where a car stood waiting to drive them both to Chinkiang. Situated near the city center, the PLA area headquarters was housed in a grand, old building adorned by a massive portrait of Mao Tse-tung. After being ushered into a room that resembled a banquet hall, Kerans and Tai were formally introduced to the waiting Communist delegation, which consisted of General Yuan, a Hunanese of about fifty years of age, Colonel Kang, a former lawyer who had practiced for ten years in Peking and was probably in his thirties, and two younger interpreters.[17] Besides the official party, Kerans was surprised to find present a few members of the press corps and propaganda representatives of the Chinkiang headquarters staff.

General Yuan opened the rather tense proceedings by stating that contrary to Brind's claim, no other talks were taking place elsewhere on resolving the Yangtze issue. Although Kerans immediately countered by saying that he had no authority to discuss anything but the steps necessary for securing a safe-conduct pass for his ship, Yuan refused to even consider this matter until the question of responsibility for the initial incident on 20 April had been satisfactorily resolved.[18] Just how difficult a settlement would be to arrange was shown by the presentation of an aide-mémoire signed by Kang and meant for Brind. Accusing the *Amethyst* and the other British vessels of invading Chinese territorial waters, the aide-mémoire went on to establish two further claims.

> The H.M.S. "Amethyst" had opened fire in a deliberate provocative challenge. Further, the British Royal Navy had subsequently repeatedly reinforced her with more warships in the shelling of the People's Liberation Army positions and villages in the liberated area, resulting in 252 casualties on the People's Liberation Army and colossal damage to the people of the liberated area. The H.M.S. "Amethyst" and other delinquent British warships in the above mentioned invasion and challenging action had acted in coordination with the fighting of the Kuomintang reactionary forces at the venue, which resulted in the impediment of the Chinese People's Liberation Army action in that area, thus precipitating a situation disadvantageous to the Chinese People's Liberation Army but advantageous to the Kuomintang troops.[19]

In the acrimonious discussion that followed General Yuan's withdrawal from the meeting, Colonel Kang claimed that the British must have realized they had no right to sail on the Yangtze, and yet they had done so knowing that the PLA had already secured a partial military occupation of the river area by April 1949. Accordingly, his contention was that the British had no option but to admit their mistake, apologize to the PLA, and pay an indemnity for the loss of life and damage caused by their warships on the Yangtze. Until this was done, the Communists would not be willing to release the *Amethyst* or her crew, and further damage would be done to Anglo-Chinese relations.[20]

Kerans tried his best to defuse the situation by pointing out that despite repeated and fruitless efforts to establish diplomatic contact with the Communists, the British had been forced to go to the Nationalist authorities for permission to send their vessels along the Yangtze from Nanking to Shanghai. His statement only served to stir Kang into action. Although he seemed to have undermined Kerans's carefully reasoned case by disclosing details of the Central Executive Committee's (CEC) proclamation of 1 February 1947, which repudiated agreements made between the KMT and foreign powers,

Kang found his adversary unwilling to concede the point on the grounds that the British government had never recognized the CEC ruling and therefore it could not have any bearing on the issues under discussion.[21]

Kerans then moved the discussion onto the practical difficulties of keeping the *Amethyst* cooped up on the Yangtze. He made it clear that besides the depletion of her fuel and food stocks, the ship was fast becoming a most uncomfortable place in which to live, particularly at night when the generators were shut down and the temperature on board rose steadily. Kang explained that he was personally not unsympathetic to the plight of the crew and saw no reason why the ship should not continue to be provisioned locally as had been the practice in the recent past. Even so, he rejected the idea that this responsibility rested solely upon the PLA. As a more constructive gesture of support for the ship's company, however, he proposed releasing Bannister and Martin, the two wounded ratings from the *Amethyst* who had been captured in Changchow in the previous month, providing an official request was made to this effect. A letter was duly written to this effect, and the two young sailors were escorted back to their ship as promised the next day (25 May).[22]

In drawing the ninety-minute meeting to a close, Kerans remarked that because the continued detention of the *Amethyst* could no longer be condoned on military grounds and in light of the British government's professed neutrality in the civil war, the only thing that would result from the situation was further unnecessary international complications.[23] At this point the meeting ended. Kerans had ample time during the 15-mile journey back from Chinkiang to reflect on what had been said in the interview. Summarizing his feelings about it later, he recorded:

> I came to the conclusion that there was reason for hope but that it might take some time to convince them that only superior authority could adjudicate the questions involved. It did appear that this first meeting was quite likely a face-saving gesture for the benefit of the local peasantry. The press alone would point to this. The fact that we were well covered by day and night by batteries made it clear that any provocation by attempted movement could only meet with disaster.[24]

Wednesday 25 May saw the return of Bannister and Martin. It also seemed to be a more interesting day than usual with various sampan journeys being made between the ship and the shore. By the time darkness fell, however, the sense of expectation had dissipated as the fans stopped and the temperature rose. What had become normal practice was reestablished: the main power and steam had been shut down, all the lights on the ship had been extinguished, and the men lay sweating profusely in their bunks.[25]

After the activity of the previous day, Thursday and Friday were devoid of incident on the river. Although a spell of bad weather ruined much of Saturday (28 May), it had slackened enough by Sunday afternoon to enable Sam Leo, an experienced and trustworthy interpreter from the British embassy in Nanking, to be ferried out to become part of the ship's company for the duration of the *Amethyst's* vigil on the Yangtze. His arrival on board ship meant that at last a reliable professional linguist was available to the captain. Kerans's relief was profound. He could now dispense with But Sai Tin's dubious services as the unskilled go-between. Kerans was never very confident that But was fluent or intelligent enough to understand the nuances in language, let alone translate them into a second and unfamiliar tongue without losing the original flavor of the text. His suspicions about But's political sympathies merely compounded the problem.[26] Therefore, the willingness of the Communists to allow Leo to make the journey from Nanking to assist Kerans was helpful and suggestive, perhaps, that they were anxious to reach a negotiated settlement with the minimum of delay.

Leo was soon put to work translating into Chinese Sir Patrick Brind's reply to the PLA version of events on the 20–21 April. Intended for dispatch to General Yuan, the message provided an account of the Yangtze incident from the British perspective. Acknowledging that there was very little common ground between the PLA aide-mémoire and his own reply, Brind stressed that the disparities in their stories could only be settled by a meeting between the highest authorities on both sides.[27] His own account of the attack upon the *Amethyst* was terse, and it reiterated all the points that by this time were well known and had already been discussed. As expected, he emphasized the most contentious point of all.

> The "Amethyst" did not repetition *NOT* fire *any guns until after she was driven aground*. The other British warships were solely concerned in helping the wounded men in "Amethyst" and in bringing the damaged ship away from her dangerous position. In no case did a British ship open fire until she was fired upon.[28]

Brind refuted all suggestions that the British were in any way responsible for the original incident and proposed that the top-level meeting he advocated ought to be convened as soon as possible in order to discuss and settle the issue before any further damage was done to Anglo-Chinese relations. In the meantime, he urged Yuan to provide the *Amethyst* with a safe-conduct pass, stressing that this decision should be seen as unrelated and without prejudice to the formal discussions on responsibility that he hoped would be held subsequently.[29] This message was eventually taken to the local garrison headquarters by Leo on Monday afternoon.[30]

Brind's resolute stand on these two issues was fully supported by the Foreign Office. In a message to the ambassador in Nanking on Saturday 28 May, the Foreign Office gave warm approval to those who sought to provide a vigorous defence of British policy on the Yangtze. Moreover, it also felt that in the wake of the recent fall of Shanghai and the lower reaches of the river to the Communists, any military reason for delaying permission for the *Amethyst* to return to the open sea had disappeared.

> We now wish the vessel to leave the Yangtse in the next few days in order that the tedium of the ship's company may be brought to an end, the wounded still on board may receive proper medical attention and the ship return to her service with His Majesty's Fleet. Since "Amethyst" was acting under orders of higher authority, her continued presence is not essential to the enquiry while her departure will equally be without prejudice to such enquiry.[31]

Kerans was given another chance to defend these views in the late afternoon of Tuesday 31 May. A ferryboat arrived unannounced alongside the *Amethyst* shortly before 4:00 P.M. with a messenger on board bearing an invitation for Kerans to go ashore for an immediate meeting with Colonel Kang in the nearest village. Taking Leo with him, the captain returned with the messenger and was soon in earnest conversation with the political commissioner.[32] Kang began the proceedings on a provocative note by calling Brind's sincerity into question. Pointing to the British admiral's recent messages as a case in point, Kang explicitly accused Brind of adopting evasive tactics so as to avoid discussing responsibility for the *Amethyst* affair. Kerans naturally protested the innocence and good faith of Brind and endorsed his proposals as concrete suggestions rather than merely skillful and disingenuous negotiating ploys designed to prevaricate and avoid having to make difficult decisions.[33]

During the next couple of hours, the two men rehashed all the old issues in an atmosphere that became more highly charged as the gulf dividing them on every one of the outstanding issues failed to narrow. If Kang could suspect Brind, Kerans made it clear that he had doubts about Kang too, and not least whether the political commissioner had the authorization to discuss the *Amethyst* affair from the higher echelons of the PLA. Kang assured him that none other than Chu Teh had approved the handling of the affair by General Yuan, and that Yuan had delegated it to him. He rationalized this decision on the basis that he had been in command of the battery at San-chiang-ying and that his men had seen the *Amethyst* fire first. Therefore, he believed he was in the best position to argue the case for the PLA.[34]

Kerans rejected the idea that he would be entrusted with the task of negotiating a final settlement of this case with Kang, Yuan, or anybody at the local level. After his request for a change of venue had been denied, he asked permission for a Sunderland flying boat to bring in a high-ranking officer who could conduct these negotiations for and on behalf of the British government. Kerans hoped that if someone like Captain Donaldson, the naval attaché from Nanking, could be brought in, a safe-conduct pass might materialize faster than if matters were left to the local officials to settle. Kang suggested that the arrival of a senior figure would not necessarily result in any immediate material improvement in the fortunes of the *Amethyst* or her crew, because a safe-conduct pass would not be granted until the British had accepted in full the terms proposed by the Communists for bringing the crisis to an end.[35]

By the time the meeting ended, the acute differences in their negotiating positions had been fully exposed, revealing little common ground—if any at all—on the various issues confronting them. Kerans's disgruntled view of the proceedings is evident in his report.

> I did feel that the time was now opportune for world wide broadcast of the true facts of the case pointing out Communist vacillation and intransigence during negotiations. It was also clear that the political machinery of the C.P.L.A. was the deciding factor and that it was hard to break, in order to make a normal approach possible. It was also obvious that Kang and his interpreters were dealing in political matters above their heads. It was only after this meeting that it dawned on me that Colonel Kang Mao-Chao and the Battery Commander with whom earlier meetings had taken place with Lieutenant Hett, were one and the same person. I now realised that Kang was probably still finding justification for his actions for the benefit of his higher authorities and at the same time to exonerate himself.[36]

Kerans felt that unless something dramatic happened, the men of the *Amethyst* probably would be forced to spend further time on the Yangtze without immediate prospect of early release.[37] It was a scenario he did not relish and with good reason. By the beginning of June, life on board the frigate was becoming daily more intolerable as the lack of adequate supplies of disinfectant, DDT, and basic medical needs, such as penicillin and ethyl chloride, began to be sorely missed. Without traps or poison to deal with them, a large number of rats had effectively taken over the after part of the ship making it totally uninhabitable, and swarms of mosquitoes made sleep tortuous for all those who were without adequate netting to put over their bunks. If these were not sufficient reasons for concern, Kerans was also worried about the effects of shutting down all power to conserve his fuel supplies, particularly because it meant that the temperature on board would rise substantially, affecting the condition and storage of explosives. Besides the problems of ensuring adequate ventilation in the armaments magazine in order to keep the temperature from rising above 100 degrees Fahrenheit, Kerans sensed that the heat and humidity below deck was wearing down the resistance of the healthy members of the crew and further torturing those who were sick or wounded.[38]

Although the men were enduring a miserable existence in what was tantamount to a floating prison on the river, at least they had enough food to eat. Malnutrition was unlikely to become a problem while adequate provisions could be obtained from local sources. Fortunately, a sampan could be relied upon to come out most days from the shore bringing supplies of fresh vegetables and eggs that could be bartered for flour, sugar, or soap. Bargaining was almost always a lengthy and taxing affair, with the local merchants succeeding, in increasing the price of their goods as the weeks went by and the ship's fate became more uncertain. In these unfavorable circumstances, with the steady depletion of the *Amethyst*'s stores of tinned food, the traders became more assertive and capitalistic. At the outset, ten dozen eggs cost 45 pounds of sugar, but as time wore on that barter price had risen to 100 pounds of sugar. At this rate, the *Amethyst*'s basic stock of barterable items was soon in danger of becoming exhausted. Therefore, alternative commodities had to be found, such as metal and winter clothing, to continue the exchange procedure.[39]

Undoubtedly the most crucial shortage throughout the long period of the ship's detention was fuel. Despite all the economies Kerans had made, the daily fuel consumption was 2.6 tons, and by 4 June only 126 tons remained in the tanks on board ship. This situation meant in effect, that the *Amethyst* could remain at anchor, if need be, for another month and still have sufficient fuel on board to make the trip downriver to Shanghai providing she was granted leave to do so.[40] This fact gave little leeway to those who might be charged with the responsibility of negotiating a settlement with the Communists.

Captain Vernon Donaldson, the British naval attaché in Nanking, knowing the vagaries of the diplomatic process and the likelihood that it might take some considerable time before a satisfactory outcome could be arranged, began looking earnestly for a method of preserving the *Amethyst*'s fuel for as long as possible. He soon discovered that there were roughly 50 tons of Admiralty boiler fuel stored in drums in the International Export Company's compound in Nanking. If the Communists could be persuaded to release this fuel in return for payment, it would provide the *Amethyst* with a temporary reprieve. Reporting his find to Brind, the naval attaché intimated that the deal would probably be more successful if he approached the Communist authorities with a strictly commercial, as distinct from political, proposal.[41]

While the British naval authorities on the Far East Station were mulling over this idea, the next round of negotiations began on the Yangtze.

13. Psychological Warfare

O N THE early afternoon of Friday 3 June, a small launch with a Chinese officer on board came alongside the *Amethyst*. Once again Kerans was asked to attend a meeting with Kang immediately. He complied with the request, although he had not been given any advance notice of the interview. He left the ship in the company of Sam Leo, his interpreter, and another member of the crew—on this occasion the electrician Blomley—who was taken along as a source of support for his captain during the wearisome discussions.

Kerans had seen on 31 May how difficult and unnerving it was to negotiate alone when faced by a phalanx of opponents, and he was determined to avoid a repetition of this fate if he could. Rather than select a senior colleague, he wisely chose someone from the ranks of petty officer or leading rating to accompany him to all subsequent talks with the Communists. This shrewd move of choosing a different individual each time provided a much-needed psychological boost for Kerans at the conference table. It also gave the men of the *Amethyst* something to look forward to, even if they were not selected to go ashore with the captain, because they would be brought up to date with the latest news about how the talks on their future were proceeding as soon as the *Amethyst* delegation returned to the ship.[1]

On 3 June, Kerans, Leo, and Blomley were taken by launch to Silver Island where Kang was waiting for them. Kerans's report of the meeting shows how difficult these sessions were becoming.

> Once again lengthy, it almost entirely consisted of Kang using every subtle device and means to force me to assume overall responsibility in negotiations. Once again I refused to acquiesce and told him most forcibly that I was not authorised. The main points of the meeting on 31st May were once more gone

through and countered with the same remarks. I asked for clearance for a Sunderland whereupon Kang made it clear that *he* did not wish a senior officer to be flown in to take over negotiations. I then tried hard to get Captain Donaldson's entry from Nanking offering the only speedy alternative; this was not acceptable. Accusations against the British Government were made and that we were using dilatory tactics and trying to separate safe conduct from the main issues of "invasion and infringement" of Chinese sovereignty.[2]

Whatever optimism Kerans had felt after the last meeting was evidently dispelled by this one.[3] Perhaps the only constructive thing to emerge from this latest encounter was the solitary concession granted by Kang allowing Leo to travel to Nanking to collect a relatively large amount of *Jen Min Piao*, the Communist currency. This money could then be used by those on board the *Amethyst* to purchase their supplies from local sources rather than relying on bartering in kind, which, as Kerans knew only too well, was rapidly becoming an unsatisfactory and increasingly expensive practice.[4]

Over the next few days, the *Amethyst* was left alone by the Communists; routine visits were made by local merchants selling eggs and potatoes, and a side party sampan came alongside each morning without fail, but no further official exchanges took place for more than a week. Regardless of the lull on the river, efforts were made to improve the morale of the ship's company by the embassy personnel at Nanking. Brind was asked, for instance, whether he would support an approach being made to the BBC in London requesting it to arrange a musical program along the lines of the ever popular "Forces Favourites." This idea was passed on to the BBC, only to be turned down reluctantly by it without adequate explanation.[5]

Subsequently, it became known that this request was rejected on advice from the government, which favored giving minimum publicity to the *Amethyst* case in the United Kingdom. According to the head of the military branch of the Admiralty, the government departments most actively involved in dealing with the Yangtze incident were acutely conscious that drawing the public's attention to the plight of the ship's company and creating widespread sympathy for those on board the *Amethyst* might actually do more harm than good. Both the Admiralty and the Foreign Office were concerned that such publicity could jeopardize the release of the ship and her crew, particularly if it aroused hostility toward the Chinese Communists among British people, as it was likely to do.[6] Lord Fraser, the chief of naval staff, was not convinced that this somewhat alarmist view should prevail, however. He wrote to Sir William Haley, the director general of the BBC, reviving the idea on the grounds that if a few special record request programs could be arranged by the corporation, they would almost certainly provide a timely boost to the morale of those on board the *Amethyst*. Haley appeared to be convinced by this argument and replied on 15 June that he agreed in principle to the first sea lord's proposal. Arrangements were subsequently made to broadcast these programs over the World Service network on alternate Sundays in July between the hours of 0815 and 0845 BST.[7]

While the idea of a nonpolitical media event was being thrashed out, other overtures of a slightly more conventional kind were being followed up elsewhere. In Shanghai the consul general had established contact with the Communist authorities through the offices of an intermediary and had received news that a deal might be struck that would allow the men to gain their freedom but at the expense of leaving their ship behind on the Yangtze. None of the British officials either in China or the United Kingdom thought this idea was even remotely feasible. P. W. Scarlett summed up their feelings when he described the offer as being rather sinister and one that must be summarily rejected before it became one of the latest demands of the Communist negotiators.[8]

Unfortunately, the alternative courses of action open to the British authorities, such as those suggested earlier by Sir Ralph Stevenson, had failed to elicit any response from the higher echelons of the Communist movement before Kerans was asked to attend another meeting on Silver Island with Kang. Petty Officer Justin McCarthy, who was actually in charge of the ship's stores, accompanied Kerans and the trusty Leo when they left the ship at 10:35 A.M. on Sunday 12 June to board a ferry for the 3-mile journey upstream. Unlike the last interview, this one was a far more harmonious and productive meeting, resulting in an agreement being reached on further provisioning of the ship from local sources. On the major questions, both men avoided a confrontational approach; Kerans talked airily of the matter being discussed at a more senior level in Nanking and Peking, a claim that Kang did not immediately refute. Cautious, as always, he merely said he would check on what, if anything, was going on in both places. Whether or not his more considerate and less obdurate mood was dictated by the retinue of propaganda and press corps present at this meeting was something about which Kerans did not bother to speculate. He saw it as being too good an opportunity to miss and used the occasion to present a formal request for the delivery of mail and urgent medical supplies to the *Amethyst* by a jeep and trailer from the British consulate in Shanghai. Kang seemed to hint that the necessary clearance for such a journey would be made within a short while, and on this relatively cordial and helpful note the interview ended.[9]

After the relative success of this meeting, Captain Donaldson, the British naval attaché in Nanking, made a swift application to the local Communist authorities for permission to transfer the 50 tons of Admiralty boiler fuel he had found in the city to the *Amethyst*. This request was turned down on a bureaucratic technicality. Apparently, the request first had to be placed with the Chinkiang headquarters of the PLA, and only if an agreement was forthcoming from this source could the local Communist officials in Nanking issue the permit for the transfer of the fuel.[10] This refusal was unfortunate, for the oil supply aboard the *Amethyst* was becoming more critically depleted with each passing day. As she was using more than 2 tons on a daily basis, Kerans decided to implement more drastic economies to conserve what fuel he had. By 18 June, his fuel stocks had fallen to 91.8 tons.[11] This level was so low that conserving fuel by imposing fairly drastic economies would not give him much more than four to six weeks before his frigate became helplessly immobile.

Brind was not pleased by this latest twist in the *Amethyst* saga, particularly because it came at a time when the other diplomatic initiatives that had been attempted from Nanking and London were looking distinctly careworn and incapable of being successful. Observing that the talks over safe conduct were evidently stalled, he became more concerned than ever about the need to replenish the ship with fuel and stores and felt that it should take precedence over all other considerations at this stage. He suggested to Donaldson that a suitable merchant ship could be hired in Hong Kong to take these essential items up the Yangtze to where the *Amethyst* lay at anchor. All that was needed to put this operation into effect would be an official clearance from the Communist authorities. Once again, however, that was likely to be the most difficult part of the plan to implement.[12]

Brind's annoyance with Kang and the deadlocked state of the discussions over the fate of the *Amethyst* spilled over into an official message, which Kerans received on Tuesday 14 June and which he was instructed to deliver to the political commissioner. It did not pull any punches and made it clear that if Kang persisted in questioning Brind's integrity, the admiral would feel perfectly justified in refusing to discuss matters with him any longer. Kerans tactfully decided to exercise a certain editorial supervision and not pass on this aide-mémoire in its entirety to the PLA at this point lest it further damage his position in the eyes of the Communists.[13]

A day later, the next and stormiest meeting thus far took place between Kerans and Kang in the village nearest to the *Amethyst*. It began with a harshly worded harangue from Kang, who was seeking to defend his status as the sole authorized representative of the PLA in dealing with the Yangtze incident. His outburst broadened into an attack on Brind's attitude to the talks and much else besides. Kerans felt that the time for careful diplomacy was over and disclosed the full contents of Brind's message, threatening a withdrawal from the talks. Kang was evidently perplexed by this new and surprising development. Kerans later described him as being "visibly shaken."[14] Regaining the initiative, the captain of the *Amethyst* suggested that a way out of the impasse would be either to move the talks elsewhere, preferably to Nanking, or to bring Captain Donaldson down to the ship to continue them as the representative of the British fleet in the Far East. Kang took a long time to respond to this unwelcome change in the way the session had been going, but in the end he agreed that this suggestion would be acceptable if Donaldson appeared in naval uniform and did not use his attaché status in the ensuing talks. Kang also agreed that Donaldson could be accompanied by an interpreter of his own choice, a job for which Kerans had Edward Youde very much in mind.[15]

While Brind was still in the throes of deciding formally in favor of Donaldson, Kerans was called for another meeting with Kang. Fortunately the meeting on Saturday 18 June was mercifully brief and consisted largely of the political commissioner asking whether Brind had actually nominated a representative for the purpose of settling the Yangtze incident. He was told that the matter was still under consideration and that no final decision had yet been made. Although strictly correct, this comment was not particularly helpful. While the Communists were kept guessing on this score, the British soon found that their adversaries were also adept at employing similar tactics; Kerans learned, for instance, that permission had not been granted for the transit of mail from Shanghai and that a further delay was anticipated.[17]

Once again the ship's log indicates that although very little may have been happening aboard the *Amethyst*, the river was an extremely busy place with fairly constant traffic in both directions as tugs, junks, steamers, ferries, and other assorted craft—some carrying civilians, others with military, and still more laden with goods—plied up and down the Yangtze. Sunday passed uneventfully, and Monday appeared to be going in the same dreary way until a sampan with several PLA officers came alongside at 3:00 P.M. with an invitation for Kerans to meet General Yuan at his headquarters in Chinkiang.[18]

Flanked by Petty Officer Venton and Sam Leo, the captain of the *Amethyst* left his ship in reasonable spirits.

After being ushered into the large dining-cum-anteroom set aside for these discussions, certain formalities had to be observed before the meeting could start officially: each person would be given a hot towel and a cup of Chinese tea, and only after the towels had been discarded and the tea drunk would the members of the two delegations shake hands and begin to take up their respective positions on either side of a large, oblong-shaped wooden table, the head of which was reserved for General Yuan.[19] Unfortunately, whatever optimism the members of the *Amethyst*'s delegation may have felt initially about this meeting soon faded as Yuan rapidly assumed the familiar, repetitive interrogation of Kerans that Kang had adopted with such relish many times in the recent past. As the official report noted,

> He asked why the British Authorities sent "AMETHYST" to relieve "CONSORT" at Nanking when it must have been realised that the City was about to fall. He backed his statement by quoting extracts from Associated Press reports of repeated crossings and bombardments between 19th April and 22nd April in the Chinkiang Area. I quickly explained that these were not evidence and as far as I was concerned totally incorrect having been ashore in the vicinity of alleged Communist held areas the entire night of 21st/22nd April. The question of press evidence was never again mentioned. He then wanted to know why "LONDON," "BLACK SWAN" and "CONSORT" were sent into his area and continued to infringe Chinese sovereignty. Humanitarian role of our warships to save life in "AMETHYST" was stressed and that this was directly attributable to the hasty attitude of the C.P.L.A. in attempting to destroy one of H.M. Ships on a peaceful mission. The General was indignant that the Commander in Chief, Far East Station should say that continued detention of "AMETHYST" would cause "unfortunate complications" and considered this intimidation of the C.P.L.A. and that the people of China were "indignant" of the incidents. It was pointed out that the fact that we did not wish to negotiate at Chinkiang and that continued requests for "AMETHYST's" safe conduct had been made, showed desire on our side to evade responsibility. He stated quite definitely that nothing had taken place in Nanking regarding settlement of the case. I was told that Kang had been unable to settle anything with myself and that I had prevaricated and delayed everything.[20]

Insisting that he was empowered by the Communist authorities to settle the *Amethyst* case, General Yuan went on to imply that a final settlement could only be reached if the British changed their attitude and became more cooperative. He urged Admiral Brind, therefore, to make a swift decision about who was to represent the Royal Navy in these talks. If it was to be Captain

Donaldson, a formal request would have to be made to the PLA Chinkiang headquarters before any decision could be made on whether or not his presence at the discussions was acceptable to the Communists. Yuan felt that if Brind stopped stalling and recognized that what had taken place in April was an unauthorized intrusion and infringement of Chinese territorial waters by British vessels, the way would be clear for an early end to the present crisis. He intimated, for instance, that if the British showed a real willingness to bring the incident to a close, it was conceivable that the *Amethyst* might be released even before questions of an apology and compensation had been addressed. Yuan ended by assuring Kerans that he personally regretted that the ship's company had been forced to endure a long spell of inactivity on the Yangtze and wished that the outstanding differences between the two sides could be resolved quickly so that the *Amethyst* might be granted her freedom and a safe passage downriver to Shanghai.[21] Summing up his views on the meeting for Brind's benefit, Kerans signaled that although the tone was reasonably friendly, the frustration and exasperation of the Communists were very evident.[22]

Two days passed before Kerans was again summoned to meet the general in Chinkiang. By this time he had received another message from Brind to pass on to Yuan, which requested that a travel permit be granted to a merchant ship bringing replenishment stores for the *Amethyst* from Hong Kong. Kerans also sought Yuan's approval for the passage to the ship of twenty cases of mail.[23]

Unfortunately, the meeting, which had been convened late in the afternoon to discuss these and other items, began on a disappointing note with Yuan rejecting Brind's request on the basis that such an operation would be both improper and an infringement of Chinese territorial waters. Kerans tried his best to counter Yuan's argument by pointing out that the Yangtze had been declared open to shipping, and that consequently the passage of a ship upstream from Shanghai could hardly be seen as a violation of Chinese sovereign rights. His defense of Brind's proposal, however, came to nought.[24] One of the contributory reasons for Yuan's opposition to the scheme may have stemmed from the increasing disruption to both river and coastal traffic as a result of the imposition of a Nationalist blockade of Chinese territorial waters from 18 June onward.[25]

Yuan went on to ask whether the views he had expressed on Monday 20 June had been passed on to Brind and stressed his wish for an exchange of notes with the admiral to resolve the crisis once and for all. This statement quite naturally led him to repeat what he had said two days earlier about the British being ready to admit that one of their warships had intruded indiscreetly into the PLA frontier area without having secured any clearance papers beforehand. He also suggested that the British should give the Communists an assurance that talks to resolve the issue finally would proceed on a mutually acceptable date in the future. If the British accepted these two suggestions, the general confirmed that he would agree to the release of the *Amethyst*. He was emphatic, however, that should the British naval authorities engage in further intransigence, it was highly likely that it would be achieved at the expense of damaged business relations with the Chinese.

Although Yuan looked forward to a swift and conclusive ending to these discussions, he no longer wished to entertain Captain Donaldson's candidacy as the British representative. No reasons were given for his change of heart, but he now appeared to be anxious for Kerans to be nominated as the bona fide plenipotentiary. Significantly, perhaps, the general had not mentioned the emotive term *invasion* nor indeed the subject of an apology and the payment of compensation before the release of the *Amethyst* could be approved. Kerans saw this as a good sign, a feeling heightened by Yuan's agreement that the overdue mail should be forwarded to the *Amethyst*'s crew without delay.[26]

There was little doubt that the British delegation, consisting of Williams, the engine room artificer, Leo, and Kerans, felt that the possibility was growing of an early release for the *Amethyst* and that it might take place before a final settlement with the Communists had been reached on the Yangtze incident. Such an event would be timely because life on board was going from bad to worse. To conserve fuel, which was expected to fall to 70 tons by the end of the month, all power was shut down in the ship for up to fifty-four hours at a time.[27] This policy had some immediate repercussions. At 6:30 A.M. on Thursday 23 June, for example, the temperature in the mess reached 86 degrees Fahrenheit.[28] As long as the crew were excited about the prospect of gaining their freedom, the harsh conditions on board could be endured with a reasonably good grace. Once those hopes were dashed, however, the frustration of all on board began mounting at a perceptible rate.

Although His Majesty's Government in London had been anxious to assist the crew of the *Amethyst* from the outset of the crisis, its diplomatic support had hitherto been relatively inadequate. Despite the fact that the government had been kept up-to-date on the latest developments in the case, and significant reports from China went beyond the departmental level to the cabinet and other top-level bodies for review and action, little practical effect had resulted from this pooling of information. By late June, however, matters had reached such a deadlocked state that it seemed likely the government might soon have to begin playing a greater role in finding a solution to the Yangtze incident. In his report to Brind of 22 June, Kerans suggested that semantic rather than factual differences now seemed to lie at the heart of the dispute. In such a sensitive situation, an agreement on what words would be used to compose a settlement between the two sides would definitely need governmental approval from London.[29]

Upon hearing the latest Chinese demand expressed by Yuan at his last meeting with Kerans and not thinking it excessive, Clement Attlee, the British prime minister, was inclined to prepare a statement worded along the lines of what the general had suggested so that the *Amethyst* could be set free. Not every minister was prepared to go quite that far, however, as Viscount Hall, the first lord of the Admiralty, discovered when he tried to get Ernest Bevin's support for surrendering some ground on this point. Indeed the foreign secretary made it plain that he did not like the word *indiscreetly* and much preferred *unfortunately*.[30] When the matter was referred to the cabinet on 23 June, the collective wish of the members was that this opportunity to save the *Amethyst* should not be lost as a result of an unwillingness to use some words rather than others. It was decided, therefore, that if Yuan insisted upon his formula, the British would have to accept it in the last resort, but if a certain flexibility was apparent, then the commander in chief might insert *unfortunately entered into* as opposed to *intruded indiscreetly* in the final exchange of notes between the two sides.[31]

Back on the Yangtze, life on the *Amethyst* improved immeasurably for a short time when Leo and a member of the mess returned from the Chinkiang post office on Friday 24 June with three bags of overseas mail that had been dispatched from Shanghai. Even the suspicion that the mail had been tampered with failed to dampen the spirits of those who received letters from home for the first time in more than two months. Although outdated, the mail still represented a tangible link with the outside world and a further reassuring sign that the men of the *Amethyst* had not been forgotten by those beyond the shores of the Yangtze. Coupled to the sending and receiving of personal telegrams, the arrival of these letters boosted morale and offered hope of a future after detention.[32]

While some temporary emotional relief was thus afforded to the men of the frigate, the continuing debate about the precise wording for any final communiqué went on without pause. After informing Yuan that he was passing his request to higher authority, Admiral Brind finally suggested on 25 June another version of the proposed communiqué that was intended for General Yuan. This message was finally sent ashore with Leo on Tuesday 28 June as soon as the bad weather in the Yangtze area had relented sufficiently for the interpreter to get back on board ship from his previous visit to Chinkiang three days before.[33]

Fortunately Leo could undertake the journey because Kerans was incapable of taking the letter himself. He had succumbed to an extremely painful attack of fibrositis, which was caused, he thought, by living for such a long time in the heat and humidity of a Yangtze summer and aggravated by a ship that offered no satisfactory relief from the oppressive temperature or dampness.[34] Leo stoically undertook the mission, returning ashore to the local garrison before lunch bearing the revised final draft of Brind's note for delivery to General Yuan in Chinkiang. It boldly stated:

> I. I am very glad to hear that you are prepared to grant a safe passage down the Yangtze River for H.M.S. "Amethyst," and I formally ask that this may be given.
> II. I recognise that H.M.S. "Amethyst" entered The China People's Liberation Army's Frontier Zone without the concurrence of the Command of the China People's Liberation Army.
> III. I am sure that you will share my very deep regret at the casualties caused on both sides.
> IV. This message is without prejudice to subsequent negotiations which will take place later by our superior authorities. I give you my assurance that there will be no objections by the British side to these negotiations taking place.[35]

Leo returned to the *Amethyst* at lunchtime with the news that a meeting to discuss the terms of Brind's note would not be held before the end of the month. This was good news for the captain because he was clearly in no condition to conduct any difficult negotiations from his sickbed.[36]

When Captain Tai, the local garrison commander, arrived alongside the *Amethyst* shortly after 9:00 A.M. on Thursday 30 June, he brought with him news that the request for the delivery of approximately 60 tons of Admiralty boiler fuel from Nanking had finally been granted by the PLA. He also indicated from a letter he had received from Kang that any further discussion of the points raised in Brind's note would probably be deferred for more than a week because of the preparations being made locally for the staging of a PLA victory celebration. In fact, the local garrison commander went on to suggest that further talks on the precise wording of a public statement on the original incident might take a fortnight before they could be satisfactorily resolved.[37]

When the commander in chief heard of this further postponement, he saw it as a devious ploy to put additional pressure upon Kerans. As Brind commented in a message to Donaldson,

> I think this is another trick on Kerans and feel he is nearing the end of his tether, the Communists know it and are playing with him. It seems that Donaldson should go to *Amethyst* to bring matters to a head and complete present negotiations.[38]

In Brind's opinion, the Communists were opposed to Donaldson conducting the talks because he would be fresh, unlike Kerans who was far from well and under extreme pressure. This fact was of considerable importance given the possibility that disputes over the wording of any communiqué would be likely to delay matters for some time to come.[39]

Leo, for example, had sensed from his discussions with the Communists that they intended to drive a hard bargain and were fully prepared to engage in a long series of discussions with the British until they had gained their objective. He had mentioned these suspicions to Kerans once he had rejoined the ship on 28 June. From his conversations with some of the lower-level military personnel, Leo had gauged that the PLA wished to force the British into admitting publicly that they had committed an indiscretion in sending their ships up and down the Yangtze without securing approval from the Communist authorities beforehand, and that anything less than such an admission would be unacceptable to Kang and could easily result in delaying the *Amethyst*'s release still further.[40]

Although he recognized the semantic problems inherent in fashioning some form of diplomatic settlement in this case, Brind still wished to avoid the use of any emotive adverb in a final statement on the Yangtze incident. He felt that if using one could not be avoided, either *unfortunately*, *imprudently*, or *indiscreetly* might be considered, in that order.[41] Although he urged Kerans not to get downhearted and to continue pressing for permission to be granted for a replenishment ship to bring much-needed supplies to the *Amethyst*, Brind was aware of the extreme pressure on the captain of the frigate. In a message to him on 2 July, the admiral stated:

> It is increasingly clear that Kang is deliberately attacking you personally with typical technique of creating suspense to get you down. This delay after hopeful situation supports this (sic) they may have read some of our plain language signals and think we are weakening our wording which we certainly are not. Do not worry too much about prejudicing your position. The exercise of impatience on your part appears to have been salutary in the past. Communists certainly have anxieties too.[42]

It was a good deal easier to say these things from the comfort of his spacious quarters on HMS *Alert* than it would have been if he had been occupying a cabin on the foul-smelling, inhospitable, disease-ridden, and rat-infested *Amethyst*. As if to prove the point, Kerans addressed a message to Brind that outlined the problem of food supplies on board ship.

> Fresh meat will be gone before end of month. Basic items will last to early August. Intend reducing to half rations shortly. Have included all N.A.A.F.I. stocks in estimates.[43]

Misfortune seemed to dog the crew at this time. Although the small emergency supplies of medicine, mosquito nets, and *Jen Min Piao* had arrived on 1 July with Mr. Khoong—the assistant naval attaché's interpreter at the consulate in Shanghai—the navigational charts of the lower Yangtze, which had been in the consignment, had been confiscated by the local garrison commander on the specious ground that they were regarded as classified material.[44] Captain Tai, who had appeared well-disposed toward Kerans in the past, was unmoved by Khoong's claim that these charts could hardly be described as secret when they were on open sale in a shop in Shanghai. Tai maintained the defense that because they had been issued by the KMT government, they were restricted.[45]

Kerans felt sufficiently vexed by this latest move that he dispatched another aide-mémoire to General Yuan on 3 July asking for an explanation of Tai's conduct and requesting further information about the reason for the prolonged delay in granting permission for the *Amethyst* and her crew to leave the Yangtze and rejoin the rest of the fleet on the British Far East Station. His description of the crew weakening under the strain of living for so long as virtual hostages on the river in a boat that was no longer habitable mirrored his own feelings most accurately. It was already becoming evident that both his health and morale were being undermined by this miserable experience.[46]

Excitement of an unwelcome kind jolted the crew out of the sweaty torpor of their lives during the night of 1–2 July when the *Amethyst* was nearly run down by two large merchant ships. Lit only by the flickering flame of a single candle set in a rudimentary lantern, the *Amethyst* was barely discernible in the dark when all power on the ship had been cut off for economic reasons. It was obvious that neither merchant vessel had detected her position in the river, and the fact that both missed ramming her was due purely to luck. Such a close brush with fate alerted Kerans and the rest on board to the inadequacy of the existing arrangements and the fact that passage on the Yangtze was now being officially encouraged at night. This situation opened up the intriguing possibility that it was now feasible to steam past Kiangyin without confronting insuperable odds.[47]

Later that Saturday (2 July), Kerans tuned the ship's wireless into a BBC news analysis program relayed from Radio Ceylon, which was devoted to the theme of "Communists in China." It mentioned the *Amethyst* and intimated that the issue of who or what caused the naval battle on the Yangtze in April had not yet been taken up at the highest levels by either government. Despite this unsatisfactory message, Kerans derived some encouragement from the fact that the ship's plight was being discussed openly. In the past there had been little mention of her confinement on the Yangtze.[48]

While Kerans waited for news from the Communists on the next stage of the negotiations, he endeavored to do something about the diminishing stores on board.[49] Replenishment was desperately needed, and yet he had been told that the PLA were not interested in dealing with anyone from the British consulate in Shanghai over this matter and that the best thing he could do was to nominate a businessman from the city who could be held responsible for obtaining and supplying the stores for the ship. A letter of authorization to H. E. Aiers, the secretary of the British Chamber of Commerce in Shanghai, was duly drawn up and taken ashore on 3 July by Leo. It gave Aiers authority to spend funds on behalf of the *Amethyst* and assume responsibility for getting the consignment intact from the city to the ship.[50]

When Leo returned on 4 July, he brought news that Kang was in Nanking and that the next stage of the negotiations was likely to be delayed until at least 8 July.[51] Kerans could do little but wait for the days to pass. By this time, however, the frustration of those on board was beginning to show. Time dragged by as if in slow motion, and both officers and men found their confinement more chafing as the days went by. It was by now a grim business living on board the HMS *Amethyst*.

14. Stalemate

OOD NEWS soon came from an unexpected source. In
the middle of Tuesday afternoon (5 July) the old, familiar sampan that had been provided for use by the ship's
company from the outset returned from the shore bringing Leo and a contractor out to the ship. Leo told the captain that Kang had returned from Nanking
unexpectedly and wished to see him forthwith. After quickly drafting a
written request for an additional interpreter and naming Edward Youde as the
man he wished to have on board to help with the future negotiations, Kerans
hurriedly selected Leading Seaman Frank and the somewhat travel weary Leo
to go ashore with him.[1]

His meeting with the political commissioner took place in the village
opposite where the frigate lay at anchor. It was notable for Kang's refusal to
accept the latest British version of what had actually happened on the Yangtze
back in April. He insisted that Brind make a number of changes to the wording
of his version of the final communiqué before the Communists would agree to
accept the document, let alone publish it. Kerans's struggle to keep the note as
neutral as possible was only partly successful. Kang demanded that the following paragraph be accepted in toto without further revision.

> I recognise that H.M.S. AMETHYST and the other three British warships
> involved in the incident, infringed into China's national river and the C.P.L.A.
> frontier zone, without the permission of the C.P.L.A. being basic fault repeti-
> tion fault on the part of the British side, regarding this matter.[2]

Despite making it clear that he could not commit his commander in chief in
advance, Kerans was told that Brind's acceptance of this vital part of the
explanatory statement was necessary without delay. After a heated exchange

between the two principal negotiators, it was agreed that Brind's authorization for Kerans to sign the document might be signaled from Japan where the
admiral was currently off station. Apart from this hopeful sign of progress,
Kang suggested it was likely that after an agreement had been signed the
Amethyst would be free to move downriver unhindered by the Communist
military forces ranged along the riverbank. Mention was also made in passing
to Leo that a final agreement might take a further week to arrange.[3]

This meeting underlined the need for Youde's presence on board to help
with technical interpreting. Sincere and hard working though he was, Leo did
not possess the linguistic fluency to translate extremely sensitive diplomatic
language from English into Chinese, as was required by the Communists for
the final communiqué. Although he trusted Leo, Kerans was concerned that
subtle nuances in language would somehow be lost on the translator, and his
choice of words could be interpreted ambiguously to the detriment of the
British cause.[4] In his message to Brind, Kerans described the meeting as "fairly
amicable but VITRIOLIC in parts." His concern for the most appropriate
diplomatic terminology was evident in the rest of his message to the commander in chief: "I only hope I have done right. I am not happy about word
INFRINGED, but this was the best I could do after an hour's discussion on
deletion of word INVADED."[5]

Selecting the correct language to settle a long-running and highly contentious dispute such as the Yangtze incident was a matter of the utmost importance involving the government in London, as well as the diplomatic and naval
personnel in China. A. V. Alexander, the minister of defense, made it clear that
he was resolutely opposed to anything stating that the British had made a basic
error in sending the *Amethyst* up the Yangtze in April. He insisted that
whatever wording was finally chosen, care would have to be taken not to give
too much away.[6] This point was echoed by Ernest Bevin, the secretary of state
for foreign affairs, in a dispatch to the British ambassador in Nanking on 6 July.

> I cannot accept any phraseology which involves our conceding that we were in
> the wrong . . . If we show willingness to make concessions which jeopardise our
> whole position in the matter even before actual negotiations begin, the Com-
> munists will score such a triumph (which will no doubt be widely publicised)
> that we may never recover from this initial step.[7]

Brind was equally determined to reject as "dishonourable and callously inhu-
mane" any changes made by the Communists to the basic formula that he had
proposed to General Yuan on 22 June. He informed Kerans that the text which
Kang had proposed on 5 July was quite unacceptable and that he should do

nothing about this message before he received further instructions from the commander in chief and until Youde was on board the frigate.[8] Brind was so incensed by what he saw as a calculated move to prevaricate by the Communists that he sent off an indignant note to Yuan, mincing few words.

In view of the sympathy expressed by you for the hardships suffered by those in "Amethyst," I am not only disappointed but extremely angry at the way her ship's company is being treated. The British fought alongside the Chinese during the War and played a large part in defeating Japan. British officers and men in H.M.S. "Amethyst" are now being treated worse than the Japanese treated their prisoners-of-war. Every difficulty and delay is being placed in the way of replenishing with stores and provisions. Some have even been confiscated.[9]

Brind's anger at the Communists for deliberately delaying the settlement of the affair was exacerbated by the amateurish way in which they had handled the case of Lieutenant Geoffrey Weston. By early July, Weston had recovered from the serious injuries that he had sustained on 20 April. Once he had been pronounced fit, he was given 24 hours notice by the local police authorities in Shanghai to leave the city and return to the *Amethyst*. Although Weston was strong enough to make the train journey to Chinkiang, the reception he found when he got there at dawn on Friday 8 July was far from friendly or helpful. After much squabbling, the local Communist party officials, claiming they knew nothing of this man, sent him back on a freight train to Shanghai some hours later.[10] Informed of these events by Leo, who had been sent ashore to wait for Weston at the railway station, Kerans feared that any embarrassment caused to the Communists by this latest event would have fairly immediate repercussions. He was right. It did.

Youde soon found himself the focus of official Communist displeasure and was denied an exit permit to leave Nanking to join the *Amethyst*. When this decision, which overturned an earlier oral statement to the contrary, was coupled with a delay in the delivery of the Admiralty fuel from Nanking, Kerans suspected that Kang had successfully exacted almost immediate revenge for the Weston incident.[11] Displaying the pent-up anger of one who had had more than his share of ill luck, he reeled off a blunt message to the political commissioner about the inexplicable action of the Chinkiang PLA in sending the unfortunate Lieutenant Weston back to Shanghai from whence he had been officially dismissed only hours before.[12]

Brind, irritated by the failure to obtain clearance for the supply ship from Shanghai to make the journey upriver to the *Amethyst* and annoyed by the bureaucratic difficulties encountered by Youde, sent a consolatory note to Kerans.

> I greatly sympathise with you in your feelings of frustration and disappointment which is of course the aim of Kang's tactics to undermine you. You are all putting up a splendid stand which is much admired on all sides.[13]

For much of Saturday 9 July, life was fairly bleak for those on board the *Amethyst*. All power in the ship had been cut off since 1:00 P.M. on the previous day and would not be restored until the middle of the afternoon nearly 27 hours later. Radical economies had managed to reduce the normal daily intake of fuel to 1 ton, but with stocks at 65 tons, the ship could not last without additional supplies for more than two to three weeks. After that time, she would reach the dire position of not having sufficient oil to make the passage downriver unaided, even if she was eventually granted a safe-conduct pass to do so.[14] As the crew languished in the fetid humidity of a midsummer evening, they were alerted to the sight and then sound of what might euphemistically be described as an oil lighter coming alongside shortly after 8:00 P.M. It says much for the plight of the men on board the *Amethyst* that they greeted with unreserved enthusiasm the arrival of what turned out to be the delayed consignment of 54 tons of Admiralty boiler fuel from Nanking.[15] Some undoubtedly saw this as a sign or omen that their situation might soon change for the better. Therefore, the men had no qualms about being up before 5:00 A.M. on Sunday morning (10 July) to begin transferring the 294 drums of furnace fuel from the junk to the ship so they could be poured into the tanks on the port side of the *Amethyst* as quickly as possible. The entire operation was graced with fine weather and was completed without undue complications in a little less than eleven hours.[16] Fortunately, the new supply had arrived just in time, for within a few hours further demands would be made upon the fuel stocks. This situation arose because the last valve on the type 60 WT set broke down, ensuring that in the future additional fuel would be required to generate sufficient power for the transmission of all messages from the ship to Nanking and the Far East Station.[17]

While the crew were laboring hard at getting the oil on board, Leo was sent ashore to discover whether a meeting was likely to be held with a representative of the PLA in the near future. He returned with the news that Kang had ruled out any meeting until he received authorization from Brind for Kerans to discuss the details of a final communiqué with the Communists and to sign his name to that document.[18] After apprising his commander in chief of this latest development and receiving the appropriate message of authorization in reply,

Kerans was given further instructions by Admiral Brind on what he should discuss with General Yuan at their next meeting.[19] Before he was able to follow these instructions, another aide-mémoire from Brind arrived and was decoded. This latest message went some way toward meeting the Communists' demands for the wording of the final statement. Brind's latest message for Yuan was short and to the point.

> I am very glad that you are prepared to grant a safe passage down the Yangtze River for H.M.S. "Amethyst," and I formally ask that this may be given.
>
> I recognise that the entry of H.M.S. "Amethyst" into the Frontier Zone without the concurrence of the China People's Liberation Army caused misunderstanding.
>
> This message is without prejudice to any investigation or negotiations which may be instituted later by our superior authorities, and I assure you that there will be no objections on the British side to discussing any aspect of the Yangtze incident.[20]

After receiving confirmation that the next meeting with the Communists would be held in Chinkiang on the following day, Kerans prepared a typed agenda and two pages of notes for what he presumed would be the final and most decisive session of the many he had already endured with Colonel Kang.[21] Lieutenant Strain, Leo, and the captain left the ship at about 2:30 P.M. on Monday 11 July and made their way to the headquarters of the local PLA regiment.

Despite his reasonably elaborate preparations, Kerans discovered that whatever initiative he had hoped to wield in this interview was seized from the outset by a hostile adversary. Kang opened the meeting with a personal broadside against the naval officer lasting some forty minutes, castigating Kerans for not only his interference in the Weston case but also his wretched failures in many other areas. Kerans's tactical plan for this meeting was undermined to a large extent by this sustained attack, so that, hard though he tried, he was never able to make the slightest impression upon the political commissioner for the rest of what proved to be a marathon session of three to four hours.[22] It was hardly surprising, given the acrimonious beginning, that the interview degenerated into a tetchy verbal brawl from which Kerans emerged somewhat the worse for wear. During this most unsatisfactory and negative series of exchanges, Kerans was told the following: he could no longer see General Yuan unless he made a formal application in writing in advance; his letter of authorization was rejected for failing to have Brind's signature upon it; the revised aide-mémoire he brandished and upon which he staked so much was refused because the word *recognise* in the second paragraph could not be construed as a synonym for *admit*, which was the only word the Communists were prepared to accept in the final communiqué; and no mention was made of *Consort, Black Swan,* and *London* in the third and final paragraph contrary to the wishes of the PLA.[23]

Kang's refusal to replenish the *Amethyst* with much-needed stores and his threat to destroy the ship if any attempt was made to move her, hardly endeared him to the British. Relations between them reached their nadir when it became unlikely that either Youde would be allowed to join the *Amethyst* or that a safe-conduct pass would be provided for the frigate before the entire affair had been settled.[24] Under the circumstances, it must have been difficult for Kerans not to believe that the *Amethyst* and her crew had become mere pawns in a game of diplomacy where the rules kept changing to their detriment. If this impression was an accurate reflection of the existing state of affairs, it was also evident that things were soon likely to get worse for everyone on board. This feeling had been intensified by the political commissioner's domineering and aggressive attitude. Kang seemed more determined than ever to cap his negotiating efforts by achieving what his political masters might regard as a brilliant political success against the British over the Yangtze incident.

Kerans's stoicism under duress was evidently being sorely tested, and his decision to go on half rations beginning the following day (12 July) showed his determination to resist whatever pressure the Communists would put on the crew of the *Amethyst* in the future.[25] His report of the latest meeting with Kang disturbed those who read it in Whitehall and on the Far East Station. Feeling that the signs of strain were beginning to show on the former assistant naval attaché, the Admiralty was now willing to allow Admiral Brind to go to the area and try to obtain a safe-conduct pass for the frigate from General Yuan. According to the Admiralty's instructions to the commander in chief, if this proved to be impossible for any reason, he ought to insist on securing an interview with Mao Tse-tung to resolve the dispute once and for all at the highest level.

> Throughout the greater part of negotiations Kerans has been obliged to depend upon Kang as intermediary between himself and the General. As you suggest, it is obvious that Kang, as the Battery Commander, is doing everything in his power to colour his reports and to keep negotiations in his own hands. In these circumstances you will no doubt refuse to have any dealings with Kang and you should emphasize to the General Kang's very unsatisfactory conduct. You may think it advisable to threaten both the General and Mao with publicity.[26]

This pronouncement said more about the ignorance of the Admiralty in dealing with the Communists than anything else. Brind was in no position to demand an interview with anyone, least of all Mao. Even if he demanded one, there was little chance of it being granted. The era of the British Raj was over; imperialism had had its day. It was, therefore, unrealistic of the Admiralty to expect the Communists to agree instantly just because the British commander in chief expected a resolution to the long-running dispute and would give them a bad press if they did not. In the past the Communists had not been unduly troubled by what the western media said about the incident on the Yangtze, so it was doubtful whether they would be extremely worried about what it would say in the future on this subject.

Brind's reaction to Kerans's interview with Kang on 11 July was less testy; he described it as disappointing but not hopeless. As far as the commander in chief was concerned, the important point about the meeting was General Yuan's absence from it.

> Kang is clearly playing his game of attrition and is entirely untrustworthy. He has several times changed his grounds. Do not have anything more to do with him except pass a message.[27]

Unfortunately, Kerans had come to the conclusion that Kang may not have been passing on Brind's notes and messages to Yuan, or if he had, it was only after opening and reading them first himself.[28] This accusation prompted Brind to review the security arrangements for passing information between the Far East Station and the *Amethyst*. Brind asked Kerans whether Kang had seen his latest aide-mémoire dated 10 July before the meeting on the next day.

> Did he seem to know the contents or be unusually quick in appreciating it? If so it is an indication he is reading our signals. So far I have not proof of this but only strong suspicions, but there may be a lag of a day or two. . . .
>
> We must be very careful now our signals do not arrive in time only saying in plain language what we do not mind KANG hearing. This code is very insecure. You can rely on me to appreciate your situation for we are all constantly putting ourselves in your shoes.[29]

Kerans made it clear that Kang had not seen the admiral's note before the meeting took place. Recalling his hostile encounter with the political commissioner, Kerans remarked that their interview had been interrupted several times by Communist officials entering the room with messages for Kang. He admitted that he had not the faintest clue whether these interruptions had anything to do with the *Amethyst*. He felt, however, that it was just conceivable these messages might have been intercepts of Brind's signals to the frigate or perhaps a series of instructions from an unseen source, such as General Yuan, who might have been lurking nearby, fully conversant with what was going on in the room and orchestrating the tactics to be used by Kang in conducting these negotiations.[30] Probably neither of these imaginative explanations was correct. Nonetheless, there were a few disturbing indications that the Chinese were now able to read at least some of the messages which passed between the Far East Station and the ship. Kang's intimate knowledge of the Weston affair and the supply question were advanced by Kerans as possible evidence that this was the case. Again, the proof is inconclusive and circumstantial. Whether or not the interruptions were designed to put more psychological pressure upon the British representatives, the captain of the *Amethyst* was left with the uncomfortable suspicion that the secrecy of his communications with the outside world could no longer be assured. This realization, although not much of a shock to those, such as French, the telegraphist, who knew they had been managing without the top-secret code and cypher books from the beginning of the crisis on the Yangtze, still rankled.[31] It also meant that unless a new code could be devised and used by the ship and those on the Far East Station without the Communists recognizing what the British were doing, the risk of sending top secret information to and from the *Amethyst* was just too great to do so. Moreover, trying to disguise it in innocent-sounding messages could be as misunderstood by the recipient as by the Communist officials the sender hoped to fool. An instance of this confusion occurred even before Kerans met Kang on 11 July.

According to the captain's official report, which he submitted some weeks later, he had been sufficiently anxious about the *Amethyst*'s unfavorable situation that he had thought about the possibility of attempting to escape ever since he had joined the ship in April. He had come to the conclusion that the only effective way to succeed in such a hazardous undertaking might be to launch his escape bid when the weather conditions were at their worst—as they were expected to be in the typhoon season. At this time of the year, the local PLA authorities would not expect any heroics from the British warship or her crew and, therefore, might be lulled into a false sense of security. If they became less vigilant than usual, they would unwittingly provide the opportunity for the frigate to mount an escape from her position on the Yangtze. Kerans knew that the exceptionally heavy rainfall that precedes, accompanies, and follows the path of a typhoon was bound to obscure visibility on the river. Therefore, if he dared to release the *Amethyst* during part of a storm, it would not only take the Communist authorities by surprise, but it would also make it difficult for the PLA gun crews to locate, let alone destroy, her as she made her way at speed down the Yangtze toward the freedom of the open sea. His report continues.

> Having no radar, risk of being wrecked was very great but in the circumstances would have to be accepted. Movement of shipping by night indicated that in fair weather navigational hazards would not be insuperable. Bearing all the above in mind I made my signal in plain language, D.T.G. 071317Z July to the Commander-in-Chief only, as follows:—"Grateful your advice please on my actions if menaced by a Typhoon. Have informed General on several occasions of this possible danger in order to hasten matters."[32]

Unaware of what Kerans was plotting, Brind began to wonder whether the strain on him might be getting too great. Nonetheless, the sheer banality of the message and the fact that the answer was obvious to any experienced sailor suggested that something odd was happening aboard the frigate. If Kerans was planning to escape, Brind did not wish to discourage him from doing so. Knowing that plain language signals were bound to be read by the Communists, the admiral attempted to hide his message of support for an escape bid in two apparently innocuous sentences. He hid it too well. Unfortunately his message became as abstruse as Kerans's original effort had been ambiguous.

> Your 071317. Typhoons are unlikely to reach you in serious strength and you are in good holding ground, the golden rule of making an offing and taking plenty of sea room applies particularly. We all listened to your special Broadcast last Sunday. I hope you heard it alright and that another will not (R) not be necessary.[33]

Kerans was understandably confused by the oblique nature of this message and wondered what it meant. He did not know for certain whether it was supposed to be a caution against leaving or an encouragement of any plan to do so. While he remained in this quandary, another signal was received on this matter from Madden, which seemed designed to dissuade Kerans from making any attempt at escape.

> Amethyst's 071317. Presumably her anchor is now deeply embedded by silt and very unlikely to drag. Best action therefore to veer as much cable as possible using second anchor either to control yaw or back up first anchor.
> I should be able to give Amethyst ample warning of approach of typhoon."[34]

Kerans interpreted this latest message, which had been addressed to the commander in chief, as a clear indication—which it certainly was not—that the

Amethyst ought to stay where she was and that he ought to conclude talks with the PLA so as not to jeopardize Britain's relations with the Communist Chinese in the future.[35] It is difficult to imagine why Madden would communicate with his chief in such an ambiguous manner when clarity could have been achieved by using a top secret code. Unfortunately, there was no way of telling whether Madden's signal had been primarily intended for Brind or Kerans. Without firm evidence to the contrary, it is feasible to assume the vice admiral was merely responding in a technical way to a practical question and that he neither intended to be vague nor expected another party to read more into his message than there was.

This unsatisfactory experience underscored the problem of trying to hide important information in ambiguous messages, for although an apparently innocuous piece of text might fool the enemy, it was conceivable that it could also have the same effect on the British, thereby devaluing the entire exercise and making it more of a lottery than a piece of sophisticated dissembling. As a result, the British naval authorities began to explore more satisfactory ways of effecting secret communications between the *Amethyst* and the Far East Station. One obvious method was to take a new code by hand to the ship. If Youde had been granted permission to leave Nanking to join the *Amethyst*, he could have been the courier for this important assignment. Once the Communists had made it clear that they were unwilling to allow him to undertake that journey, however, another way had to be found to establish secure contact between Admiral Brind and Lieutenant-Commander Kerans.[36]

In the end, the authorities favored devising a one-time pad system. Such a code could not be constructed without a great deal of laborious effort and a certain element of luck. In essence the one-time pad would have to be built up by transmitting a series of several hundred four-figure number groups from the *Amethyst* at great speed, the messages bearing dummy indicators and delivery groups to C-in-C FES (Afloat). Using the Government Telegraph Code, which was probably far from secure, the British authorities on the Far East Station signaled the *Amethyst* with instructions on how to make the one-time pad.[37] Jack French, the telegraphist, was told to form column one by putting the surnames of all the British naval officers and men aboard ship in alphabetical order. In column two and opposite each name was to be written the first Christian name of the next of kin. French's next step was to place in column three in correct sequence the name of the town or village given in the address of the next of kin. When column three had been compiled, he could then ignore the information in column one. French was to work his way down column two, converting letters into four-figure groups. In this way the name Joan would become 1015 0114. These groups were to be written across the page, with five four-figure groups to a line. Once column two had been completed, he was told to do the same thing for column three. It was acknowledged that before such a scheme could be implemented, those on board the *Amethyst* would have to know the exact time when these FF (Fox Fox) broadcasts were scheduled to take place and have all the information correctly converted into numbers for the proper transmission and receipt of messages between the ship and the British naval authorities on the Far East Station in Singapore.[38] A few practical difficulties were experienced in building up this pad because some of the ratings forgot whom they had originally listed as their next of kin, and a number of them could not remember exactly what address they had used when they had provided this information for the Admiralty upon joining the navy several months or even years before.[39] Eventually, however, all the information was collated and *In* and *Out* pads were fashioned from this material in accordance with the instructions received from the Far East Station. Naturally enough, the success of this scheme would depend to a great degree on the abilities of the Communists to unravel the code. Both Brind and Kerans worked on the assumption that the sheer quantity and speed of the coded transmissions would be sufficient to prevent discovery and an accurate reading of these signals. They were almost certainly right on both counts.[40]

While these arrangements were being worked out, further developments on the Yangtze reemphasized the degree of difficulty facing Kerans as he tried to negotiate with representatives of the PLA. Shortly after 9:00 P.M. on Wednesday 13 July, after all power on the frigate had been shut down for the night, Kerans received a surprise visitor from the shore. Captain Tai, the local garrison commander, had brought a message from General Yuan, which was to be passed on to Admiral Brind. It was basically a message of reproach for failing to provide Kerans with the power of attorney that Colonel Kang had been given to negotiate a settlement of the Yangtze incident.

> I should like to remind you that the present case attracts great attention from the people and army men all over China. Our aims for reaching a settlement of the issue in question have been conveyed to Lieutenant Commander Kerans for forwarding to you during the two talks on 20th and 22nd June respectively. If you will agree to a speedy rational solution of the matter, I certainly hope that you will lose no time in investing on your representative the (necessary) power of attorney for partaking the formal negotiations and for signing on your behalf any agreement reached in the negotiations.[41]

Yuan finished his memorandum with a warning that if the British did not comply with his request they would be held responsible for any further complications that might arise from failing to resolve the dispute.[42] Kerans raised steam and sent the message using the DTG (date time group) code to Brind forthwith. While he waited for the reply from his commander in chief, Kerans wrote another letter to General Yuan asking for Edward Youde's assistance as an interpreter.[43]

It was to be a request that Brind would echo when sending his message to Yuan on 14 July. Brind welcomed the idea of direct communication between the two commanders as being the best means of solving the dispute, but he was aware of the risks of worsening the situation by going to Chinkiang in person—particularly if he was unable to secure the release of the *Amethyst*. Brind had to try to establish a procedure that would enable him to do long-distance negotiating with Yuan on a personal basis using Kerans as the official British go-between, who would deliver messages from one to the other until an acceptable settlement could be found. Brind's message seemed to indicate that while he did not wish Kerans to become engaged in thrashing out the details of any final communiqué between the two sides on the circumstances of the Yangtze incident, he was quite prepared for the captain of the *Amethyst* to sign any agreement that might be worked out by the two commanders in chief at some time in the future. In addition, he had no objection to Kerans signing a safe-conduct pass for the *Amethyst* to go downriver to Shanghai upon the completion of these discussions.[44] If such a system could be established, it would have two distinct advantages: it would obviate the need for Kang's unsatisfactory involvement in the negotiating process, and it would ease some of the pressure off Kerans in the process.

Whatever hopes the admiral may have entertained about giving a fresh impetus to the talks surrounding the *Amethyst*, he had first to confront the practical problem of providing the Communists in Chinkiang with a letter of authorization for Kerans to act in an official capacity as his personal representative. This problem was complicated by the unreliability of mail deliveries to the interior of China. As a result, he ordered Donaldson, the naval attaché in Nanking, to sign a letter on his behalf and give it to Edward Youde in the hope that the PLA would grant him permission to take it to the frigate and remain on board the *Amethyst* thereafter to act as an additional and much-needed interpreter.[45]

Brind's irritation with the existing situation on the Yangtze was evident in the personal message he sent on 14 July to all those on board the *Amethyst*. Designed to reassure the crew that the government had not forgotten them, despite the lack of publicity given to their case by the news media, his signal stated:

It is clear that the Communists have been holding you hostage to wring admissions from the British government which would not only be untrue and dishonourable but would harm the cause of free nations in the future…For the present therefore you are in the forefront of what is called the cold war in which the cause of freedom is being attacked. I know it is a pretty hot war as far as you are concerned & your stand is widely recognised & greatly admired.[46]

Stirring words about not submitting to intimidation, insults, or perversions of the truth followed, and the dispatch ended on the hopeful note that the men of the *Amethyst* would be buoyed up by the good wishes of the British government and people.

Looking at the problem from the dubious vantage point of the British Embassy in Nanking, Sir Ralph Stevenson had little doubt that the talks on the Yangtze incident had become deadlocked, and that neither Kang nor Kerans were the appropriate people to settle some of the outstanding issues raised by this case. In his view the only effective way forward would be for Brind and Yuan to meet and thrash out an accommodation on this controversial matter.[47] Despite the desirability of holding such a meeting from the British perspective, it was doubtful whether the Communists would agree to taking the negotiations away from their local representatives.

Before any reply had been received from Yuan, the *Amethyst* received a new consignment of foodstuffs from local contractors, as well as the emergency supplies of medicine, disinfectant, soap, rat traps, matches, sweets, cigarettes, and a large quantity of *Jen Min Piao* in cash that had been ordered from the British Chamber of Commerce in Shanghai.[48] Although these items brought temporary and much-needed relief to the crew of the frigate, the physical demands made of them aboard the *Amethyst* could not be easily forgotten. On Tuesday 19 July the temperature on board reached 110 degrees Fahrenheit in the engine room and 128 degrees Fahrenheit in the boiler room, a fact that caused considerable concern and prompted a signal to Vice-Admiral Madden asking for advice on how to reduce the heat on board ship to a more acceptable level.[49]

Madden's technical experts quickly came up with several practical tips to make life more bearable for those on board the frigate. Besides improvising windsails on canvas scoops, Kerans was advised to keep the floorplates of his ship wet at all times and to spray water onto the sides of the *Amethyst* to cool them down. In addition, he could make a few modifications to the funnel and wash through the bilges when it was practical to do so. Unfortunately, most of these suggestions were unlikely to have a major impact on the problem.[50] From a practical point of view, unless main power could be restored to the ship for more than a few daylight hours at a time—a possibility that could not be even remotely countenanced given the severe shortage of fuel in her tanks—the frigate would hardly get the chance to cool down. By Thursday 21 July, for example, Kerans was bowing to the inevitable need to conserve fuel by shutting down the ship's generators at 6:00 P.M. daily even though he realized that doing so would make life on board even more intolerable than before.[51]

On that day, Sam Leo, returning from a short spell ashore, brought a note from Colonel Kang that asked Kerans to meet him on the following morning at 9:00 A.M. A sampan with a soldier on board duly arrived at 8:40 A.M. and left for the shore taking Kerans, Leo, and Lieutenant Strain for their meeting at General Yuan's headquarters in Chinkiang.[52] Yuan began the interview by rejecting much of Brind's message to him of 14 July, including his final proposed letter of exchange. He adamantly refused to accept any signaled authorization from the commander in chief of the Far East Station that nominated Kerans as the official British representative at talks with the PLA; he also rejected the idea that Donaldson could be used to sign any official document to this effect on Brind's behalf and refused to consider him the Royal Navy's representative at the talks.[53] This decision not to allow another delegate to enter the negotiations spelled doom for Kerans's hopes that Youde would arrive on board. After such a negative start, the meeting careered on in a similar manner for roughly forty minutes before the general withdrew. By now it was obvious to Kerans that the Communists were no longer just interested in finding a solution to the *Amethyst* situation; they had become more determined than ever to widen the scope of the talks to involve the action of the *Consort, Black Swan,* and *London* as well. Yuan had stressed in this interview that until such time as the British authorities acknowledged their "fundamental guilt" for the incidents concerning all four British vessels on the Yangtze in April, the *Amethyst* would remain on the river under Communist supervision. He had also branded as libelous Brind's remarks about the redoubtable Kang, whom the general described in flattering terms as someone in whom he reposed trust and who, contrary to the admiral's allegations, had done much to help the crew of the frigate in the past.[54]

After Yuan had departed, Kerans spent more than two hours trying to convince Kang that permission ought to be given for Youde to travel from Nanking to join the *Amethyst*. Every time the captain thought that Kang appeared to be wavering and ready to accept his call for an extra translator, the political commissioner would think of some additional reason why this permission could not be granted. Frustrated by these near misses and irked by the accusation that the British were deliberately using delaying tactics in these talks, Kerans went to lunch in a pensive mood. He sensed that everything hinged on whether or not Brind would be willing to follow Yuan's demands on the authorization procedure. If not, the likelihood of Youde being able to make the trip down the Yangtze was very small.[55]

Lunch was much less tense. In the more relaxed atmosphere induced by a six-course meal and quantities of Shanghai beer, Kang began speaking in fluent English to Lieutentant Strain about conditions on board the *Amethyst*. Kerans was astonished to hear Kang's grasp of the language, as the political commissioner had previously denied having any knowledge of English and had always relied exclusively upon his interpreters when communicating with the British in the past. Neither expressing surprise at Kang's excellent command of English, nor musing over his motives in raising this issue, Strain launched into a vivid description of how wretched life had become for those still aboard the frigate. His graphic account left the Communist official in no doubt about the grim situation on the floating prison.[56] It would have been difficult after hearing this plaintive and melancholy tale not to become convinced that time was on the Communists' side and that sooner or later the whole *Amethyst* saga would be resolved in their favor.

After lunch, the meeting resumed but did not get very far before it was called off for the day. Although the afternoon session accomplished little, Kerans did use the time constructively in trying to get permission for the replenishment of the *Amethyst*'s stock of oil, food, and general stores from Chinese sources in Shanghai. Failing to give an assurance on this point, Kang did seem to suggest that it might be allowed.[57] This prospect provided a temporary fillip to Kerans's hopes for an early end to the dispute and ensured that Strain, Leo, and he returned to the frigate slightly encouraged by the events of the day.

Any confidence in the future that this threesome may have entertained soon evaporated once they were back on board ship and nothing of substance materialized in the next few days to show that their efforts had been rewarded with success. None of the 250 tons of oil that Kerans had asked for at the meeting on 21 July appeared, and no message was passed to the vessel about finalizing the arrangements for the delivery of stores from Shanghai. Meanwhile Kerans had to rely on the local contractors and merchants who continued to come out to the ship with a restricted range of foodstuffs.[58]

Assessing the situation in light of what had happened at Chinkiang, Kerans decided that he could afford to send the overworked Leo back to his home at Nanking for a couple of days rest. He reasoned that if permission was granted by the PLA for this visit, Leo could use the opportunity to drop in at the British Embassy in the city and find out what the ambassador felt about the progress or lack of it in the talks that Kerans had been having with the Communists.[59] After receiving approval for his trip home, Leo sent word to the *Amethyst* before he left Chinkiang that Kang had come to a similar conclusion and had sent his two interpreters on leave until the following Thursday (28 July).[60] He had also learned that it had become firm PLA policy to link the clearance papers for Youde's visit to the *Amethyst* to the receipt of Brind's personal signature authorizing Kerans as his personal representative for all future discussions with the Communists.[61]

Annoying though this undoubtedly was for Kerans, he soon received news of a totally different kind, which managed to divert his attention away from the stalled negotiations with the PLA. Vice-Admiral Madden sent him a signal about the menacing presence of typhoon *Gloria*, which had formed off the southern tip of Formosa and was approaching the mainland with winds of 80 knots per hour.[62] According to the latest meteorological information available to Madden from the observatory at Hong Kong, *Gloria* was expected to strike inland to the west of Shanghai and sweep across the Yangtze valley during Sunday night (24–25 July) bringing with it the usual accompaniment of heavy rain and flooding.[63]

Beginning early Sunday evening, preparations were made on board the *Amethyst* to secure the ship, should the center of the typhoon pass close to it. Sunday night passed without incident, but by first light on Monday morning (25 July), the barometer began falling rapidly. By 8:00 A.M. the wind had risen to between gale force 6 and 7. In the next four hours the weather closed in, and the storm increased in intensity. At noon the wind had reached gale force 9, and conditions on the river had become extremely rough with high waves and a treacherously swift current. Despite the lack of adequate shelter from the storm, the *Amethyst*—attached by a heavy cable slung over her port side and a light cable on the starboard beam—was able to ride out the worst of the weather as the afternoon drew on. By 3:00 P.M., for instance, the typhoon was measured at force 10 with torrential rain restricting visibility almost to nil. A slight improvement gradually became discernible as the wind velocity slackened over the next couple of hours. Nonetheless, the storm was still raging at force 8–9 at 5:00 P.M. It remained steady at this point for several hours before dropping gradually to gale force 7 by 11:00 P.M.[64] An anchor watch was set for the night, but no insuperable difficulties were anticipated as the wind was easing appreciably and relative calm was returning to the Yangtze region. It took about twenty-four hours for the bad weather to blow over, even though the actual center of the storm had passed about 50 miles away from where the *Amethyst* was anchored.[65]

While the storm had been approaching its height on Monday afternoon, Kerans had received a further communication from Admiral Brind.

I am very interested in how you fare. Typhoon Gloria has already been chasing some of us. I think you should be quite safe. My previous advice applies and you may think it wise to warn Kang that it may be essential for you to move downstream because of weather. I shall of course support your judgment.[66]

This signal, a little less ambiguous than his previous advice on what action to take if menaced by a typhoon, went some way toward convincing Kerans that his commander in chief was urging him to escape if he still had time.[67] Unfortunately and ironically, given the amount of it he had had on his hands in the recent past, time was no longer on his side. In order to escape, the *Amethyst* would have to slip her anchor cable free and under cover of the driving rain and poor visibility execute a 180 degree turn in the river before proceeding downstream at high speed on the flood tide. Although tempted, Kerans decided against making a run for it at this time because turning his vessel in the narrow part of the Yangtze would have been an extremely lengthy and hazardous procedure under these appalling conditions.[68] Moreover, steaming downriver would have brought the *Amethyst* into or near the eye of the storm, and he doubted whether the frigate was structurally sound enough to cope with the battering she would receive from the typhoon and the heavy swell that was expected in the estuary.[69] Nonetheless, he came to the conclusion that if the anchor cable parted at any stage, he would make a run for it. He signaled Brind that if he did so and an accident occurred, he would attempt to blow up what was left of the wreck and try to get his officers and men to Shanghai by any available means.[70] Kerans's suspicions about Brind's intentions and his approval of an escape bid were soon confirmed in a signal, drafted in the new secret code, which he received from the admiral during Monday night just as the storm in the wake of the typhoon began to relent.[71] By then, of course, it was too late for him to do anything about the lost opportunity, if indeed one had ever really existed.

After the excitement brought about by typhoon *Gloria*, the normal routine was quickly reestablished on board the *Amethyst* in the days that followed. Little of note happened—save the landing of more local stores, hardly a pulsating event in itself—to break the tedium of an existence dominated by enforced idleness, squalid living conditions, and unrelenting humidity. When his fuel stocks had fallen to 65 tons, despite the imposition of the most stringent economies, Kerans knew that unless adequate replenishment came within the next day or two he would be faced with making a momentous decision about the future of his ship and her crew. He had one of two choices: either to try to escape while he still had enough oil on board to make the 150-mile journey downriver to Shanghai or to remain at anchor and trust in the Communists' good faith to supply the *Amethyst* with additional quantities of fuel before her tanks became empty.[72]

This dilemma was identified by Ambassador Stevenson in a message to the Foreign Office on 28 July. He used this dispatch and one he had sent a couple of days before as a means of alerting the government in London to the possibility that unless an acceptable solution could be speedily found to the *Amethyst* dispute, the British might have to contemplate taking grave action to solve the problem at its source, even though the risks involved would be considerable. Stevenson mentioned the possibility, for instance, of scuttling the frigate, an idea already mooted by the Admiralty a few days before.[73] Alternatively, he suggested using this plan as a last resort if any attempted escape bid failed for one reason or another. Whatever was finally decided upon, the ambassador believed that the time had arrived for the government to revise its news embargo on the *Amethyst* crisis and begin publicizing the extent of the problem facing the British in resolving the Yangtze incident with the Communists.

> What I have in mind is the release of some more detailed account of the course of events in contradiction of the false versions given out by the Communists. It could be pointed out for instance that despite the conciliatory attitude maintained by us in the face of considerable provocation in the hope that this might be rewarded by an amicable and equitable settlement of this unfortunate affair, the recent attitude of the Communists suggested that their intention was to hold up the ship as hostage regardless of the welfare of the crew with a view to extracting from the Junior Officer Far East Land Forces Command an acknowledgment of guilt which was obviously inadmissable and contrary to the facts of the case.[74]

He thought this publicity could be best achieved through a parliamentary question, which could then solicit an official answer from a minister.[75] Although this approach had some obvious merits, it was doubtful whether many on the China desk in the Foreign Office would relish the handling of the story by the popular tabloids. If they indulged in their usual mixture of strident nationalism and exaggerated, destructive xenophobia, their stories could well enflame matters and lead to a further deterioration in Anglo-Chinese relations.[76]

A day before Stevenson's suggestions were sent off to London, Kerans had received the latest aide-mémoire from his commander in chief for onward

dispatch to General Yuan. Alluding to the degree of misunderstanding between the two sides, Brind's message had stressed his conviction that the PLA
were wrong to deny the *Amethyst* free passage down the Yangtze and underlined his serious objection to the Communists' idea that permission for such a
journey would depend upon the British admitting their guilt in causing the
incidents that had taken place on the river in April. Indicating that the negotiations ought to be confined to the *Amethyst* incident solely and must not be used
as an excuse for delving into the actions of other British naval vessels, the
admiral's note intimated that matters of considerable international significance
could not be discussed by someone of the comparatively junior rank of lieutenant-commander.[77] His signal had included yet another revised version of a
proposed final communiqué on the *Amethyst* dispute. By avoiding the word
fault, this one went even further in meeting the demands of the Communists.

> I recognise that the entry of H.M.S. "Amethyst" into the Frontier Zone on the
> 20th April, 1949, without the concurrence of the China People's Liberation
> Army was a basic factor in causing a misunderstanding. H.M. Ships "Lon-
> don," "Consort" and "Black Swan" also entered the Frontier Zone without
> the agreement of The China People's Liberation Army.[78]

Brind had also prepared an as yet unsigned letter of authorization for Kerans,
the wording of which he hoped would be approved, and inserted a request that
the *Amethyst* be released from her detention and allowed to steam downriver to
rejoin the rest of the British fleet. In his view this would be a suitable quid pro
quo for his agreement to the terms of a public statement about the original
incident. If this request could not be accommodated for any reason, the admiral
proposed a personal meeting between Yuan and himself at any location the
former might choose. Apart from reiterating the urgent necessity for having
Edward Youde aboard the frigate to iron out difficulties in translating messages
from English into Chinese and vice versa, Brind's aide-mémoire had ended by
suggesting that the admiral was planning to send an aircraft to Nanking with
his letter of authorization if Yuan granted him permission to do so.[79]

Leo returned from his short holiday at Nanking on the morning of Thursday 28 July and immediately began his translation of Brind's letter into Chinese. When he had finished his draft of the message, he took the sampan back
to the shore in the late afternoon and handed the admiral's dispatch to the local
garrison commander who was to arrange for its delivery to General Yuan or
Colonel Kang.[80] On the following day before any reply had been received to
this communication, Kerans instructed Leo to take a message to Kang asking
for clearance to be given for delivery from Chinese sources in Shanghai of 280

tons of oil and a consignment of stores that could not be obtained from the few local contractors who supplied the ship with fresh food. If Kerans had hoped for a positive response from the political commissioner, he was soon sadly disabused of this notion. Leo returned later in the day with news that Kang had left the garrison headquarters and traveled to Nanking on the previous day for an unspecified period. This development involved yet more waiting and uncertainty for the men of the *Amethyst*. In Kang's absence, no one in the PLA garrison was willing to speculate about when the next meeting between the Communists and the British might take place, let alone what might result from such an encounter.[81]

Whether valid or not, it began to look as though the Communists were stalling for time—much as the British ambassador feared they were—in the belief that ultimately a deal could be struck in which the British would be forced to accept the responsibility for the entire Yangtze incident in return for the release of the frigate.[82] Suspecting as much and having little confidence in an early end to the *Amethyst*'s vigil on the river, Kerans's mind turned away from the frustrations of seeking a negotiated settlement to the crisis and began to concentrate exclusively on mounting an escape bid instead. There was little time to be lost, as the official report reveals.

> Total oil fuel remaining onboard on 30 July was now reduced to 55 tons, subtracting 16 tons as estimated for loss of suction—this left me 39 tons operationally with a day's power ahead of me for W/T and distillation. By nightfall and flashing up a second boiler this would only leave me some 33 tons. Clearly I had to make my decision now or face operational immobility to leave the Yangtze.[83]

Kerans chose freedom.

15. Escape in the Dark

KERANS WAS a practical man not given to idealistic notions; he accepted the challenge of attempting to escape from Communist detention on the Yangtze because he felt the risks were worth taking, not because he was a historical romantic who savored the idea of adding a new adventure to the swashbuckling sea legends of the distant past. He did not need reminding that if anything went wrong on the headlong dash downriver, he would ultimately be held responsible for the safety of his ship and the lives of the seventy-three men aboard the *Amethyst*. It was unlikely that a courts martial would be unduly impressed by spirited talk of wresting the initiative from the enemy if the escape attempt ended in failure and loss. Nevertheless, the idea of taking action rather than settling for a further indefinite period of virtual imprisonment on the river had some considerable attractions for the former assistant naval attaché. Quite apart from the moral support he had received in the recent past from Admiral Brind, Kerans felt that with Kang still in Nanking and Communist vigilance perhaps not what it ought to have been, the time had finally arrived for the *Amethyst* to try to steal away from her anchorage on the Yangtze. He knew that in order to do so, the night would have to be as black as possible with little or no moonlight. It just so happened that the moon was due to set at 11:15 P.M. on Saturday 30 July.[1] He hoped that in the dead of night the Communist artillery would not be able to spot the moving figure of the *Amethyst* or hit it even if they could see it. Not simply banking on the poor eyesight or indiscipline of the PLA troops, although these would be contributory factors in any successful escape attempt, Kerans imagined that the Communists would have to overcome certain practical problems created by the intensity of the recent storms in the area. He knew from conversations between his crew and local contractors that typhoon *Gloria* had caused severe flooding along much of the lower Yangtze valley, and it was reasonable to assume, therefore, that this situation would have forced the PLA to relocate their battery positions from the riverbanks to drier areas further inland. If so, the further they had to go to get to dry land, the greater the odds became that the *Amethyst* might be able to slip past them undetected and unharmed.[2]

According to his official report, Kerans finally reached his decision to make a run for it at 3:00 P.M. on Saturday 30 July.[3] Once he had resolved to go, he knew he would have to improve the vulnerable position of his hard-working Chinese translator Sam Leo whose family lived in Nanking and were at risk should Leo be implicated in the plot to escape. Kerans decided to dispense with his services and devise a scheme for getting him off the ship before the crew were ordered to make last minute preparations for the breakout later that evening. Leo, who had worked enthusiastically and outstandingly for Kerans in the past few weeks, was now put ashore by the captain with a letter for Colonel Kang requesting permission for the interpreter to travel to the Stevenson Mission Hospital in Chinkiang in order to obtain medical supplies that were desperately needed on board the *Amethyst*.[4] Kerans told Leo nothing about the escape attempt, and the translator left the ship in total ignorance of what was being planned. It was a callous thing for Kerans to have done because he was repaying a loyal employee with certain incarceration. Leo only found out that something was dreadfully amiss when he was arrested on his way back to Nanking and charged with complicity in the escape. His innocence did not prevent an irate Kang from dealing severely with him, regardless of whether his alibi was plausible or not. Referring to this action later, Kerans noted laconically:

> I much regret having taken this course, but obviously I could not bring him into my confidence and his reactions might have jeopardised the whole operation. It was one man's life against the rest of us onboard.[5]

Although the captain claimed he was trying to do Leo a favor by not including him in the escape bid, he was unable to do the same for the other eight Chinese members of the crew on board, men whose reliability was, he thought, far more suspect than that of the faithful and dependable translator. Kerans decided that they should be kept under surveillance at all times and remain ignorant of his intention to escape until the ship was on its way. Some, in fact, were locked up below decks to ensure that even if they heard what was afoot they would be unable to warn anyone on shore of the planned action. This precaution was sensible and infinitely preferable to the drastic solution of "eliminating them," which Kerans later admitted he had contemplated if they had threatened to ruin the operation by alerting the PLA troops ashore to unusual activity on the frigate.[6]

When he had reached his decision, Kerans called for Lieutenant-Commander George Strain.[7] After telling him of his intention to escape, the captain needed to spend little time in convincing the electrical officer that there was basically no effective alternative to that of making a run for it.[8] Both men knew that the damage repair team had done sterling work throughout the ship and nowhere more effectively than in the engine room where Leonard Williams and his men had managed to overhaul the turbines and replace virtually all the defective pieces of equipment during the frigate's prolonged stay on the Yangtze. This fact alone was a vitally important consideration to Kerans because the *Amethyst* could not afford to have her engines working at anything less than full capacity for the entire passage downriver toward Shanghai. In simple terms it came down to this: if the engines could not provide such a service for an unbroken stretch of roughly eight to nine hours, the escape bid would be as good as over before it started. Kerans and Strain both realized this fact, but pinned their faith on their engineers and hoped their confidence in the men would be rewarded by a trouble-free passage down the Yangtze.[9]

Once convinced of the soundness of the engines, the two men began encrypting the message that the *Amethyst* would send to Admiral Brind by flash procedure using the one-time pad code that had been recently devised by the Far East Station and built up in conjunction with those on board the frigate. It said simply: "TOP SECRET. I AM GOING TO TRY AND BREAK OUT 2200 I (R) 2200 I TONIGHT 30TH JULY. CONCORD SET WATCH 8290."[10] It was almost 4:00 P.M. by the time the message had been patiently encrypted and sent off.

This occasion was not the first one in which the special code had been used. Brind had already sent two messages in it, the first during the night of 25 July when typhoon *Gloria* was raging along the Yangtze. He had disclosed that in the past his advice on how to cope with freak weather conditions had been merely a cover for supporting any escape plan that Kerans might favor.[11] Brind used the same procedure three days later in reminding the captain of the *Amethyst* that an escape bid should only be launched if the visibility and weather conditions were definitely favorable for such an attempt.[12] This more restrained signal appears to have been sent in response to a lengthy message he had received from Kerans indicating that he would not let pass another opportunity to escape without acting upon it.[13] Although Kerans's eagerness to escape was understandable, Brind was anxious to ensure that he did not condone any foolhardy exploit.

Neither the Admiralty nor the Foreign Office in London had been consulted by Brind before he sent his coded dispatches to the *Amethyst*. When both departments were informed on 29 July about what had passed between the commander in chief and the frigate, the Admiralty was at first inclined to give its unqualified support to Admiral Brind. This attitude changed when Lord Fraser, the chief of naval staff, ruled that no escape attempt should be made by Kerans without further reference to the Admiralty.[14] His attitude of cautious restraint matched that of the Foreign Office. Although both departments felt great sympathy for all those on board the *Amethyst* and wished to bring their ordeal to a timely end, each remained hopeful that it could be secured by diplomatic means. Therefore, they preferred Kerans to take the less dynamic option of continuing with negotiations rather than staging a decisive plan of action that might come to grief in a painful way in the near future. A Foreign Office minute explained this view:

> An attempt to break out, whether successful or unsuccessful, might have grave repercusions on British interests, possibly even on British lives, in Communist China. Our efforts to reach some sort of accommodation with the Communists and the preservation of our economic interests would receive a serious—conceivably fatal—setback. For these reasons, it is submitted that we should resist any suggestion that the Commander of *Amethyst* should be authorised to break out until Sir R. Stevenson has been given a full opportunity to provide an assessment of the political risks involved.[15]

By the time the Admiralty had taken its cue from Lord Fraser and sent a signal to Brind countermanding his advice to Kerans and ordering him instead to refrain from any action that might enflame the tense situation on the Yangtze, the *Amethyst* was on her way downriver and could not be recalled.[16]

While the government bureaucracy in London ground on relentlessly and to little effect, activity of an altogether more purposeful kind was taking place on board the frigate. Kerans knew that before his escape plan could be activated much remained to be done on board. At 6:30 P.M. he told the engine room artificer what was afoot and swore him to secrecy. A little over an hour later, as Williams tacked his duties below decks with renewed vigor, the captain invited seventeen chief and petty officers into his cabin together with a small number of ratings to divulge what he had already revealed to his fellow officers on board. His news was greeted with a mixture of excitement and relief that the waiting was over. This "gung-ho" attitude was infectious and demonstrated that morale on board had remained astonishingly high after such a long period of confinement. Kerans admitted that the journey downriver was bound to be dangerous but that it constituted perhaps their only chance of doing something for themselves. If they waited much longer, they would not be masters of their own destiny.[17]

Aware that the odds against success were still fairly considerable, the men showed no hesitation in accepting the risks involved and immediately began to discuss the practical details. It was agreed, for instance, that a number of damage control parties would be selected and given their instructions before the frigate got under way, and that some of the men would be detailed to camouflage the outline of the *Amethyst* and try to make her pass for an LST. Kerans hoped that this ruse might work if her silhouette could be changed. Arrangements were made, therefore, to rig some black canvas from the area of the rear of the bridge and funnel forward along the upper part of the deck to A gun mounting and beyond. At the same time other men were to use the cover of darkness to splash black paint on the off-white-colored superstructure and side of the ship, and the anchor chain was to be lagged with hammock bedding that had been soaked in soft soap so as to sharply reduce the noise when it was weighed. At the same time, another party of men supervised the flooding of the forward ballast tank, X magazine, and numbers 1, 2, 7, and 8 oil fuel tanks to ensure that the increase in weight would lower the ship's center of gravity and improve her overall stability in what was bound to be a flood tide.[18] Another group was charged with splinter protection duties, which involved placing hammocks, cushions, and bedding around the bridge, the WT office, and on both sides of the after mess deck. Bags of flour were also used for this purpose on the bridge and around the WT office on the starboard side.[19]

All of these things were done by the men in the sure knowledge that if the worst happened and the ship was damaged beyond repair, the captain would attempt to beach and destroy her once the crew had been put ashore. Kerans had made it clear that under those circumstances, it was the duty of the men to use their initiative to try to get to Shanghai or the relative safety of the open sea by any means at their disposal.[20]

As the men scurried around the ship intent on finishing as many of the duties assigned to them as possible before departure, a most unexpected and thoroughly unwelcome development took place. At about 8:25 P.M. a sampan was spotted coming toward the ship from the shore bearing vegetables, eggs, and beer ordered from the traders who had been out to the ship earlier in the day. If a local contractor came on board, noticed any untoward activity, and mentioned it to the Communist authorities on his return to the shore, it would compromise the entire mission. Kerans had to act quickly to stave off such a threat and to keep the crew from panicking. He rapidly issued a set of instructions to his men as the sampan drew alongside the *Amethyst*. This attempt to appear calm in the face of adversity paid off; the men immediately stopped work and some hurriedly undressed and got into their bunks as though they were turning in for the night. Meanwhile the stores petty officer was ordered to go down the gangway to the sampan, unload the supplies, and ensure that the traders did not come up on deck. Even though he did not have the services of an interpreter, Justin McCarthy produced an inspired performance in the best traditions of British vaudeville. Adopting an air of aggrieved surprise and complaining loudly about shortages in the supplies, he kept up a stream of mildly reproachful banter for the entire seventeen-minute period it took to transfer the provisions. As the sampan pushed off from the side of the ship and moved toward the shore, the relief of all those watching and waiting apprehensively for its departure was palpable.[21]

After plotting the desired course that he wished the *Amethyst* to follow downriver on the incomplete set of navigational charts of the Yangtze he had on board, Kerans went up to the darkened bridge at about 9:00 P.M. and remained there for over an hour so that his eyes might become accustomed to the nighttime gloom. Although he may have hoped for cloudy, overcast conditions to enhance the chances of the *Amethyst* succeeding in her escape bid, the evening was far from ideal, being both dry and reasonably clear.[22] Knowing what was required of his ship if she was to make it downriver to the open sea by dawn, Kerans could not afford to wait around indefinitely in the hope that the weather would worsen. Shortly after 10:00 P.M. as he wrestled with the problem of when to give the order to cut the anchor cable, he had an enormous stroke of luck. A fully lit merchant ship rounded Tasha Island on its way downriver. As the *Kiang Ling Liberation* approached the *Amethyst*, Kerans sensed that the time to begin the perilous descent of the Yangtze had arrived. He realized that if his frigate could leave her berth, execute a 180-degree turn in the river and follow closely in the wake of the Chinese ship as she steamed toward Shanghai, the major problem of trying to navigate the first few miles of a tricky stretch of water without the aid of a reliable chart would be overcome. For this reason, if for no other, Kerans did not hesitate. He gave orders to start the port engine, slip the anchor cable in such a way that it would swing the bows of the *Amethyst* 45 degrees to starboard and allow the fast-running current to assist in bringing the vessel around to point downstream. At 10:12 P.M., the frigate slipped her anchor cable and moved off without making much noise. Initially, nearly everything went to plan, and nothing disastrous happened; the ship made her turn in under half a minute amid a flurry of yellow sparks from her funnel and began forging downriver at 10 knots astern of the *Kiang Ling Liberation*.[23]

According to the official report, the next few minutes were among the most nerve-racking of the entire journey.

> In a very short space of time the "Kiang Ling Liberation" was challenged by a flare from the batteries and she replied with the usual siren signal. I noticed another small vessel on my port bow fully lit which appeared to be an L.C.I.(L) or H.D.M.L. converted. A second flare went up which was obviously intended for me, I did not reply but continued on my way. The L.C.I.(L) or H.D.M.L. opened fire at the batteries across my bows. My first impression was that he was trying to stop me and I was prepared to ram him if necessary. Within a very few seconds I came under heavy artillery and small arms fire. The 75 m.m. and 105 m.m fire was accurate but Bofors and Oerlikon were well over. I gave orders for "full ahead" and was hit forward of the bridge on the water line on the starboard side. My first impression was that we were badly hit in the starboard engine or boiler room. We heeled well over to starboard and I thought it possible we might sink soon. I weaved heavily but it was some minutes before "full ahead" was reached and with shallow water, steering was extremely difficult. By then the "Kiang Ling Liberation" had switched off all her lights, had turned to port (to the Northern Bank) and appeared to have stopped. I managed to get past the "Kiang Ling Liberation" with a few feet to spare, made black smoke and continued on my way.[24]

In the midst of all the action and with the ship listing some 35 degrees to starboard, Kerans told French to send a flash signal to Admiral Brind. It said simply: "I AM UNDER HEAVY FIRE AND BEEN HIT."[25] It was exactly 10:33 P.M. Fortune continued to smile on the *Amethyst*, however, because the frigate had not suffered serious damage, only sustaining a relatively light blow from what appears to have been a 75-mm shell exploding near the waterline on the starboard side. Apart from causing extreme underwater turbulence, the shell did nothing more than buckle and loosen a few plates in the vicinity of the naval stores. As a result there was some flooding, but it was easily contained and promptly dealt with by the damage control parties; the ship only lost speed momentarily and thereafter moved to full ahead both without any major difficulty.[26]

Although the *Amethyst* virtually got away unharmed from this first encounter with the PLA artillery, the *Kiang Ling Liberation* was not so fortunate. Whether by accident or design, the Communist batteries singled her out for a withering barrage of shells. Caught up in something that must have taken her captain completely by surprise, the ship moved to port, switched off all her lights, and began using her siren in an almost demented way. It failed to do any good. As she moved toward the Communist gun positions, the shells continued to rain down on her. She soon became a smoking wreck and sunk with the loss of roughly forty lives.[27]

By this time *Amethyst*, which had only managed one round from the B gun, had stopped firing at the shore with her Bren guns and Oerlikon because Kerans did not wish to draw attention to her position in the middle of the river.[28] Even so, the captain estimated that a minimum of four batteries were still engaging his ship, as his next signal to Brind indicated: "STILL UNDER HEAVY FIRE. JUST PASSED ESPIGLE POINT."[29] Fortunately the *Amethyst*'s speed and darkened form made her a difficult target to hit in the murky light. Although they did their best, the PLA gun crews failed to register any more direct hits on the frigate as she sped on her way through the Tan-tu Reach toward Rose Island, the point where the Yangtze incident had begun over three months before. At 10:50 P.M. Brind sent a flash signal to Kerans: "WELL DONE. WE ARE ALL WATCHING AND HOPE IT WILL BE DIFFICULT TO HIT YOU."[30] At precisely the same moment, Kerans had fired off another signal to his commander in chief pointing out that he was off Rose Island. Surprisingly the ship encountered no opposition as it passed to the north of the island and to the south of San-chiang-ying where Kang's battery had once been located.[31] Both banks of the river remained dark and silent as *Amethyst* forged on toward Kiangyin at maximum speed aided by a fast-flowing current. Nothing untoward happened as she closed with and then passed to the east of Bate Point. This news was disclosed by Kerans in another flash signal sent at 12:24 A.M. It crossed with an anxious query from Brind asking for an update on the ship's progress. Kerans quickly issued a reply: "SO FAR O.K."[32]

It did not remain so for long. As the *Amethyst* approached Kiangyin, a flare revealed her position, and she came under fire immediately. Kerans wasted no time in ordering the engine room to produce as much black smoke as possible in an effort to lay an impenetrable screen across the river and obscure the ship. He had realized in advance that things were bound to be more hazardous at Kiangyin because the town had become a military stronghold of the Communists.[33] It was reasonable to assume, therefore, that there would be a number of batteries situated along the waterfront of the port. If the *Amethyst* could get past these guns unscathed, a more formidable obstacle still had to be overcome: a submerged boom, consisting of a row of sunken ships laid by the Chinese at the start of the last Sino-Japanese War and placed in the river in such a way as to leave only a relatively small navigable channel for ships to pass through on their way up- or downriver. Flanked by what Kerans feared were nests of guns, the boom was bound to be an exceedingly dangerous barrier for the frigate to circumvent.[34] At 12:57 A.M. *Amethyst* flashed the disconcerting signal: "UN-DER HEAVY FIRE OFF KIANGYIN."[35] As she neared the boom, the firing naturally became more intense, even if the artillery troops failed to find the correct range or inflict any further damage on the ship.[36] Kerans responded only with Bren gun fire because he did not wish to illuminate the ship by sending any 4-inch salvos from B gun. At 1:09 A.M. another flash signal announced that the frigate was rapidly approaching the boom.[37] According to the navigation chart he possessed, Kerans expected the boom's presence in the river to be indicated by two lights. He knew that the course to steer was between the lights in the narrow lane indicated by two rows of white buoys. Unfortunately, all he could see from the bridge of the *Amethyst* was a solitary light in the middle of the river. If the buoys marking the narrow channel existed, he claimed he did not see them, and as a result, he was now in a real quandary about which side of the light he should attempt to pass. He knew that if he chose wrongly, the escape bid of the *Amethyst* would almost certainly end explosively with the ship smashing into the boom at speed. If this collision occurred, it was inconceivable that the frigate could remain afloat for long. In all probability, the bottom of the vessel would be immediately ripped open or peeled off by the hidden barrier, thereby ensuring that the *Amethyst* would soon join the other sunken wrecks littering the river bed and tragically form a new layer of the boom. Without any real clue as to which side of the light the navigable channel lay, Kerans opted to steer close to the port side. Once he had chosen his course, there was nothing to do but pray that luck or the Almighty was on his side. As the *Amethyst* careered toward the light and passed to the port side of it, Kerans waited for the sickening impact that would spell instant disaster. Miraculously, perhaps, it never came. Instead the ship went through the gap in the boom without the slightest damage and on past the town to the immense relief of her captain and crew.[38]

Half an hour later at 1:39 A.M. Kerans dictated another signal to French. It informed Brind that they had covered half the distance to Shanghai.[39] This flash signal inspired a longer reply than usual from the commander in chief.

YOUR 301639 SPLENDID. IF YOU CANNOT GET ABOUT TEN MILES PAST WOOSUNG BEFORE DAWN SUGGEST YOU EITHER LAY UP DURING DAYLIGHT OR TAKE THE TSUNG MING CROSSING AND NORTH CHANNEL WHICH SHOULD BE NAVIGATED AT SLOW SPEED.[40]

A mere fifty minutes later, *Amethyst* announced that she had passed the 100-mile mark.[41] She was now five-eighths of the way down the Yangtze, and the next major test would come when she reached the area of Woosung forts close to the end of her heroic 160-mile journey to the open sea. Brind labelled it "A MAGNIFICENT CENTURY," which it clearly was, given that the ship was tearing down one of the most dangerous stretches of navigable water in the world in the dark and without an experienced local pilot on board to assist in choosing the correct course.[42] This aspect of the escape bid alone justifies it as a brilliant piece of helmsmanship. Although batteries and fortifications presented real dangers to the *Amethyst*, the river Yangtze itself was the most obvious source of constant threat. A slight error or a bad stroke of luck at any moment could bring this whole effort to a shuddering halt. No one could afford to think that the worst was over when there was still several hours of hazardous steaming to go.[43]

Kerans estimated that if everything went according to plan, he would reach Woosung at about 5:30 A.M. He sent a message to Brind asking for HMS *Concord* to cover him at this point just in case the Communists tried to bombard the ship as it passed the forts.[44] Brind acknowledged that he would do so, then sent a message to *Concord*, repeated for the benefit of *Amethyst*, which was very explicit in this regard: "IF AMETHYST PASSES WOOS-UNG NEAR DAWN SUPPORT HER BY ENGAGING BATTERIES FROM SEAWARD IF THEY OPEN FIRE. YOU SHOULD NOT GO ABOVE IDENTIFIED BATTERIES EXCEPT IN EMERGENCY."[45] This order was amended in a later signal to read "DO NOT GO ABOVE QUAR-ANTINE BOUY (sic) EXCEPT IN EMERGENCY. SMOKE MAY BE USEFUL."[46] At 3:50 A.M. *Amethyst* flashed a signal to the destroyer *Concord* asking her to be in position off Woosung and indicating her own progress: "CENTAUR LOWER BUOY COME QUICK."[47] Shortly afterward at about 4:00 A.M., the *Amethyst*, making good progress on the swollen tide at roughly 22 knots, suddenly struck something. She shuddered sickeningly for a few seconds before returning to normal. Leslie Frank, who had been at the wheel from the time that the *Amethyst* had slipped her moorings just over five hours before, had been asked by Kerans to steer "Hard a starboard" and then "Hard a port," but these orders had come too late for the frigate to avoid running down and cutting in half a darkened junk that had drifted into her path.[48] Kerans did not stop to survey the scene of the accident or pick up any survivors. Although he felt bad about the innocent and unnumbered victims who had been on board the junk, he realized that the collision had been unavoidable. If he stopped and conducted a search for survivors in the murky and swirling waters of the Yangtze, the *Amethyst* could not make it downriver to the open sea by daybreak. Not wishing to jeopardize the entire mission or put all his men at risk once again, Kerans took the pragmatic option and did not look back.[49]

After this mishap, the *Amethyst* continued to make good progress down the ever-widening river. It was surprising that her machinery held up as magnificently as it did under the strain of being continuously used flat out for the first time in over three months. Those working down in the engine room soon realized, however, that top speed could only be obtained at the cost of working in temperatures in excess of 150 degrees Fahrenheit.[50] Their determined efforts to keep things going in a most taxing environment rate as one of the most grueling and commendable feats of the entire enterprise.[51]

An hour after the unfortunate ramming of the junk, Brind was informed by French that Woosung was in sight.[52] It was 5:03 A.M. Kerans could see the searchlights from the fort sweeping back and forth across the river and sensibly decided to steer a course that took his ship as far from both the Paoshan and Woosung forts as possible. As the *Amethyst* approached Woosung at 22 knots, dawn broke. Kerans ordered those on the B gun mounting to be ready to fire on the forts some 4¹/₂ miles away if the searchlight picked up the silhouette of the frigate and drew the attention of the Communist artillery to her position on the Yangtze. Although the searchlights did move across the *Amethyst* twice, they did not stop on either occasion but swept past the vessel. As a result, the guns of Woosung, the last major hazard of this epic voyage, remained silent. *Amethyst* passed the Quarantine Buoy at Woosung at 5:25 A.M. Four minutes later, she signaled Brind that *Concord* was in sight.[53] As the two ships of the Royal Navy closed on each other, the relief and jubilation of all those on deck who could see what was happening was unconfined. *Concord*'s cheery and almost incredulously worded welcoming signal, "FANCY MEETING YOU AGAIN," was greeted by Kerans with the response "NEVER, NEVER HAS A SHIP BEEN MORE WELCOME."[54] In a separate signal to Brind, repeated for the benefit of the Admiralty in London, Kerans issued a stirring message that would soon be emblazoned across much of the world's press: "HAVE REJOINED THE FLEET SOUTH OF WOOSUNG, NO DAMAGE OR CASUALTIES. *GOD SAVE THE KING*."[55] It soon received the following acknowledgment from the commander in chief of the Far East Station:

YOUR 302032. WELCOME BACK TO THE FLEET. WE ARE ALL EX-
TREMELY PROUD OF YOUR MOST GALLANT AND SKILFUL ES-
CAPE AND THAT ENDURANCE OF AND FORTITUDE DISPLAYED
BY EVERYONE HAS BEEN REWARDED WITH SUCH SUCCESS.

YOUR BEARING IN ADVERSITY AND YOUR DARING PASSAGE TONIGHT WILL BE EPIC IN THE HISTORY OF THE NAVY.[56]

King George VI responded enthusiastically to the news of the *Amethyst*'s escape. In a dispatch to Brind, which was made public and reprinted in *The Times* on 1 August, the king praised everyone aboard the frigate for their courage, skill, and determination throughout their long vigil on the Yangtze. He ended with the familiar refrain, "Splice the mainbrace."[57]

Before the crew could do so in some style, however, the battered frigate had a few more hours steaming to do. Accompanied by *Concord, Amethyst* made her untroubled way out of the estuary into the open sea. Her success, astounding as it undoubtedly was, could be judged a fine one in every sense of the word; nothing illustrated this better than the fact that when she hove to off the North Saddles in midmorning, *Amethyst* had only 9 tons of usable fuel left in her tanks.[58]

16. Aftermath

*A*FTER ALLOWING his men to rest during the day, Kerans sailed for Hong Kong on Sunday evening (31 July) in an effort to make the best of the good weather prevailing in the region at this time. *Amethyst*, accompanied initially by *Concord* and subsequently by the destroyer HMS *Cossack*, made reasonable progress down the Chinese coastline at 14 knots in light seas. After an emotional rendezvous with the cruiser HMS *Jamaica* at sea north of Formosa on the evening of 1 August, the frigate continued on her passage southward.[1] Very little happened to spoil the *Amethyst*'s party on this voyage, not even the difficulties she experienced with one of her boilers, which forced her to limp into harbor in Hong Kong later than expected. When she did finally arrive at 11:00 A.M. on Wednesday 3 August, she was given a rousing welcome by hundreds of spectators who had waited patiently on the dock to greet her.[2]

While the British were naturally ecstatic about the heroic exploits of their small ship, the Communists reacted to her escape with ferocity. Despite protesting his innocence most vehemently, Leo was immediately taken into custody in Chinkiang and transferred to Nanking handcuffed and in irons on the day after the escape. He was interrogated and threatened with death for allegedly conspiring with the enemy. According to his wife, he remained in irons for three days. After enduring three sessions of close questioning, Leo was told that the PLA believed his version of what had taken place. Nevertheless, he was given a mandatory course of political indoctrination and remained in custody for seventy-nine days.[3]

After apprehending Leo, the Chinese wasted no time in accusing the *Amethyst* of the most heinous crimes. According to the lurid account provided on 2 August by *Hsin Min Pao,* the Shanghai local evening newspaper, it was the

213

British vessel that had fired at and sunk the Chinese merchant ship the *Kiang Ling Liberation* on the Yangtze on 30 July. Not content with stealing away from the scene of the crime, HMS *Amethyst* was alleged to have deliberately fired upon the numerous lifeboats that had come out to rescue the survivors, an act of calculated wickedness that needlessly condemned several hundred innocent passengers to a watery grave. Basing its story on the statement made by General Yuan on 31 July, the *Hsin Min Pao* ended its report with a succinct warning: "The Chinese people, who will never forget this incident, will ask the British imperialists to pay back in blood."[4]

Yuan's version of the story, broadcast over Communist radio on the evening of 2 August, differed only in emphasis from the newspaper account. He asserted that besides compelling the *Kiang Ling Liberation* to shield the *Amethyst* from the PLA batteries, the British frigate had fired upon the steamer when the ruse was discovered, which caused the passenger vessel to catch fire and sink. In making her getaway, the *Amethyst* was accused of callously disregarding the plight of the passengers and crew of the merchant ship who jumped overboard and were trying to swim to safety.[5] Addressing himself to other less emotive matters, Yuan reminded his audience that the British commander in chief, Admiral Brind, had accepted the fact that the *Amethyst* had entered the frontier zone on the Yangtze in April without the agreement of the PLA and that this violation was the basic cause of the misunderstanding between them.[6] He contended that whereas the Communist authorities were lenient with the crew of the *Amethyst*—allowing them to receive local supplies, oil, and overseas mail during their detention on the Yangtze—this generous attitude had been met with various forms of insincerity from the British side inspired by the unscrupulous Brind. Yuan's statement concluded by saying that the entire personnel of the PLA and the Chinese people as a whole would never forget or forgive the double crime of the *Amethyst* and that of her accomplices *London, Black Swan,* and *Consort.*

> Do not make haste in celebrating the success of the flight of the Amethyst. The whole case will not be closed so long as the culprits are not punished and an apology and compensation for the crimes are not made by the British Government.[7]

This theme was echoed and expanded upon in a commentary supplied by the Communist New China News Agency on 2 August: "The whole course of the incident profoundly teaches the Chinese people the viciousness, hypocrisy and shamelessness of Imperialists no matter who they are."[8] Referring to British policy in China, the wire service suggested that it would eventually reap what it had sown, much as the Americans had paid for their excesses in China during the recent past.

> As long as the British Government still exists the Chinese people must continue to go into the responsibility of the crime and insist on meting out severe punishment for the two atrocities committed by Amethyst.[9]

The *People's Daily* joined in the chorus of protest branding the British ship as being solely responsible for the death and injury of many innocent Chinese. Evocative words such as *revenge* and *justice* for the victims of this piratical act were used with telling effect by the journalists who summarily rejected the Admiralty's denial of the *Amethyst*'s guilt in sinking the *Kiang Ling Liberation*.[10]

Whether these warnings were more bluster than an actual statement of intent was something that could not be determined at the time by the British officials in China. Ambassador Stevenson believed that some reprisals were bound to be resorted to by the Communists against British interests in the country. To minimize the repercussions, he urged Attlee's government not to gloat over the escape of the *Amethyst*, but to respond soberly to the barrage of public denunciation it was receiving at the hands of the PLA-inspired media.[11]

Robert Urquhart, the British consul in Shanghai, was also eager to limit the damage the *Amethyst*'s escape had done to the British cause in China. He believed that something constructive should be done by the Foreign Office to divert the attention of the national and local media from the negative effects of the Yangtze incident.[12] Quite how this could be achieved when press agitation over the sinking of the *Kiang Ling Liberation* was at its most vociferous in the early days of August remained another matter. In truth, everything hinged upon the attitude of the Communist authorities, and there was probably nothing the British government could have done to bring this highly charged affair to an end if the PLA wished it to remain an issue between them.

In the meantime, as the *South China Morning Post* indicated in an article on 3 August, British citizens in Communist-held areas of China remained at risk should the PLA decide that official protests and media assaults were insufficient methods of punishment for the litany of crimes allegedly committed by the *Amethyst* on behalf of her imperialist government in London. If the PLA resorted to a policy of direct reprisals against the British government, its citizens, and interests in China, there was much that it could attack. Apart from more than 4,000 of its citizens in Shanghai and sizable groups of them in Tientsin and Hankow, the British had a number of large investments scattered throughout the country, ranging from warehouses and factories in Shanghai, to egg packing plants in Hankow and Nanking and coalmines in northern China. Knowing this and appreciating the volatile nature of the problem, it is difficult not to agree with the sentiments expressed by Hong Kong's English language daily newspaper the *South China Morning Post* on 3 August that Britain had gambled its commercial future in Red China against the lives of its men on the *Amethyst*.[13]

Although the British government naturally wished to protect its people and interests while avoiding a massive confrontation with the Chinese Communists, it was far from convinced that it could devise an effective policy that would secure these longed-for objectives. Despite the advantages of maintaining a low profile in the aftermath of the *Amethyst*'s escape, Attlee's government was forced into the open by the sheer hostility of the Communist media's campaign against it. Although it hoped that the storm of protest would soon pass over, the British government could not allow the kind of stories the Chinese press was printing to go unchallenged for long, even if a protest risked enraging the Communists still further. If Britain did not refute what it saw as fictitious and highly damaging accounts of the action on the Yangtze, these stories might soon begin to take on a cloak of respectability and authenticity in the eyes of other nations watching the Chinese imbroglio from different parts of the world. A good deal of the luster shining from the *Amethyst*'s successful dash for freedom would be lost if independent nations began to suspect that the frigate only achieved her coup by the most craven imperialistic methods.

Admiral Brind tried to remove this imputation of guilt against the *Amethyst* by issuing a carefully reasoned press statement from his headquarters in Singapore on 6 August. Rejecting the Communist version of events on the night of 30 July, the commander in chief made the telling point that if the *Kiang Ling Liberation* was being used as a shield by the British frigate, as the PLA had claimed, what would be the purpose of *Amethyst* mowing down the merchant vessel and thereby losing the protection that she was being supposedly afforded by the Chinese ship?

> There was evidently much confusion in the battery positions and the Amethyst saw very clearly that the shore guns fired at their own ships. The firing continued for a considerable time, estimated at 15 minutes, after the Amethyst had passed on and the firing at her had ceased. It is clear, therefore, that the ship had not sunk and the Amethyst could not have harmed the survivors when she passed.[14]

Interestingly, despite the virulence of the press reaction in China, the survivors of the *Kiang Ling Liberation* who had begun arriving in Shanghai in early August did not join in this orchestrated campaign. According to Urquhart, those who were on board the ship at the time the liner was fired upon and disabled evidently felt no compunction about disagreeing with the official verdict on the sinking of their ship. Not echoing the trenchant anti-British tone of the media, the survivors and relatives of the passengers and crew made it clear to whoever was willing to listen that the ship had run into artillery fire from the shore and not from the *Amethyst*.[15] On 5 August they took their vociferous complaints to the Shanghai offices of the China Merchants Steam Navigation Company, the owners of the ill-fated *Kiang Ling Liberation*.

> They are claiming damages brushing aside the newspaper reports of British responsibility and saying that they know perfectly well the ship was fired on from shore.
>
> Associated Press correspondent interviewed the captain on August 4th. The captain gave the true story saying that he was under fire from "three directions from the shore." He saw the Amethyst pass. He had 70 passengers and crew on the ship when he left Ching Kiang and thinks some 30 passengers and ten of the crew were unaccounted for.[16]

Urquhart revealed that the Associated Press account had subsequently been seized by the censors and the captain arrested by the Communist authorities.[17]

If this action was expected to kill the story before it hit the pages of the world's press, it proved to be a total failure. On 20 August the *South China Morning Post* appeared with the unexpurgated account of the interview held in early August with Chen Lo-sen, the experienced master of the *Kiang Ling Liberation*. Chen was reported to have said that after loading 400 tons of coal and beans at Hankow, his vessel had also taken on board a large number of passengers bound, like the cargo, for Shanghai. He claimed that on 29 July the *Kiang Ling Liberation* docked at Chinkiang, and most of the passengers left the ship to continue their journey by rail. After leaving port on 30 July, he proceeded downriver—again without incident—until suddenly he was engaged by intense artillery and machine gun fire from three directions on the shore. His ship was struck several times, which caused her highly inflammable cargo to burn out of control. At this moment, with his ship ablaze and under attack, he noticed that a large unidentified ship running without lights had stationed herself close up behind the stern of his 600-ton steamer. This ominous discovery increased the pandemonium on board his own vessel. Soon both passengers and crew began throwing themselves overboard in the hope that they might be able to swim to safety. Chen abandoned ship in a similar fashion and struck out for the shore once the *Kiang Ling Liberation* began to swing broadside into the Yangtze currents. Before he threw himself into the river, however, he noticed the large craft passing him but never saw her firing at either his own ship or the shore as she did so.[18]

Although these disclosures were a terrific boon to the British, there were other more disquieting aspects to the *Amethyst* story, which Attlee's government in London would have greater difficulty explaining if they were revealed. Ambassador Stevenson was well aware of the potentially damaging revelations that could be made about the sinking by the *Amethyst* of the Chinese junk and informed the Foreign Office on 2 August that he thought the Communists were likely to exploit this incident to the full when they learned about what had happened on the Yangtze. In Stevenson's view, there was no need for them to fabricate any part of this story, for the truth was bad enough if it was treated in a less than sympathetic way.[19] A long minute on this subject written on the following day by P. D. Coates, of the China desk in the Foreign Office, appeared to agree with the ambassador that the British government should not attempt to cover up the accident because these efforts would almost certainly come to naught when the *Amethyst*'s ratings reached Hong Kong and began talking about their experiences on the river.

> We should however not ignore that if we do admit it we shall be accused, probably correctly, of having caused loss of life, and compensation will be demanded. Even if the Communists cannot trace the wreck or the victims they will have no difficulty in manufacturing bogus ones.
> We are batting on a very tricky wicket, because, quite apart from present politics, anything a foreign warship does on the Yangtze is capable of being worked up into a major source of trouble, in view of the touchiness of Chinese chauvinism about foreign warships in inland waters.[20]

Coates believed that a statement expressing regret for the unfortunate incident ought to be issued by the government, but that it should try to tie the responsibility for the junk's destruction to the Communist authorities whose continued detention of the *Amethyst* had forced her captain to escape with his ship down the Yangtze in the dead of night. This action was in line with the expressed opinion of G. G. Fitzmaurice, the legal advisor to the Foreign Office, who had been asked by Coates whether the government could be held liable in international law for the loss of the junk and those of her crew who may have perished when she was cut in half by the British vessel. Owing to the fact that Fitzmaurice had rejected the imputation of negligence by the *Amethyst* in respect of the junk, Coates concluded that it would be in Britain's interests to forestall any possible claim for compensation by stating categorically that the blame for this event lay with the PLA, its political masters, or both. He summed up his feelings about the matter by stating, "If we do not take the offensive I feel that we may find ourselves forced onto the defensive."[21]

These concerns paled, however, in the face of what was arguably an even more graphic and contentious story that the British Sunday newspapers published on 7 August. Only a week before, Stevenson had urged the government not to publicize the fact that HMS *Concord* had entered Chinese territorial waters under cover of darkness in the early morning of 31 July without first obtaining the necessary permission from the Nationalist authorities. Although that act would have been sufficient in itself to warrant censure from the KMT, the *Sunday Pictorial* ran a banner headline that boldly proclaimed: "Navy was ready to fight for *Amethyst*." It informed its readers that *Concord* had trained her big guns on the Woosung forts guarding the mouth of the Yangtze.

> And a whole flotilla of destroyers was closing in to join her and if necessary go up river between the sandbanks and wrecked sampans to blast a passage for the sloop that had been bottled up for 101 days.[22]

According to the report, this destroyer flotilla, comprising *Cossack, Comus,* and *Constance,* was fully prepared to launch a full-scale battle against the PLA, should the *Amethyst* have needed any assistance getting past Woosung and out of the Yangtze.[23] It is just as well that punitive measures were not taken by the Royal Navy in this instance because such action could have been construed by the Chinese Communists as an act of war. Once again this disclosure caught the British Foreign Office off guard. Coates minuted caustically: "We, of course, had not previously heard of this plan, and to divulge it at this stage is criminal folly."[24] In a dispatch to its embassy in Nanking, the Foreign Office expressed the hope that the *Amethyst* episode might be allowed to die a natural death and that under no circumstances should any new startling revelations find their way into print as they would only keep the issue alive to the detriment of British interests in China.

> *Amethyst* is out, but we still have a large stake in China. Our chances of eventually reaching some sort of accommodation with the Chinese Communists are slender enough as it is, and we do not want to jeopardise them further by embarking on a prolonged propaganda war if it can possibly be avoided.
>
> In this connexion we think it unfortunate that the preparations for attacking the Woosung Forts etc should have been quite unnecessarily divulged after the event.[25]

It soon transpired that the facts of the *Concord* case had been provided as background information to the international press by none other than Sir Patrick Brind, commander in chief of the Far East Station. He confirmed that the journalists at his press conference on Saturday 6 August had not kept this information off the record as they should have done.[26] If Brind did make it clear to the assembled journalists that the information he was revealing was top secret and not for publication, it does not say much for their ethics that these instructions were ignored. If, however, Brind failed to spell out the terms under which he was providing this information, he had little reason to complain. Regardless of whether or not the stories about *Concord* should have been published, they certainly succeeded in capturing the headlines in Britain much to the embarrassment of Attlee's government. In apportioning blame for this latest controversy, one should not forget that Brind was under no compulsion to tell the journalists about *Concord*'s operations or the activities of the destroyer flotilla and to do so was simply crass and extremely tactless. Brind ought to have known better. Once again, however, as in other aspects of this saga, a naval officer had exceeded his instructions and helped to compromise his government's China policy.[27]

It was not just a case of British policy offending the Communists; the action of *Concord* in going upstream had infuriated the Nationalists as well, just as Stevenson had predicted it would.[28] According to a memorandum submitted by the Ministry of Foreign Affairs to the British Embassy in Nanking, the destroyer *Concord* was accused of virtually encroaching upon the sovereignty of China in her foray up the Yangtze during the night of 30–31 July. This memo claimed that a Chinese naval patrol craft had spotted the British ship sailing upriver from the mouth of the Yangtze at about 1:30 A.M. on 31 July. When the *Concord* was challenged by lamp, she was alleged by the Nationalists to have replied that she was going to anchor close to the lightship at Chiu Tuan Sha, which she did. Nonetheless, at 4:00 A.M. she was seen getting under way again and moving upriver. Challenged again by the signal lights of another KMT vessel, *Concord* allegedly responded that she was under orders to go to the assistance of *Amethyst*. Shortly afterward she extinguished her lights and proceeded up the Yangtze in defiance of the regulations imposed by the Chinese government, which expressly forbade foreign ships from making any unauthorized journey on the river.[29] By issuing an official protest to the British Embassy for onward transmission to the government in London, the Nationalists let it be known that they did not appreciate their rules being flouted by anyone, not even friends and former allies.

Nationalist blockade restrictions, already chafing, worsened as August wore on, bringing protests from leaders of the British community in China that unless Attlee's government could apply pressure on the KMT authorities to remove the embargo—or at least ease some of the rules they had imposed on marine traffic—a number of British businesses particularly in Shanghai were likely to face bankruptcy. Owing to the abnormal trading conditions they had been forced to endure for more than two months, the firms were desperately short of local funds with which to pay their employees and had been forced to remit sterling from Britain to the value of more than £350,000 per month in order to settle their outstanding accounts. Besides damaging mercantile interests, the blockade had caused a growing number of shortages for British trading and industrial concerns in both Shanghai and Tientsin. Relief supplies were badly needed in each of these cities, but landing them would be difficult if the embargo was maintained by the Nationalist authorities for any length of time.[30]

Since this situation could not be allowed to continue indefinitely, the Foreign Office began to consider what action might have to be taken if the Nationalists refused to accommodate foreign mercantile interests in an effort to ease the plight of the expatriate community in China. Its report, which was tabled at a meeting of the cabinet on 29 August, made grim reading because it revealed that although relations with the KMT were bad, those with the Communists were far worse. This accurate assessment of the current situation in China underlined the gravity of the problem for the Attlee administration. It was clear that the British government found itself in a deplorable situation: caught between two enemy forces and perceived by each of them to be imperialistic and untrustworthy. Despite the scale of their problems, however, the British were not totally bereft of ideas about how to react and what policies to adopt in China. It had already become obvious to the Foreign Office that whatever policy His Majesty's Government decided to follow, it could do nothing to reverse the steady erosion of the Nationalist's position in the civil war. Apart from experiencing reverses on land, the KMT had fared little better at sea. Gaps were now beginning to appear in its naval blockade as a result of the fall to the PLA of some of the strategic Miao Islands at the entrance to the Gulf of Pechili. Appreciating the significance of this trend, Bevin and his experts felt they could afford to take some chances with the KMT as its fortunes were on the wane. In making a couple of recommendations for dealing with this part of the strategic equation—including the controversial one of running the blockade in order to keep British commercial interests going—the memo assumed a less trenchant tone when addressing the subject of the appropriate line to adopt in coming to terms with the Communists.[31]

It was the growing military and political power of the Communists, which now seemed unlikely to be arrested by the KMT, that spelled trouble for the British in China. Although Attlee's government undoubtedly wished to "keep a foot in the door," along the lines of the foreign secretary's statement of December 1948, the key to the future success of this policy lay to a large extent beyond its control. Instead, it was the political hierarchy of the Communist party, which could hardly claim to be neutral toward Britain or its imperial interests in the wake of the *Amethyst* episode, that would determine the fate of British firms in China. Without mentioning this aspect of the problem, the report rather optimistically suggested that if the leading cadres of the CCP could be somehow induced to see the advantages of trading with foreign capitalists—a process that not only defied description but would also take some time to come to fruition—a future Communist government might allow the British to maintain their small commercial foothold on the mainland. The Foreign Office report, although occasionally engaging in wishful thinking, as in this case, did make some amends by admitting that if this measure of political will was lacking for any reason, the British would be in an intensely vulnerable position and one that they could do little about.[32]

It was evident from the tone of the Foreign Office memo that the PLA was expected to win a crushing victory in the civil war and to establish a Communist regime over much of China within a matter of months. In the meantime there was little for the British merchants in China to do other than to wait until conditions improved and try to ensure that no offense was caused to the Communists by any of their trading activities. This strategy may have been sound in theory, given the uncertainty of the expatriates' position and the ease with which it could be undermined, but in practice it was extremely difficult to keep a low and uncontentious profile in this war-torn country. A clear illustration of this problem had been graphically provided by the latest Yangtze incident. As a result, regardless of China's abundant sources of raw materials and foodstuffs and its rich potentialities as an export market, trade prospects between the British and a future central Communist government were almost impossible to gauge at this time. In line with these reservations and those of its diplomats in Nanking and Shanghai, the Foreign Office report mentioned the fear expressed by some merchants that when the Communists had won the war they might decide to impose excessive and penalizing taxation upon the British business enterprises still operating in some of the coastal cities of China in a concerted effort to drive them out. If the Communists resorted to such an anticapitalist policy, the British firms would be forced to withdraw from the country because they would not possess the financial resources to absorb such a blow. Clearly the Foreign Office hoped that a withdrawal could somehow be avoided and that a *modus vivendi* might be struck between the British merchants and the Communist authorities so as to ensure their future coexistence and preserve the possibility, at least in theory, of a semblance of mutual dependence on economic matters in the future.[33]

Choosing a policy that might be expected to secure these goals was not easy, although the use of diplomatic means was to be canvassed with increasing fervor by those in China as the autumn proceeded. If the British government was to live down its image in the eyes of the Communists as a collaborator of the KMT, it would have to adopt measures that would prove beyond doubt that this ''alliance'' was over once and for all. Nothing could accomplish that objective more starkly than by withdrawing *de jure* recognition from the Nationalist government and transferring it to any Communist regime that Mao might establish in China. Adopting a balanced view on this most contentious of subjects, the Foreign Office appreciation made the following observation:

> The political objections to precipitate recognition of a Communist regime are obvious. On the other hand, to withhold recognition from a Government in effective control of a large part of China is legally objectionable and leads to grave practical difficulties regarding the protection of Western interests in China. It is most unlikely that the fulfilment of any special conditions can be exacted in return for recognition of the Communist regime, and it is therefore probable that after a certain stage delay in proceeding with recognition might seriously prejudice Western interests in China without any compensating advantages being obtained. The Chinese Communists themselves are unlikely to be seriously inconvenienced by the withholding of recognition. For their part they will probably decline to enter into diplomatic relations with any Power which continues to recognise the Nationalist Government.[34]

Whatever the British Cabinet might finally decide to do about this question—and nothing could be done until a Communist government was established in China—the omens for a vastly improved relationship with Mao's forces were not promising. As a result there was little room for doubt about where the ideological battle lines were drawn between the two sides: quite apart from the acrimony caused by the escape of the *Amethyst*, the military buildup of Hong Kong that had been going on since May 1948—with the scarcely concealed intention of thwarting any Communist takeover of the colony—and the vigorous, uncompromising attitude adopted by the British against the MCP in the Malayan Emergency ensured that Anglo-Chinese relations remained poor.[35] Mao's equally unequivocal public statements, which extolled the virtues of forming an antiimperial front with the Soviet Union against the western powers and scoffing at the idea that the Chinese needed any assistance from their class enemies, demonstrated graphically that if any improvement in bi-lateral relations was desired by either London or Peking it would only come about in a slow, painstaking way.[36]

These portents were not misleading. In the absence of mutual willingness to cooperate, it is scarcely surprising that no overall or discernible improvement in relations between Britain and the PLA could be detected during the rest of the summer or early autumn of 1949. Although the establishment of the People's Republic of China (PRC) on 1 October seemed at the time to hold out the hope of better times ahead, the prospects proved to be only illusory. Attlee's government eventually shrugged off American objections and hastened to grant *de jure* recognition of the PRC on 6 January 1950, but the act itself did not bring the immediate rewards British officials at home and expatriate businessmen in China appear to have expected.

To the dismay of the Foreign Office, the Chinese government drew a distinction between recognition and the establishment of normal diplomatic links between the two powers. According to the Communists, further negotiations were necessary before this advanced stage in their relationship could be reached. This announcement ushered in the likelihood of a further indeterminate delay and one that could not easily be bridged, particularly because the principal Communist demand involved an issue of extreme sensitivity, namely, the total severance of relations between the British government and the Nationalist regime in Taiwan.[37] Although formal talks between London and Peking on normalizing their relations began shortly after *de jure* recognition had been granted by the British, these diplomatic efforts soon floundered as the sceptics imagined they would. It is not difficult to see why.

The British government's risky and muddleheaded attitude to the China question, characterized by a desire to maintain its existing links with the Nationalists while forging new ones with the Communists, was soon revealed in the most imposing of official forums, with dire results for relations between London and Peking. On 13 January 1950, Sir Alexander Cadogan, leader of the United Kingdom delegation to the United Nations (UN), abstained from voting on a Soviet motion in the Security Council to remove UN accreditation from the KMT government and award it instead to the PRC. Cadogan's unwillingness to commit his government fully to this course of action was resented by the Chinese Communist regime, which saw it as yet another instance of British insincerity toward the PRC and partiality for the Nationalists of Taiwan.[38] This belief in the innate hostility of the democratic powers was further fueled by Ernest Bevin's injudicious remarks made during a parliamentary debate on 24 May 1950, when he referred to the "unpleasant decision" his government had had to make in recognizing Mao's regime. Although Hansard's version of his speech quoted him as saying that it had been an "awkward decision," the Chinese media treated the revision with scant respect.[39] It cannot have helped the British cause or made the Communist leadership view Attlee's administration as anything other than a reactionary elite and one of which it should be wary. Soon, all hope of a new commercial dawn for British firms in China had been dispelled. Trading conditions deteriorated and losses mounted for those businessmen who had stayed on in Shanghai and other coastal ports in the mistaken belief that things would get better once the British government had granted *de jure* recognition of the PRC.[40] Their problems were mirrored by those who had the virtually impossible task of reconciling the two powers on the diplomatic stage.

John Hutchison, who was sent out to Peking on 13 February 1950 as British chargé d'affaires, soon came to appreciate the scale of the problem at firsthand. Although he did not hold ambassadorial rank, he had nonetheless assumed the position of leading British diplomat in China and might have expected to receive the customary treatment accorded to such individuals from the government in Peking. Instead, his presence as head of the British mission was never officially recognized by the Communist authorities during the frustrating year he spent in the Chinese capital, nor was he ever afforded the chance of meeting Mao, Foreign Minister Chou En-lai, or any of the other top chance of leaders of the PRC.[41] His extraordinary diplomatic isolation demonstrated most vividly the depths to which Anglo-Chinese relations had plunged in recent months and the unfulfilled wishes of those British officials and businessmen who had hoped that a formal recognition of the Communist regime would lead to a more harmonious and profitable future for all concerned. What was left of this once rich and alluring image evaporated altogether when the first shots of the Korean War rang out on 25 June 1950. Gone was the anticipated commercial success and likewise gone were the talks designed to normalize Anglo-Chinese relations. Britain's failure in China was complete.

Aside from the ideological antipathy that separated the Attlee administration and its peculiar brand of social conservatism from that of Mao's idiosyncratic version of Marxism-Leninism, the roots of Britain's failure in China can be traced back to the civil war and to the kind of policies with which the British were identified during that hectic period. Whether accidental or deliberate, justified or not, the fact remains that to the Communists the British government did not appear to be neutral even if it constantly claimed that it was. Perhaps nothing illustrates this situation more clearly than the *Amethyst* episode. Looking back to the origins of that crisis, one is forcibly struck by the mistaken belief of British officials in China that their country, as a great power, could not be trifled with and certainly not by a creaking fascist state or its upstart adversary.

Not all commentators have viewed the stationing of a gunboat at Nanking in this unflattering light, however, and they have stressed the very real humanitarian motives underlying the original decision to keep a British vessel up the Yangtze on guard duty. According to the apologists for this scheme, such a ship was needed to ensure adequate protection for British lives and property in Nanking when it looked as though a dangerous power vacuum might occur there after the collapse of the KMT and before the establishment of the PLA in the city. This theme was taken up by the *Spectator,* as its leader of 29 April 1949 makes clear:

> Conditions were then such that a destroyer could have acted either as a stabilising influence locally or as a means of escape if the situation deteriorated. At that time such Communist elements as had reached the north bank consisted only of scattered reconnaissance parties, unsupported by heavy equipment and incapable of opposing effectively the passage of one of H.M. ships on an errand of mercy. The original decision, therefore, to order a destroyer to stand by at Nanking was a perfectly proper one, since the destroyer could in those days have done without serious risk any of the things that she might have been required to do.[42]

Although the rationale for this decision sounds plausible enough when addressed in these terms, at closer inspection the laudable aims of the policy appear less defensible, especially when one remembers Bevin's exhortation to the diplomatic corps to remain at their posts in China regardless of which party wielded power at the national or local level. For these individuals, therefore, evacuation aboard a British gunboat was hardly the option they were likely to exercise unless the KMT or PLA decided to go on a rampage. By the same token, those civilian personnel working in China knew the risks of staying in a likely war zone and could have left of their own volition by rail, road, or air before the onset of fighting. They could not say that they had not been warned of the potential dangers they were running by remaining behind in a country engulfed by civil war. If they chose to ignore these warnings, it is at least arguable whether the British government had a moral duty to rescue them in an emergency.

By stationing a warship at Nanking, the British government assumed a responsibility for these people and in so doing exposed itself to a far greater danger than the one its solitary naval vessel was designed to prevent. Whatever possessed the author(s) of this Yangtze policy to propose such an extraordinary plan in the first instance, or the government to approve it, still defies logical explanation, unless an excuse can be found in what apologists are wont to describe as "the exigencies of the time." One can only imagine that the remarkable gains made by the Communists in the civil war during the late autumn of 1948 must have touched off a collective sense of panic among British officials in China, impairing their judgment and that of the senior members of the Admiralty and Foreign Office in London who were monitoring the latest phase in the PLA-KMT struggle and who were anxious to preserve British interests from the ravages of either side.

Although it is clear from the primary source naval records that Stevenson first proposed the idea of having a Nanking guardship to the Foreign Office on 9 November 1948, the files say nothing about how this policy was born. Fortunately, the evidence of His Excellency U Myint Thein, the Burmese ambassador to China, reveals that the idea was agreed upon unanimously by the most senior figures in the Commonwealth diplomatic community resident in Nanking in the autumn of 1948. This much has been confirmed by Rear-Admiral Vernon Donaldson. Unfortunately, neither can recall who was the first person to propose the scheme. Tempting though it is to think of the chain-smoking British ambassador as the prime suspect, Sir Ralph Stevenson would hardly have proposed such an initiative without first consulting Sir Denis Boyd, the commander in chief of the Far East Station in Singapore, or his deputy in Hong Kong, Vice-Admiral Alexander Madden. Despite the lack of evidence to confirm or deny this link, the suspicion remains that the naval personnel, like their mercantile brethren, would have encouraged any plan that opened up the Yangtze to foreign vessels once again and at the same time supplied the operational means to evacuate British nationals from Nanking and its environs smoothly and without delay should the situation demand it. Without Boyd's support, or failing that the Admiralty's, the Nanking guardship could not have become a practical proposition.

A change of fleet commander from the irascible and haughty Boyd to the less bellicose and usually more enlightened Sir Patrick Brind on 11 January 1949 failed to have any immediate impact upon and merely served to perpetuate the British naval presence in Chinese waters. Vice-Admiral Madden, the flag officer associated with the policy from its infancy, continued to be responsible for supervising it and arranging the selection of the Nanking guardship from the force at his disposal on the Far East Station. A torpedo specialist, Madden had been retained on the active list in December 1948. He was a popular figure in naval circles—an amusing extrovert, well liked by his fellow officers and men. He was also known to be a reliable and experienced sailor, even though he was by no means an intellectual powerhouse.[43] It is clear from the decisions he made in April 1949 that he saw no reason for overhauling or suspending the Yangtze policy at that time. It is doubtful whether the idea of scrapping it ever seriously entered his head.

Although it is easy enough to blame the local officials for committing the British government to a disastrous policy, the responsibility for the Yangtze incident is a shared one. It is simply inconceivable that neither major department of state was informed about this extension of the Royal Navy's role in China or that official approval was never actually given for this measure. Whether the Admiralty or the Foreign Office were the initiators of this policy or merely willing accomplices of their local officials in its execution, the fact remains that the evacuation scheme ought to have been reviewed in light of the disciplined conduct exhibited by the PLA when it had assumed power in such cities as Mukden, Peking, and Tientsin by the end of January 1949. Those events and the impasse in the civil war ought to have persuaded the government to think again on this question. It did not. Inertia triumphed over wisdom. Besides the cabinet, which remained blissfully ignorant of this novel way of alienating the most probable victors in the civil war, the other official committees dealing with defense matters or foreign affairs in London were never alerted to the dangers of this curiously benighted and offensive policy. It is a moot point whether the British Defence Coordination Committee in Singapore ever discussed the issue, but even if it did—and its papers have never been fully released so verification is impossible—the significant fact is that this grossly irresponsible policy remained untouched. As a result, the British continued to flaunt their indifference to Chinese sensitivities by retaining a solitary gunboat at Nanking, an action that involved sending either a destroyer or frigate 200 miles upriver from Shanghai at roughly fortnightly intervals to relieve it. It does not seem to have occurred to them that the Communists might have resented this singular demonstration of British superiority, or that the PLA would be moved to object to what they could construe as an unauthorized incursion into Chinese territorial waters, until the attack upon the *Amethyst* awoke them to the reality of the situation in the most dramatic way possible. Whatever blame one apportions among the various parties for constructing and maintaining this policy, the plain fact is that by the spring of 1949 its retention had become an act of incredible folly.

If the British can be accused of being excessively myopic over the matter of the Nanking guardship, the question of who or what was responsible for the

Yangtze incident still remains to be solved. According to those on board the *Amethyst*, the facts are clear and indisputable: the British frigate was twice attacked without warning by Communist batteries situated on the northern shore of the Yangtze on the morning of 20 April. This was the story that was reproduced faithfully and often in graphic detail by most organs of the western press. These newspapers were already predisposed to seeing things in confrontational terms because the crisis had arisen during the cold war, which pitted the western allies against the Communist world. All claims by the PLA that the *Amethyst* fired first were generally dismissed by the Anglo-American media barons as mischevious propaganda designed to cover up the culpability of the Communist military in attacking the frigate.[44] Unless the men aboard the *Amethyst* had fired a stray round or two at some undisclosed target along the Yangtze—an act strenuously denied by all those on the frigate that morning—it is difficult to imagine what the *Amethyst* could have done to convince the PLA that she had opened the exchange of gunfire on the river.

Yet despite the disavowals of the *Amethyst*'s crew concerning the indiscriminate or deliberate firing of blanks or live shells by them on their journey upriver from Kiangyin, the ship's report, written several weeks after the fact by John Kerans, refers mysteriously to the possibility that a noise may have been created by testing the frigate's firing circuits. What Kerans meant by this statement is almost impossible to deduce. He died without clarifying what he had written on this point. In any case, as he was not even on board the vessel when the original incident occurred, one is entitled to assume that either he made a genuine mistake when compiling the report or he must have received his information from someone who was on board the frigate and in a position to know what happened on her ill-fated passage upriver.

Sir Peter E. C. Berger, who at the time was the navigating officer on board the frigate, denies vehemently that the *Amethyst* was in any way responsible for her own downfall on that early spring morning of 20 April. He insists that Kerans's statement makes no sense because the mere act of testing the firing circuits, usually a virtually noiseless procedure, could hardly have been heard by the Communist forces drawn up on the northern bank of the river. Nevertheless, an element of doubt persists and cannot be conveniently swept away or ignored. One should not forget that in the weeks that followed, the Communists never once wavered from their original negotiating stance that the British ship unleashed the first shots in the affair.

Although it vehemently dismissed the allegations made by the Communists, the British Foreign Office was inclined from the outset to accept the view of Sir Ralph Stevenson, its ambassador in China, that the PLA action in opening fire upon the *Amethyst* was not premeditated.[45] This view was made apparent in an analysis of the encounter written specifically with Attlee's parliamentary speech of 26 April in mind.

> It is now known with some certainty that the People's Liberation Army had general orders not to fire on British vessels unless they fired first. And FO 2 i/c has confirmed that he is satisfied there is no question of a deliberate "trap." This is supported by the action of the first battery . . . in ceasing fire when *Amethyst* was fully identified. It is also fairly clear that fire was not opened by individual guns' crews without orders, as eyewitnesses reports show that the discipline, etc., of the rank and file is very good.[46]

This assessment led the Foreign Office to infer that the first engagement off Low Island was probably the result of an error made by the PLA battery commander in failing to identify the *Amethyst* as a British frigate and not a vessel of the KMT navy.

Although the first incident could be explained away in this fashion, could the same be said about the battery at San-chiang-ying, which did so much damage to the British ship? In this case, as we have seen, the battery's concentrated shell fire had wrought immediate havoc with the frigate, disabling her and contributing to her grounding on the western shore of Rose Island. In addressing this particular incident, the Foreign Office memo offered the government two possible explanations: either the PLA battery commander at San-chiang-ying exceeded his brief in ordering his men to open fire upon the *Amethyst* or he did so because he initially mistook the gunboat to be hostile and a fair target for his men to engage.[47] Beyond the initial onslaught, however, the battery continued to pound the ship unmercifully for a total of one and a half hours, long after the *Amethyst* had stopped using her own guns against the PLA and presumably some time after the vessel must have been positively identified as belonging to the Royal Navy. Why it did so remains a mystery; the Foreign Office did not speculate on the reasons for this prolonged bombardment and seems to have regarded it as a quirk of fate.

Although it had no more evidence to go on, the British government stood by this assessment of the situation, attributing the shelling to a reckless decision made in the first instance by Major Kung (alias Colonel Kang Mao-chao), the battery commander at San-chiang-ying. Its view was reinforced by Kang's uncompromising conduct in the seemingly interminable and tedious series of negotiations for the release of the *Amethyst* that took place during the spring and early summer of 1949. His determination to pin the blame for the Yangtze incident solely on the British was seen by His Majesty's Government as nothing more than a cynical attempt to deflect attention and future criticism from the role he and the PLA had played in the crisis. While the British officials did not resist the temptation of ascribing Kang's querulous behavior in these terms, their explanation for his conduct would look a little careworn if it could be proved that the political commissioner was not actually present when the incident broke out. All along, the British officials suspected that Kang was the individual who had issued the orders to fire upon the *Amethyst*, and they steadfastly refused to see him as anything less than a self-serving individual anxious to make amends for his original mistake by securing what would be tantamount to the unconditional defeat of the Royal Navy in Chinese waters.

Despite the fact that no solid evidence to the contrary was published by the PRC until 1988, the account written by Kang Maozhao, which appeared in three installments of *Shi Jie Zhi Shi* (World Knowledge) in that year, reveals that the obdurate Colonel Kang was not with his battery at the time of the shelling. Instead he and Li Ang Bong, the battalion commander, had left the third battery unit at San-chiang-ying early in the morning in order to attend a conference at Yang Chow on the preparations for the impending cross-Yangtze offensive against the KMT when the *Amethyst* incident had occurred.[48]

If this account is accurate, the question of who or what was responsible for this most unfortunate incident has still to be finally resolved. At first glance it seems to suggest that the San-chiang-ying incident could have arisen through a misunderstanding much as the first one at Low Island had, the major difference being the contrasting fortunes of the two gun crews. While the artillery group north of Low Island had struggled to find the range of the *Amethyst* and had not hit her once before the attack was called off, the San-chiang-ying battery had displayed a lethal accuracy in striking its target with only its second shell. Its sheer effectiveness in rapidly disabling the British frigate transformed what might otherwise have been a local skirmish into an international incident. Once an exchange of gunfire had taken place between the PLA and the *Amethyst*, the encounter could no longer be contained; the extent of the damage caused and the number of casualties inflicted on both ship and shore were bound to provoke further hostility among those involved and lead to demands from them for revenge and retribution. Whether these inflammatory sentiments can account for the PLA's decision to continue strafing the *Amethyst* long after she had been driven aground remains unclear. Whatever the explanation, the damage had already been done; a costly mistake at the local level on 20 April had resulted in an international crisis that proceeded to get far worse as *Consort, London,* and *Black Swan* came onto the scene and were thwarted in their rescue attempts for the *Amethyst* during the next 28 hours.[49]

It was later alleged by the Communists that the British had received considerable aid from the Nationalists during those first hectic hours after *Amethyst* had gone aground. Although the Admiralty confirms that the KMT was willing to offer various forms of assistance to the men of the stricken frigate after the attack on 20 April, it totally rejects all Communist claims that there was any actual collusion between the task force assembled by the Far East Station and ships of the Nationalist Chinese on the following day's sortie toward Rose Island. For their part the Communists have not presented any convincing evidence to prove their claim that there was a conscious effort on behalf of the two navies to mount a concerted rescue operation for the *Amethyst*. Nonetheless, it must be admitted that it would have been customary for an officer of Madden's rank to pay a courtesy call on the senior KMT naval officer aboard the destroyer *Yat Sen* after *London*'s arrival at Kiangyin on the evening of 20 April. It is unbelievable that such a meeting could have taken place without the two men discussing the extraordinary events of that day and the next steps that Madden was inclined to take in striving to rescue the *Amethyst* from the custody of the Communists. Whether an offer of support was forthcoming from the KMT admiral is unknown, as is Madden's reply, if any. Once again, alas, the official record is silent on this matter.

Although irrefutable evidence is lacking on the question of what, if any, direct naval involvement took place between the Nationalists and the British at this time, some information has leaked out subsequently concerning the kind of assistance rendered by the Marine Department of the Chinese Maritime Customs in helping to keep the navigational lights burning and other aids on the Yangtze operational in order to facilitate the *Amethyst*'s progress downriver on the night of 30–31 July. Madden acknowledged later that without this assistance, the *Amethyst* would not have been able to make her heroic passage downriver to the open sea.[50] This aspect of the great escape was not revealed to the world in any of the press conferences that were arranged following the momentous events of that long night on the run. A premature disclosure of this form of cooperation would have been most indiscreet and not served the future interests of either the British or the Maritime Customs. An official silence on this issue, therefore, became a matter of policy.

Besides the largely unknown but intriguing role played by the Maritime Customs in the escape bid and the implication that it was aware from an early stage of what was afoot, there were other elements of the *Amethyst*'s successful dash for freedom of which the Communists were unaware and that are still worth considering now. In deciding to abandon all hope of a negotiated end to the Yangtze incident and staking everything on attempting a river passage at night, Kerans was giving vent to his true feelings. He was an inspirational leader whose flair and charisma, which had not always been appreciated by the Admiralty in the past, were a redeeming feature throughout the *Amethyst*'s long vigil on the Yangtze. A complex and rather rebellious character, Kerans's resolve even under desperately difficult conditions to face down the Communists had been buttressed to a large extent by the loyal support he had consistently received from Lieutenant George Strain. Although Kerans was depicted by the non-Communist press as the dashing hero of the Yangtze crisis, the relatively unsung qualities of George Strain during the entire episode deserved more attention than they received. Strain helped Kerans cope with the very intense pressures he was under throughout the long, drawn-out crisis on the river and helped his captain build up a very loyal following among his men on board the frigate. As a result, if either man was prepared to risk his life for freedom so were they. To be fair, however, it must be acknowledged that it was basically Kerans's show. Far from being unreliable or reckless, as many in the Admiralty were wont to see him, he had shown a remarkable amount of restraint in the painfully frustrating series of negotiations he had endured with the PLA delegation. The little progress made in these sessions had convinced him that something more drastic was required to extricate his ship and men from their predicament. Sensing that Admiral Brind was restless for some action and supportive of any decision within limits that he might take to supply it, Kerans had little difficulty in choosing an adventurous end to the Yangtze story.

When this decision was conveyed to the first sea lord and the British ambassador by the commander in chief, however, they were aghast that Kerans had taken matters into his own hands without consulting higher authority in advance. Both Fraser and Stevenson would have preferred to carry on the official talks in the hope of bringing about a negotiated settlement of the affair.[51] Whether these talks would have succeeded is far from clear, although the prospects of a settlement on anything less than the Communists' terms were probably out of the question by this stage. Neither Yuan nor Kang had seemed ready for a compromise; time was on their side, so they could afford to wait for the British to accept the inevitable, apologize, and pay some form of indemnity. Regardless of whether they acted on their own initiative or, as seems more likely, received their orders directly from leading members of the CCP, the end result can best be summed up in the phrase *No surrender*. This firm and unyielding attitude personified by Kang, whom the British saw as being unscrupulous and incorrigible, left the Attlee administration with little room to maneuver.

As a result of the fact that the Chinese appeared to be unimpressed by British stoicism or undeterred by the thought that they were negotiating with one of the great powers, the options available to Kerans, Brind, and the government in London were rather limited. No naval solution, even if one could be found, would eliminate the PLA and CCP from their position of ascendancy in China. Short of spiriting the *Amethyst* away from under the gaze of the Communists, therefore, no other realistic alternatives to reaching an agreement with the PLA were on offer at this time. Knowing that there was only a limited range of options available, the British government had supported its local and regional officials who were striving to find a diplomatic solution to this question on the best terms that they could get. In fact, other than the loss of pride and an undisclosed sum of money, the government really had very little to lose by issuing a public apology and paying some form of indemnity for the Yangtze incident, particularly if it hoped to maintain, let alone increase, its commercial stake in China after the end of the civil war. Therefore, it had gradually shifted its position to become more accommodating in the talks and doubtless would have gone further still along this road if it had been allowed to. Quite how far it would have gone in pursuit of a settlement if the Communists had continued to remain intransigent is, however, unclear.

Kerans's decisive action in launching his escape bid may have spared the Attlee administration from further embarrassment by removing all element of choice about what it ought to do for the best, but his decision was not initially welcomed by either Nanking or Whitehall. Although understandable, Kerans's willingness to tempt fate in this cavalier manner was obviously a gamble whose chances of success were incalculable. Sir Ralph Stevenson, who admitted later that he would not have given his assent to such a risky enterprise if he had been consulted in advance, spent a sleepness night waiting for news of the *Amethyst* as she sped downriver on the flood tide.[52] Both he and Lord Fraser, who had actually turned down the plan when he learned of its existence, admired Kerans's boldness and courage but were fearful of the complications that would result if the bid failed and anxious lest the brave men who risked their lives to get free from Communist detention ended up condemned by the PLA artillery to a watery grave. In the event, they had no need to worry because the frigate made it to the open sea virtually unscathed.[53]

By escaping against the odds the *Amethyst*, battered but defiant to the last, achieved instant fame. She was depicted by the western media as a symbol of spirited democratic resistance to the steady and deadening encroachment of communism around the world. Her exploits, which were recalled with such avidity and relish by much of the western press, became a cause for unre-

strained—some would say excessive—national rejoicing in the United Kingdom. Kerans and his crew became folk heroes overnight. Their epic voyage
seemed to catch the imagination of a people depressed by postwar austerity and
the unrelieved hostility of the cold war. It is not, therefore, surprising that
their arrival was eagerly awaited and noisily acclaimed by huge crowds at every
port of call on their homeward voyage to the United Kingdom through the
Indian Ocean, Suez Canal, and the Mediterranean. Wherever she docked,
HMS *Amethyst* supplied a ready excuse for merrymaking on a lavish and vast
scale, and the opportunity to stage parades, assemble bands, host banquets, and
hold press conferences was not forsaken by the citizens of the Commonwealth
who had not had much to cheer about in recent years. She eventually arrived
back in Plymouth on 1 November 1949 to scenes of euphoria eclipsing even
those witnessed in Hong Kong on 3 August.[54]

Although it is tempting to regard the escape of the *Amethyst* as a triumph for
the Royal Navy, not everyone found this prolonged celebration of British
stealth and deliverance to their taste. Consul General Urquhart was one who
felt that the *Amethyst* saga had done no favors for the British community in
China. As a resident of Shanghai, it was a good deal easier for him not to get
caught up in the wave of patriotic fervor that was sweeping his native country.
Writing on 3 August about the popular and jingoistic celebrations going on in
Britain over the escape of the frigate, he offered the Foreign Office a perceptive
analysis of what he saw as a curious inversion of the truth.

> The parable needs re-writing to cover a case of such loud rejoicing over one
> sheep lost and found while ninety and nine are still outside the fold and without
> defence against the wolves. A happy ending is not easy to contrive.[55]

It was a cautionary message that the government may have understood and
yet failed for various reasons to appreciate fully in the immediate aftermath of
the *Amethyst*'s escape. Despite its anxiety lest some of the more unsavory
aspects of the Yangtze incident got into print and encouraged a xenophobic
reaction among the public at large, the government did not court unpopularity
by belittling the significance of the *Amethyst*'s achievements. On the contrary,
a conscious decision was made from the outset to honor her men when they
returned home. Meticulous plans were drawn up to do justice to the crew
whose sterling deeds had been an inspiration to the British public. On 16
November 1949 the City of London had its chance to pay its respects to these
unlikely heroes of the ill-timed intervention by the Royal Navy in the Chinese
civil war. After assembling on Horse Guards Parade, Kerans and his men
marched to St. Martins-in-the-Fields for a thanksgiving service and from there

onto Guildhall for a luncheon given by the lord mayor of London. Cheering crowds lined the entire route. On the next day a smaller delegation drawn from the officers and crew of the ship was received by the king at Buckingham Palace.[56] HMS *Amethyst* had been rewarded the ultimate accolade.

Fame had its price, however, for while the democracies celebrated the safe return of the frigate in grand style, the Communists regarded the escape as a source of bitter embarrassment and intense anger. Whichever way one looked at it, they had lost face: their quarry had slipped away unnoticed and defied the batteries that had once pounded larger ships than the *Amethyst* into submission. This fact alone pointed to lamentable inefficiency on the part of the PLA, a feature that could not be effectively disguised even by the Communist media.[57] Although public humiliation may be instructive, it is also painful. It is not easily forgotten or forgiven.

At the same time it is important to keep the *Amethyst* episode in perspective; after all it only represented a mere hiccup in the otherwise quite remarkable military rise to power of the Communists in China. Yet to dismiss it as an issue of only marginal importance may be as much a mistake as treating it as a matter of the greatest possible significance. In making a negative contribution to Anglo-Chinese relations, the Yangtze incident could be said to have confirmed the feeling already held in Communist circles that the British were insincere, cunning, ruthless, and untrustworthy. Is it therefore surprising that relations between Attlee's administration and Mao's regime stagnated in the weeks and months that followed the *Amethyst*'s perilous trip down the Yangtze on that dark night in late July?

Ironically, what was seen initially by the British as a victory soon became a comprehensive defeat. Their gamble of using old-style imperialism in a new setting had proved to be very costly. In a very real sense, therefore, the *Amethyst* episode represented the end of an old adventure and not the beginning of a new one.

Appendixes

Appendix 1

Casualties on Royal Navy Ships, 20–21 April 1949

Casualties	Amethyst	London	Consort	Black Swan
Killed	22[a]	13	10	0
Missing	1	0	0	0
Wounded	31[b]	32	23	7
Total	54	45	33	7

Sources: "Admiralty Command Report," 6 May 1949, F6522/1219/10, F0 371/75891; App. 5, "*Amethyst* Report," 271.

[a]Includes two Chinese ratings and one Yangtze pilot.

[b]Includes one Chinese rating.

Note: There is a discrepancy in the figures supplied by the two sources listed above. In the "Admirality Command Report" (ACR), only twenty-nine people are classified as wounded on the *Amethyst*. Part of the explanation lies in the fact that the ACR only lists British officers and ratings and does not include local Chinese employees.

Appendix 2

British and Japanese Ships Entering and Clearing
Chinese Ports, 1900–1938

Year	Number of British Ships	Total Weight, tons	Number of Japanese Ships	Total Weight, tons
1900	22,618	23,052,459	4,917	3,871,559
1910	28,000	34,253,439	31,197	18,903,146
1911	28,885	34,712,440	21,259	19,172,727
1912	31,909	38,106,732	20,091	19,913,385
1913	32,186	38,120,300	22,716	23,422,487
1914	32,705	38,795,409	22,143	23,684,774
1918	31,034	29,911,369	24,961	25,283,373
1919	36,074	36,284,312	27,182	27,532,449
1920	39,543	40,315,707	25,152	28,191,592
1921	38,855	42,326,445	25,385	31,738,783
1922	40,075	47,698,139	25,281	32,961,333
1923	44,055	51,965,230	25,063	33,288,617
1924	48,886	55,715,925	26,294	34,759,884
1925	36,937	42,942,484	27,261	35,081,116
1926	36,474	47,645,090	29,654	38,938,844
1927	33,791	40,258,049	27,105	35,745,535
1928	48,523	56,036,567	29,839	39,065,724
1929	50,845	57,926,507	31,705	42,349,647
1930	49,402	57,246,927	33,755	45,630,705
1931	50,534	60,560,794	31,589	43,042,411
1932	49,517	59,430,602	13,441	19,775,917
1933	47,574	58,215,213	12,863	20,168,140
1936	48,154	57,345,515	17,911	24,913,576
1937	35,232	36,105,795	10,435	12,815,014
1938	23,398	28,403,147	7,242	8,743,975

Sources: Bell and Woodhead, *China Year Book, 1912–20;* Woodhead, *China Year Book, 1921–30;* Woodhead, *China Year Book, 1931–39.* These volumes used information collated on an annual basis by the Chinese Maritime Customs.

Note: What these figures do not reveal, however, is the extent to which the Japanese were using Chinese-flagged vessels in the period after the Manchurian incident of September 1931 to carry their trade for them.

Appendix 3

HMS *Consort*'s Narrative of Events on 20 April 1949

The following narrative is recorded in *Consort* to C-in-C FES (Afloat), 110540, May 1949, Adm 1/21299.

On receipt of F.O. 2 I/C signal ordering CONSORT to "Proceed to assistance of AMETHYST," we advanced our time of sailing and got away at 1130 instead of 1200 which had previously been our scheduled time.

After jettisoning £160 worth of empty beer bottles and cases, proceeded through Nanking cut off (1/4 mile wide) at 20 knots, increasing to 28 knots when clear.

We hoisted 7 ensigns and displayed 3 Union Jacks and at 1300 went to action stations. We were travelling down the Yangtse faster than any ship had ever done before and our wash would have been destructive to the numerous craft that ply in normal times. In point of fact there was an ominous calm over the entire river except for some automatic machine gun fire coming from the North bank in the vicinity of Icheng.

Although our guns were peacefully fore and aft, we were keeping a very close watch on the North bank and after we'd been hit several times we fired one salvo which scored a hit on a machine gun emplacement. All enemy fire immediately ceased.

We were keeping in touch with F.O. 2 I/C and Nanking by wireless, giving them a SITREP every ten minutes and at 1345 we were able to report that AMETHYST was in sight. This was earlier than expected as her position proved to be further up than calculated and we had apparently made a good 30 knots.

She signalled to us advising us to turn back but naturally we went on, and we were approaching her at 15 knots, when suddenly "bang-whoosh" and a shell landed 100 yards away on our starboard quarter followed rapidly by another one.

That was enough invitation for us and we let them have it back with "knobs on" (those were the captain's actual words). We went on past the "AMETHYST" and right round the Rose Island bend passing within 1000 yards of their batteries. We knocked out three by direct hits but missed others because of our spread at that very short range. However they must have been well shaken up because when we were two miles below "AMETHYST" their firing ceased and so did ours. We stopped the ship, turned round and moved slowly back in order to take "AMETHYST" in tow. We paused long enough to acertain that our own damage was superficial and our casualties none. "AMETHYST" did not look too badly aground and we signalled that we would send Medical assistance, and for her to be ready to be taken in tow.

As we moved back into "Hell Fire Corner" we were again fired at and succeeded in picking off four more emplacements whilst our Bofors beat up enemy concentrations. While this was going on the 1st Lieutenant (Lieut. B. C. Hutchinson R.N.) came up to the bridge and calmly reported "All ready to tow Aft Sir." After travelling slowly abour [sic] mile we started getting hit again, and it was pretty accurate fire coming from concealed positions well behind the bend. The wheelhouse was hit, killing the coxswain and putting the forward steering position out of action. We were ready for that one, because the torpedo tube's crew were manning the tiller flat, instead of the tubes, so it was an easy matter to telephone the wheel order direct to them from the bridge.

The Captain sent the navigator Lieut J. Consadine R.N. to the wheelhouse for a quick estimation of the situation there, and as he returned on [sic] the bridge his tin hat was removed from his head. When he picked it up it had a hole straight through the front centre made by a .5 bullet. He reported that the wheel was wrecked the coxswain killed and the other occupants wounded. At this time the bridge was hit twice by 37mm shells and the first Chinese Pilot was knocked out. The second pilot had to be dragged up from down below and pinned in position by the navigator's dividers. Although we appeared to have knocked out all the emplaced guns there was a lot of this lighter stuff flying about and pieces were being chipped off the ship rather fast. "A" and "B" guns were put out of action, the trainer in each case later dying of wounds whilst many others were wounded.

It was then about 1500 and the captain reluctantly decided to withdraw. We could do nothing for AMETHYST, we could not even send a doctor as ours had 25 wounded on his hands. If we'd had a seaworthy boat, we knew it was unlikely to survive in that concentration of fire for long. The dressing station (Wardroom) was inches deep in blood and whilst the Medical Officer (Surgeon Lieut. Bentley R.N.) ably continued his grisly work, the wardroom was hit three times putting the lights out, re-wounding casualties and sweeping away the surgical instruments. Luckily the doctor was untouched and he was ably assisted by the one Sick Berth Attendant (Ldg. S. B. A. Harwood) whilst the radar ratings were of great value as stretcher bearers.

While the survivors of "A" and "B" guns went aft to man "Y" gun, "X" gun had a stoppage and for a brief unhealthy few minutes none of our main armament was in action. However, the Bofors were still firing and so was a Bren gun on the after bridge which was continuously at the shoulder of Lieut. Birks R.N. who was stationed there in case either the Captain or Navigator dropped. Actually the Captain had at this stage been wounded and though one leg was dripping blood he was not badly hurt.

When "X" gun jammed the gunner's mate (Petty Officer Robinson) got so excited that in his exhortations to the supply party to keep the Bofors in action his upper plate fell out and he promptly flung it at the supply parties and when the next belt of ammunition ran out, he said that one half was no good without the other and so hurled the lower half at those "bloody Communists." Supply parties were short handed and were mostly made up of Chinese cooks, stewards and mess boys and the dhoby firm. As the crisis drew on they were discovered to be sending up any projectile they could lay hands on, even starshell. The stokers of fire and repair parties when not putting out fires, of which there were several, hurled themselves into the magazine in order to send up more ammunition. Not counting the unexploded shell which was discovered many days later sitting on top of one of the boilers, the engine and boiler rooms had only [sic] hit, which was very lucky. The engine room had a big part to play. On no less than three occasions, that afternoon they received the order "Emergency full astern together," when that wasn't on the order of the day was "full ahead together."

We turned only 500 yards from the North bank down river, slowly, signalling to AMETHYST "We'll be back in the morning" in order to cheer them up. As all our signal projectors had been put out of action, and two leading signalman wounded we made the signal by W/T and got it through only a few minutes before that equipment, too, was wrecked.

As we cleared Rose Island we went on again to 28 knots hugging the south bank of the river. We had about 10 minutes breather, which was hardly long enough to reorganise, when the batteries on Low Island opened up.

As our director circuits had been shot away, we could only answer back with "X" and "Y" guns firing independently and the enemy had apparently 8 75mm guns in emplacements on the bund. At least one of their guns did some very accurate shooting and we were hit in rapid succession, in the gyro room, radar office, W/T office, T.S. etc. The first shot had the effect of swinging the ship in towards the bank, but she was soon conned back by telephone order from the bridge, although not before the engines had been ordered astern and then put ahead again.

The second shot killed two and wounded three of the forward repair party, the third shot wrecked the W/T transmitter and mortally wounded the operator in the middle of an emergency message. The other occupants were either killed or wounded except a young acting leading telegraphist Miller, who disentangled himself from the mess and immediately went aft to get the emergency set going.

The fourth shot wrecked the T.S. killing the whole crew of three. The Electrical Officer who had been visiting the T.S. came up to report to the Captain looking like a negro covered with the debris of the explosion. Although alongside the crew he was himself untouched.

The fifth shot started a fire amongst the Oerlikon supply line forward, but this was soon dealt with by the remainder of the forward fire party ably led by Leading Stoker Mechanician Johnson.

Meantime we were answering back and knocked out one emplacement. At a speed of about 28 knots we were fairly soon clear, but there was another drama to come. Owing to a misunderstood order the wheel in the tiller flat was put the wrong way and the ship turned directly towards the South bank which was only 200 yards away. It seemed unlikely that we could fail to end up a permanent feature of the landscape. However for the 3rd and last occasion that day Emergency Full Astern was passed to the engine room and it was a tonic to hear the Engineer Officer calmly repeat back "Emergency Full Astern Together" as his staff leapt into action down below. By the time we hit the bank bows on, all 40,000 horse power was drawing the ship astern and we came off with not trouble at all, turned round and once more headed down stream. We slowed down as we approached Kiangyin and anchored in the spot we chose, not that chosen by the Chinese pilot, who was obviously for anchoring as soon as possible and getting his head down. He must have had some sort of headache, not being used to the amount of noise.

A Chinese sloop anchored "Have you been caught by the Communist gunfire" to which we replied "Yes but we gave them rather more than we got." Although we'd taken severe punishment we [were] far from downhearted. As some wag remarked "Might have been worse, it could have been raining." It had been a perfectly glorious sunny day, almost too warm for the sort of work we'd had that afternoon.

Appendix 4

The following statement was submitted on 8 October 1949 by Lieutenant Geoffrey Weston and included as an appendix to the "HMS *Amethyst*'s Final Report on Yangtse Incident," 22 May 1950, M0118/50, Adm 1/21851/50.

In Shanghai and Nanking

Commander Kerans had told me to leave, if I was going without delay, as the railway was expected to be cut. The ship was anchored about 7 miles below Ching Kiang and I reached this town in the K.M.T. assault craft about an hour later. After some delay I succeeded in getting a jeep, went to the Nationalist Naval Headquarters, met the Chief of Staff, and telephoned the Military Attache who came to meet me. Lieutenant Colonel Dewar-Durie took me to the station in another jeep; Miss Dunlap of the local American hospital gave me an injection on the platform and some hours later I boarded an overdue train for Nanking. This was the last train to run before Nanking fell. No trains were running to Shanghai for the reason, unknown to us at the time, that the railway line between Ching Kiang and Shanghai was already cut. Colonel Dewar-Durie himself had to stay behind and only left Ching Kiang while the town was being taken over by the Communists the next day.

2. This train never actually reached Nanking as the railway station there had been blown up by the retreating Nationalists. It finally stopped, many hours late, at a station outside the Capital called Hu Ping. I was met here at about 0130 (23rd April) by the assistant Military attache, Major Cook, who had been searching for me all evening. He took me to the Nanking University Hospital in the embassy car. I had become very ill on the train, probably in consequence of jeep journeys over cobbled streets, and could hardly speak or move at the end of the journey. After X ray later the same morning (23rd) the doctors pronounced that the piece of shrapnel (about matchbox size) had passed through the lung and entered the liver, where they proposed to leave it and where it still is. I wanted it removed but the surgeon replied that this would entail a very serious operation unnecessarily and he would only remove it if my condition deteriorated. A seat had been reserved for me on an aircraft which left for Shanghai at 1600 that afternoon (24th), but when the time came I was considered unfit to travel. This was to be the last link with Shanghai for some time.

3. Nanking was occupied by the Communists on 24th April. The Naval Attache, Captain Donaldson, removed my uniform from the hospital and he and his wife came to see me every day except when they were prevented from leaving their house by the Communists early on. By 12th May I had recovered and went to stay at the embassy with Sir Ralph and Lady Stevenson, being employed during the day in the Naval Attache's office.

4. Captain Donaldson and Mrs. Donaldson showed me very great kindness, and supplied me with food, clothes and many other basic needs. I thought I could rejoin my ship by taking a sampan downstream from Hogee (on the Nanking water front) but Captain Donaldson would not allow me to do so. He was concerned with getting me out of the country and back to Hong Kong when it should be possible. About a month later Shanghai fell and a few foreign ships

entered the now Communist port. However foreigners* in Nanking were not allowed to leave the city. By the time this ban was lifted and foreigners were permitted to travel to Shanghai, the Nationalist blockade effectively prevented any shipping from entering or leaving the port. This being so the Naval attache eventually allowed me to try and rejoin, because this seemed at the time to afford my best chance of leaving China. Negotiations at the time (end of June) between Commander Kerans and the Communists seemed to be making favourable progress.

5. However Captain Donaldson stipulated that I should first go to Shanghai for medical examination to ensure that I would not burden the ship by falling sick onboard. So on 30th June (after a false start on 26th) I arrived in Shanghai; saw various specialists who passed me fit to return, and obtained a police pass to travel to H.M.S. AMETHYST on 7th July.

6. Commander Kerans was not keen about my returning onboard as he had to get permission from the local Communist Commander (Colonel Kang) before any stores or personnel joined or left the ship. Two ratings† who had been left wounded ashore had been allowed to rejoin after repeated applications and negotiations, but Commander Kerans told me later at Hong Kong that he considered that there had been no hope of an officer being allowed to do so. I was naturally very anxious for my own part to get back to H.M.S. AMETHYST. Shanghai was pleasant enough but I felt there as Uriah felt during the siege of Rabbah. But my presence onboard was not vitally necessary to the ship, and I did not want Kang to use his permission as a bargaining point in the negotiations. However the Commander-in-Chief now wished me to rejoin, and Commander Kerans could not know that I had been given instructions to pass on to him which could not be sent by plain language signal, or that I had memorised a code for his use. However Commander Kerans told me to come, because, he said later, he received the impression from a signal that the police had 'ordered' me to leave Shanghai.

7. With two suitcases full of cigarettes, sweets, soap and other stores, I left Shanghai on the evening of 7th July with Mr. Khoong in company as interpreter. The police at the station thoroughly searched my suitcase and person and read my letters and papers which were all fortunately harmless. I arrived at Ching Kiang about 0530 next morning (8th July) but was prevented from leaving the station by sentries. They took me to an office where I argued for a few hours with Communist officers. They said that my pass was not in order and out of date, that Commander Kerans had not applied for permission for me to board and that it was an insult to Chinese National Sovereignity that I should travel on Chinese National soil and so on. I was able to prove the fallacy of their first two arguments but their other points were academic. However they said that they would convene a meeting of the soi-disant ' "Amethyst" Committee' to consider the matter and returned to say that it had been decided that I was to proceed straight back to Shanghai without leaving the station. All this was in Chinese through Mr. Khoong. Although they could speak English they would not use it, except occasionally for abuse.

8. After more passes had been made out I returned to Shanghai that night, and applied to

---

* Foreigners here is used in the sense of non Chinese, both here and hereafter.
† Ordinary Seaman Martin and Stoker Bannister.

the police headquarters next morning for a new pass to rejoin. I pointed out that they would have to get covering approval from the Ching Kiang frontier headquarters first for the pass to be valid. Although I paid further visits to the police station no new pass was forthcoming. I still believe that the only way to have got onboard without a pass was downriver by sampan from Nanking. Both riversides near H.M.S. AMETHYST were guarded by a military force stationed there to "protect" the ship. To penetrate this without a pass and without speaking Chinese was impossible.

9. This report does not describe the situation in the Communist cities or the progress of the negotiations as they appeared in Nanking and Shanghai. These will have been covered by others more qualified to do so. Nor have I mentioned the kindness I received from our Embassy's consulate or from other foreigners in China; they were so many. While in Shanghai I was employed in the office of the assistant Naval attache, Commander Pringle, who was, of course, constantly pre-occupied with H.M.S. AMETHYST and in getting stores for her and in applying pressure through commercial channels to secure her release. After endless permit troubles only a trickle of stores could be got by rail to the ship, chiefly owing to the difficulties created by Kang. These stores were only allowed to be accompanied by a Chinese and this was always done by Mr. Khoong, ANA's chief driver. I often wondered whether Mr. Khoong would get into trouble with the Communists for his open devotion to our interests. By the middle of July H.M.S. AMETHYST was reported to be running short of fuel and food. Ample quantities of both were ready at Shanghai for delivery and despatch by rail or river, together with other items such as rat poison, valves, toothpaste, beer and hairclippers. Kang had promised clearance for the fuel at any rate, but it was eventually delayed for frivolous reasons, and it is doubtful whether he ever intended to give it. An attempt at escape or the destruction of the ship seemed to be becoming inevitable. Fortunately when the Commander-in-Chief asked for information governing a possible attempt to escape a person came to call at the office who had seen round the Communist batteries at Ta Tu riverside near Ching Kiang. The river at this time was extremely high, but the river pilots considered that this would obscure all landmarks on the banks and make navigation much more difficult. We felt that this was not so material except to a river pilot and that the extra depth of water provided compensating advantages.

10. However no one in Shanghai knew that a definite attempt to escape was going to be made. I was staying with the American A/Naval attache (Commander Morgan Slayton, U.S.N.) when the great news came through on the B.B.C. My host was not staying at his house because he had been locked up for several days in his office at the U.S. Consulate by his former employees but he rang me up and told me the news. I went to church at the cathedral (where we sang a hymn of thanksgiving) and met the British Consul General there. He told me to go to the office and burn all secret and relevant papers. The British newspaper (The China Daily News) did not dare to publish the news, but there was unreserved jubilation amongst the foreigners at Shanghai, which was by no means confined to the British community. The Consul General felt that although the outcome was extremely satisfactory, the Communists might take reprisals against the British community. The Communist press did not mention the subject for two days, but when they did their reaction was violent. They called for repayment in blood and I believe tried to stir up riots against the Consulate, but unsuccessfully. If the escape had been

made a month or so before at a cost (alleged by the Communists) of "hundreds of Chinese lives" there might have been violence. When it did happen the populace were not so enthusiastic as they had been for the new government, and the only result appeared to be a bevy of protests from the students bodies, unions and other people's organisations. The escape was also well timed in that the S.S. ANCHISES had left Shanghai under tow only the day before.

Appendix 5

Biographical Data of Leading Personalities, 1949–89

The information below was found in the following sources: *Who Was Who*, vol. 6, *1961–70; Who Was Who*, vol. 7, *1971–80; Who's Who 1989;* Bartke, *Who's Who in China.*

Admiral Sir Patrick Brind (1892–1963)

Awarded Knight Grand Cross of the Order of the British Empire (1951); commander-in-chief Far East Station (1949–51), Allied Forces, Northern Europe (1951–53); retired from Royal Navy (1953).

Colonel Kang Mao-chao

Counselor, embassy in India (Dec. 1950–55), Lebanon (Aug. 1955–59); deputy director, Information Department, Ministry of Foreign Affairs (June 1959–64); chargé d'affaires, embassy in Yugoslavia (Oct. 1964–66); ambassador to Cambodia (June 1969–74), Mauritania (1974–Feb. 1978), Belgium (May 1978–81), Luxemburg and European Economic Community (June 1978–81); retired from diplomatic corps (1981).

Commander John Simon Kerans (1915–85)

Awarded Distinguished Service Order (Aug. 1949); promoted to commander (Dec. 1949); RN staff course, Greenwich (1950); head, Far East section, Naval Intelligence, Admiralty (1950–52); i/c HMS *Rinaldo* (1953–54); British naval attaché, Bangkok, Phnom Penh, Vientiane, Saigon, Rangoon (1954–55); senior officers technical course, Portsmouth (1957); retired from Royal Navy (1958). Conservative MP for the Hartlepools (1959–64); civil servant, Pensions Appeal Tribunals (1969–80), retired (1980).

Vice-Admiral Sir Alexander Madden (1895–1964)

Awarded Knight Commander of the Order of the Bath (1951); flag officer commanding Fifth Cruiser Squadron and flag officer second-in-command, Far East Station (1948–50); lord commissioner of the Admiralty, second sea lord and chief of naval personnel (1950–53); commander-in-chief Plymouth (1953–55); retired from Royal Navy (1956).

Sir Ralph Stevenson (1895–1977)

Ambassador to China (1946–50, effective Oct. 1949), Egypt (1950–55); retired from diplomatic corps (1955); captain of the Parish of Arbory, Isle of Man (IOM); member, Legislative Council, IOM (1955–70); member, executive council, IOM (1962–69).

Sir Edward Youde (1924–86)

Third secretary, Nanking and Peking (1948–51); Foreign Office (1951); second secretary, Peking (1953–56); first secretary, Washington, D.C. (1956–59), Peking (1960–62); Foreign Office (1962–65); Counselor and head of chancery, United Kingdom Mission to United Nations (1965–69); private secretary to prime minister (1969–70); IDC (1970–71); head of personnel services dept., Foreign and Commonwealth Office (FCO; 1971–73); assistant under secretary of state, FCO (1973–74); ambassador to China (1974–78); deputy under secretary of state (chief clerk), FCO (1978); deputy to permanent under secretary of state and chief clerk, FCO (1980–82); governor and commander-in-chief, Hong Kong (1982–86).

General Yuan Chung-hsien (1894?–1956)
Ambassador to India (Jan. 1950–56).

Notes

PREFACE

1. *The Times,* 21 Apr. 1949.
2. Translation of statement issued by the New China News Agency in its *Yangtse Front* bulletin of 22 April 1949. A copy of this translation was sent by Ambassador Stevenson to the Foreign Office, number 488, 24 Apr. 1949, F5715/1219/10, FO 371/75888. This dispatch and all other official correspondence cited in this book, unless otherwise indicated, can be consulted in the Public Record Office (PRO) at Kew Gardens, London.

For those unfamiliar with the filing system in operation at the PRO, the reference cited above indicates the internal piece number (F5715), subject reference (1219), and regional classification, for example, China (10) of the large General Correspondence class (FO 371). Armed with this information, a researcher would have little difficulty in discovering the specific file number (75888) from the PRO's register of all FO 371 General Correspondence files.

CHAPTER ONE. GUNBOAT DIPLOMACY

1. Morse, *International Relations* 1:51. For the purposes of maintaining consistency with the contemporary documents, I have adopted the old practice of writing Chinese names, terms, and titles of periodicals in accordance with the Wade-Giles system of transliteration that was used in 1948–49. Nonetheless, citations to recent work published in Hanyu Pinyin have been left in that form. I have also retained the spelling of Chinese place names as they were transliterated into English in the late 1940s.
2. Ibid. 1:51–53, 67.
3. Ibid. 1:53–55, 102–3; Keeton, *Extraterritoriality* 1:14–20, 40–41; Beeching, *Chinese Opium Wars,* 15–21.
4. Beeching, *Chinese Opium Wars,* 21–23; Remer, *Foreign Trade of China*, 16–18; Morse, *International Relations* 1:90–91; Fay, *Opium War,* 15–19.
5. Fay, *Opium War,* 41–52; Morse, *International Relations* 1:90–91.
6. Fay, *Opium War,* 53–64.

7. Morse, *International Relations* 1:209–10; Remer, *Foreign Trade,* 24–26.

8. Fay, *Opium War,* 142–79; Morse, *International Relations* 1:213–40; Beeching, *Chinese Opium Wars,* 63–93; Graham, *China Station,* 85–107.

9. Keeton, *Extraterritoriality* 1:143–70.

10. Morse, *International Relations* 1:262–97; Fay, *Opium War,* 213–355, Graham, *China Station,* 108–229; Wakeman, "Canton Trade and the Opium War," 163–212.

11. Morse, *International Relations* 1:298–337; Fairbank, "Creation of the Treaty System," 213–63.

12. Morse, *International Relations* 1:400–18; Graham, *China Station,* 230–98; Beeching, *Chinese Opium Wars,* 164–205.

13. Morse, *International Relations* 1:419–37, 479–538; Selby, *Paper Dragon,* 46–62; Graham, *China Station,* 299–364; Beeching, *Chinese Opium Wars,* 206–57.

14. Morse, *International Relations* 1:571–87; Beeching, *Chinese Opium Wars,* 258–72; Graham, *China Station,* 365–78; Hurd, *Arrow War,* 181–84.

15. Morse, *International Relations* 1:589–617; Graham, *China Station,* 378–406; Beeching, *Chinese Opium Wars,* 272–331; Hurd, *Arrow War,* 189–241; Selby, *Paper Dragon,* 63–87.

16. Fox, *British Admirals and Chinese Pirates,* 40–45; Gregory, *Great Britain and the Taipings,* ix–169.

17. Kuhn, "Taiping Rebellion," 264–317; Selby, *Paper Dragon,* 109–51; Morse, *International Relations* 2:25–63, 90–112, 138–62.

18. *The Times,* 19 Feb. 1869. The background to this important declaration is dealt with in Williams, *Anson Burlingame,* 173–76 and Fox, *British Admirals,* 67–71.

19. Fox, *British Admirals,* 68.

20. Morse, *International Relations* 2:239–61, 283–306.

21. Ibid. 2:303–6, 313–15.

22. Ibid. 2:395.

23. Woodhead, *Yangtsze and Its Problems,* 1–2.

24. Morse, *International Relations* 3:18–56.

25. Ibid. 3:101–27; Young, *British Policy in China,* 1–99. For a brutal critique of Britain's gain from the Scramble, see Pratt, *War and Politics in China,* 13–14.

26. Morse, *International Relations* 3:119–20; Wesley-Smith, *Unequal Treaty 1898–1997,* 21–44.

27. Morse, *International Relations* 3:128–92; Young, *British Policy,* 100–119; Purcell, *Boxer Uprising.*

28. Morse, *International Relations* 3:193–210; Selby, *Paper Dragon,* 178–83.

29. Tan, *Boxer Catastrophe;* Morse, *International Relations* 3:211–88; Selby, *Paper Dragon,* 182–91.

30. Young, *British Policy,* 160–213.

31. Morse, *International Relations* 3:330–59; Hsu, "Late Ch'ing Foreign Relations," 70–141.

32. Marder, *Anatomy of British Sea Power,* 427–29.

33. Young, *British Policy,* 295–318; Lowe, *Reluctant Imperialists* 1:225–51; Nish, *Anglo-Japanese Alliance* 174–228.

34. Lowe and Dockrill, *Mirage of Power* 1:1–11. Even so, neither country was prepared

to sign an entente without trying to gain the best bargain it could. P. J. V. Rolo shows in his book *Entente Cordiale* (149–270) that the desire for territorial compensation was a more persuasive factor in arranging the entente than was the fear of entanglement in a Far Eastern war.

35. Admiral Jacky Fisher's program to rationalize the Royal Navy, which he began devising and implementing after becoming first sea lord in October 1904, had fairly immediate effects in the Far East. Shortly after the destruction of the Russian fleet at Tsushima in May 1905, Fisher felt confident enough about the naval situation in the Far East to withdraw all five of the British battleships from Chinese waters and redeploy them elsewhere in European waters (Kennedy, *British Naval Mastery,* 217).

36. Tz'u-hsi had been seriously ill for some time, and her death had long been expected. Kuang-hsü, by contrast, had been in robust health before his sudden and highly suspicious death occurred on 14 November 1908. At the time, it was rumored that there was evidence of the empress dowager's handiwork in Kuang-hsü's rapid demise. Although conclusive proof has never been established, the temptation to regard his death as murder is overwhelming. Besides the fact that her hatred for the emperor was well known, the prospect of such an individual exercising full powers after her own death is thought by most scholars to have been a sufficient inducement for Tz'u-hsi to have conspired with Yuan Shih-k'ai to poison the emperor and prevent him from gaining his rightful inheritance (Hsu, *Rise of Modern China,* 510). A quite different version of the background to this event is supplied by J. O. P. Bland and E. Backhouse in their hagiographical account of Tz'u-hsi's life and times (*China Under the Empress Dowager,* 443–67). They contend that the emperor had been seriously ill for at least a year before he died. This is confirmed to some extent by Jerome Ch'en in his book (*Yuan Shih-K'ai*, 74–75).

37. According to the Far Eastern Survey (vol. 6, no. 13, 13 June 1937), quoted by S. L. Endicott in his book *Diplomacy and Enterprise* (Table 1, p. 186), 590 British firms were engaged in trading enterprises in China in 1913, a figure amounting to 15 percent of all foreign concerns in the country. It also revealed that 8,966 British citizens lived in China at this time. For an estimate of the value of this business, see the Board of Trade file on British investments in China and especially a minute by P. M. Wack on 1 Apr. 1947 in BT 11/3390.

38. Marder, *From the Dreadnought,* 2:104.

39. Marder suggests that at least for the first few months of the war, the British had nineteen warships in Chinese waters. Some of these were withdrawn subsequently. HMS *Triumph*, for example, was transferred to the Dardanelles in the early months of 1915. Allen, et al., described the British naval contingent in Chinese waters in 1914 as comprising one battleship (*Triumph*), two armored cruisers, two light cruisers, eight destroyers, four torpedo boats, three submarines, and a number of small, mainly river, vessels (Marder, *From the Dreadnought* 2:103; Allen, Whitehead, and Chadwick, *Great War* 3:412; Preston, *Battleships of World War I,* 92, 108).

40. Chow, *May Fourth Movement,* 84–94; Wang, *Chinese Intellectuals*, 307–61; Schwartz, "Themes in Intellectual History" 406–50.

41. Tolley, *Yangtze Patrol*, 90.

42. Pollard, *China's Foreign Relations*, 205–47.

43. Sir James Cable in his standard work on the subject entitled *Gunboat Diplomacy 1919–1979* classifies four different types of force used by governments during this period to support their diplomatic endeavors. Cable asserts that the British government resorted to the use of "definitive," "purposeful," and "catalytic" force in its dealings with the Chinese during the 1920s and 1930s (see 57–81, 198–209).

44. Iriye, *After Imperialism*, 60–61; Woodhead, *China Year Book, 1926–27*, 895–1016.

45. Woodhead, *China Year Book, 1928*, 666–72; Tolley, *Yangtze Patrol*, 139–43.

46. Pollard, *China's Foreign Relations*, 296–98; Iriye, *After Imperialism*, 99–101.

47. Woodhead, *China Year Book, 1928*, 737–55; Cable, *Gunboat Diplomacy*, 203; Tolley, *Yangtze Patrol*, 135–37.

48. Woodhead, *China Year Book, 1928*, 723–36; Cable, *Gunboat Diplomacy*, 204. According to Tolley's account of the action in *Yangtze Patrol* (152–64), *Noa* fired nineteen flat-nosed, high explosive shells from her 4-inch guns. *Preston* fired fifteen more similar shells, and HMS *Emerald* fired seventy-six rounds from her 6-inch 100-pounders.

49. Tolley, *Yangtze Patrol*, 165.

50. Pollard, *China's Foreign Relations*, 330–38; Iriye, *After Imperialism*, 133–42, 145–49.

51. Woodhead, *China Year Book, 1929–30*, 775–79; Cable, *Gunboat Diplomacy*, 205.

52. Woodhead, *China Year Book, 1931*, 481–87; Pollard, *China's Foreign Relations*, 354–56, 372–87.

53. Tolley, *Yangtze Patrol*, 192–94; Cable, *Gunboat Diplomacy*, 207.

54. Iriye, *After Imperialism*, 285–88.

55. One should consult the following material for further information on this emotive subject: Hajime Shimizu, "Senkanki Nihon Keizaiteki 'nanshin,' " 11–44; Shimizu, "Nanshin-ron: Its Turning Point," 386–402. See also Frei, *Japan's Southward Advance*; and Schalow, "Transforming Railroads," 55–67.

56. Cable, *Gunboat Diplomacy*, 209.

57. Friedman, *British Relations with China*, 217–25. As can be seen from Appendix 2, however, the Japanese shipping trade in China fell at an even faster rate than that of the British in the period 1936–38. In fact, it had experienced a loss in trade in terms of vessels entering and clearing Chinese customs every year from 1932 onward. Why this occurred has not been adequately researched; it deserves further study.

58. For a full account of this extraordinary period in British foreign policy, see Murfett, *Fool-proof Relations*, 3–161. Japanese action in China is covered in Woodhead, *China Year Book, 1939*, 437–43.

59. Because the problems of accurately gauging British investments in China have never been satisfactorily resolved, all statements about the value of these investments should be treated with caution. Nevertheless, a consensus has emerged among scholars and experts that places the value of these investments in the 1930s in the range of two hundred million to three hundred million pounds sterling (see Endicott, *Diplomacy and Enterprise*, 19; Friedman, *British Relations*, 219–20).

60. Brice, *Sino-Japanese Incident*, 135–47.

61. Ibid., 145–63.

CHAPTER TWO. RENEWAL OF AN OLD ADVENTURE

1. A report by the Foreign Office Economic Intelligence Unit (FOEIU) in April 1949 points out that Malaya was "overwhelmingly the greatest dollar earner among the colonies." It estimated that in 1948 Malayan exports to the United States were worth more than $178 million. When added to the earning capacity of Singapore, the total exceeded $230 million or 12.8 percent of the total sterling area dollar deficit (FOEIU, Apr. 1949, F5704/1114/61, FO 371/76049).

2. A concise account of the British government's opposition to British intervention or mediation in the Chinese civil war, on the basis that it would compromise its relations with the two belligerents, is contained in Foreign Office (hereafter FO) to Washington, 391, 11 Jan. 1949, F392/1015/10, FO 371/75735.

3. For a detailed appreciation of the situation in China at the end of 1948, see Far Eastern Official Committee, FE(O)8th and 9th mtg, 4 and 8 Dec. 1948; Memo FE(O)(48)34(Revise), 10 Dec. 1948, Cab (Cabinet Office) 134/285. Additional material about the supposedly orthodox nature of the Chinese Communists is in FE(O)(49) 1st mtg, 16 Feb. 1949, Cab 134/286; a useful memo devoted to this subject (F2807/1016/10) was taken as an appendix to FE(O)(49)8(Revise), 1 Mar. 1949, Cab 134/287; see also FO to Singapore (commissioner general in Southeast Asia), 242, 17 Feb. 1949, F2705/1015/10G, FO 371/75741. Secondary literature on Britain and China in the 1945–49 period remains sparse. Of those books published on this theme in recent years, the following are some of the best available: R. Boardman, *Britain and the People's Republic of China, 1949–1974*, 6–27; E. Luard, *Britain and China*, 50–82; R. Ovendale, *The English-Speaking Alliance*, 185–200; B. E. Porter, *Britain and the Rise of Communist China*, 1–24; A. Shai, *Britain and China 1941–47*, 126–52. It is hoped that Steve Tsang's *Democracy Shelved* will be the start of a new series of studies to be published on Anglo-Chinese relations in the postwar period. A doctoral thesis submitted in the summer of 1989 by Shao Wenguang, a member of the Chinese Ministry of Foreign Affairs and a graduate student at St. Antony's College in Oxford, ought to break new ground. It would be encouraging if his work on Anglo-Chinese commercial relations in the 1949–57 period and that of J. T. H. Tang on "Diplomatic Relations with a Revolutionary Power" might find a suitable publisher in due course.

4. Report of Sir William Strang's tour of Southeast Asia and the Far East, 27 Feb. 1949, Strn (Strang) 2/5, Churchill College Archive Centre, Cambridge; Record of Meeting in FO, 4 Mar. 1949, F4396/1015/10, FO 371/75746.

5. Sir Ralph Stevenson, the British ambassador, did not take an impartial stand on this issue. In a radio program broadcast to the Chinese people over the Far Eastern Service of the BBC (British Broadcasting Corporation) on 10 October 1948, he described communism as "death to any kind of liberty, either of the nation, the family or of the individual." He went on to state:

Today the world pattern of that insidious but barren creed is all too clear. Under the guise of apparently national and patriotic movements, Communist influence is gradually but inexorably extended in one country after another until one day whole nations wake up to find themselves powerless in the grip of the Kremlin. (His Majesty's Ambassador's Speeches File, Sir Ralph Stevenson Papers, [hereafter Stevenson], Gardenfield, Castletown, Isle of Man. [hereafter IOM])

For a jaundiced view of his speech see editorial in the *Daily Worker*, 7 Feb. 1949, and minutes attached in F2022/1015/10, FO 371/75740.

6. Minute by P. W. Scarlett, 17 Feb. 1949, F3305/1023/10, FO 371/75810; FO to Washington, 3067, 17 Mar. 1949, F3305/1023/10, FO 371/75810.

7. As an indication of what the British were up against, see Mao's attack on imperialism in his address on the thirty-first anniversary of the October Revolution:

The working class and the people as a whole cannot be successfully led in their struggle against imperialism and its lackeys without a revolutionary party based on the ideological, organisational and theoretical principles of Marxism and Lenism [sic] and guided by the all-powerful ideas of Marx, Engels, Lenin and Stalin. (From *Chinese Cominform*, no. 21(24), 1 Nov. 1948, sent as paraphrased dispatch FO to Nanking, 903, 25 Nov. 1948, F16917/33/10, FO 371/69542).

See also his trenchant article in the Tientsin *Jih Pao* of 23 January 1949 and the FO minutes covering this polemic, which can be found in F11127/1015/10, FO 371/75764.

8. Minute by P. D. Coates, 8 Nov. 1948, F15805/361/10G, FO 371/69608; official expression for this policy was provided by Ernest Bevin, the British foreign secretary, in his speech during the debate on foreign affairs held in the House of Commons on 9 Dec. 1948 (U.K., *Hansard (Commons)*, vol. 459, col. 566–67; see also Cabinet Paper [CP](48)299, 9 Dec. 1948, Cab 129/31).

9. Stevenson to FO, 154, 4 Feb. 1949, F2130/1015/10, FO 371/75740; Stevenson to FO, 368, 31 Mar. 1949, F4793/1023/10, FO 371/75810. Much the same story of diplomatic impotence emerged from Franklin, the British consul at Tientsin (Stevenson to FO, 162, 7 Feb. 1949, F2137/1015/10, FO 371/75740). Sadly, the situation did not improve as is clear in the following dispatches: Stevenson to FO, 709, 26 May 1949, F7715/1015/10, FO 371/75757 and 929, 28 June 1949, F10110/1015/10, FO 371/75762.

10. Minute by P. W. Scarlett on Stevenson to FO, 154, 4 Feb. 1949, F2130/1015/10, FO 371/75740.

11. U.K., *Hansard (Commons)*, vol. 418, col. 53; Memo by P. W. Scarlett, 12 May 1948, F7028/364/10, FO 371/69610.

12. U.K., *Hansard (Commons)*, vol. 462, col. 1704; Memo by P. W. Scarlett, 12 May 1948, F7028/364/10, FO 371/69610. HMS *Mendip*, a *Hunt* class destroyer, was only loaned to the Chinese government for five years; see Bevin to Stevenson, 169, 18 May 1949, F7162/364/10, FO 371/69610.

13. Stevenson to FO, 192, 28 Mar. 1949, F5316/1013/10, FO 371/75733.

14. Letter from D. F. Allen (U.K. shipping representative for Far East, Hong Kong) to F. V. Cross (British Embassy in Washington), 7 Jan. 1948, F1664/37/10, FO 371/69559.

15. Minute by P. W. Scarlett on "British Shipping in China," 26 Feb. 1948, F3285/37/10, FO 371/69559.

16. After the successful completion of its Liaohsi-Shenyang (Mukden) campaign had ended on 2 November 1948 with the shattering defeat of the KMT armies in Manchuria, the battle for Huai-hai commenced on 6 November. It lasted until 10 January 1949 and proved to be another significant victory for the PLA, providing it with the opportunity to move south to the banks of the Yangtze. For a succinct account of these two campaigns and that of the battle for northern China fought in the Peking-Tientsin campaign of 21 November–31 January 1949 see "The KMT-CCP Conflict 1945–1949" by Suzanne Pepper, 774–82.

17. Naval Attaché (Nanking) (hereafter NA Nanking) to Flag Officer, second in command, Far East Station, (hereafter FO2 i/c FES), 210448Z/December, 21 Dec. 1948, F17440/33/10, FO 371/69545. Consul General at Tientsin (Smyth) to Secretary of State, 86, 19 Jan. 1949, U.S. Dept. of State, *Foreign Relations of the United States, 1949*, 8:190–91. (hereafter *FRUS, 1949*, 8).

18. Stevenson to FO, 261, 9 Nov. 1948, DTC 090343Z, found in F5738/1611/10, FO 371/75939; letter from U. Myint Thein (formerly Burmese ambassador to China in 1949) to the author, 7 June 1989.

19. Stevenson to M. E. Dening (FO), 54/1086/48, 13 Dec. 1948, F18602/33/10, FO 371/69550. In December 1948, the number of Commonwealth nationals in Nanking was as follows:

	Males	Females	Children
British civilians	25	18	10
British Embassy personnel	28	22	
British Council employees	2	21	
Canadian Embassy personnel	6		
Canadian missionaries		3	
Australian Embassy staff	7		
Total	68	64	10

For its subjects, the Indian Embassy had already worked out a contingency plan for emergency evacuation by air directly to India, should this be necessary:

	Males	Females
Indian civilians	52	13
Indian Embassy personnel	21	18
Total	73	31

Source: Commander in Chief (hereafter C-in-C), FES to Admiralty, (hereafter Adm), 060616Z, 6 Dec. 1948, F17440/33/10, FO 371/69545.

20. In a message relayed by the British consul general in Shanghai to the Foreign Office on 9 November 1948, Mr. Ogden indicated that the Shanghai community was pressing him to secure the services of a cruiser in the port to reassure both locals and expatriates. Responding to this dispatch on 12 November 1948, Peter Scarlett minuted: "I assured Mr.

Mitchell that this thought would be present in the minds of the naval authorities in the Far East and of H.M. Embassy." (Consul General Ogden to FO, 274, 9 Nov. 1948, F15724/33/10, FO 371/69541.)

21. In reply to a question in the House of Commons on 17 November 1948, Christopher Mayhew, under secretary of state for foreign affairs, indicated that in 1941 the value of British investments in Shanghai was estimated at £107 million and that the replacement value for these investments at 1948 prices was probably still not less than this figure. (U.K., *Hansard [Commons]*, vol. 458, col. 357–58).

22. At this time there were estimated to be 2,480 American citizens in Shanghai and an additional 476 in the area of Kiangsu, Anhwei, Chekiang, and Fukien. Various plans had been made for their evacuation for many months. Information about these arrangements is to be found in U.S. Dept. of State, *FRUS, 1948* 8:809–946.

23. Hall to Attlee, 21 Apr. 1949, Prem (Prime Minister's Office) 8/944; FO2 i/c FES to Adm, 021549Z, 3 May 1949, F6398/1219/10G, FO 371/75891.

24. Stevenson to FO, 557, 2 May 1949, F6301/1219/10, FO 371/75891; Memo by first sea lord, undated, F6448/1219/10, FO 371/75891. For a critical view of the decision to discontinue the air link to Nanking, see the *Spectator,* 29 Apr. 1949.

25. FO2 i/c FES to Adm, 021549Z, 3 May 1949, F6398/1219/10G, FO 371/75891.

26. *The Times,* 29 Nov. 1948; C-in-C FES to Adm, 060616Z, 6 Dec. 1948, F17440/33/10, FO 371/69545; Memo by P. W. Scarlett, 20 Apr. 1949, F5476/1219/10, FO 371/75887.

27. Stevenson to FO, 750, 1 June 1949, F8040/1219/10, FO 371/75892.

28. FO2 i/c FES to Adm, 021549Z, 3 May 1949, F6398/1219/10G, FO 371/75891.

29. Ibid.

30. Mao, "Statement on the Present Situation" in *Selected Works of Mao Tse-tung,* 4:315–19.

31. Tong and Li, *Memoirs of Li Tsung-Jen,* 480–505.

32. Memo by P. W. Scarlett, 20 Apr. 1949, F5476/1219/10, FO 371/75887.

33. Ibid.; despite the existence of a naval defense plan for the Yangtze announced by the KMT in Dec. 1948, the Chinese government admitted privately in January that the most it could do would be to retain control of the river between Nanking and the sea. By February 1949 even this hope looked ambitious (Stevenson to FO, 24, 13 Jan. 1949, F1675/1013/10, FO 371/75733).

34. NA Nanking to War Office (hereafter WO), 191145, 201515, 20 Jan. 1949; "Situation Reports from Military Advisers, Nanking," F83/1015/10, FO 371/75734.

35. FO 2 i/c FES to Adm, 021549Z, 3 May 1949, F6398/1219/10G, FO 371/75891. In his report to the flag officer, I. G. Robertson, the commanding officer of HMS *Consort,* wrote:

> From our point of view though we could, in fact, have stayed some weeks more by eke-ing out our fuel, it was felt that four weeks were quite a long enough stay for single destroyers in an isolated place. (I. G. Robertson to FO2 i/c FES, 74/47/1, 26 Apr. 1949, Adm 1/21800.)

36. Chassin, *Communist Conquest of China,* 217; Stevenson to FO, 382, F4794/1013/10, FO 371/75733.

37. U.S. Ambassador J. Leighton Stuart (Nanking) to U.S. Secretary of State, (hereafter Stuart to Secy. State), 716, 6 Apr. 1949, U.S. Dept. of State, *FRUS, 1949*, 8:229–30; Stevenson to FO, 402, 6 Apr. 1949, F5011/1015/10, FO 371/75748; Stevenson to FO, 422, 11 Apr. 1949, F5226/1013/10, FO 371/75733.

38. Stuart to Secy. State, 742–43, 11 Apr. 1949, U.S. Dept. of State, *FRUS, 1949*, 8:236–37; 771, 16 Apr. 1949. U.S. Dept. of State, *FRUS, 1949*, 8:242–43. Stevenson to FO, 431, 12 Apr. 1949, F5262/1015/10, FO 371/75748.

39. Stuart to Secy. State, 771, 16 Apr. 1949, U.S. Dept. of State, *FRUS, 1949*, 8:242–43; Stevenson to FO, 422, 11 Apr. 1949, F5226/1013/10, FO 371/75733.

40. Stuart to Secy. State, 768, 15 Apr. 1949, U.S. Dept. of State, *FRUS, 1949* 8:240–41.

41. Stuart to Secy. State, 782, 18 Apr. 1949, U.S. Dept. of State, *FRUS, 1949*, 8:244–46; Stevenson to FO, 442, 18 Apr. 1949, F5571/1013/10, FO 371/75733.

42. Stevenson to FO, 443, 18 Apr. 1949, F5404/1015/10, FO 371/75748.

43. *Ibid.*

44. Stuart to Secy. State, 805, 20 Apr. 1949, U.S. Dept. of State, *FRUS, 1949* 8:255.

45. Madden technically was acting commander in chief because his superior Sir Patrick Brind was attending the *Trident* naval staff exercise in Greenwich (FO2 i/c FES to Adm, 021549Z, 3 May 1949, F6398/1219/10G, FO 371/75891).

46. *Comnavfe* is an acronym for the U.S. Navy and stands for Commander Naval Forces Far East.

47. FO2 i/c FES to Adm, 021549Z, 3 May 1949, F6398/1219/10G, FO 371/75891.

48. In a sharply critical editorial, the *Spectator* (29 Apr. 1949) indicated that far from experiencing shortages, the city of Nanking enjoyed a glut of food at this time. Moreover, it questioned the premise on which the relief of *Consort* rested, namely, the replenishment of the destroyer.

In the past gunboats of the Royal Navy, stationed at remote upriver ports like Changsha and Chungking, lived off the country for months on end as a matter of routine. It may have seemed convenient, but it can hardly by the wildest stretch of imagination have been called necessary that H.M.S. 'Consort' should be relieved.

49. Stevenson to FO, No. 454, 21 May 1949, F5550/1219/10, FO 371/75887.

50. *Ibid.*

51. *Ibid.*

52. FO2 i/c FES to Adm, 021549Z, 3 May 1949, F6398/1219/10G, FO 371/75891.

53. Stevenson to FO, 443, 18 Apr. 1949, F5404/1015/10, FO 371/75748.

54. *Ibid.*

55. NA Nanking to FO2 i/c FES, 180234Z, app. 1, Adm 116/5740A. Reflecting upon the crisis some weeks later, Stevenson noted rather wistfully, "The Yangtze incident could not have been foreseen but it happened. . ." (Stevenson to FO, 600, 10 May 1949, F6681/1015/10, FO 371/75752)

56. "INTEND TO SAIL AMETHYST ZERO ZERO ZERO ONE ZEBRA TOMORROW TUESDAY ONE NINE (19) UNLESS N.A. NANKING INFORM ME CLEARANCE HAS NOT BEEN GRANTED." (FO2 i/c FES to NA Nanking, 180657Z, app. 1, Adm 116/5740A)

57. NA Nanking to FO2 i/c FES, 190839Z, 19 Apr. 1949, Adm 116/5740.

58. NA Nanking to FO2 i/c FES, 190417Z, 19 Apr. 1949, F5476/1219/10, FO 371/75887.

59. FO2 i/c FES to Adm, 021549Z, 3 May 1949, F6398/1219/10G, FO 371/75891.

60. Stevenson to FO, 454, 21 Apr. 1949, F5550/1219/10, FO 371/75887; SBNO (Senior British Naval Officer) Nanking to FO2 i/c FES, 190501Z, 19 Apr. 1949, Adm 116/5740.

61. *The Times,* 1 and 6 Nov. 1948; FO notes for China debate, 5 May 1949, F6588/1219/10, FO 371/75891.

62. Minute by P. D. Coates, 8 Nov. 1948, F75805/361/10G, FO 371/69608. These sentiments, crudely depicted as "keeping a foot in the door" were reechoed by the foreign secretary in his Cabinet Paper CP (48)299, 9 Dec. 1948, Cab 129/31 and less emotively described by him in his speech on foreign policy in the House of Commons on 9 Dec. 1948 (U.K., *Hansard [Commons],* vol. 459, col. 566–67).

CHAPTER THREE. UNDER ATTACK

1. Enclosure to G. L. Weston's letter, 8 October 1949, submitted as app. 3 to "HMS *Amethyst's* Report on the Yangtze Incident, 1949" (hereafter Weston,), 248, Adm 116/5740.

2. A frigate of the modified *Black Swan* class, HMS *Amethyst* was built on Clydeside and completed on 2 November 1943. Designed to carry a full complement of 192 men, *Amethyst* began her war service escorting convoys in the Atlantic. She achieved a certain distinction during the last months of the war by being involved in the stalking and destruction of two German submarines, *U-483* on 6 January 1945 and *U-1208* on 20 February 1945. She was also responsible, along with the sloop HMS *Magpie,* for bringing the *U-249* into Portland on 9 May 1945, after the submarine had surrendered off the Cornish coast with her crew of four officers and forty-three ratings. After the European phase of the war, *Amethyst* was sent to the Far East and was present at the surrender of Japanese forces at Rabaul in New Guinea on 25 August 1945. She remained east of Suez for the postwar period ("HMS *Amethyst* Scrapbook," vol. 2, J. S. Kerans Collection [hereafter Kerans], 69/45/1, Imperial War Museum, London [hereafter IWM]; *Illustrated London News,* 26 Nov. 1949, 823–24).

3. It was customary for the pilots to work in hourly relays—one hour on, one hour off—using large-scale Chinese Maritime Customs charts that divided the river into approximately 20-mile sections (I. G. Robertson, "HMS *Consort's* Part in the 'Amethyst' Incident," 55, "*Amethyst* Scrapbook," vol. 2, Kerans, 69/45/1, IWM).

4. "HMS *Amethyst's* Final Report on Yangtse Incident" (hereafter "*Amethyst* Report"), 22 May 1950, M0118/50, 21, Adm 1/21851/50.

5. Weston, 248; Adm 116/5740.

6. *The Times,* 19 Apr. 1949; these reports were amplified somewhat in the *South China Morning Post,* 19 and 20 Apr. 1949.

7. *The Times,* 21 Apr. 1949.

8. "*Amethyst*" Report, 21.

9. Weston, 248; Interview with Sir Peter Berger, Cambridge, 2 June 1988.

10. "*Amethyst* Report," 21.

11. Ibid.

12. Phillips, *Escape of the "Amethyst,"* 23.

13. *"Amethyst* Report," 21; Interview with Sir Peter Berger, Cambridge, 2 June 1988.

14. Earl, *Yangtse Incident,* 13, see also J. A. Jerome (Dept. of Chief of Naval Information, Adm) to W. A. Fletcher, CNI 269/49, 7 Sept. 1949, Adm 116/5704.

15. *"Amethyst* Report," 21.

16. Weston, 248; Enclosure A of Adm to R. F. Wood, 3 May 1949, Earl Attlee Papers (hereafter Attlee), dep. 82, fol. 56–63, Bodleian Library, Oxford (hereafter BL); Earl, *Yangtse Incident,* 14–15.

17. All times with the suffix Z are in Greenwich mean time. In the period up to 30 April 1949 the time differential was eight hours. After 1 May 1949 for the duration of the summer it would be nine hours. (*Amethyst* to FO 2 i/c FES, 200111Z, 20 Apr. 1949; 290507, 29 Apr. 1949, *"Amethyst* Signal Log" [hereafter ASL], Apr. 1949, Kerans, 69/45/1, IWM).

18. The original message read:

HAVE BEEN FIRED ON FROM NORTH BANK AT BEAVER ISLAND, LAT. 32 DEGREES 13 MINUTES NORTH, LONG. 119 DEGREES 53 MINUTES EAST BY MEDIUM ARTILLERY, TEN SINGLE GUN SALVOES AND SOME SMALL ARMS. SHIP WAS FLYING MASTHEAD ENSIGN. UNION JACKS WERE SHEWN [sic] BOTH SIDES AFTER FIRST SALVO. NO HITS. FIRE WAS NOT RETURNED AS NO DEFINITE TARGET COULD BE IDENTIFIES [sic] DUE TO MIST. *Amethyst* to NA. Nanking, 200111Z, 20 Apr. 1949, Adm 116/5740.

19. *"Amethyst* Report," 21.

20. "Action Damage Report: HMS *Amethyst,"* (hereafter "ADR *Amethyst"*), undated, Adm 116/5740A; E. G. Wilkinson, "HMS 'Amethyst' in the Yangtze—Engineering Exploits," (hereafter "Engineering Exploits"), 417–25, *"Amethyst* Scrapbook," vol. 2, Kerans, 69/45/1, IWM; Earl, Yangtse Incident, 16–17, 19.

21. "ADR *Amethyst,"* Adm 116/5740A; Earl, *Yangtse Incident,* 17.

22. Weston, 248.

23. Earl, *Yangtse Incident,* 18–19; *"Amethyst* Report," 21–22.

24. Earl, *Yangtse Incident,* 21.

25. "ADR *Amethyst,"* Adm. 116/5740A; *"Amethyst* Report," 22; Phillips, *Escape of the Amethyst,* 45.

26. Weston, 249.

27. *Amethyst* to All Ships, TOO (time of origin)/20 Apr. 1949, F5544/1219/10, FO 371/75887.

28. *"Amethyst* Report," 22.

29. Weston, 249.

30. *"Amethyst* Report," 22; Interview with Sir Peter Berger, Cambridge, 2 June 1988.

31. *"Amethyst* Report," 22.

32. "Rate of Fire was about once every Half Minute but allowing for pauses average

fire was about one every one and a half minutes. Firing was most accurate and nearly all rounds hit. Machine gun fire kept decks and nearby water clear during late forenoon and afternoon." (*Amethyst* to FO2 i/c FES, 210627Z, 21 Apr. 1949, ASL Apr. 1949, Kerans, 69/45/1, IWM.)

33. Ibid., 22–23; Weston, 249.

34. "*Amethyst* Report," 23.

35. Ibid.; Weston, 249.

36. Interview with Sir Peter Berger, Cambridge, 2 June 1988.

37. "*Amethyst* Report," 23–24, 271.

38. Ibid., 23.

39. Earl, *Yangtse Incident,* 29–30.

40. "*Amethyst* Report," 23.

41. Ibid.; Weston, 249.

42. "*Amethyst* Report," 23–24.

43. Ibid., 23; Earl, *Yangtse Incident,* 34–35.

44. French worked incredibly long hours in the WT office while *Amethyst* was detained on the Yangtze. His outstanding devotion to duty was duly recognized by an announcement in the *London Gazette* on 6 May 1949, indicating that he had been awarded the Distinguished Service Medal.

45. Report by P. E. C. Berger (hereafter Berger), undated, 2, Adm 1/21299.

46. Ibid.

47. "*Amethyst* Report," 24; Earl, *Yangtse Incident,* 36–38.

48. Earl, *Yangtse Incident,* 27–28; Diary by Leslie Frank, 20 Apr. 1949, "*Amethyst* Scrapbook," vol. 2, Kerans, 69/45/1, IWM.

49. Although the time mentioned on page 24 of the *Amethyst* Report was 2:30 p.m., Robertson maintains in his letter to FO2 i/c FES, 74/47/1, 26 Apr. 1949, Adm 1/21800, that the frigate was sighted at 1:40 p.m. In the "Monthly Intelligence Report" (hereafter MIR) for May 1949, no. 41, 10 June 1949, Adm 223/229, the time quoted is 1:45 p.m.

50. "*Amethyst* Report," 24; I. G. Robertson to FO2 i/c FES, 74/47/1, 26 Apr. 1949, app. 1, Adm 1/21800.

51. "*Amethyst* Report," 24. TCS was the pattern number of a radio transceiver and is not significant in itself. Far more important was the fact that the order was for voice contact and not WT.

52. Ibid.; Earl, *Yangtse Incident,* 38–39.

53. By the time she reached Kiangyin and anchored for the night at 4:45 p.m., *Consort* had been hit by sixty-eight projectiles; five were 105-mm shells, twelve were 75 mm, thirty-seven were 37 mm, and fourteen were from small arms. ("Action Damage Report of HMS *Consort,*" M041/50, I. G. Robertson to FO2 i/c FES, 8 Oct. 1949, Adm 1/21800).

54. *Daily Telegraph,* 22 Apr. 1949.

55. I. G. Robertson to FO2 i/c FES, 74/47/1, 26 Apr. 1949, app. 1, Adm 1/21800.

56. About ten minutes after leaving the vicinity of Rose Island, *Consort* came in for another pounding from a PLA battery on the northern bank of the river. This one was established on Low Island and it succeeded in knocking out the gyro, WT office, and T.S., as well as inflicting fifteen further casualties among the crew (MIR, May 1949, no. 41, 10 June 1949, 12, Adm 223/229).

57. Ibid.

58. Weston, 250.

59. *"Amethyst* Report," 25.

60. Ibid.

61. Ibid; Earl, *Yangtse Incident,* 42–43.

62. *"Amethyst* Report," 25.

63. Ibid; Weston, 250.

64. *"Amethyst* Report," 25; *Amethyst* to FO2 i/c FES, 201400Z, 20 Apr. 1949, ASL Apr. 1949, Kerans, 69/45/1, IWM.

65. *"Amethyst* Report," 25; Earl, *Yangtse Incident,* 48–49.

66. *"Amethyst* Report," 25.

67. Berger, 5; *"Amethyst* Report," 26. *Amethyst's* fully laden oil fuel capacity was 391 tons of furnace fuel and 28.6 tons of diesel. When she went aground she had 365 tons of furnace fuel and 14 tons of diesel left in her tanks. (Wilkinson, "Engineering Exploits," 419; *"Amethyst* Scrapbook," vol. 2, Kerans, 69/45/1, IWM).

68. Berger, 5; *"Amethyst* Report," 26.

CHAPTER FOUR. NO CHANCE OF AN UNDERSTANDING

1. Stevenson to FO, 491, 20 Apr. 1949, F5476/1219/10, FO 371/75887; *The Times,* 21 Apr. 1949. When news of the attack was intercepted in Hong Kong at 10:58 A.M. on 20 April, work on refitting the destroyers HMS *Cossack* and HMS *Constance* was rapidly accelerated. *Constance* left for Shanghai during the afternoon of the following day.

2. Earl, *Yangtse Incident,* 24.

3. FO2 i/c FES to Assistant Naval Attaché (Shanghai) (hereafter ANA), 200235Z, 20 Apr. 1949, F5544/1219/10, FO 371/75887.

4. FO2 i/c FES to *Consort,* 200253Z, 20 Apr. 1949, F5544/1219/10, FO 371/75887.

5. MIR May 1949, no. 41, 10 June 1949, 12, Adm 223/229.

6. FO2 i/c FES to ANA Shanghai, 200312Z, 20 Apr. 1949, F5544/1219/10, FO 371/75887.

7. Astalusna (Singapore) to Chief of Naval Operations (Washington), 201005Z, 20 Apr. 1949, F5590/1219/10, FO 371/75887.

8. ANA Shanghai to NA Nanking, 200416Z, 20 Apr. 1949, F5544/1219/10, FO 371/75887.

9. *Consort* to FO2 i/c FES, 200442Z, 20 Apr. 1949, F5544/1219/10, FO 371/75887.

10. *Consort* to FO2 i/c FES, 200704Z, F5589/1219/10, FO 371/75887. Although *Consort* was lavishly bedecked in British colors, it is quite possible that those artillery troops at the PLA battery positions in the Nanking-to-Rose Island sector of the Yangtze front may not have recognized the destroyer as a Royal Navy vessel.

11. SOFF3 (Senior Officer 3rd Frigate Flotilla) to FO2 i/c FES, 201041Z, 20 Apr. 1949, F5590/1219/10, FO 371/75887.

12. *Amethyst* to FO2 i/c FES, 2201400Z, 20 Apr. 1949, F5591/1219/10, FO 371/75887.

13. Stevenson to Peking, 48, 21 Apr. 1949, F5551/1219/10, FO 371/75887.

14. Stevenson to FO, 463, 21 Apr. 1949, F5598/1219/10, FO 371/75887; Minute by P. D. Coates, 20 Apr. 1949, F5483/1219/10, FO 371/75887.

15. Stevenson to Peking, 49, 21 Apr. 1949, F5595/1219/10, FO 371/75887.

16. At a press conference held at the Royal Naval College, Greenwich, on 20 April, Lord Fraser, the chief of naval staff, confirmed this situation by stating, "Our principle of course is the same; leave it to the man on the spot, except where you can give him assistance." (Lord Fraser's Press Statement, 20 Apr. 1949, Adm 1/21508.)

17. Although a number of the dispatches have a restricted access, those released by the Foreign Office can be found under file numbers 5476, 5483, 5550, 5551, 5596, 5598, 5599/1219/10, FO 371/75887.

18. FO to Stevenson, 394, 20 Apr. 1949, F5476/1219/10, FO 371/75887.

19. Stevenson to FO, 454, 21 Apr. 1949, F5550/1219/10, FO 371/75887.

20. Ibid.

21. COS (Chiefs of Staff) (49) 57th mtg, 20 Apr. 1949, Defe (Ministry of Defence) 4/21.

22. SAC (Strategic Appreciation Committee) (49), 2d mtg, 20 Apr. 1949, Cab 134/669.

23. Ibid. Attlee was asked in an unsigned note dated 21 April whether he wished to meet Admiral Brind, the commander in chief of the Far East Station in Singapore. Brind was attending the *Trident* naval planning conference at Greenwich. Attlee wrote: "Not necessary, I think." (Prem 8/944)

24. FO2 i/c FES to NA Nanking, 201147Z, 20 Apr. 1949, Adm 116/5696.

25. NA Nanking to FO2 i/c FES, 201543Z, 21 Apr. 1949, Adm 116/5696.

26. ANA Shanghai to FO2 i/c FES, 201200Z, 20 Apr. 1949, F5591/1219/10, FO 371/75887.

27. Commander Hong Kong (hereafter COM Hong Kong), to FO2 i/c FES, 201425Z, 20 Apr. 1949, F5591/1219/10, FO 371/75887.

28. COM Hong Kong to FO2 i/c FES, 201528Z, 20 Apr. 1949, F5591/1219/10, FO 371/75887.

29. *Amethyst* to FO2 i/c FES, 201400Z, 20 Apr. 1949, F5591/1219/10, FO 371/75887.

30. FO2 i/c FES to NA Nanking, 201434Z, 20 Apr. 1949, F5591/1219/10, FO 371/75887. According to Vice-Admiral Sir Ballin Robertshaw's map of the battery positions on the Yangtze, the distance between the battery on Low Island to the one situated at the eastern edge of Sinnimu Creek and to the north of Rose Island was approximately 9 miles. There is another battery position marked on Robertshaw's map on the opposite bank of Sinnimu Creek and to the northwest of Rose Island. Nonetheless, it is difficult to reconcile the positions of these batteries with the extent of the firing zone mentioned by Ian Robertson, the captain of the *Consort* (Map of the Yangtse Incident, 15 May 1949, included in Vice-Admiral Sir Ballin Robertshaw Papers, (hereafter Robertshaw, 72/75/1, IWM.)

31. FO2 i/c FES to NA Nanking, 201434Z, 20 Apr. 1949, F5591/1219/10, FO 371/75887.

32. NA Nanking to FO2 i/c FES, 201516Z, 20 Apr. 1949, F5591/1219/10, FO 371/75887.

33. *Amethyst* to Hong Kong Wireless, 201610Z, 20 Apr. 1949, Adm 116/5696.

34. FO2 i/c FES to *Amethyst*, 201715Z, 20 Apr. 1949, F5592/1219/10, FO 371/75887.

35. *Amethyst* to FO2 i/c FES, 201818Z, 20 Apr. 1949, F5592/1219/10, FO 371/75887.

36. Ibid.

37. FO2 i/c FES to *Amethyst*, 201950Z, 20 Apr. 1949, F5592/1219/10, FO 371/75887.

38. *Amethyst* to FO2 i/c FES, 202150Z, 21 Apr. 1949, F5593/1219/10, FO 371/75887.

39. FO2 i/c FES to COM Hong Kong, 210058Z, 21 Apr. 1949, F5594/1219/10, FO 371/75887.

40. FO2 i/c FES to *London, Black Swan, Amethyst,* NA Nanking, 210137Z, 21 Apr. 1949, F5594/1219/10, FO 371/75887.

41. FO2 i/c FES to *Black Swan*, 210140Z, 21 Apr. 1949, F5594/1219/10, FO 371/75887.

CHAPTER FIVE. MOUNTING A RESCUE ATTEMPT

1. *"Amethyst* Report," 26.

2. Ibid., 11.

3. Ibid., 26.

4. Ibid.

5. Weston, 250.

6. *"Amethyst* Report," 26.

7. Ibid.

8. Ibid.

9. Earl, *Yangtse Incident,* 61.

10. Report by J. Hodges (hereafter Hodges), 221/139, 28 Apr. 1949, 1, in letter CO (Commanding Officer) HMS *London* (Capt. P. G. L. Cazelet) to COM Hong Kong, 439/139, M2158/49, 24 May 1949, Adm 1/21508.

11. According to *Black Swan*'s "Action Damage Report" (PR 4186/49, in CO HMS *Black Swan* [Capt. A. D. H. Jay] to FO2 i/c FES, 15 June 1949, Adm 1/21312), the battery was situated 1.6 miles from Bate Point Beacon. In a map drawn on 15 May 1949 and found in Vice-Admiral Sir Ballin Robertshaw's papers, however, the distance appears to be closer to 3 miles (Map, 15 May 1949, Robertshaw, 72/75/1, IWM).

12. Cazelet to COM Hong Kong, 439/139, 24 May 1949, Adm 1/21508 and Hodges, 2; see also Narrative Report by Capt. A. D. H. Jay in his letter to FO2 i/c FES, 15 June 1949, Adm 1/21312.

13. Hodges, 2.

14. Ibid; *The Times,* 7 Sept. 1949. According to Robertshaw's map of the Yangtze incident, however, *London* was somewhere between 13–15 miles from the *Amethyst* when she was fired on. He plots her as having turned and set course downriver when the distance between the cruiser and the stranded frigate was only 13 miles (Map, 15 May 1949, Robertshaw, 72/75/1, IWM).

15. Hodges, 3; App. A to Hodges, 1–3; App. B to Hodges, 3; Grove, *Vanguard to Trident,* 131–32.

16. Hodges, 2.

17. "Action Damage Report and Narrative," HMS *Black Swan,* PR 4186/49, in Jay to FO2 i/c FES, 15 June 1949, Adm 1/21312; Hodges, 3.

18. Cazelet to COM Hong Kong, 439/139, M2158/49, 24 May 1949, Adm 1/21508.

19. FO2 i/c FES to C-in-C, FES, 210423Z, 21 Apr. 1949, F5595/1219/10, FO 371/75887; FO2 i/c FES to *Amethyst,* 210424Z, 21 Apr. 1949, ASL Apr. 1949, Kerans, 69/45/1, IWM.

20. "*Amethyst* Report," 26.

21. FO2 i/c FES to C-in-C FES, 210423Z, 21 Apr. 1949, F5595/1219/10, FO 371/75887.

22. FO2 i/c FES to C-in-C FES, 210737Z, 21 Apr. 1949, F5851/1219/10, FO 371/75888.

23. FO2 i/c FES to C-in-C FES, 211435Z, 22 Apr. 1949, F5853/1219/10, FO 371/75888.

24. Ibid.

CHAPTER SIX. KERANS ENTERS THE PICTURE

1. Kerans's naval career up to this point had been a checkered one. Although an intelligent and resourceful man, his potential strengths had to a large extent been undermined by certain personal shortcomings, most notably a growing dependency on alcohol and an incorrigible desire for women. As a result of his past misdemeanors, the Admiralty had been unwilling to give him a seagoing command worthy of his rank and had instead kept him out of harm's way by shipping him off to Hong Kong in 1947 on security intelligence work and then on to Malaya in October 1948 for a three-month attachment with the Selangor police. While Kerans was completing his assignment in Kuala Lumpur, Captain Vernon Donaldson, the naval attaché at the British Embassy in China, was seeking an assistant to help him cope with the additional workload that had been created since the British had begun retaining a warship at Nanking in November 1948. Sir Patrick Brind, the newly appointed commander in chief of the Far East Station, signaled Donaldson with the news that Kerans was immediately available should he decide to have him. Brind informed Donaldson that although he had considered court-martialing Kerans for committing an undisclosed offense in the past, he would give him a second chance even though he would be "Under Report" status for an indefinite period. Donaldson decided to risk having Kerans on his staff, and his newly appointed assistant naval attaché duly arrived in Nanking on 3 February 1949. Donaldson soon began to regret his decision to give Kerans a fresh start in his naval career, as the flaws in his assistant's character already alluded to manifested themselves once again. Overall, therefore, he was not very satisfied with his brash assistant or his work methods in the period before the Yangtze crisis occurred in April 1949. (Correspondence with Rear Admiral Vernon Donaldson, 3 Oct. 1989; Interviews with Nicholas Rodger, London, 10 June 1988; Sir Peter Berger, Cambridge, 2 June 1988; MIR Oct. 1949, no. 46, 10 Nov. 1949, 28, Adm 223/230).

2. Earl, *Yangtse Incident,* 50–52.

3. Ibid; "Report on Evacuation of Wounded from H.M.S. *Amethyst*" by R. V. Dewar-Durie (hereafter Dewar-Durie), 30 Apr. 1949, FO 371/75897; "*Amethyst* Report," 26.

4. *"Amethyst* Report," 26; Earl, *Yangtse Incident,* 52.

5. Dewar-Durie, 1.

6. *"Amethyst* Report," 26; Earl, *Yangtse Incident,* 52–53.

7. AHQ Hong Kong to FO2 i/c FES, 210208Z, 21 Apr. 1949, F5595/1219/10, FO 371/75887.

8. Earl, *Yangtse Incident,* 52, 55.

9. *"Amethyst* Report," 27; NA Nanking to FO2 i/c FES, 210749Z, 21 Apr. 1949, F5595/1219/10, FO 371/75887.

10. *"Amethyst* Report," 27; Earl, *Yangtse Report,* 55–56; Dewar-Durie, 1.

11. *"Amethyst* Report," 27.

12. Ibid.

13. Earl, *Yangtse Incident,* 69–70.

14. Ibid, 70–71.

15. *"Amethyst* Report," 27.

16. *Amethyst* to FO2 i/c FES, 211122Z, 21 Apr. 1949, F5852/1219/10, FO 371/75888.

17. *"Amethyst* Report," 27; Earl, *Yangtse Incident,* 71–72.

18. Dewar-Durie, 1; Earl, *Yangtse Incident,* 56; "Amethyst Report," 27–28.

19. *"Amethyst* Report," 27–28.

20. Dewar-Durie, 1.

21. *Amethyst* to FO2 i/c FES, 211302Z, 21 Apr. 1949, F5853/1219/10, FO 371/75888.

22. *Amethyst* to FO2 i/c FES, 211605Z, 21 Apr. 1949, F5853/1219/10, FO 371/75888.

23. *"Amethyst* Report," 27.

24. Dewar-Durie, 1–2; Earl, *Yangtse Incident,* 57–58.

25. *"Amethyst* Report," 28.

26. Dewar-Durie, 2.

27. Earl, *Yangtse Incident,* 75; *"Amethyst* Report," 28.

28. Dewar-Durie, 2.

29. Earl, *Yangtse Incident,* 76.

30. Dewar-Durie, 2.

31. Ibid.

32. Weston, 251; Earl, *Yangtse Incident,* 74–75.

33. FO2 i/c FES to *Amethyst,* 211520Z, 21 Apr. 1949, F5853/1219/10, FO 371/75888.

34. Earl, *Yangtse Incident,* 74–75.

35. *Amethyst* to FO2 i/c FES, 212040Z, 21 Apr. 1949, F5854/1219/10, FO 371/75888.

36. *"Amethyst* Report," 29.

37. *Amethyst* to FO2 i/c FES, 212040Z, 21 Apr. 1949, F5854/1219/10, FO 371/75888.

38. FO2 i/c FES to *Amethyst,* 220008Z, 22 Apr. 1949, F5854/1219/10, FO 371/75888.

39. Weston, 251.

40. Dewar-Durie, 2; "*Amethyst* Report," 28–29.

41. Dewar-Durie, 3; "*Amethyst* Report," 28–29.

42. Dewar-Durie, 3; Earl, *Yangtse Incident*, 77–78; "*Amethyst* Report," 29.

43. Dewar-Durie, 3.

44. "*Amethyst* Report," 29; Earl, *Yangtse Incident*, 78.

45. Dewar-Durie, 3; "*Amethyst* Report," 29.

46. Dewar-Durie, 3; "*Amethyst* Report," 29; Earl, *Yangtse Incident*, 78–79.

47. "*Amethyst* Report," 29; Earl, *Yangtse Incident*, 80.

48. Weston, 251.

49. Ibid.

50. Ibid.; "*Amethyst* Report," 29–30.

51. Weston, 251; Earl, *Yangtse Incident*, 81–82.

52. Earl, *Yangtse Incident*, 82–83.

53. *Amethyst* to FO2 i/c FES, 220731Z, 22 Apr. 1949, F5914/1219/10, FO 371/75889; "*Amethyst* Report," 30.

54. FO2 i/c FES to *Amethyst*, 220734Z, 22 Apr. 1949, F5914/1219/10, FO 371/75889.

55. "*Amethyst* Report," 30; Earl, *Yangtse Incident*, 84.

56. NA Nanking to FO2 i/c FES, 220327Z, 22 Apr. 1949, F5913/1219/10; 220737Z, 22 Apr. 1949, F5914/1219/10, FO 371/75889.

57. FO2 i/c FES to *Amethyst*, 220954Z, 22 Apr. 1949, F5914/1219/10, FO 371/75889.

58. FO2 i/c FES to C-in-C FES, 221111Z, 22 Apr. 1949, F5915/1219/10, FO 371/75889.

59. FO2 i/c FES to *Amethyst*, 221152Z, 22 Apr. 1949, F5915/1219/10, FO 371/75889.

60. *Amethyst* to FO2 i/c FES, 221222Z, 22 Apr. 1949, F5915/1219/10, FO 371/75889.

61. "*Amethyst* Report," 30.

62. Ibid., 30–31.

63. Ibid.

64. FO2 i/c FES to *Amethyst*, 221346Z, 22 Apr. 1949, F5915/1219/10, FO 371/75889.

65. "*Amethyst* Report," 31.

66. Dewar-Durie, 3.

CHAPTER SEVEN. YOUDE'S MISSION

1. Stevenson to FO, 464, 21 Apr. 1949, F5599/1219/10, FO 371/75887.

2. Stevenson to FO, 463, 21 Apr. 1949, F5599/1219/10, FO 371/75887.

3. Stevenson to FO, 466, 22 Apr. 1949, F5741/1219/10; Stevenson to FO, 468, 22 Apr. 1949, F5782/1219/10; Stevenson to FO, 472, 22 Apr. 1949, F5693/1219/10; Stevenson to FO, 488, 24 Apr. 1949, F5715/1219/10, FO 371/75888.

4. "Report on an Attempt to Secure a Safe-Conduct Pass for H.M.S. Amethyst After She Had Been Crippled by Communist Gunfire" by Edward Youde (hereafter Youde), n.d., 2, FO 371/75897.

5. Youde had graduated with a B.A. Honours degree in Chinese from the School of Oriental and African Studies at London University before joining the Foreign Office in 1947. He had been promoted to third secretary and appointed to the embassy in Nanking and the consulate in Peking in 1948.

6. Youde, 1.

7. Ibid.

8. Ibid., 6

9. Ibid., 1.

10. Ibid.

11. Ibid.

12. Ibid.

13. Ibid.

14. Ibid., 2.

15. Ibid.

16. Ibid.

17. Ibid.

18. Ibid., 2–3.

19. Ibid., 3.

20. Ibid.

21. Ibid.

22. Ibid.

23. Ibid.

24. Ibid., 3–4.

25. Ibid., 4.

26. Ibid., 5–6.

27. Ibid., 6.

28. Ibid.; see also Military Attaché, Nanking to WO, unnumbered, DTO (date time of origin) 271815GH, 28 Apr. 1949, F6783/1015/10, FO 371/75733.

29. Youde, 4.

30. Stevenson to FO, 485, 24 Apr. 1949, F5713/1219/10, FO 371/75888.

31. Ibid.

32. Youde, 4.

33. Ibid.

CHAPTER EIGHT. EXPLORING OTHER POSSIBILITIES

1. Stevenson to FO, 463, 21 Apr. 1949, F5598/1219/10, FO 371/75887.

2. Minute by P. D. Coates, 22 Apr. 1949, on Stevenson to FO, 460, 21 Apr. 1949, F5596/1219/10, FO 371/75887.

3. Minute by S. Burgess, 22 Apr. 1949, on Stevenson to FO, 463, 21 Apr. 1949, F5598/1219/10, FO 371/75887.

4. Stevenson to FO, 488, 24 Apr. 1949, F5715/129/10, FO 371/75888. Commander J. M. Pringle, assistant naval attaché in Shanghai, found a report in the local press that declared emphatically that the Royal Navy and the KMT had been cooperating with one another: "Chinese Mosquito press today alleged that *Amethyst* was carrying stores and

ammunition for the Nationalists and nothing for Embassy in contradiction to our official report." ANA Shanghai to FO2 i/c FES, 230436Z, 23 Apr. 1949, F5977/1219/10, FO 371/75889.

5. Stevenson to FO, 490, 24 Apr. 1949, F5717/1219/10, FO 371/75888. For a very different view on this statement, see Urquhart to FO, 238, 24 Apr. 1949, F5723/1611/10, FO 371/75939.

6. Stevenson to FO, 488, 24 Apr. 1949, F5715/1219/10, FO 371/75888.

7. *People's Daily,* 24 Apr. 1949.

8. Ibid.; see also Urquhart to FO, 238, 24 Apr. 1949, F5723/1611/10, FO 371/75939.

9. Stevenson to FO, 466, 22 Apr. 1949, F5741/1219/10, FO 371/75888.

10. Stevenson to FO, 472, 22 Apr. 1949, F5693/1219/10 FO 371/75888.

11. Stevenson to FO, 473, 22 Apr. 1949, F5694/1219/10, FO 371/75888.

12. Ibid.

13. FO to Stevenson, 408, 23 Apr. 1949, F5694/1219/10, FO 371/75888.

14. Stevenson to FO, 465, 22 Apr. 1949; Minute by P. D. Coates, 22 Apr. 1949, F5623/1015/10, FO 371/75749.

15. Ibid.

16. Stevenson to FO, 476, 480, 23 Apr. 1949, Adm 116/5698.

17. MIR Apr. 1949, no. 40, 10 May 1949, Adm 223/229; Stevenson to FO, 480, 23 Apr. 1949, F5711/5712/1015/10, FO 371/75749.

18. Stevenson to FO, 485, 24 Apr. 1949, F5713/1219/10, FO 371/75888.

19. COS (49)57th mtg, 20 Apr. 1949, Defe 4/21; Adm to FO2 i/c FES, 202330A, 20 Apr. 1949, F5593/1219/10, FO 371/75887.

20. COS (49)58th mtg, 22 Apr. 1949, F5593/1219/10, FO 371/75887.

21. FO2 i/c FES to Adm, 220306A, 22 Apr. 1949, F5913/1219/10, FO 371/75889.

22. Adm to FO2 i/c FES, 221352A, 22 Apr. 1949, F5915/1219/10, FO 371/75889.

23. FO2 i/c FES to Adm, 221526Z, 22 Apr. 1949, F5916/1219/10, FO 371/75889; Minute for prime minister, 23 Apr. 1949, Prem 8/944.

24. *Amethyst* to FO2 i/c FES, 221932Z, 22 Apr. 1949, F5916/1219/10, FO 371/75889.

25. FO2 i/c FES to *Amethyst,* 221346Z, 22 Apr. 1949, F5915/1219/10, FO 371/75889.

26. FO2 i/c FES to *Amethyst,* 23 Apr. 1949, F5976/1219/10, FO 371/75889.

27. *Amethyst* to FO2 i/c FES, 222352Z, 23 Apr. 1949, F5876/1219/10, FO 371/75889.

28. All damage repair parties worked under the supervision of Lieutenant George Strain. While the engineers somehow carried out a quite sophisticated program of repairs and replacement of equipment in the heart of the ship, other groups made do with what they could get their hands on. Cushions and hammocks were stuffed unceremoniously into the gaping shell holes left in the mess decks, WT office, bridge, wheelhouse, and chartroom. Surplus hardwood was used to make shores, and flour became a substitute for nonexistent good quality cement (MIR Oct. 1949, 46, 10 Nov. 1949, 30–32, Adm 223/230; "*Amethyst* Log," 23 Apr. 1949, Adm 53/125421).

29. *Amethyst* to FO2 i/c FES 230127Z, 23 Apr. 1949, ASL Apr., Kerans, 69/45/1, IWM.

30. *"Amethyst* Report," 32.

31. Ibid.; *Amethyst* to FO2 i/c FES, 230455Z, 23 Apr. 1949, F5977/1219/10, FO 371/75889.

32. *"Amethyst* Report," 32.

33. *Amethyst* to FO2 i/c FES, 230554Z, 23 Apr. 1949, ASL Apr., Kerans, 69/45/1, IWM.

34. FO2 i/c FES to *Amethyst,* 230659Z, 23 Apr. 1949, F5978/1219/10, FO 371/75889.

35. *"Amethyst* Report," 33.

36. Ibid.

37. Ibid.

38. Ibid.; FO 2 i/c FES to C-in-C FES, 240700Z, 24 Apr. 1949, F6065/1219/10, FO 371/75890.

39. *"Amethyst* Log," 24 Apr. 1949, Adm 53/125421.

40. *"Amethyst* Report," 33–34.

41. Stevenson to FO, 484, 24 Apr. 1949, Adm 116/5698. Strangely enough, the wording of the cancellation telegram received in the Admiralty is slightly different from that sent to the Foreign Office. A further peculiarity exists in that the original telegram (261 of 9 Nov. 1948) could not be traced within the archives of the Foreign Office. (Minute by P. W. Scarlett, 25 Apr. 1949, on Stevenson to FO, 484, 24 Apr. 1949, F5738/1611/10, FO 371/75939.)

42. FO2 i/c FES to Adm, 241627Z, 24 Apr. 1949, referred to in CP (49), 25 Apr. 1949, CAB 129/34.

43. Ibid.; see also Stevenson to FO, 489, 24 Apr. 1949, F5716/1611/10, FO 371/75939.

44. Stevenson to FO, 503, 25 Apr. 1949, F5785/1611/10, FO 371/75939.

45. Urquhart to FO, 248, 25 Apr. 1949, F5787/1611/10, FO 371/75939. This suggestion ought to be compared to the text of his stirring, patriotic speech to celebrate St. George's Day, in which the heroic deeds of the *Amethyst* and other British naval vessels on the Yangtze figured prominently (*China Daily Tribune,* 24 Apr. 1949).

46. COS (49) 59th mtg, 25 Apr. 1949, Defe 4/21.

47. Aide-mémoire of mtg, 25 Apr. 1949, F6128/1015/10G, FO 371/75751.

48. *Ibid.*

49. According to Madden, Urquhart and he had decided unilaterally on 25 Apr. not to implement Operation *Legionary* (the plan for the evacuation of British nationals from Shanghai in an emergency) in its original form. Instead, travel arrangements were made for those women and children who wished to leave the city. They were to be given berths on the Dutch vessel *Boissevain,* which was scheduled to depart from the port on 28 April (FO2 i/c FES, "Report of Proceedings from 26 March–28 May 1949" to C-in-C FES, M01702/49, 4 Aug. 1949, F02FE/2960/11, Adm 1/21493).

50. Aide-mémoire of mtg, 25 Apr. 1949, F6128/1015/10G, FO 371/75751.

51. On the same day (25 April), Mao had issued an eight-point proclamation that was published by the New China News Agency on 26 April. Its final point referred to the intention to protect the security of the lives and property of all foreign nationals in China. It exhorted them to do their work as usual and preserve order (BBC Intercept,

F5710/1015/10, FO 371/75749; Stevenson to FO, 555, 2 May 1949, F6386/1015/10, FO 371/75751).

CHAPTER NINE. A POLITICAL STORM IS BREWING

1. U.K. *Hansard (Commons)*, vol. 464, col. 25–26.

2. Ibid., col. 26–27.

3. Ibid., col. 27–33; see also the draft speech written for Attlee (Prem 8/944) and note the significant omissions from this draft in the address he delivered in parliament.

4. U.K., *Hansard (Commons)*, vol. 464, col. 31–32.

5. Ibid.

6. Ibid., col. 32–33.

7. At its meeting at 10:00 A.M. on 26 April, the cabinet revised the draft statement that both Attlee and Viscount Hall, the first lord of the Admiralty, would use in the Commons and Lords, respectively, that same afternoon. See Cab mtg. (28)49, 26 Apr. 1949, Cab 128/15; CP (49)93, 25 Apr. 1949, Cab 129/34.

8. Ibid., col. 33–34.

9. Ibid., col. 34.

10. Ibid., col. 34–35; in the draft speech referred to in Note 3 above, the prime minister was to have made the following remarks:

> The passage has always been regarded as one of some risk in case irresponsible elements on either bank opened fire. Nevertheless, the Naval Commander-in-Chief decided that, since there had been no opposition and our aim was peaceful, the passages should be continued; I fully endorse his decision. The House will of course appreciate that if passages had been stopped because of the uneasy situation, or because of individual scares, the requirements of the Embassy and the British community in Nanking would not have been met. The Navy has always been prepared, and I hope will always be prepared, to take justifiable risks in carrying out its tasks. (Prem 8/944)

11. U.K., *Hansard (Commons)*, vol. 464, col. 35.

12. Ibid., col. 36.

13. Ibid.

14. Ibid.

15. Ibid.

16. Ibid., col. 36–37.

17. Ibid., col. 37.

18. Ibid.

19. Ibid., col. 38–39.

20. Ibid., col. 39.

21. Ibid., col. 39–46.

22. Ibid., col. 46.

23. Ibid., col. 34, 42.

24. Alexander had announced the decision to withdraw the two aircraft carriers from the China Station in parliament on 27 October 1947. Harold Macmillan, the Conservative

MP for Bromley, would raise this matter again when opening the debate on British policy in China on 5 May (Ibid, col. 1227).

25. U.K., *Hansard (Lords)*, vol. 162, col. 23–42.

26. Minute by G. Burgess, Far East Dept., FO, 29 Apr. 1949, F5827/1219/10, FO 371/75888.

27. Minute by News Dept., 2 May 1949, F5827/1219/10, FO 371/75888.

28. Ibid.

29. Notes of the Week, *Economist*, 30 Apr. 1949; see also Urquhart to FO, 232, 22 Apr. 1949, F5720/1611/10, FO 371/75939.

30. *Economist*, 30 Apr. 1949; A Foreign Office minute summed up the piece in the following words: ". . . not up to the usual standard of the paper." Quite what that meant is obscure and perhaps should remain so!

31. *Spectator*, 29 Apr. 1949.

32. Mao, "On the Outrages by British Warships," 30 Apr. 1949, in *Selected Works of Mao Tse-tung* 4:401.

33. Ibid., 401–2; see also *Wen Wei Po*, 1 May 1949.

34. Mao, "On the Outrages by British Warships," 30 Apr. 1949, in *Selected Works of Mao Tse-tung* 4:401; *Wen Wei Po*, 1 May 1949.

35. Ibid.; memo by P. W. Scarlett, 12 May 1948, F7028/364/10, FO 371/69610; Stevenson to FO, 192, 28 Mar. 1949, F5316/1013/10, FO 371/75733.

36. Stevenson to FO, 559, 2 May 1949, F6246/1219/10, FO 371/75890.

37. Ibid. In a dispatch to the Foreign Office on 30 April, Stevenson revealed that although the Communist press had taken a uniformly aggressive tone toward the clashes on the Yangtze between the Royal Navy and the PLA, these articles had not inspired any anti-British demonstrations either in Nanking or elsewhere. He strongly supported the view expressed in London that the British should remain in China and try to look after their interests in the country come what may (Stevenson to FO, 547, 30 Apr. 1949, F6211/1015/10, FO 371/75751).

38. Admiralty notes for parliamentary question no. 32 by Mr. Low, undated, Attlee, dep. 82, fol. 60–61. BL.

39. U.K., *Hansard (Commons)*, vol. 464, col. 642.

40. "Yangtse Incident," an Appreciation by Lord Fraser, undated, F6448/1219/10, FO 371/75891; Admiralty notes for parliamentary question no. 32 by Mr. Low, undated, Attlee, dep. 82, fol. 60–61, BL.

41. COS (49)65th mtg, 6 May 1949, Defe 4/21.

42. It is difficult to know how effective this committee was in giving advice to the government because its papers have been embargoed under the Official Secrets Act. Despite this element of uncertainty, however, it is evident from other references to it in published documents that it was extremely busy. Indeed the vast number of telegrams exchanged with the COS in London and coded COSSEA and SEACOS attest to that. Unfortunately, apart from the period 1945–46 (Cab 105 series), the rest of the BDCC material has not yet been released under the thirty-year rule.

43. Stevenson to FO, 565, 3 May 1949, F6292/1219/10, FO 371/75890.

44. These articles were not wide of the mark, however, as Admiral Brind revealed in a message to Commander J. M. Pringle, the assistant naval attaché in Shanghai, on 30 May 1949 (C-in-C FES (Afloat) to ANA Shanghai, 290629Z, 30 May 1949, F8240/1015/10,

FO 371/75759; see also notes by S. P. Osmond for C. R. Attlee, 3 May 1949, Attlee, dep. 82, fol. 41, BL).

45. Stevenson to FO, 561, 3 May 1949, F6297/1219/10, FO 371/75891. At this time the disposition of ships of the Far East Station in Chinese waters was as follows: at Woosung—HMS *Constance* (destroyer); at Alacrity Anchorage (80 miles east of Woosung)—HMS *Belfast* (cruiser), HMS *Black Swan* (frigate), and HMS *Green Ranger* (oiler); at Hong Kong—HMS *Cossack* (destroyer), HMS *Consort* (destroyer), and HMS *Concord* (destroyer); at sea—HMCS *Crescent* (destroyer), HMAS *Shoalhaven* (frigate), HMS *London* (cruiser), and HMS *Hart* (frigate) (Attlee, dep. 82, fol. 82–85, BL).

46. Nonetheless as late as 30 May, the commander in chief, while anxious to redeploy his naval force from the mouth of the Yangtze following the fall of Shanghai, was reluctant to leave the area altogether: "We must plan for one destroyer or frigate in North China for some time. One cruiser is to be within 48 hours repetition 48 hours of Shanghai. Request you arrange cruiser programme accordingly." (C-in-C [Afloat] to FO2 i/c FES, 30 1437Z, 30 May 1949, F8240/1015/10, FO 371/75759).

47. FO2 i/c FES to Adm, 011611/May, 1 May 1949, F6471/1219/10, FO 371/75891.

48. FO2 i/c FES to Adm, 021308Z, 2 May 1949, F6471/1219/10, FO 371/75891.

CHAPTER TEN. OPENING NEGOTIATIONS ON THE YANGTZE

1. Despite the ingenuity shown by the damage repair parties led by George Strain, the hole on the waterline in the tiller flat and in the wardroom could not be plugged successfully. Persistent flooding in these areas affected the after flat causing it to be shut down as well.

2. "*Amethyst* Report," 33–34.

3. Ibid., 35.

4. Earl, *Yangtse Incident,* 93–94; "*Amethyst* Log," 26 Apr. 1949, Adm 53/125421.

5. Ibid., "*Amethyst* Log," 26 Apr. 1949, Adm 53/125421.

6. Ibid. This so-called Major Kung was none other than Colonel Kang Mao Chao, the political commissioner, who would become Kerans's major adversary in the protracted series of negotiations conducted between the PLA and the *Amethyst* in the weeks to come. Kerans only discovered that Kung and Kang were the same person at the end of May 1949. (*Amethyst* to C-in-C FES, 311237Z, 31 May 1949, F8060/1219/10, FO 371/75892).

7. *Amethyst* to FO2 1/c FES, 261221Z, 26 Apr. 1949, F6104/1219/10, FO 371/75890.

8. Ibid.

9. Ibid.

10. "*Amethyst* Report," 35.

11. Ibid.

12. Ibid., 36.

13. Ibid.

14. Ibid., 177.

15. Ibid., 36.

16. Ibid.

17. Ibid, 36–37.

18. Ibid.

19. Ibid.

20. Ibid., 37.

21. *Amethyst* to FO2 i/c FES, 290507Z, 29 Apr. 1949, "Captain's Log: *Amethyst*," Kerans, 69/45/1, IWM; Kang Maozhao, "Hong Dong Yi Shi De Ying Jian Chang Jiang Shi Jian," *Shi Jie Zhi Shi* (World Knowledge) 1988, 8:25–26; 10:22–23; 11:22–25.

22. Stevenson to FO, 509, 26 Apr. 1949, F5796/1219/10, FO 371/75888.

23. Ibid.

24. Minute by P. D. Coates, 27 Apr. 1949 on 509, F5796/1219/10, FO 371/75888.

25. "*Amethyst* Log," 28 Apr. 1949, Adm 53/125421.

26. Ibid., 30 Apr. 1949.

27. Ibid., 1 May 1949; Earl, *Yangtse Incident,* 95.

28. Tai's role in the negotiations during the next two months was to take verbatim notes in Chinese of the proceedings whenever the two sides met. According to Kerans, Tai was not as staunch a Communist as the rest of his team. This suspicion seems to have been confirmed by the fact that Tai was always being watched by a PLA security agent (MIR Oct. 1949, 46, 10 Nov. 1949, pp. 34–35, Adm 223/230).

29. "*Amethyst* Report," 37.

30. Ibid.

31. Ibid., 37–38.

32. Ibid.

33. Ibid., 38.

34. Ibid; see also Leslie Frank's Diary, 5 May 1949, 5., "*Amethyst* Scrapbook," vol. 2, Kerans, 69/45/1, IWM.

35. As evidence of the growing might of the PLA, Hangchow was captured on 2 May ensuring that the last railway link was broken between Shanghai and the rest of China (MIR Apr. 1949, no. 40, 10 May 1949, Adm 223/229).

36. "*Amethyst* Report," 38.

37. *Amethyst* to FO2 i/c FES, 080121Z, 8 May 1949, F6748/1219/10, FO 371/75891.

38. "*Amethyst* Report," 39.

39. Ibid.

40. *Amethyst* to FO2 i/c FES, 170852Z, 17 May 1949, F6748/1219/10, FO 371/75891.

41. "*Amethyst* Report," 242.

42. *Amethyst* to FO2 i/c FES, 180745Z; 180814Z, 18 May 1949, F7168/1219/10, FO 371/75891.

43. "*Amethyst* Report," 41.

CHAPTER ELEVEN. MORE QUESTIONS THAN ANSWERS

1. U.K., *Hansard (Commons),* vol. 464, col. 1224–25.

2. Ibid.

3. Ibid., col. 1225.

4. Ibid., col. 1226.

5. Ibid., col. 1226–27.

6. Ibid., col. 1227–28.

7. Ibid., col. 1228.

8. Ibid., col. 1229.

9. Ibid., col. 1229–31.

10. Ibid., col. 1231–36. In fact on the same day (5 May), Attlee's government announced a substantial reinforcement program for Hong Kong. Besides increasing the garrison's strength to two brigade groups in size, the government would send fighter aircraft to the colony and add an additional cruiser to the forces at the disposal of the commander in chief of the Far East Station. It was also revealed that Brind could call upon an aircraft carrier in certain circumstances. Although this kind of situation was not spelled out in advance, the official statement took pains to explain that the military buildup ought not to be seen as an indication of the British government's wish to interfere in Chinese internal affairs (Attlee, dep. 82, fol. 133, BL).

11. U.K., *Hansard (Commons)*, vol. 464, col. 1236–47.

12. Ibid., col. 1239–40.

13. Ibid., col. 1241.

14. Ibid., col. 1242. After an inquiry from the Admiralty about the existence of any precedents for using a Nanking guardship, Esler Dening—the assistant under secretary of state at the Foreign Office with overall responsibility for the Far East—responded by pointing out that ships of the Royal Navy had gone to Japan in 1923 to assist British citizens and evacuate them from the scene of the Yokohama earthquake (R. Barclay [FO] to J. L. Pumphrey [10 Downing St.], 5 May 1949, Attlee, dep. 82, fol. 91, BL). See also fol. 94–95 for a list of other instances where British warships entered the territorial waters of an independent power for similar purposes. Besides HMS *Sandwich* at Taku in August 1937, at Chefoo in December 1937, and at Wei-hai-wei in the spring of 1938, the only other example cited was that of the allied fleet in Shanghai in 1937.

15. U.K., *Hansard (Commons)*, vol. 464, col. 1242–45.

16. Ibid., col. 1245–46.

17. Ibid., col. 1246–47.

18. Ibid., col. 1252–53.

19. Ibid., col. 1254.

20. Ibid., col. 1252–54.

21. Ibid., col. 1257.

22. Ibid., col. 1258–60.

23. Ibid., col. 1259.

24. Ibid., col. 1259–60.

25. Ibid., col. 1263.

26. Ibid., col. 1263–66.

27. Ibid., col. 1267–68.

28. Ibid., col. 1269–80.

29. Ibid., col. 1280–81.

30. Ibid., col. 1281–82.

31. Ibid., col. 1282–84.

32. Ibid., col. 1284–85. Salter's criticism was similar to that published in a recent issue of the *Economist,* which queried the role to be played in the future by the British ambassador in China:

He is marooned in a city where he is virtually a hostage; he cannot expect from the invaders any of the courtesies of international diplomatic usage until the British Government has granted them that recognition which it is their purpose to obtain by any means of pressure available. The legal successor of the head of state to whom the British Ambassador presented his credentials has gone elsewhere; the presence of His Majesty's envoy in the deserted capital is merely ridiculous and humiliating, an unnecessary gift of face for the murderers of British sailors and an invitation to blackmail. (*Economist*, 30 Apr. 1949)

33. U.K., *Hansard (Commons)*, vol. 464, col. 1286–88.
34. Ibid., col. 1290.
35. Ibid., col. 1290–92.
36. Ibid., col. 1293–94.
37. Ibid., col. 1295.
38. Ibid., col. 1296.
39. Ibid., col. 1296–1300.
40. Ibid., col. 1301–1323.
41. Ibid., col. 1317–18.
42. Ibid., col. 1323–27.
43. Ibid., col. 1325.
44. Ibid., col. 1326–29.
45. Ibid., col. 1330.
46. Ibid.
47. Ibid., col. 1330–32.
48. Ibid., col. 1333–38.
49. Ibid., col. 1335–36.
50. Ibid., col. 1336–37.
51. Ibid., col. 1337.
52. Ibid., col. 1337–41.
53. Ibid., col. 1343–44.
54. Ibid., col. 1344–46.
55. Ibid., col. 1344–45.
56. Ibid., col. 1345.
57. Ibid., col. 1345–46.
58. Ibid.
59. Ibid., col. 1346, 1349.
60. Ibid., col. 1341–42.
61. Ibid., col. 1348–49.
62. Ibid., col. 1349.

CHAPTER TWELVE. THE LIMITATIONS OF NAVAL DIPLOMACY

1. Stevenson to FO, 646, 16 May 1949, F7018/1219/10, FO 371/75891.
2. Admiral Brind was a gunnery specialist known throughout the navy as "Daddy Brind." Donaldson describes him as a "tall spare man with very dark hair and rather

beetling eyebrows" who had been a very intimidating parade ground officer at Whale Island, the naval gunnery school. He came to the Far East Station with an excellent war record and a record of achievement in peacetime commands.

After attending Exercise *Trident,* the naval staff conference at Greenwich, Brind left London by air for the Far East Station in Singapore on 29 April. He arrived in Hong Kong on 7 May and sailed in HMS *Alert* for Alacrity Anchorage three days later. He returned to Hong Kong on 18 May and left by air for Singapore on the same day (*The Times,* 21 Apr. 1949; "Action at Hong Kong" report by Commodore C. L. Robertson, 81/H.K.16/61/ g, M01203/49, 4 June 1949, Adm 1/21508; Correspondence with Rear-Admiral Vernon Donaldson, 3 Oct. 1989).

3. C-in-C FES to NA Nanking, 190758Z, 19 May 1949, F7352/1219/10, FO 371/75892. Kerans's past disciplinary record may have affected the policy of both Brind and the Admiralty in this respect.

4. C-in-C FES to NA Nanking, 201010Z, 20 May 1949, F7347/1219/10, FO 371/75892.

5. Ibid.

6. Adm to C-in-C FES, 201908A; 202020A, 20 May 1949, F7353/1219/10, FO 371/75892. Shanghai was finally "liberated" by the PLA five days later, see ANA Shanghai to FO2 i/c FES, 250326Z, 25 May 1949, F7705/1015/10, FO 371/75757; Minute by Far Eastern Dept. of FO, 25 May 1949, F7825/1015/10, FO 371/75758.

7. "*Amethyst* Report," 181–82.

8. Stevenson to FO, 673, 20 May 1949, F7326/1219/10, FO 371/75892.

9. Stevenson to FO, 682, 21 May 1949, F7417/1219/10, FO 371/75892.

10. *Amethyst* to FO2 i/c FES, 200454Z, 20 May 1949, ASL May, Kerans, 69/45/1, IWM; FO to Nanking, 560, 21 May 1949, F7018/1219/10, FO 371/75891.

11. Stevenson to FO, 691, 23 May 1949, F7440/1219/10, FO 371/75892.

12. Urquhart to FO, 381, 23 May 1949, F7419/1015/10, FO 371/75756.

13. Stevenson to FO, 697, 24 May 1949, F7442/1015/10, FO 371/75756.

14. C-in-C FES to *Amethyst,* 210610Z, 21 May 1949, ASL May 1949, Kerans, 69/45/1, IWM.

15. Notes by Kerans on 210852Z, 21 May 1949, ASL May 1949, Kerans, 69/45/1, IWM.

16. C-in-C FES to *Amethyst,* 221310Z, 22 May 1949, F7595/1219/10, FO 371/75892.

17. *Amethyst* to C-in-C FES, 201131Z, 20 June 1949, ASL June 1949, Kerans, 69/45/1, IWM; Earl, *Yangtse Incident,* 112–14. Kerans later described Yuan as being "politically highly trained" and Kang as "a clever and unscrupulous Communist." Both PLA interpreters were university trained and had been undercover agents for the CCP in Nanking before the fall of that city to the PLA (MIR Oct. 1949, no. 46, 10 Nov. 1949, 34–35, Adm 2234/230).

18. *Amethyst* to C-in-C FES, 240952Z, 24 May 1949, F7595/1219/10; 241037Z, 24 May 1949, F7550/1219/10, FO 371/75892.

19. "*Amethyst* Report," 242–43.

20. *Amethyst* to C-in-C FES, 241037Z, 24 May 1949, F7550/1219/10, FO 371/75892.

21. "*Amethyst* Report," 42.

22. Ibid.

23. Ibid.

24. Ibid. By this time, the naval arm of the PLA had been substantially reinforced mainly as a result of a series of defections from the KMT Second Coastal Defense Fleet and its vessels stationed in the middle reaches of the Yangtze. Fifty-four KMT vessels had changed sides in less than a month (New China News Agency, Weekly Bulletin 103, 24 May 1949, F7731/1015/10, FO 371/75757).

25. "*Amethyst* Report," 245; "*Amethyst* Log," 25 May 1949, Adm 53/125421. "When shut down the only power available was 24 volts from the Type 60 Emergency W/T set and enough for a handful of pilot lamps on the mess decks and the wardroom." Temperatures below decks would rise to as much as 110 degrees Fahrenheit on some of the worst nights (MIR Oct. 1949, no. 46, 10 Nov. 1949, pp. 40–41, Adm 223/230).

26. "*Amethyst* Report," 38, 43.

27. Ibid., 187–89.

28. Ibid., 188.

29. Ibid., 189.

30. Brind sent another signal (300159Z) revising his original message to Yuan (270545Z) and stressing that *Amethyst* withheld her fire until she had been hit, disabled, and driven ashore. There is no evidence available to suggest whether these revisions were incorporated in the translated dispatch to Yuan that Leo carried ashore on the afternoon of 30 May (ASL May 1949, Kerans, 69/45/1, IWM).

31. FO to Nanking, 589, 28 May 1949, F7440/1219/10, FO 371/75892.

32. "*Amethyst* Report," 43.

33. *Amethyst* to C-in-C FES, 311149Z, 31 May 1949, F7595/1219/10, FO 371/75892.

34. Ibid.

35. "*Amethyst* Report," 44.

36. Ibid.

37. Ibid.

38. *Amethyst* to C-in-C FES, 020404Z, 2 June 1949, Adm 116/5740A; *Amethyst* to FO2 i/c FES, 080257Z, 8 June 1949, Adm 116/5740A.

39. Earl, *Yangtse Incident*, 103–6; *Amethyst* to C-in-C FES, 020312Z, 2 June 1949, Adm 116/5740A.

40. *Amethyst* to C-in-C FES, 040037Z, 4 June 1949, Adm 116/5740A.

41. NA Nanking to C-in-C FES, 020747Z, 3 June 1949, F8238/1219/10, FO 371/75892.

CHAPTER THIRTEEN. PSYCHOLOGICAL WARFARE

1. MIR Oct. 1949, no. 46, 10 Nov. 1949, p. 35, Adm 223/230; Earl, *Yangtse Incident*, 114.

2. "*Amethyst* Report," 45.

3. Kerans repeated Kang's threat to destroy the *Amethyst* if any attempt was made to move it without first obtaining permission from the PLA, and he added a personal observation about the atmosphere in which these negotiations were taking place.

VEIL of FRIENDLINESS noticeably thinner and all my efforts to CONVINCE them met with indifference and illogical answers. (*Amethyst* to C-in-C FES [Afloat], 031007Z, 3 June 1949, ASL June 1949, Kerans, 69/45/1, IWM.)

4. *Amethyst* to C-in-C FES, 031007Z, 3 June 1949, F8238/1219/10, FO 371/75892; "*Amethyst* Report," 45.

5. SBNO Nanking to C-in-C FES, 070057Z, 7 June 1949, F8423/1219/10, FO 371/75893; FO2 i/c FES to Adm, 080831Z, 8 June 1949, F8423/1219/10, FO 371/75893.

6. Head of Military Branch, Adm to FO2 i/c FES, 081513A, 8 June 1949, F8423/1219/10, FO 371/75893.

7. Lord Fraser to Sir W. Haley, 9 June 1949, Adm 1/21508; Haley to Fraser, 15 June 1949, Adm 116/5704.

8. Consul General Urquhart (Shanghai) to FO, 446, 10 June 1949, F8523/1219/10, FO 371/75893; Minute by P. W. Scarlett, 14 June 1949, attached to 446.

9. "*Amethyst* Log," 12 June 1949, Adm 53/125422; "*Amethyst* Report," 45–46.

10. BNA (British Naval Attaché) Nanking to FO2 i/c FES, 130059Z, 13 June 1949, F8762/1219/10, FO 371/75893; NA Nanking to FO2 i/c FES, 140244Z, 14 June 1949, F8762/1219/10, FO 371/75893.

11. *Amethyst* to FO2 i/c FES, 131027Z, 13 June 1949; 180044Z, 18 June 1949, ASL June 1949, Kerans, 69/45/1, IWM.

12. C-in-C FES to NA Nanking, 140931Z, 14 June 1949, F8762/1219/10, FO 371/75893.

13. "*Amethyst* Report," 46, 193.

14. *Amethyst* to C-in-C FES, 150555Z, 15 June 1949, F8762/1219/10, FO 371/75893; "*Amethyst* Report," 46.

15. *Amethyst* to C-in-C FES, 150555Z, 15 June 1949, F8762/1219/10, FO 371/75893; "*Amethyst* Report," 46.

16. C-in-C FES to NA Nanking, 170456Z, 17 June 1949, F9043/1219/10, FO 371/75893.

17. *Amethyst* to C-in-C FES, 180921Z, 18 June 1949, F9043/1219/10, FO 371/75893; "*Amethyst* Report," 46–47.

18. "*Amethyst* Log," 19–20 June 1949, Adm 53/125422; Leslie Frank's Diary, 18 June 1949, "*Amethyst* Scrapbook," vol. 2, Kerans, 69/45/1, IWM.

19. MIR Oct. 1949, no. 46, 10 Nov. 1949, 35, Adm 223/230.

20. "*Amethyst* Report," 47.

21. Ibid.

22. *Amethyst* to C-in-C FES, 201131Z, 20 June 1949, ASL June 1949, Kerans, 69/45/1, IWM.

23. Ibid., 195–96.

24. *Amethyst* to C-in-C FES, 221202Z, 22 June 1949, F9043/1219/10, FO 371/75893; "*Amethyst* Report," 48.

25. For the background to the Nationalist blockade and the attack by KMT aircraft on the Blue Funnel liner SS *Anchises* in the Whangpoo River on 21 and 22 June 1949, see memo by Viscount Hall, first lord of the Admiralty (CP [49]133, 22 June 1949, Cab 129/35). In his paper, Hall criticized the existing arrangements that had prevented British

vessels from entering the Whangpoo to render assistance to the beleaguered *Anchises,* and he made a number of recommendations for a drastic revision of those rules. In the cabinet discussion at which his proposals and those of Sir Patrick Brind were aired, Ernest Bevin and Lord Tedder made it plain they were not in favor of such a radical change of policy as that envisaged by either the first lord or his C-in-C of the Far East Station (Cab mtg 42[49], 23 June 1949, Cab 128/15).

Further material on this incident and the British government's response to it is available in minutes by P. W. Scarlett, 21 June 1949, F9209/1261/10, FO 371/75900; 29 June 1949, F9820/1015/10, FO 371/75762; C-in-C FES to FES, 219P, 241630Z, 24 June 1949, F9282/1261/10, FO 371/75900; GHQ (General Headquarters) Far East Land Forces to Minister of Defence, SEACOS 923 and 928, 21 and 28 June 1949, F9121/1015/10, FO 371/75760; Adm 116/5713; and DO (49)16th mtg, 21 June 1949, Cab 131/8. For a KMT response see editorial in *Chung Cheng Jih Poh,* 25 June 1949. A translation of this editorial is available in F10255/1015/10, FO 371/75763.

26. *"Amethyst* Report," 48.

27. There is a major discrepancy between the figures for oil entered in this message and that of the *"Amethyst* Log," 23 June 1949, Adm 53/125423; *Amethyst* to FO2 i/c FES, 220227Z, 22 June 1949, ASL June 1949, Kerans, 69/45/1, IWM. Wilkinson arrives at yet another figure. He claims that on 15 June there were 106 tons of fuel remaining on board the *Amethyst* and that steam was raised every other day to economize further (Wilkinson, "Engineering Exploits," 423, *"Amethyst* Scrapbook," vol. 2, Kerans, 69/45/1, IWM).

28. It became so intensely humid at night that Jack French, the sole telegraphist, had someone pump air on him with a set of bellows so that he could send and receive messages. Kerans observed that French often perspired so much that his written signals became so stained with the drops of his sweat that the words were barely legible. Sufficiently concerned about overtaxing his telegraphist, Kerans asked the Far East Station to cut its signal traffic to the *Amethyst* at night (MIR Oct. 1949, no. 46, 10 Nov. 1949, 41, Adm 223/230).

29. *Amethyst* to C-in-C FES, 221202Z, 22 June 1949, F9043/1219/10, FO 371/75893; Stevenson to FO, 892, 23 June 1949, F9190/1219/10, FO 371/75893.

30. FO minute by R. E. Barclay, 23 June 1949, F9391/1219/10, FO 371/75893.

31. Minute by P. W. Scarlett, 23 June 1949, F9430/1219/10, FO 371/75893; Adm to C-in-C FES, 231920, 23 June 1949, F9450/1219/10, FO 371/75893.

32. *Amethyst* to C-in-C FES, 241451Z, 24 June 1949, Adm 116/5740A; *"Amethyst* Report," 49. According to Kerans, 265 personal telegrams were sent from the *Amethyst* during the 101 days spent on the Yangtze (MIR Oct. 1949, no. 46, 10 Nov. 1949, 39, Adm 223/230).

33. C-in-C FES to Adm, 230601Z, 23 June 1949, F9430/1219/10G, FO 371/75893; C-in-C FES to *Amethyst,* 250801Z, 25 June 1949; 270251Z, 27 June 1949, F9450/1219/10, FO 371/75893.

34. *Amethyst* to C-in-C FES, 280224Z, 28 June 1949, F9450/1219/10, FO 371/75893; *Amethyst* to C-in-C FES, 281047Z, 28 June 1949, Adm 116/5740A.

35. *"Amethyst* Report," 49–50, 201.

36. Ibid., 50.

37. *Amethyst* to NA Nanking, 300057Z, F9752/1219/10, FO 371/75893; *Amethyst* to C-in-C FES, 300107Z, 30 June 1949, F9752/1219/10, FO 371/75893.

38. C-in-C FES to NA Nanking, 301420Z, 30 June 1949, F9752/1219/10, FO 371/75893.

39. Ibid.

40. "*Amethyst* Report," 50. During these negotiations in 1949, Edward Youde was the first to draw Captain Donaldson's attention to a curiously revealing situation that seemed to have an uncanny bearing on the progress of these talks with the Communists. In a letter to this author on 6 May 1989, Donaldson wrote the following:

> Jardine Matheson had not long before published a book about an event which had taken place about the time of the Opium Wars: one of H.M. Ships had got trapped up the Canton River. The book gave an account of the negotiations to obtain her release, and in several cases gave the texts of the "exchanges." His [Youde's] comment was how closely the Chinese negotiators with whom our Embassy was having to deal were following the pattern set by their pre-decessors of 100 years before, once one had ignored the "ceremonial" beginnings and endings to the dispatches—the meat, & therefore the attitude of mind was identical. He went on to say that it was possible consequently to forecast with great accuracy what the Chinese response was likely to be to any line we might take.

41. C-in-C FES to Adm, 301955Z, 1 July 1949, F9752/1219/10, FO 371/75893.

42. C-in-C FES to *Amethyst*, 021219Z, 2 July 1949, F9752/1219/10, FO 371/75893. Brind sent another signal to *Amethyst* (030225Z, 3 July 1949), which virtually repeated this message word for word. It is difficult to understand why he needed to do so unless it was sent in error or to test the code system being developed between the Far East Station and the ship (ASL July 1949, Kerans, 69/45/1, IWM).

43. *Amethyst* to C-in-C FES (Afloat), 030027Z, 3 July 1949, ASL July 1949, Kerans, 69/45/1, IWM.

44. According to the British naval authorities in Shanghai, the exchange rate was 4,100 *Jen Min Piao* to £1 (ANA Shanghai to *Amethyst*, 080615Z, 8 July 1949, ASL July 1949, Kerans, 69/45/1, IWM). Hyperinflation soon made nonsense of these figures. According to Captain Donaldson, the rate had become 5,000 *Jen Min Piao* to £1 by 25 July.

45. "*Amethyst* Report," 51.

46. Ibid., 205.

47. Kerans took immediate precautions to ensure that this kind of incident would not happen again. French duly sent off the following cable later the following morning:

> Can you inform communist shipping companies of my position and warn them that I show no lights at night as there is no power and I must abide by their military orders. I show a white lantern with candle only. Have no torch batteries left. 2 large merchant ships nearly hit us last night. (*Amethyst* to ANA Shanghai, 020001Z, 2 July 1949, ASL July 1949, Kerans, 69/45/1, IWM).

48. "*Amethyst* Report," 51.

49. Ibid. It may well have inspired the following signal, which was dispatched that same evening:

> Grateful confirmation that no (R) No contact has yet been made by other persons

with higher authorities concerning Yangtse incidents. Especially, whether General here has in fact, need to refer exchange of notes to a superior authority. (*Amethyst* to C-in-C FES, 021317Z, 2 July 1949, ASL July 1949, Kerans, 69/45/1, IWM).

50. "*Amethyst* Report," 204.
51. Ibid., 52.

CHAPTER FOURTEEN. STALEMATE

1. "*Amethyst* Log," 5 July 1949, Adm 53/125424; "*Amethyst* Report," 52, 206; Diary of L. Frank, 5 July 1949, 15, "*Amethyst* Scrapbook," vol. 2, Kerans, 69/45/1, IWM.
2. "*Amethyst* Report," 52.
3. Ibid., 52–53.
4. Ibid.
5. *Amethyst* to C-in-C FES (Afloat), 051117Z, 5 July 1949, ASL July 1949, Kerans, 69/45/1, IWM.
6. R. F. Woods (Ministry of Defence) to R. D. C. McAlpine (FO), 6 July 1949, F10022/1219/10, FO 371/75894.
7. FO to Nanking, 767, 6 July 1949, F10022/1219/10, FO 371/75894.
8. C-in-C FES to NA Nanking, 051810Z, 6 July 1949, F10022/1219/10, FO 371/75894.
9. "*Amethyst* Report," 211.
10. Ibid., 53–54, 208. For a full account of this incident, see Appendix 4.
11. Ibid., 54; SBNO to C-in-C FES, 070312Z, 7 July 1949, F10023/1219/10, FO 371/75894; "*Amethyst* Report," 54.
12. "*Amethyst* Report," 212. A measure of Kerans's anger is evident in his message to Brind of 8 July: "Have learnt now that everything connected with 'Amethyst' is going to continue to meet with frustration and opposition. KANG is behind all this." (*Amethyst* to C-in-C FES [Afloat], 081017Z, 8 July 1949, ASL July, Kerans, 69/45/1, IWM).
13. C-in-C FES to *Amethyst*, 081505Z, 9 July 1949, F10023/1219/10, FO 371/75894.
14. "*Amethyst* Log," 9 July 1949, Adm 53/125424; *Amethyst* to C-in-C FES, 090001Z, 9 July 1949, Adm 116/5740A; *Amethyst* to FO2 i/c FES, 09020Z, 9 July 1949, Adm 116/5740A.
15. "*Amethyst* Report," 54.
16. *Amethyst* to C-in-C FES (Afloat), 100707Z, 10 July 1949, ASL July, Kerans, 69/45/1, IWM.
17. *Amethyst* to C-in-C FES, 091439Z, 9 July 1949, F10023/1219/10, FO 371/75894.
18. *Amethyst* to C-in-C FES 100637Z; 101121Z, 10 July 1949, F10402/1219/10, FO 371/75894.
19. C-in-C FES to *Amethyst*, 100825Z; 100827Z, 10 July 1949, F10402/1219/10, FO 371/75894; C-in-C FES to Adm, 100501Z, 10 July 1949, F10402/1219/10, FO 371/75894.
20. "*Amethyst* Report," 219.
21. Ibid., 214–17.

22. Ibid., 54–56; *Amethyst* to C-in-C FES, 111207Z, 11 July 1949, F10440/1219/10, FO 371/75894.

23. "*Amethyst* Report," 55.

24. *Amethyst* to C-in-C FES, 111627Z, 111717Z, 111317Z, 11 July 1949, F11095/1219/10, FO 371/75894; C-in-C FES (Ashore) to C-in-C FES (Afloat), 112330Z, 12 July 1949, F10402/1219/10, FO 371/75894.

25. *Amethyst* to C-in-C FES, 111207Z, 11 July 1949, F10440/1219/10, FO 371/75894.

26. Minute by P. M. Scarlett, 12 July 1949, F10440/1219/10, FO 371/75894; Adm to C-in-C FES, 131219A, 13 July 1949, F10402/1219/10, FO 371/75894.

27. C-in-C FES to *Amethyst,* 111420Z, 11 July 1949, F11095/1219/10, FO 371/75894.

28. *Amethyst* to C-in-C FES, 111717Z, 11 July 1949, F11095/1219/10, FO 371/75894.

29. C-in-C FES to *Amethyst,* 120515Z, 12 July 1949, ASL July, Kerans, 69/45/1, IWM. A somewhat different version of the signal without the grammatical inaccuracies of the original cited above is to be found in F10562/1219/10, FO 371/75894.

30. *Amethyst* to C-in-C FES, 131350Z, 14 July 1949, F10562/1219/10, FO 371/75894.

31. "*Amethyst* Report," 56.

32. Ibid. DTG is an abbreviated form of date time group.

33. C-in-C FES to *Amethyst,* 091246Z, 9 July 1949, Adm 116/5740A.

34. FO2 i/c FES to C-in-C FES, 112358Z, 12 July 1949, Adm 116/5740A; *Amethyst* to C-in-C FES (Afloat), 130307Z, 13 July 1949, ASL July, Kerans, 69/45/1, IWM.

35. "*Amethyst* Report," 57.

36. "Can you send with Khoong Chinese Commercial code for telegraphic purposes. Tarr may have one. Alternatively Giles numerisation of Charaders." (*Amethyst* to ANA Shanghai, 121038Z, 12 July 1949, app. 1, Adm 116/5740A).

37. C-in-C Report to Adm, 2 Dec. 1949, Adm 116/5695.

38. Twenty-four-hour trials on the Fox Fox system were established on 30–31 May in a signal from SO Force 68 to *Amethyst* and ANA Shanghai, 300254Z, 30 May 1949, ASL May, Kerans, 69/45/1, IWM.

39. C-in-C Report to Adm, 2 Dec. 1949, Adm 116/5695.

40. Ibid. Further trials using the Chinese commercial code were conducted on 17 July, see *Amethyst* to FO2 i/c FES, 1708382Z, 17 July 1949; *Amethyst* to COM Hong Kong, 170731Z, 17 July 1949, ASL July, Kerans, 69/45/1, IWM.

41. "*Amethyst* Report," 57, 246.

42. Ibid., 246–47.

43. Ibid., 57, 221.

44. C-in-C FES to *Amethyst,* 140545Z, 14 July 1949, F10562/1219/10, FO 371/75894.

45. C-in-C FES to NA Nanking, 141103Z, 15 July 1949, F10562/1219/10, FO 371/75894.

46. C-in-C FES to *Amethyst,* DTG 140825Z, 14 July 1949, ASL July, Kerans, 69/45/1, IWM.

47. Stevenson to FO, 1040, 15 July 1949, F10514/1219/10, FO 371/75894.

48. "*Amethyst* Report," 227–28; "*Amethyst* Log," 17 July 1949, Adm 53/125424. In the original report, mention was made of $300,000 of *Jen Min Piao*. I am convinced that the figure was 300,000 units of *Jen Min Piao* and *not* the dollar equivalent. At the exchange rate mentioned by ANA Shanghai in Chapter 13, note 44, this sum would amount to a little over £73.

49. *Amethyst* to FO2 i/c FES, 200144Z, 20 July 1949, Adm 116/5740A. Maximum temperatures recorded in the engine room and boiler room at the end of July were 120 degrees and 130 degrees respectively (Wilkinson, "Engineering Exploits," 420, "*Amethyst* Scrapbook," vol. 2, Kerans, 69/45/1, IWM).

50. FO2 i/c FES to *Amethyst*, 200825Z, 20 July 1949, Adm 116/5740A.

51. "*Amethyst* Log," 18–21 July 1949, Adm 53/125424.

52. Ibid., 22 July 1949.

53. *Amethyst* to C-in-C FES (Afloat), 220727Z; 220757Z; 220827Z, 22 July 1949, F10857/1219/10, FO 371/75894; *Amethyst* to C-in-C FES (Afloat), 220721Z, 22 July 1949, ASL July 1949, Kerans, 69/45/1, IWM; "*Amethyst* Report," 58–59.

54. Ibid.

55. Ibid.

56. Ibid.

57. Ibid.

58. "Amethyst Log," 23 July 1949, Adm 53/125424.

59. *Amethyst* to C-in-C FES (Afloat), 232239Z, 24 July 1949, ASL July, Kerans, 69/45/1, IWM; "*Amethyst* Report," 59.

60. *Amethyst* to C-in-C FES, 240057Z, 24 July 1949, F11096/1219/10, FO 371/75894; Letter by Leo to Kerans, 24 July 1949, ASL July, Kerans, 69/45/1, IWM.

61. "*Amethyst* Report," 59.

62. *Amethyst* had been receiving daily weather reports from HMS *Hart* at 1700 hours since early June. *Hart* had been stationed off the Saddles, but with the approach of Typhoon *Gloria* she had moved away in search of a more sheltered anchorage for the duration of the storm (*Amethyst* to HART [repeated to C-in-C FES (Afloat)], 050827Z, 5 June 1949, app. 1, Adm 116/5740A).

63. FO2 i/c FES to *Amethyst*, 240742Z, 24 July 1949, Adm 116/5740A.

64. "*Amethyst* Log," 25–26 July, Adm 53/125424.

65. *Amethyst* to C-in-C FES (Afloat), 251104Z, 25 July 1949, ASL July, Kerans, 69/45/1, IWM.

66. C-in-C FES to *Amethyst*, 250110Z, 25 July 1949, Adm 116/5740A.

67. "*Amethyst* Report," 59–60.

68. *Amethyst* to C-in-C FES, 250314Z, 25 July 1949, Adm 116/5740A.

69. "*Amethyst* Report," 60.

70. *Amethyst* to C-in-C FES, 250314Z, 25 July 1949, Adm 116/5740A.

71. C-in-C FES to *Amethyst*, 250942Z, 25 July 1949, Adm 116/5695.

72. *Amethyst* to C-in-C FES, 250314Z, 25 July 1949, Adm 116/5740A; "*Amethyst* Log," 26 July 1949, Adm 53/125424.

73. Stevenson to FO, 1110, 26 July 1949, F11088/1219/10; 1125, 28 July 1949, F11234/1219/10, FO 371/75894.

74. Stevenson to FO, 1125, 28 July 1949, Prem 8/944.

75. A parliamentary question about the current position of the *Amethyst* was written

by L. Gammans (Unionist MP for Hornsey) and answered on 27 July 1949 by John Dugdale (Labour MP for West Bromwich) in his capacity as parliamentary and financial secretary to the Admiralty. In his answer, Dugdale disclosed that there were seventy-three officers and men aboard the frigate and that the BBC had kindly provided facilities for overseas broadcasts to the ship's company on alternate Sundays between the hours of 0815 and 0845 BST (U.K., *Hansard [Commons]*, vol. 467, col. 142–43).

76. Admiralty CNI to P. N. N. Synnott (Adm), 15 July 1949 and Synnott to Adm CNI, 18 July 1949, Adm 1/21508.

77. C-in-C FES to *Amethyst*, 270742Z, 27 July 1949, F11096/1219/10, FO 371/75894; see also C-in-C FES to *Amethyst*, 270748Z, 27 July 1949, ASL July, Kerans, 69/45/1, IWM.

78. "*Amethyst* Report," 236.

79. Ibid., 60–61, 233–37.

80. "*Amethyst* Log," 28 July 1949, Adm 53/125424.

81. "*Amethyst* Report," 61, 238. Kerans had increased his fuel order by 30 tons to compensate for having used extra quantities of oil during the height of the typhoon.

82. Stevenson to FO, 1110, 26 July 1949, F11088/1219/10, FO 371/75894.

83. "*Amethyst* Report," 61. According to Wilkinson, when Kerans decided to make his escape bid, there was only 47.3 tons of fuel remaining on board the *Amethyst* (Wilkinson, "Engineering Exploits," 423, "*Amethyst* Scrapbook," vol. 2, Kerans, 69/45/1, IWM).

CHAPTER FIFTEEN. ESCAPE IN THE DARK

1. "*Amethyst* Report," 62. Strangely enough, an undated and unsigned memo—presumably from the Admiralty's naval information department—that recorded local conditions on the night of the escape for the benefit of newspaper editors, states that the moon set at 0018 hours and not 2315 as the "*Amethyst* Report," suggests (Adm 116/5707).

2. "*Amethyst* Report," 62–63. During the escape, the river level was 12 feet above normal at Chinkiang and an extra 3 feet in the lower reaches of the Yangtze (Adm 116/5707).

3. "*Amethyst* Report," 61.

4. In a message to the naval attaché in Nanking on 9 August, Kerans indicates that Dr. Fearnley, the RAF medical officer on board the *Amethyst* was involved in the scheme to keep Leo ashore and had supported his captain's letter with a list of the medical supplies required by the ship. Leo was told to remain in Chinkiang overnight in order that he might see Colonel Kang early the next day (31 July) to inform him that the frigate was running dangerously short of fuel and that more oil was desperately needed from Shanghai if the ship was to continue functioning (*Amethyst* to NA Nanking, 090515Z, 9 Aug. 1949, F12026/1219/10, FO 371/75896).

5. "*Amethyst* Report," 63. Leo was in an unusually vulnerable position because he was employed as an interpreter-translator by the British Embassy in Nanking. His situation, already complicated by this connection, was worsened because one of his two sons was in the KMT navy and the other was in the Nationalist army somewhere in the area of Canton (*Amethyst* to NA Nanking, 090515Z, 9 Aug. 1949, F12026/1219/10, FO 371/75896).

56. C-in-C FES to *Amethyst* (R) Adm, 302100Z, July 1949, in *"Amethyst* Report," 71.

57. *The Times*, 1 Aug. 1949. Notified that the *Amethyst* was safe, Clement Attlee offered his congratulations to Kerans and his crew in a personal message to them relayed by the Admiralty and Admiral Brind. See Adm to C-in-C FES, 302339A, T170/49, 30 July 1949, Prem 8/944.

58. *The Times*, 1 Aug. 1949; Adm to C-in-C FES, 302339A, T170/49, 30 July 1949, Prem 8/944.

CHAPTER SIXTEEN. AFTERMATH

1. According to the *South China Morning Post* of 2 August 1949, *Amethyst* met *Jamaica* at 0914 GMT (6:14 p.m. local time) on 1 August to the accompaniment of lusty cheering and good-natured ribaldry from the officers and men lined up on the cruiser's upper deck. At the same time, the band of the Royal Marines played a musical tribute to the crew of the *Amethyst*, featuring such old favorites as "Cruising Down the River on a Sunday Afternoon," "See the Conquering Hero Comes," and "For They Are Jolly Good Fellows."

2. *"Amethyst* Report," 18.

3. He was finally released on 18 October 1949. After considering the matter for more than two months, the British authorities decided to pay him £1,000 compensation for the trouble he had endured on their behalf. Unfortunately, the matter did not end there because the Communists insisted that Leo should resign from the staff of the British Embassy and work for them instead (Stevenson to FO, 1244, 16 Aug. 1949; 1258, 17 Aug. 1949, F12191/1219/10; 1268, 18 Aug. 1949, F12346/1219/10; 1317, 23 Aug. 1949, F12596/1219/10, FO 371/75896; 1409, 5 Sept. 1949, F13415/1219/10, FO 371/75897). See also Hutchinson (Nanking) to FO, 1772, 20 Oct. 1949, F13415/1219/10; 1949, 21 Nov. 1949, F17449/1219/10, FO 371/75897; P. M. Scarlett (FO) to Cardo (Adm), 3 Dec. 1949; Minute by Scarlett, 6 Dec. 1949, F18109/1219/10, FO 371/75897; F.O. to Nanking, 44, 5 Jan. 1950, F18109/1219/10, FO 371/75897.

4. *Hsin Min Pao*, 3 Aug. 1949; *Ta Kung Pao*, 3 Aug. 1949; *The Times*, 3 Aug. 1949.

5. *Hsin Min Pao*, 3 Aug. 1949; *Ta Kung Pao*, 3 Aug. 1949; *The Times*, 3 Aug. 1949; Stevenson to FO, 1158, 3 Aug. 1949, F11476/1219/10, FO 371/75895.

6. *Hsin Min Pao*, 3 Aug. 1949; *Ta Kung Pao*, 3 Aug. 1949; *The Times*, 3 Aug. 1949; Stevenson to FO, 1158, 3 Aug. 1949, F11476/1219/10, FO 371/75895.

7. *The Times*, 3 Aug. 1949.

8. *Ta Kung Pao*, 3 Aug. 1949; *South China Morning Post*, 4 Aug. 1949.

9. *Ta Kung Pao*, 3 Aug. 1949; *South China Morning Post*, 4 Aug. 1949.

10. *People's Daily*, 5 Aug. 1949.

11. Stevenson to FO 1138, 31 July 1949, F11301/1219/10, FO 371/75895. This point was well made, given the reception that the *Amethyst* story received at the hands of the American press. The *New York Times* of 1 August 1949 was typical of many newspapers that heaped great praise upon the frigate and her crew, describing the escape as a moral victory after a period in which the democracies had lost much of their self-respect.

12. One of the most bizarre suggestions of all came from the consul general himself. He wrote the following to the probable amazement of the Foreign Office China specialists

on 4 August—in other words, barely four days after the *Amethyst* had escaped from the Yangtze:

> It may have been overlooked that in Chinese Civil Wars it is traditional for mails and [travellers?] to pass lines freely. I suggest that if His Majesty's Government announced a ship would bring the mails in and carry passengers, Nationalists would think it a perfectly natural proceeding. It would be a pity if our Western ideas of efficiency were responsible for making the blockade harsher than it need be. (Urquhart [Shanghai] to FO, 648, 4 Aug. 1949, F11541/1219/10, FO 371/75895)

13. *South China Morning Post,* 3 Aug. 1949.

14. Malcolm MacDonald to FO, 575, 6 Aug. 1949, F11640/1219/10, FO 371/75895.

15. Urquhart to FO, 655, 6 Aug. 1949, F11641/1219/10, FO 371/75895.

16. Ibid.

17. Ibid.

18. *South China Morning Post,* 20 Aug. 1949.

19. Stevenson to FO, 1152, 2 Aug. 1949, F11420/1219/10, FO 371/75895, citing *Amethyst* to C-in-C FES, 302241, 31 July 1949, F11466/1219/10, FO 371/75895.

20. Minute by P. D. Coates, 3 Aug. 1949, F11420/1219/10, FO 371/75895.

21. Ibid.

22. *Sunday Pictorial,* 7 Aug. 1949.

23. Ibid. See also *South China Morning Post,* 7 Aug. 1949.

24. Minute by P. D. Coates, 9 Aug. 1949, F11687/1219/10, FO 371/75896.

25. FO to Nanking, 911, 9 Aug. 1949, F11767/1219/10, FO 371/75896.

26. C-in-C FES to Adm, 110827Z, 11 Aug. 1949, F11767/1219/10, FO 371/75896.

27. Although the files on the *Amethyst* crisis that have been opened to the public say nothing about this plan, it appears to be a radical extension of Viscount Hall's memo on the "Bombing of British Shipping in the Yangtse," which he submitted to the cabinet as CP (49)133, 22 June 1949, Cab 129/35.

28. Stevenson to FO, 1139, 31 July 1949, F11302/1219/10, FO 371/75895.

29. Counselor (Chinese Affairs) Canton to E. Bevin, 57, (2570/49/45), 18 Aug. 1949, Adm 116/5698.

30. Memo by E. Bevin, "China," CP (49)180, 23 Aug. 1949, par. 7–11, Cab 129/36; Cab mtg. 54(49), 29 Aug. 1949, Cab 128/16.

31. "China" memo, par. 22; annex A, para. 1–16. For a contrasting opinion, however, see Stevenson to FO, 912, 25 June 1949, F9310/1261/10, FO 371/75900.

32. "China" memo, annex A, par. 1–16.

33. Ibid., annex B, par. 1–6.

34. Ibid., annex A, par. 14; this paragraph had first appeared in an undated Foreign Office minute that was received in the registry on 6 August 1949 and devoted to an assessment of the general situation in China (F11653/1023/10, FO 371/75813).

35. CP (1949)118, 24 May 1949, Cab 129/35; Cab mtg 38(49), 26 May 1949, Cab 128/15; JP (Joint Planning Committee) (48)124 (Final), 12 Jan. 1949, Defe 4/19; *The Times,* 7 May 1949; JP (49)50 (Final), 17 May 1949, Defe 4/21; COS (49) 73rd mtg, 18 May 1949, Defe 4/21; JP (49)55 (Final), 24 May 1949, Defe 4/22.

36. "On the People's Democratic Dictatorship," New China News Agency, *Special Supplement*, 21(1), 1 July 1949, F9742/1015/10, FO 371/75761; MIR July 1949, no. 43, 10 Aug. 1949, 74, Adm 223/230.

37. Tang, "Diplomatic Relations," 150–54.

38. Ibid., 158.

39. Ibid., 171, 199; U.K., *Hansard (Commons)*, vol. 475, col. 2083.

40. Tang, "Diplomatic Relations," 162–63.

41. Ibid., 156–59; Sir Ralph Stevenson had been withdrawn from Nanking by the British government in mid-October 1949 and brought home to London for "consultations" on the question of extending diplomatic recognition to the PRC. The *Economist* fully concurred with the decision, having severely criticized the idea of maintaining an ambassador on Chinese soil from the very beginning of the Yangtze incident on the grounds that it lent greater weight and the dignity of the state to the Communists than was called for under the circumstances (Scrapbook File, Stevenson, IOM; *Economist*, 30 Apr. 1949).

42. *Spectator*, 29 Apr. 1949.

43. Vice-Admiral Sir Alexander C. G. Madden's career did not appear to be adversely affected by the Yangtze incident. He went on to become second sea lord in charge of naval personnel (1950–53) and afterwards C-in-C Plymouth from 1953–55 before retiring from the service in 1956. He died at the age of 69 in Sept. 1964.

44. Not surprisingly, the most vehement critics of the PLA's action on the Yangtze were those organs of the British press—such as the *Daily Mail, Daily Sketch, Daily Express,* and *Daily Telegraph*—that were seen as mouthpieces for conservative and imperialistic interests. Nonetheless, the rest of the non-Communist press in both the United Kingdom and the United States showed remarkably little objectivity in their reporting; in most cases the stories they printed implied that the Communists were as guilty as the Royal Navy believed them to be.

45. Sir R. Stevenson to Prof. D. B. Copland (vice chancellor of ANU), 25 May 1949, "China—Correspondence File," Stevenson, IOM.

46. Attlee, dep. 82, fol. 57–58, BL.

47. Ibid.

48. Kang Maozhao, "Hong Dong Yi Shi De Ying Jian Chang Jiang Shi Jian," *Shi Jie Zhi Shi* (World Knowledge) 1988, 8:25–26; 10:22–23; 11:22–25.

49. In his papers at the Liddell Hart Centre for Military Archives at King's College, London, Admiral Brind has left a press cutting of an interview he gave to the *Sunday Tribune* upon his arrival back at Tengah airbase in Singapore on 30 April 1949. In response to a question about the outbreak of the Yangtze incident, he is reputed to have stated:

> The shelling of the sloop Amethyst and destroyer Consort by Chinese Communists on the Yangtze was not a deliberate hostile act. The excitement when blood is up between two forces often involves a third in disaster. (*Sunday Tribune*, 1 May 1949)

50. Capt. F. L. Sabel to L. K. Little (inspector general, Chinese Maritime Customs, Hong Kong), 18 Oct. 1949; Madden to Little, 19 Oct. 1949, Stevenson, IOM.

51. Interview with Mark B. Stevenson, Castletown, Isle of Man, 7 June 1988; Minute by P. D. Coates, 5 Aug. 1949, F11480/1219/10, FO 371/75895; Minute by F. S.

Tomlinson, 30 July 1949, F11508/1219/10, FO 371/75896; FO to Nanking, 862, 30 July 1949, F11480/1219/10, FO 371/75895.

52. Interview with M. B. Stevenson, Castletown, Isle of Man, 7 June 1988.

53. Fraser to Brind, 2 Sept. 1949, 2750/66B, Adm 205/72.

54. "*Amethyst* Scrapbook," vol. 2–3, Kerans, 69/45/1, IWM.

55. Urquhart to FO, 644, 3 Aug. 1949, F11490/1015/10, FO 371/75765.

56. A large file of correspondence on the arrangements for the *Amethyst*'s reception after arriving in the United Kingdom on 1 November 1949 is contained in Adm 116/5704; photographs and press cuttings from her triumphant voyage home are in the "*Amethyst* Scrapbook," vol. 1–2, Kerans, 69/45/1, IWM.

57. The *Economist* in its issue of 6 August 1949 gave the following explanation for this puzzling feature of the inept showing of the PLA on the night of 30–31 July 1949:

> The escape was rendered possible by the fact that the Communist élite troops which had lined the north bank of the Yangtse in April, and so severely punished even the heavy cruiser *London,* have now gone elsewhere; the fire of the batteries was, therefore, of no more than average Chinese efficiency.

Select Bibliography

MANUSCRIPT SOURCES

Official Records
Public Record Office, Kew Gardens, London.
Admiralty

Adm 1/16242; Adm 1/18549; Adm 1/18691; Adm 1/21299;
Adm 1/21312; Adm 1/21493; Adm 1/21508; Adm 1/21525;
Adm 1/21696; Adm 1/21718; Adm 1/21800; Adm 1/21851/50;
Adm 53/125421–6; Adm 53/125604–9; Adm 53/126346–50;
Adm 116/5093; Adm 116/5132; Adm 116/5690; Adm 116/5695–6;
Adm 116/5698; Adm 116/5704; Adm 116/5707; Adm 116/5713;
Adm 116/5740; Adm 116/5740A; Adm 116/5752–4; Adm 167/124;
Adm 167/130–4; Adm 205/50; Adm 205/72; Adm 223/228–30.

   Board of Trade
BT 11/2157; BT 11/2234; BT 11/2542; BT 11/2560; BTG 11/3290; BT 11/3390;
BT 11/3406; BT 96/206.

   Cabinet Office
Cab 78/33; Cab 78/36; Cab 80/99; Cab 105/162–6; Cab 122/418;
Cab 128/10; Cab 128/15–18; Cab 129/21; Cab 129/26–29;
Cab 129/31–9; Cab 131/3–4; Cab 131/6–8; Cab 134/280;
Cab 134/285–8; Cab 134/657; Cab 134/669.

   Ministry of Defence
Defe 4/5–6; Defe 4/8; Defe 4/11–12; Defe 4/16; Defe 4/19;
Defe 4/21–23; Defe 5/6; Defe 5/9; Defe 5/14–15; Defe 6/8–9.

   Foreign Office
FO 371/69526; FO 371/69528; FO 371/69539–46; FO 371/69550;
FO 371/69557–61; FO 371/69608–10; FO 371/75731;
FO 371/75733–38; FO 371/75740–69; FO 371/75771;
FO 371/75785–7; FO 371/75810–16; FO 371/75818–9;
FO 371/75821; FO 371/75824–9; FO 371/75837;

FO 371/75839; FO 371/75855; FO 371/75864–68;
FO 371/75883–97; FO 371/75900; FO 371/75939; FO 371/75945;
FO 371/76049; FO 371/83415; FO 371/83417; FO 371/83424–38;
FO 371/84086; FO 371/84091; FO 800/462.
 Prime Minister's Office
Prem 8/944.
 Treasury
Although neither the Treasury's Supply files (T 161 series) nor those relating to
Imperial and Foreign Divisions (T 220) provided any real assistance on the *Amethyst* issue,
both they and the general correspondence files ought to be consulted for the earlier period
when extraterritoriality and a certain element of gunboat diplomacy held sway.

Private Papers

 Bodleian Library, Oxford
  Earl Attlee Papers; Baron Inverchapel Papers.
 Churchill College Archive Centre, Cambridge
  Earl Alexander of Hillsborough Papers; Ernest Bevin Papers;
  Sir Alexander Cadogan Papers; Lord Strang Papers.
 National Maritime Museum, Greenwich
  Lord Bruce Fraser Papers.
 Gardenfield, Castletown, Isle of Man
  Sir Ralph Stevenson Papers.
 Imperial War Museum, London
  Admiral Sir Peter Cazelet Papers; Commander John Simon Kerans Papers;
  Admiral Sir Ballin Robertshaw Papers.
 Liddell Hart Archive Centre, King's College, London
  Sir Patrick Brind Papers.
 Rhodes House Library, Oxford
  Arthur Creech-Jones Papers.

Interviews & Correspondence

Captain Charles Baker; Vice-Admiral Sir Peter Berger;
Richard Burton; Dr. Chan Lau Kit-ching;
Rear-Admiral Vernon Donaldson; Professor Barry Gough;
Dr. Nicholas A. M. Rodger; Mark B. Stevenson; Dr. Shao Wenguang;
Dr. James T. H. Tang; Dr. Steve Tsang;
Professor Mary Turnbull; His Excellency U. Myint Thein; Sir Edward Youde.

PRINTED SOURCES

Primary Sources

Official and Semiofficial Papers
U.S. Dept. of State. FRUS (*Foreign Relations of the United States*), vol. 8–9 (1948), vol. 8–9
(1949), Washington, D.C., 1973.

U.K. (United Kingdom). *Hansard Parliamentary Debates* (Commons), 5th ser., vol. 418 (1945–46); vol. 458, 459, 462, 464, 467 (1948–49); vol. 475 (1950).
U.K. (United Kingdom). *Hansard Parliamentary Debates* (Lords), 5th ser., vol. 162 (1948–49).
London Gazette
Who's Who 1989. London, 1989.
Who Was Who, vol. 6, 1961–70. London, 1972.
Who Was Who, vol. 7, 1971–80. London, 1981.

Newspapers and Periodicals

Boston Daily Globe; John Bull; China Daily Tribune; China Mail; China Pictorial; Chung Cheng Jih Poh; Daily Mail; Daily Express; Daily Graphic; Daily Herald; Daily Telegraph; Daily Worker; Economist; Illustrated London News; Keesing's Contemporary Archives; New York Times; New China News Agency Weekly Bulletin; North China Herald; Observer; People's Daily; Readers Digest; South China Morning Post; Spectator; Sphere; Straits Times; Sunday Express; Sunday Graphic; Sunday Herald; Sunday Pictorial; Sunday Times; Sunday Tribune; Ta Kung Pao; The Times; Washington Post; Wen Wei Po.

Secondary Sources

Articles, Books, and Theses

Allen, G. H., H. C. Whitehead, and F. E. Chadwick. *The Great War,* vol. 3. Philadelphia, 1916.
Barber, Noel. *The Fall of Shanghai.* New York, 1979.
Bartke, Wolfgang. *Who's Who in the People's Republic of China.* Armonk, N.Y., 1981 (2nd edition, Munich, 1987).
Beeching, Jack. *The Chinese Opium Wars.* New York, 1975.
Belden, Jack. *China Shakes the World.* New York, 1970.
Bell, H. T. Montague, and H. G. W. Woodhead. *The China Year Book,* 5 vols., 1912–1920. London, 1912–19.
Beloff, Max. *Britain's Liberal Empire, 1897–1921.* London, 1969.
Bernard, W. D. *Narrative of the Voyages and Services of The Nemesis from 1840 to 1843.* 2 vols. London, 1844.
Bishop, J. F. *The Yangtze Valley and Beyond.* London, 1899.
Bland, J. O. P., and E. Backhouse. *China Under the Empress Dowager.* London, 1910.
Boardman, Robert. *Britain and the People's Republic of China, 1949–1974.* London, 1976.
Booker, Michael. "H.M.S. Amethyst. The Yangtse River Crisis of 1949." Unpublished paper, Wilfred Laurier University, Waterloo, Ontario, March 1987: 1–20.
Brice, Martin H. *The Royal Navy and the Sino-Japanese Incident 1937–41.* Shepperton, 1973.
Broome, Jack. *Make Another Signal.* London, 1973.
Cable, James. *Gunboat Diplomacy, 1919–1979.* London, 1981.
Carrington, C. E. *The Liquidation of the British Empire.* London, 1961.
Chan Lau, Kit-ching. *Anglo-Chinese Diplomacy, 1906–1920.* Hong Kong, 1978.
Chassin, Lionel M. *The Communist Conquest of China: A History of the Civil War, 1945–49.* London, 1966.
Ch'en, Jerome. *Yuan Shih-K'ai.* Stanford, Calif. 1972.
Chow, Tse-tsung. *The May Fourth Movement.* Cambridge, Mass., 1967.

Clark, Grover. *Economic Rivalries in China.* New Haven, Conn., 1932.

Clifford, Nicholas R. *Retreat from China: British Policy in the Far East, 1937–1941.* London, 1967.

Clubb, O. Edmund. *20th Century China.* New York, 1964.

Collis, Maurice. *Foreign Mud.* Singapore, 1980.

Costin, W. C. *Great Britain and China, 1833–1860.* Oxford, 1937.

Dingman, Roger. *Power in the Pacific.* Chicago, 1976.

Dixon, Norman F. *On the Psychology of Military Incompetence.* London, 1979.

Dreyer, Frederick C. W. *The Sea Heritage.* London, 1955.

Eames, James B. *The English in China.* London, 1974.

Earl, Lawrence. *Yangtse Incident.* London, 1973.

Ehrman, John. *Grand Strategy,* vol. 6. London, 1956.

Endicott, Stephen L. *Diplomacy and Enterprise.* Vancouver, B.C., 1975.

Fairbank, John K. "The creation of the treaty system." In Twitchett and Fairbank, eds. *Cambridge History,* vol. 10, 1978: 213–63.

———, ed. *The Cambridge History of China,* vol. 12. Cambridge, 1983.

Fairbank, John K., and A. Feuerwerker, eds. *The Cambridge History of China,* vol. 13. Cambridge, 1986.

Fairbank, John K., and Kwang-ching Liu, eds. *The Cambridge History of China,* vol. 11. Cambridge, 1980.

Fay, Peter Ward. *The Opium War, 1840–1842.* Chapel Hill, N.C., 1975.

Fishel, Wesley R. *The End of Extraterritoriality in China.* Berkeley, 1962.

Fox, Grace. *British Admirals and Chinese Pirates.* London, 1940.

Frei, Henry. *Japan's Southward Advance and Australia.* Honolulu, 1991.

Friedman, Irving. *British Relations with China: 1931–1939.* New York, 1940.

Furuya, Keiji. *Chiang Kai-Shek: His Life and Times.* New York, 1981.

Graham, Gerald S. *The China Station: War and Diplomacy, 1830–1860.* Oxford, 1980.

Gregory, J. S. *Great Britain and the Taipings.* London, 1969.

Grenville, J. A. S. *Lord Salisbury and Foreign Policy.* London, 1964.

Grove, Eric J. *Vanguard to Trident.* Annapolis, Md. 1987.

Gull, E. M. *British Economic Interests in the Far East.* London, 1943.

Gwynn, Charles. *Imperial Policing.* London, 1943.

Haines, Gregory. *Gunboats on the Great River: A History of the Royal Navy on the Yangtse.* London, 1975.

Hampshire, A. Cecil. *The Royal Navy Since 1945.* London, 1975.

Harris, Kenneth. *Attlee.* London, 1982.

Harrison, James P. *The Long March to Power: A History of the CCP, 1921–72.* New York, 1972.

Hatano, Sumio. "Nihon kaijun to 'nanshin': sono seisaku to riron no shiteki tenkai" [The Japanese navy and the southward advance: the historical development of its policies and theory]. In Shimizu, Hajime, ed., *Ryo taisenkanki Nihon.* Tokyo, 1986: 207–36.

Hewlett, William M. *Forty Years in China.* London, 1943.

Holt, Edgar. *The Opium Wars in China.* London, 1964.

Howard, C. J. *Britain and the Casus Belli, 1822–1902.* London, 1974.

Hsu, Immanuel C. Y. *The Rise of Modern China*. Oxford, 1975.

_____. *"Late Ch'ing-Foreign Relations, 1866–1905."* In Fairbank and Kwang-ching Liu, eds., *Cambridge History*, vol. 11, 1980, 70–141.

Hubbard, G. E. *British Far Eastern Policy*. London, 1939.

Humble, Richard. *Fraser of North Cape*. London, 1983.

Hurd, Douglas. *The Arrow War*. New York, 1967.

Inglis, Brian. *The Opium War*. London, 1976.

Iriye, Akira. *After Imperialism*. Cambridge, Mass., 1965.

Jones, A. Philip. *Britain's Search for Chinese Cooperation in the First World War*. New York, 1986.

Jones, F. C. *Shanghai and Tientsin*. New York, 1940.

Joseph, Philip. *Foreign Diplomacy in China, 1894–1900*. London, 1928.

Kang, Mao Chao. "Hong Dong Yi Shi De Ying Jian Chang Jiang Shi Jian" [The Controversial British Warship Incident on the Yangtse], *Shi Jie Zhi Shi* [World Knowledge], 1988: 8:25–26; 10:22–23; 11:22–25.

Keeton, G. W. *The Development of Extraterritoriality in China*, 2 vols. London, 1928.

Kennedy, Paul. *The Rise and Fall of British Naval Mastery*. Atlantic Highlands, N.J., 1986.

Kiernan, E. V. *British Diplomacy in China, 1880 to 1885*. Cambridge, 1939.

Kuhn, Philip A. "The Taiping Rebellion." In Twitchett and Fairbank, eds., *Cambridge History*, vol. 10, 1978: 264–317.

Kuo, P. C. *A Critical Study of the First Anglo-Chinese War*. Westport, Conn., 1973.

Liu, F. F. *A Military History of Modern China, 1924–1949*. Princeton, 1956.

Loh, Pichon P. Y., ed. *The Kuomintang Debacle of 1949, Conquest or Collapse?* Boston, 1966.

Louis, William R. *British Strategy in the Far East, 1919–1939*. Oxford, 1971.

Lowe, Cedric J. *The Reluctant Imperialists*, 2 vols. London, 1967.

Lowe, C. J., and M. L. Dockrill. *The Mirage of Power*. 2 vols. London, 1972.

Lowe, Peter. *Britain in the Far East*. London, 1981.

_____. *Great Britain and Japan, 1911–1915*. London, 1969.

Luard, Evan. *Britain and China*. London, 1962.

Lubbock, Basil. *The Opium Clippers*. Glasgow, 1946.

Mao Tse-tung. *Selected Works of Mao Tse-tung*, vol. 4. Peking, 1961.

Marder, Arthur J. *The Anatomy of British Sea Power*. New York, 1976.

_____. *From the Dreadnought to Scapa Flow*. 5 vols. London, 1961–70.

_____. *Old friends, new enemies*. Oxford, 1981.

Millard, Thomas F. *The End of Exterritoriality in China*. Shanghai, 1931.

Monger, G. W. *The End of Isolation*. London, 1963.

Morse, Hosea B. *The International Relations of the Chinese Empire*. 3 vols. London and Shanghai, 1910–18.

Murfett, Malcolm H. "British Naval Policy on the Yangtse in 1949: A Case of Diplomacy on the Rocks." *War & Society* 6 (no. 1, May 1988): 79–92.

_____. *Fool-proof Relations: The Search for Anglo-American Naval Cooperation During the Chamberlain Years, 1937–1940*. Singapore, 1984.

_____. "An Old Fashioned Form of Protectionism: The Role Played by British Naval Power in China from 1860–1941." *American Neptune* 50 (no. 3, Summer 1990): 178–91.

————. "Old Habits Die Hard: The Return of British Warships to Chinese Waters After the Second World War." In Murfett and Hattendorf, eds., *The Limitations of Military Power.* London, 1990: 203–17.

————. "The Perils of Negotiating From an Exposed Position: John Simon Kerans and the Yangtse Talks of 1949." *Conflict* 9 (May 1990): 271–300.

————. "Strategic Necessity or Naval Extravagance? The Role of Hong Kong and Singapore in British Defence Policy in the Far East, 1945–49." *Pointer* 14, no. 4 (July–Sept. 1988): 48–69.

————. "What a Difference a Day Makes: The Royal Navy and the Yangtse Incident of 20–21 April 1949." *American Neptune* 49 (no. 3, Summer 1989): 208–25.

Murfett, Malcolm H., and John B. Hattendorf, eds. *The Limitations of Military Power.* London, 1990.

Murphey, Rhoads. *The Treaty Ports and China's Modernization, What Went Wrong.* Ann Arbor, Mich., 1970.

Nagai, Yōnosuke, and Akire Iriye, eds. *The Origins of the Cold War in Asia.* Tokyo, 1977.

Navy League. *The Glorious Story of H.M.S. AMETHYST.* London, 1950.

Nish, Ian. *The Anglo-Japanese Alliance.* London, 1966.

Olver, A. S. B. *Outline of British Policy in East and Southeast Asia, 1945–50.* London, 1950.

Osterhammel, Jürgen. *CHINA und die Weltgesellschaft.* Munich, 1989.

Ovendale, Ritchie. *The English-Speaking Alliance.* London, 1985.

Padfield, Peter. *Rule Britannia.* London, 1981.

Parkes, Oscar. *British Battleships.* Hamden, Conn., 1970.

Pelcovits, Nathan A. *Old China Hands and the Foreign Office.* New York, 1969.

Pepper, Suzanne. *Civil War in China, The Political Struggle, 1945–1949.* Berkeley, 1978.

————. "The KMT–CCP Conflict 1945–1949." In Fairbank and Feuerwerker, eds., *Cambridge History,* vol. 13, 1986: 774–82.

Phillips, C. E. Lucas. *Escape of the "Amethyst."* London, 1958.

Platt, D. C. M. *Finance, Trade and Politics in British Foreign Policy 1815–1914.* Oxford, 1968.

Pollard, Robert. *China's Foreign Relations 1917–1931,* New York, 1933.

Porter, Brian. *Britain and the Rise of Communist China.* London, 1967.

Pratt, John. *War and Politics in China.* London, 1943.

Preston, Anthony. *Battleships of World War I.* New York, 1972.

Preston, Anthony, and John Major. *Send a Gunboat! A Study of the Gunboat and its Role in British Policy, 1854–1904.* London, 1967.

Pritchard, Earl H. *Anglo-Chinese Relations During the Seventeenth and Eighteenth Centuries.* New York, 1970.

————. *The Crucial Years of Early Anglo-Chinese Relations, 1750–1800.* New York, 1970.

Purcell, Victor. *The Boxer Uprising.* Cambridge, 1963.

Rea, Kenneth W., and John C. Brewer, eds. *The Forgotten Ambassador: The Reports of John Leighton Stuart, 1946–1949.* Boulder, Colo. 1981.

Remer, Charles. *Foreign Investments in China.* New York, 1933.

————. *The Foreign Trade of China.* Taipeh, 1967.

Ridley, Jasper. *Lord Palmerston.* London, 1970.

Rolo, P. J. V. *Entente Cordiale.* London, 1969.

Schalow, Thomas R. "Transforming Railroads into Steamships: Banking with the Matsukata Family at the 15th Bank." *Hitotsubashi Journal of Commerce and Management* 22, (no. 1, Dec. 1987): 55–67.

Schwartz, Benjamin I. "Themes in Intellectual History: May Fourth and After." In Fairbank, ed., *Cambridge History,* vol. 12, 1983: 406–50.

Selby, John. *The Paper Dragon.* New York, 1968.

Shai, Aron. *Britain and China 1941–47.* London, 1984.

————. "Imperialism Imprisoned, the Closure of British Firms in the People's Republic of China." *English Historical Review* 104 (no. 410, Jan. 1989): 88–109.

Shimizu, Hajime. "Nanshin-ron: Its Turning Point in World War I." *The Developing Economies* 25 (no. 4, Dec. 1987): 386–402.

————. *"Ryo taisenkanki Nihon-Tonan'ajia kankei no shoso"* [Various aspects of Japanese southeast Asian relations between the two world wars]. Tokyo, 1986.

————. "Senkanki Nihon keizaiteki 'nanshin' no shisoteki haikei" [Intellectual foundations of Japan's economic "southward advance" between the two world wars]. In Sugiyama Shinya and Ian Brown, eds., *Senkanki Tonanazia.* Tokyo, 1990: 11–44.

————. "Southeast Asia in Modern Japanese Thought: The Development and Transformation of 'Nanshin-Ron.' " Unpublished paper deposited at the Department of Pacific and Southeast Asian History, Research School of Pacific Studies, Australian National University, (June 1980): 1–56.

Shoup, David M. *The Marines in China, 1927–1928.* Hamden, Conn. 1987.

Sprout, Harold, and Margaret Sprout. *Toward a New Order of Sea Power.* Princeton, 1940.

Steiner, Zara. *The Foreign Office and Foreign Policy, 1898–1914.* Cambridge, 1970.

Stuart, John L. *Fifty Years in China.* New York, 1954.

Stokesbury, James L. *Navy and Empire.* New York, 1983.

Sugiyama, Shinya, and Ian Brown, eds., *Senkanki Tonanazia no keizai masatsu* [International Commercial Rivalry in Southeast Asia in the Inter-war Period: Japan, Southeast Asia, and the West]. Tokyo, 1990.

Tan, Chester C. *The Boxer Catastrophe.* New York, 1967.

Tang, James Tuck Heng. "Diplomatic Relations With A Revolutionary Power," London School of Economics, Ph.D. diss. (Economics), 1987.

Teow, See Hong. "The Acting-Presidency of Li Tsung-Jen: A Critical Analysis on the Chiang-Li Factional Rivalry in 1949," National University of Singapore, Academic Exercise (History), 1986–87.

Tolley, Kemp. *Yangtze Patrol.* Annapolis, Md., 1971.

Tong, Te-kong, and Tsung-jen Li. *The Memoirs of Li Tsung-Jen.* Boulder, Colo., 1979.

Tsang, Steve Yui-sang. "Great Britain and Attempts at Constitutional Reform in Hong Kong, 1945–52," Oxford, Ph.D. diss. (Mod. Hist.) 1987.

————. *Democracy Shelved.* Oxford, 1988.

Twitchett, Denis, and John K. Fairbank, eds. *The Cambridge History of China,* vol. 10. Cambridge, 1978.

Van Slyke, Lyman P. *Yangtze.* Reading, Mass., 1988.

Wakemen, Frederick, Jr. "The Canton Trade and the Opium War." In Twitchett and Fairbank, eds. *Cambridge History,* vol. 10, 1978: 163–212.

Waley, Arthur. *The Opium War Through Chinese Eyes.* London, 1958.

Wang, Y. C. *Chinese Intellectuals and the West, 1872–1949.* Chapel Hill, N.C., 1966.

Watt, Donald C. "Britain and the Cold War in the Far East, 1945–58." In Yōnosuke Nagai and Akira Iriye, eds., *The Origins of the Cold War in Asia*. Tokyo, 1977: 89–122.

Wesley-Smith, Peter. *Unequal Treaty 1898–1997*. Oxford, 1984.

Whyte, Frederick. *China and Foreign Powers*. London, 1927.

Wilbur, Martin C. *Sun Yat Sen*. New York, 1976.

Wilgus, Mary H. *Sir Claude MacDonald, the Open Door, and British Imperial Empire in China, 1895–1900*. New York, 1987.

Williams, Frederick W. *Anson Burlingame and the First Chinese Mission to Foreign Powers*. New York, 1912.

Woodhead, H. G. W. *The Yangtsze and Its Problems*. Shanghai, 1931.

_____. *The China Year Book*, 7 vols., 1921–30. Tientsin, 1922–30.

_____. *The China Year Book*, 8 vols., 1931–39. Shanghai, 1931–39.

Wolf, David C. "To Secure a Convenience, Britain Recognises China, 1950," *Journal of Contemporary History* 18, (1983):299–326.

Wright, Stanley. *China's Struggle for Tariff Autonomy: 1843–1938*. Shanghai, 1938.

Young, Leonard, *British Policy in China*, vol. 1. Oxford, 1970.

Index

About the Author

Malcolm Murfett completed his undergraduate studies at Leeds University and won a scholarship to New College, Oxford, in 1974. While working on his doctorate in modern history, he was chosen to be the principal research assistant to the earl of Birkenhead. After spending five years on the officially commissioned single-volume biography of Sir Winston Churchill, he was appointed a lecturer in modern history at the National University of Singapore and subsequently promoted to senior lecturer in 1986. Dr. Murfett has also been a senior associate member of St. Antony's College, Oxford, and a visiting professor in modern history at York University, Toronto. He was elected a fellow of the Royal Historical Society in January 1990.

He has written many articles on British naval history and is the author of *Fool-proof Relations: The Search for Anglo-American Naval Cooperation During the Chamberlain Years, 1937–1940* and the coeditor with John B. Hattendorf of *The Limitations of Military Power*. He is the editor of a forthcoming volume on the British first sea lords and a joint author of a military history of Singapore. He is also engaged in gathering material for a biographical study of Sir Eric Geddes.

An Oxford blue in hockey, Malcolm Murfett also played cricket for the Republic of Singapore for several years. He now lives in semisporting retirement with his wife and four children in Singapore.

The **Naval Institute Press** is the book-publishing arm of the U.S. Naval Institute, a private, nonprofit professional society for members of the sea services and civilians who share an interest in naval and maritime affairs. Established in 1873 at the U.S. Naval Academy in Annapolis, Maryland, where its offices remain today, the Naval Institute has more than 100,000 members worldwide.

Members of the Naval Institute receive the influential monthly magazine *Proceedings* and discounts on fine nautical prints, ship and aircraft photos, and subscriptions to the quarterly *Naval History* magazine. They also have access to the transcripts of the Institute's Oral History Program and get discounted admission to any of the Institute-sponsored seminars regularly offered around the country.

The Naval Institute's book-publishing program, begun in 1898 with basic guides to naval practices, has broadened its scope in recent years to include books of more general interest. Now the Naval Institute Press publishes more than forty new titles each year, ranging from how-to books on boating and navigation to battle histories, biographies, ship and aircraft guides, and novels. Institute members receive discounts on the Press's more than 375 books.

Full-time students are eligible for special half-price membership rates. Life memberships are also available.

For a free catalog describing the Naval Institute Press books currently available, and for further information about U.S. Naval Institute membership, please write to:

Membership & Communications Department
U.S. Naval Institute
Annapolis, Maryland 21402

Or call, toll-free, (800) 233-USNI. In Maryland, call (301) 224-3378.

THE NAVAL INSTITUTE PRESS

HOSTAGE ON THE YANGTZE

Britain, China, and the Amethyst *Crisis of 1949*

Designed by Pamela L. Schnitter

Set in Bembo
by BG Composition
Baltimore, Maryland

Printed on 50-lb. Antique Cream
and bound in Holliston Kingston Natural
by The Maple-Vail Book Manufacturing Group
York, Pennsylvania